PIRE AND THE ENGLISH CHARACTER

EMPIRE
AND
THE ENGLISH CHARACTER

Kathryn Tidrick

I B TAURIS & Co Ltd.
Publishers
London

Published in 1992 by
I.B.Tauris & Co Ltd
45 Bloomsbury Square
London WC1A 2HY

First published in hardback in 1990 by I.B.Tauris

175 Fifth Avenue
New York
NY 10010

In the United States of America
and Canada distributed by
St Martin's Press
175 Fifth Avenue
New York
NY 10010

A full CIP record for this book is available from the British Library

Library of Congress catalog card number: available
A full CIP record is available from the Library of Congress

ISBN 1-85043-561-8 (paperback)

Printed and bound in Wales by
WBC Limited, Bridgend, Mid Glamorgan.

To Gene

ACKNOWLEDGEMENTS

I would like to record here the friendly assistance I received from the staffs of the following institutions: the Library of Congress; the Rhodes House Library, Oxford; the Tanzania National Archives; the Kenya National Archives; the British Library; the Public Record Office, Kew; the Boston Public Library; the New York Public Library; the Library of the University of Zimbabwe.

Chapter 5, 'The Masai and their Masters', is a much revised and developed version of an article which appeared in the *African Studies Review* in 1980.

CONTENTS

Justice: once that word is uttered, where will it all end? Easier to shout *No!* Easier to be beaten and made a martyr. Easier to lay my head on a block than to defend the cause of justice for the barbarians: for where can that argument lead but to laying down our arms and opening the gates of the town to the people whose land we have raped?

J.M. Coetzee, *Waiting for the Barbarians*

. . . it is a lucky society in which despicable behaviour at least has to be disguised.

Nadezhda Mandelstam, *Hope Abandoned*

Introduction

Many attempts have been made to define the motive force of British imperialism. None has succeeded. A phenomenon so complex and yet so fraught with the appearance of inevitability admits of no final explanation and this book does not aspire to give one. I assume throughout that the full range of human motives was at work in the empire and that it would serve no useful purpose to attempt to catalogue and assess them all. I assume furthermore that what was distinctively English about the enterprise was not people's motives for going where they did but what they believed themselves to be doing when they got there. *Empire and the English Character*, then, is about the play of character within the context of empire once empire was an established fact, and is only incidentally and implicitly about the role of character in acquiring it. The term 'English character' is used, of course, merely as a convenient shorthand for an untidy bundle of thoughts and feelings which seem to have occurred with some regularity among the people described in this book; and 'English' is used in preference to 'British' because, though Scots and Irish and even Welsh proliferated throughout the empire, the ideas by which they were consciously guided as imperialists were English in origin.

Even after arriving at a relatively modest definition of the scope of my inquiry, a multitude of questions of fascinating largeness immediately suggested themselves – far too many indeed to raise, let alone answer, in a book of manageable dimensions. The ones which eventually formulated themselves in my mind and on which I chose to concentrate were these. What might be said to be the British ideal of themselves as a ruling race? How did the men in the outposts, doing the work of settlement and administration, develop and give

1

practical expression to this ideal? And how did they come to terms
with the moral dilemmas implicit in their ascendancy? The last
question led naturally to another: how did they reconcile the use of
force with an imperial conception of themselves with which, it soon
became apparent, it was completely at odds? The British ambivalence
towards the use and acknowledgement of armed compulsion
provides one of the main themes of this book. I hope to show how
the men of empire preferred to avoid it, or, if it were unavoidable,
ignore it – not only because they had moral reservations about
physical coercion but because they believed that they were blessed
with attributes of character which enabled them to prevail without
it.

The formulation of the questions inevitably influenced the
formulation of the answers. I was soon conscious of concentrating
my attention on people who were sufficiently morally and intellec-
tually evolved to think and write intelligibly about the rights and
wrongs of what they were doing, and why they did it. This meant
that a host of inarticulate ruffians was relegated to the wings: they
must be imagined there, doing the usual ruffianly things. In the end
I found myself writing about individuals and groups who were
believed by large numbers of people to represent what was best in
the empire. This seemed to me interesting in itself, as well as
revealing the face the British wished to show the world. There are
some, of course, who would contend that it is in the nature of an
empire to bring out the worst in people, but this is a belief which,
though it has seemed to me at times very plausible, I am unable to
share. The general expansion of personality which is such a
fundamental part of the imperial experience can also bring out the
best.

There was no shortage of candidates for a gallery of imperial *beaux
idéals*, and my choice was based on my own interests and the
accessibility of the material. This meant that Africa was over-
represented and India under-represented.

For two reasons, I decided to begin this study in the 1840s. By
that time the British, though only represented by a chartered trading
company – the East India Company – had acquired control of most
of India and had begun to think in terms of permanent dominion
there. Before 1818, writes Percival Spear in *The Oxford History of
India*, we can speak of the British power in India; after 1839 it is
more correct to speak of the British empire in India. In that year the
British mounted a large, costly, and ultimately catastrophic invasion
of Afghanistan – an undertaking which they would never have
embarked upon had they not now thought of India as their *imperium*,
and the preservation of their power there as a sufficient reason for

extravagant geopolitical adventures. Afghanistan was the first of many such adventures; Suez in 1956 was the last.

In the eighteenth century the British still thought of India as a business proposition entailing some necessity to govern. By the middle of the nineteenth century they had acquired the habit of rule, and it had come to be supposed that government *was* the chief business of the British in India. And it is in the 1840s, in the Punjab, the last remaining corner of India to be brought under British control, that we find the first signs of a distinctive governing ethos which was to capture the imagination of the public and the imperial civil service alike, and which was to find its most developed expression sixty years later in the doctrine of Indirect Rule.

This governing ethos owed much of its character to evangelical religion. Evangelicalism, as Eric Stokes showed nearly thirty years ago[1], opened English eyes to India's existence as a vast field for social and spiritual reform: it showed the English what work they could do. But it also, and equally importantly, supplied a conception of authority which, because it happened to take root in India under conditions which were highly mythogenic, was of immense importance in defining the ideal to which men of empire thereafter aspired. This conception of authority was rooted in the evangelical cult of personal example.

There have been few varieties of religious experience in which the human personality has assumed a more important role than in evangelical Christianity. With its emphasis on self-scrutiny and the reforming power of the transfigured life, evangelicalism succeeded, in the early decades of the nineteenth century, in identifying to a degree unknown in England since the Middle Ages the moral power of the Christian message with the moral power of the messenger. To be 'changed', it was understood, was to be visibly so, and to effect thereby changes in others. A doctrine so inspiring could not, and did not, remain confined to the sphere of religious life. It found a general application in social relations, where it collided productively with aristocratic conceptions of honour to emerge as the Victorian ideal of the gentleman, acknowledged by his equals and adored by his inferiors. Evangelicalism was never a revolutionary movement. It was High Church in origin and, notwithstanding its devotion to philanthropy, was and remained politically conservative. The reforming energy of many of its leading proponents was directed almost exclusively to the conversion of the upper classes, in the hope and expectation that they would continue to preside, albeit in a more humane and spiritual fashion, over a society in which hierarchy was a principle of unalterable law.

The evangelical contribution to Victorian political life has often been identified as the doctrine of paternalism. But paternalism, if we understand by it the exaltation of an omniscient governing class, probably owed more to utilitarian philosophy with its implicitly Platonic theory of the state than to evangelicalism with its impulsive and unsystematic enthusiasm for reform. Evangelicalism's political legacy was the idea of a society in which the governing classes, regenerated through Christian fellowship, inspired in the lower classes an obedience based not merely on duty – for this was not forgotten – but on love. That is to say, the evangelical belief in the changing power of personal example became conflated, in the political sphere, with a belief in its power to control.

Such a conception of government was essentially pre-modern. It involved indeed little more than the sanctification of the traditional aristocratic claim to 'leadership'. It was thus ideally suited for export to the empire, where those to be governed seemed also eminently qualified by their primitiveness to be led. But the really profound significance of the revival of this ancient notion of government was in its extension, through the channels of institutional religion, to the middle classes. In appropriating to themselves hitherto supposedly aristocratic qualities they asserted their fitness for political power. And the empire, more than anywhere else, was the place which provided them with the opportunity to prove themselves the equals of the aristocracy, not only in the practical, but also in the inspirational, arts of government. 'His course', wrote Sir Richard Temple, reviewing John Lawrence's career '. . . should have a spirit-stirring effect on the middle class from which he sprung.'[2] It would require another book to explore the influence of such thoughts upon the political history of England in the nineteenth century; but they may be noted here as contributing to the deceptively aristocratic appearance possessed by that generally very middle-class enterprise, the British empire.

A word, finally, about the organization of the book. It is not possible, of course, to trace a straight line from John and Henry Lawrence and the 'Punjab creed' to Frederick Lugard and Indirect Rule in Nigeria in the 1900s: that is another reason why I have chosen to write about individuals and their lives rather than directly about the development of ideas. The first chapter covers relatively familiar ground and tries to trace the development through the activities of certain widely celebrated imperial heroes – the Lawrences and their assistants in the Punjab; Rajah James Brooke of Sarawak; General Gordon of Khartoum – of some of the fundamental notions of imperial conduct and style. The Punjab, quite fortuitously, through the influence of John and Henry Lawrence in circumstances dramatically receptive to it, was the breeding ground of that sense of high risk, high endeavour, and high personal importance which we see reflected in the activities of some lesser known, but no less interesting, individuals in the chapters which follow.

The subjects of these chapters were selected with some care, and it is hoped that one of them at least, the administrator Hugh Clifford, will be rescued from an undeserved oblivion: his imperial career, though a tragic one in certain respects, involved him in heroic efforts at intellectual and emotional honesty, and he was a man who can be judged not merely by the standards of his own time but of any time. The big game hunter, explorer and Rhodesian pioneer, Frederick Courtenay Selous, on the other hand, was a man who enjoyed immense celebrity in his lifetime but whose subsequent oblivion has been deserved. Famous as much in his day because he was the personification of an ideal imperial type as for his success in shooting elephants – he was the reputed original of Rider Haggard's Allan Quatermain, the hero of *King Solomon's Mines* and other wildly popular romances – Selous' moral evasiveness is what strikes us now. Nevertheless, his life repays study for what it meant to people at the time, and for what it shows us about how the imperialism of the moral imagination fared in contact with the brute reality which was Cecil Rhodes. The white settlers of Kenya, the subject of Chapter 4, were perennially at the centre of controversy and were as much disliked as admired even in their heyday, which was probably the 1920s. But they consistently thought of themselves as custodians of the pure imperial flame, representative in every way of all that was best in their own civilization, and how they managed to do this is the subject of their chapter. The British administrators of the Masai who form the subject of Chapter 5 acquired and have retained the reputation of being a special breed of men: their inclusion requires no justification.

A final section attempts to deal with the wider significance, for British imperial policy and other matters, of assumptions which by 1900 had become deeply impervious to rational analysis.

1

Nicholson to Peshawar, Gordon to Khartoum: The Punjab Creed and its Disciples

John and Henry Lawrence came from exactly the sort of background where evangelical enthusiasm was most likely to express itself in an impulse towards the leadership of men. Though in no sense members of the governing class as it then constituted itself, they were nevertheless brought up in an atmosphere of command, their father being an Anglo-Irish colonel of foot who spent most of his life on active service in India and expected his sons in due course to do the same. Their mother, the daughter and sister of clergymen, was the source of religious inspiration in the home. She instilled in her children a profound Christian piety, which in Henry's case took the form of a lifelong compulsion to be conspicuously good. His last request, as he lay dying of wounds at the siege of Lucknow, was that there be inscribed on his tombstone the words: 'Here lies Henry Lawrence, who tried to do his duty'. At school he was remembered for a precocious decency and scorn for wrongdoing, and for showing no interest in frivolity, 'unless,' his biographer records, 'it were a drama improvised to while away the dreariness of holidays at school, and then he would fling himself into it heart and soul, and be the hero of the piece'.[1] As a young man in India he gravitated naturally to Fairy Hall, Dum Dum, where the Reverend George Craufurd, chaplain to the Bengal Artillery, presided over a group of religious officers who lived together and prayed together in an atmosphere of mutual fascination and concern – a young male coterie of a kind very common in evangelical circles at the time. John's character was less complex, and his religious aspirations less public: he set himself without ostentation to meet the standards of conduct imposed on him by a just god. His dying words were: 'I am so weary'.

The two Lawrences were very uneconomic imperialists, united in their contempt for gain. In office, they kept no state. John was famous for losing the Koh-i-noor diamond, which he put in his waistcoat pocket and forgot about; Henry was all his life conspicuously bereft of possessions. They occupied a very different mental world from that of Clive, who had been 'astonished at his own moderation' in extracting from the Nawab of Bengal a fortune of only a quarter of a million pounds. India was to them a route not to wealth but to authority and, in true evangelical fashion, they perceived authority as legitimating itself through the established purity of intention of those who practised it. This meant for Henry that even the appearance of enrichment – private or public – at the expense of Indians had to be avoided. He consequently opposed Lord Dalhousie's policy of annexing native states which were misgoverned, or whose rulers died without issue, because to do so meant taking over their revenues. 'We have no right', he wrote, 'to rob a man because he spends his money badly, or even because he ill-treats his peasantry. We may protect and help the latter without putting the rents into our own pockets.'[2]

Both brothers had originally hoped for a military career, but though Henry went to Addiscombe, the East India Company's training college for artillery officers and engineers, John, thanks to the intervention of a family friend, found himself at Haileybury to be prepared for a civil appointment. In later life neither was content with positions which allowed them to exercise only one of what they came to regard as two integrated aspects of the governing art. Their ideal was to combine military with civil command, and it was to be a cardinal feature of the system of administration they designed for the Punjab that civil and military authority were united in the person of a single officer – a practice which brought into focus with extreme clarity the question of the role of force in upholding British authority.

Henry's opportunity to make his mark in Indian government came in 1838, with his appointment as administrator of Ferozepore on what was then the north-west frontier of British India. Here for some years he occupied himself in getting to know the Sikhs, acquiring that knowledge of them which was to be the foundation of his later career.

In 1838 the Sikhs, under their great leader Ranjit Singh, were still an independent power in wary alliance with the British. But after Ranjit Singh's death in 1839 the Sikh state fell into disarray and the policy of alliance with the British collapsed. In 1845 the Sikh army crossed the Sutlej into British India and succumbed to defeat in a series of bloody battles with the British army. These were not the usual unequal encounters of colonial warfare: Ranjit Singh had employed European officers to teach his men the arts of civilized warfare, and their prowess contributed mightily to their casualties.

The Punjab was not annexed right away – this came about only in 1849 after a rebellion and another equally bloody series of battles – but under the treaty of Lahore the size of the army was reduced, Kashmir was sold for £1 million to the Dogra chief Golab Singh, who had come in on the British side, the Jallandhar *doab* (Urdu = 'space between rivers') was ceded to the British, and a British Agent (later to acquire the title, British Resident) was installed in Lahore to advise the Sikh government. This Agent was Henry Lawrence, and the administrator of the Jallandhar *doab* was his brother John.

Though technically no more than adviser to the Sikh Durbar, or ruling council, Henry plunged headlong into the administration of the Punjab. He rationalized the tax system and the legal system, got rid of officials who leeched the peasants, built roads and canals, planted trees, established caravanserais and police posts along his new roads, and in general turned the country into a safer and more civilized place. But before all this could be done he had to confront two crises of authority. His handling of both was distinctive; and that of the second contributed substantially not only to his reputation but to what became his legend, and thereby to the public perception of the nature of British authority in India.

The first crisis was a riot in Lahore in April 1846 after British troops killed some cows – whether for food, or, as was improbably claimed at the time, in self-defence, is not clear. Lawrence was stoned in the street, but he forbade his escort to fire on the crowd. Instead he had the ringleaders arrested and sent in irons to Ferozepore, where the chief culprit was hanged. This 'did much', he later remarked, 'to insure the peace of the town'.[3] Already we see here Lawrence's coolness, deliberateness, and preference for judicial punishments such as hanging, which established legitimacy, over the spontaneous application of firepower, which did not. We see also his concern to make clear the purity of his own intentions. 'I thought', he wrote, 'of flogging the three chief offenders, and should have done so, had I not been personally affected by their offence.'[4]

The second, and more serious, challenge to British authority was the refusal of the governor of Kashmir, acting in complicity with the minister Lal Singh at Lahore, to hand over his province to Golab Singh. At first Henry Lawrence took no action, preferring to wait for Golab Singh to claim his reward. But when the latter proved unable to do so, he was obliged to act. First he informed the Durbar that unless they saw that Kashmir was handed over he would cancel the treaty of Lahore. This was a threat of war and resulted in a Sikh army being put in the field, with Lawrence himself at the head of it, to march on Kashmir. To discourage the soldiery from mutinous thoughts, a British army under General Wheeler was deployed in the rear. John Lawrence was installed as acting British Agent at Lahore, and before Henry departed he let it be known that, should harm befall him on the way to Kashmir, Lal Singh would find himself clapped into prison. Finally, diplomacy was not neglected. Henry's young assistant, Herbert Edwardes, was despatched to see what negotiations might produce. So successful was he that the rebellious governor surrendered before the army reached Kashmir, induced to do so by a promise that he could keep the vast sums squeezed out of the peasantry and not remitted to Lahore. When Henry Lawrence arrived in Kashmir after mopping up what remained of the resistance, all he had to do was accept the governor's not unwilling surrender and hand the country over to Golab Singh. He then returned to Lahore and had Lal Singh tried, convicted of treason, and removed to Ferozepore.[5]

One reflects with awe upon the skilful mixture of bribery and intimidation employed in Henry Lawrence's handling of the Kashmir crisis. No oriental potentate could have improved upon it. Yet we are dealing here with the actions of an enthusiastically Christian personality, who gave everything connected with his own and others' moral well-being an immense amount of anxious thought. How did he reconcile bribery – at the expense of the government he supposedly advised – with his conscience? We do not know. But even more mysterious is the way the exploit caught the popular imagination and came before long to be regarded, not as the inspired piece of statecraft which it was, but as 'one of the most striking examples of moral force in the history of India'. 'So great was the force of character and the *ikbal* (prestige) of Henry Lawrence', a biographer of the Lawrences was later to write, '. . . that everything happened as he had planned.'[6] Herbert Edwardes' transactions were not, of course, advertised at the time or later, but most of the other circumstances were publicly known, so the misapprehension can only partly be attributed to the fact that the sinews of power in India were not clearly discernible from England. It seems that the force of Henry Lawrence's character impressed itself not only upon Indians but on his compatriots at home. By the time accounts of his life came to be written, he had passed into history as the saintly defender of Lucknow – a man presumed to be without guile or selfishness, of whom it was repeatedly said that he inspired in both Indians and Europeans who knew him awe and love in equal measure. It thus seems to have come about that all his more striking achievements were attributed to the beauty and power of his personality.

This process was without doubt assisted by the fact that his first biographer was Sir John Kaye, whose histories of British India were written with the intention of showing what men of the British middle classes, 'merely by the force of their own personal characters, can do for their country in India, and what they can do for themselves'.[7] Kaye saw Britain's achievements in India as vindicating the political virtue, indeed the political innocence, of the rising middle classes against the political sophistication of the aristocracy. 'It is only by consummate honesty and transparent truthfulness,' he wrote, 'that the Talleyrands of the East have been beaten by such children in the world's ways as . . . Henry Lawrence.'[8] It was entirely natural to Kaye that he should ascribe Lawrence's success in inducing Golab Singh to abolish suttee and female infanticide to 'the moral power which such a man as Lawrence may exercise over the princes of India'.[9] The possibility that Golab Singh, a ruler described by Sir Charles Napier as 'a modern Tiberius'[10], might have calculated that the man who had established him on the throne of Kashmir might just as easily remove him was one he overlooked.

Henry Lawrence himself was inclined to see his adventures in the same transfiguring light as his admirers. 'It would be no unpleasant theme', he wrote,

> to dilate on the Cashmere campaign, on the extraordinary fact, never before witnessed, of half a dozen foreigners taking a lately-subdued mutinous army through as difficult a country as there is in the world, to put the chief, formerly their commander, now in their minds a rebel, in possession of the brightest gem in their land. Roman history shows no such instantaneous fellowship of the vanquished with the victors.[11]

Fellowship – that evangelical word! It was Henry Lawrence also who was responsible for the claim, true only in the most literal sense, that the pacification of the Punjab in the years after annexation in 1849 was accomplished without firing a shot.[12] So emphatic was he on this point that after his death the *Westminster Review* said of his achievements in the Punjab that 'all this had been done without any recourse to violence'.[13] There were, of course, other methods, not requiring the actual use of firearms, for striking terror into the hearts of wrongdoers, and these Henry Lawrence used apparently without compunction. 'We have hunted down all the Dacoits', he wrote to Kaye in 1852. 'During the first year we hanged nearly a hundred, six and eight at a time, and thereby struck such a terror that Dacoitee is now more rare than in any part of India.'[14] Possibly he was unaware that dacoity was a traditional expression of political discontent in the Punjab[15], but with his knowledge of the country this does not seem likely. Incorrigibles such as the Afridis were encouraged to submit by having their villages burnt and their crops destroyed. When this was revealed to the world by Sir Charles Napier in 1853[16], Henry Lawrence responded by pointing out that, though it was indeed standard practice on the border under his administration to destroy ripening corn and put villages to the torch, the inhabitants were always evacuated beforehand; then they had 'nothing but their cattle, grain, and houses to lose'.[17]

The point to be noted here is not that the British subdued the Punjab by the usual methods of conquerors, though that is what they did, or even that these methods were so little acknowledged, but that they were positively and vigorously denied and quite contrary claims advanced. Proud though he was of his military rank and record of service – and realistic as he could occasionally be in recognizing that India was, in the last analysis, held by the sword[18] – Henry Lawrence was nevertheless much concerned to suggest that whatever he accomplished in the Punjab owed little or nothing to the use of force and everything or almost everything to qualities which he modestly left it to others to describe. Such preoccupations simply did not allow the unambiguous acknowledgement of the extent to which force had actually been employed, outside the legitimate context of the battlefield.

None of this was cynically intended. Henry Lawrence's concern, besides being for his reputation, was also an authentically moral concern, and he sought to invest the necessary murder – for violence could scarcely be avoided altogether on the frontier – with an authentically moral quality. It was the essence of the famous 'Punjab creed', the unwritten rules which governed the administration of the Punjab under Henry Lawrence, and later under the joint tenure of the two brothers, that action when necessary should be swift and decisive; and this was not quite the straightforward response to frontier conditions which it at first appears to be. The origins of the principle in Henry Lawrence's mind, if we are to judge from its earliest articulation in his youthful novel of 1840, *Adventures of an Officer in the Service of Runjeet Singh*, were not expedient but moral.

This work of semi-fiction, based on Lawrence's contacts with the European adventurers employed in Ranjit Singh's army, contains portraits of a number of them, most prominently Paolo di Avitabile, the Neapolitan soldier of fortune who was governor of Peshawar. Avitabile was that fascinating thing, a European ruling natives by 'native', that is to say barbarous, methods, a prototype of Joseph Conrad's Kurtz and a host of other Europeans, fortunately for the most part fictional, whom the wilderness found out. He kept order by hanging wrongdoers fifty at a time, and skinning alive and

amputation also featured in his repertoire of disciplinary techniques.[19] Like Kurtz he seems to have had the power of making an
impression; Henry Lawrence met him and, evangelical principles
notwithstanding, declared him to be 'one of the world's master
minds'.[20] A discussion of his methods occupies several pages of
Adventures of an Officer, and the author's rather surprising conclusion
is that Avitabile, though indeed excessively severe,

> at the expense of his own character for humanity, by the terror of his
> name, *saved* much life. . . Believed to fear neither man nor devil, [he]
> keeps down by grim fear what nothing else *would* keep down – the
> unruly spirits around him, who, if let slip, would riot in carnage; his
> severity may therefore be extenuated, as the least of two evils.[21]

Later in the novel, in a scene where the hero Bellasis, a European of
unspecified nationality, explains to a friendly Sikh the need for
timely severity in managing troops, Avitabile's name is again
invoked, critically but nevertheless with an implicit sense of kinship.
What would Bellasis do, asks the Sikh, to discipline the unruly
soldiery? 'Hang up a score', replies Bellasis. 'Is the *Sahib* of
Avitabile's school', asks his friend, 'does he delight in blood?' 'No
. . .' replies Bellasis, 'I do not, and that is the very reason I would
shed a little. . .'[22]

It was a consistent theme with Lawrence that prompt and
moderately severe punishment possessed the moral virtue of
rendering severer punishment at a later date unnecessary. For this
reason he supported the use of the lash as a disciplinary measure in
both the native and European armies in India; it was preferable to
execution later on.[23] This seems a curiously unregenerate view of
human nature for one so preoccupied with improvement in himself
and others, but it was rooted in that consciousness of the weight of
inborn sin which darkened and confused the moral optimism of the
evangelicals. It should, of course, also be pointed out that in
endowing resort to violence with a moral quality Henry Lawrence
endowed it with legitimacy: to be cruel in order to be kind is to
inflict legitimate punishment, rather than to practise illegitimate
oppression.

There was another way of making force morally acceptable and
reducing its perceived importance, and this was to display it rather
than use it. It happened that the men who ruled the Punjab were
adepts in this art, for the simple if ironical reason that they were, for
the most part, not civilians ignorant of military matters but

professional soldiers, who furthermore had received their military training in days when the memory of the wars of manoeuvre of the eighteenth century was still green. Repeatedly, they extracted capitulation by confronting their opponents with indisputable evidence of superior military resources. Henry Lawrence employed this technique in the Kashmir crisis, and later in his swift and efficient disarming of the Punjab after annexation. No violence was directly employed, but village after village was made conscious of the armed majesty of the state.[24]

Though not a military man, John Lawrence possessed an instinctive capacity for this form of warfare. 'John was pulling up his shirt-sleeves and feeling his muscles, a very favourite attitude of his', an acquaintance interestingly recorded of a meeting with him in 1846.[25] Shortly before Henry was to grapple with the crisis in Kashmir, John was dealing with recalcitrance of his own, in the Jallandhar *doab*, and the manner in which he did so was a textbook example of how force could be used to terrify and overawe, without resorting to the actual shedding of blood.

In April of 1846 the commander of the ancient fortress of Kangra, which had passed to the British under the treaty of Lahore, refused to give it up. He had good reason to be bold: Kangra was one of the great strongpoints of India, standing on a rock 400 feet high and accessible only by a heavily fortified neck of land twenty yards wide. When John Lawrence arrived there he saw that the only hope of victory lay in finding some way of bringing up heavy guns to the citadel. A route was found, and within a week the engineers had constructed a temporary road and brought the guns as far as Lawrence's camp at the foot of the hill. Meanwhile, Henry Lawrence had appeared on the scene, bringing with him Raja Deena Nath of the Sikh Durbar at Lahore, who had agreed to bring his influence to bear. The terms he offered were rejected and the Kangra deputation was about to return to the fort from the British camp when John Lawrence suggested that they might stay and see the guns make the ascent to the citadel at daybreak. Not bothering to disguise their incredulity, they nevertheless agreed, and found themselves awakened just before dawn by cheering which they thought at first signified a sally from the garrison. 'They were soon undeceived', wrote John Lawrence,

> for a few moments later there appeared a couple of large elephants slowly and majestically pulling an eighteen-pounder, tandem fashion, with a third pushing behind. In this manner gun after gun wound its way along the narrow pathway, and, by the help of hundreds of sepoys, safely rounded the sharp corners which seemed to make

further progress impossible. The Sikh elders looked on with amazement, but said not a word. When the last gun had reached the plateau, they took their leave and returned to the fort. In an hour the white flag was raised. The garrison defiled out man by man, and, throwing down their arms, quietly took their way to the plains. Thus passed by what might have developed into a very serious affair.[26]

Here indeed was a bloodless victory which there was no mistaking for the result of personal influence. Nor would John Lawrence have wished it to be; he was clearer in his mind about such things than Henry. But a not dissimilar exploit, Herbert Edwardes' reduction of Bannu in 1847–8, was mistaken for precisely that, partly because of the memorializing efforts of Edwardes' wife, and partly because of his own insistence, in the style of Henry Lawrence whom he deeply revered and much resembled, that all he had done was accomplished '*without a single shot being fired*'.[27]

Bannu was a remote valley near the Afghan border whose inhabitants neither Sikh nor Afghan, nor even the mighty Alexander, had been able to subdue. Herbert Edwardes, not yet thirty, was sent there by Henry Lawrence to bring the Bannuchis into a taxable condition. On his first visit nothing was accomplished; on the second, he subdued the Bannuchis, promulgated and began to administer a code of laws, founded a town, and began a road and a canal. Edwardes had discovered in the course of his previous adventures in the Punjab that 'There is no arguing in this country without force to back you'[28], and this was the principle he now proceeded most successfully to apply.

'He was despatched', wrote his wife in her biography of 1886, 'with five hundred men and two troops of Horse Artillery' to conquer Bannu.[29] In fact, by the time Edwardes arrived at the entrance to the valley for the second time, in December 1847, he had with him, by his own account, 'eighteen guns, one hundred and thirty zumbooruhs [a small gun usually mounted on a saddle], two thousand cavalry, and five regiments of infantry', and he eventually assembled in Bannu an army, consisting mostly of Sikhs and Punjabi Muslims, of about 5,000 men.[30] He also had with him a Eurasian officer, General van Cortlandt, who had spent eighteen years in the Sikh army. His services in command of the Sikh contingent received a handsome acknowledgement from Edwardes in his *A Year on the Punjab Frontier* but were forgotten by his admirers, who liked to think of their hero as 'the only European' in a mob of unpredictable natives.

Arriving at Bannu, Edwardes issued a series of proclamations to the Bannuchis, telling them how large a force he had and exactly what would happen to anyone who proved recalcitrant. The main objective was to destroy the 400 Bannuchi forts – actually walled villages but invariably referred to in the literature as forts – which were scattered about the valley. Edwardes had no objection in principle to shelling them but felt doubts about the practicality of attempting to take all of them in this fashion. He therefore decided to proceed by indirect means, thus, as it turned out, opening the way to bloodless victory, with all that that implied.[31]

First he began work on a fort of his own, of impressive dimensions and situated so as to command the irrigation canals on which the Bannuchis depended for their crops. When work on this was sufficiently advanced, he ordered the Bannuchis to tear down the walls of their villages. The chief of each village was held responsible for carrying out the order and Edwardes let it be known that any village whose walls were still standing in fifteen days would be treated as hostile and its chief removed. Villages which failed to get to work were fined twenty rupees and had five horsemen quartered on them till they paid. As the Bannuchis laboured at their task, their new master looked on 'with equal shares of satisfaction and contempt'. Had his proclamation been sent back to him as gunwadding, he mused, and the Bannuchi chiefs united in defiance, 'the valley of Bunnoo, for aught I know, might have been free at this moment. To be sure it would have been a hell; but what of that? The Bunnochees liked it.'[32] He was in fact obliged to fire one shot in the course of his campaign – to defend himself against a native who tried to assassinate him in his tent. The body was displayed on the gallows, though Edwardes knew full well that in the eyes of the Bannuchis no Muslim so humiliated could enter paradise.[33]

Thus was Bannu subdued, by means which showed how, once the existence of superior British military strength was established, minimum force could be used with maximum effect. Or, as Edwardes put it, how 'one well-intentioned Englishman accomplished in three months, without a struggle, a conquest which the fanatic Sikh nation had vainly attempted with fire and sword, for five and twenty years'.[34]

Perhaps it is worth quoting for the sake of comparison at this point Henry Lawrence's instructions to officers in charge of the disarming of villages in the Punjab. 'Immediately on your arrival', he ordered,

> call the head men, and inform them that it is the order of the Durbar that they give up *all* arms and ammunition, and allow two hours for their doing so; keep your men together, and on the alert; do not search, but give the head men distinctly to understand, that if arms

are hereafter discovered to be in their villages, they will be individually held responsible, and will be liable to imprisonment and to have all their property confiscated.

Take a note of the names of the head men who appear before you. Inform them that no man in their village is henceforth permitted to carry arms, unless he is in the service of the State.[35]

In the same fashion as that employed by Edwardes at Bannu, leaders were efficiently separated from led, and individual miscreants singled out for exemplary punishment. By such highly professional methods Indians were brought to submission almost before they knew it.

The second and supplementary article of the Punjab creed, after swift and decisive action, was the autonomy of the junior officer. Together, these were the underpinning of what was known in the Punjab as the 'responsibility system', which meant that a junior officer who acted with the desired decision could expect his superior to back him up. In practice there were limitations to this autonomy. Public support by no means excluded private reprimand, and both Henry and John Lawrence, though impatient of restraint from above, were sticklers for accountability in those below. Assistant officers had to send in detailed monthly reports and were brought sharply to heel when instructions were not carried out to the letter. With Henry, terrible snubs alternated with flattering displays of affection, disconcerting even the most worshipful of his subordinates: in his youthful days his temper had been the subject of prayers at Fairy Hall.[36] Nevertheless, the responsibility system was the first institutional expression of that exaltation of the man-on-the-spot, his judgement and his capacity, which became perhaps the most distinctive feature of the British system of imperial administration.

Responsibility was, of course, implicit in the integration of military with civil command, but it also reflected independently Henry Lawrence's earliest aspirations with respect to the proper organization of authority, should he ever acquire it. In 1841 he published in the *Delhi Gazette* a fantasy entitled 'Anticipatory Chapters of Indian History', in which the rising in Afghanistan which occurred later that year was predicted and in which he imagined himself, or rather a narrator who is clearly his fictional counterpart, being given the command of the expedition to put it down. The conditions of his appointment are that he shall possess 'supreme political as well as military authority', and that 'from highest to lowest, he fill up all staff situations, and that, as responsible for the result, he have the selection of his own instruments'.[37], the justification being the necessity of choosing subordinates who also, at their own level, are capable of command. These suggestions had a definite plausibility. It was already apparent that the division of authority between the military commander in Afghanistan, General Elphinstone, and the British envoy, Sir William Macnaghten, was potentially disastrous, and the jobbery involved in the selection of staff had been notorious. Henry Lawrence, avid for responsibility and feeling his oats in his first civil appointment, thought he had the answer.

In 'Anticipatory Chapters' the selection of officers, destined without exception to add lustre to the hero's command, is most carefully described. All in one way or another have proved themselves capable of initiative: the Quartermaster-General obtains his appointment by reminding the hero that they ran away from school together. In 1847, after the treaty of Byrowal following the disgrace of Lal Singh placed Henry Lawrence in a position of supreme power in the Punjab, he was to experience the pleasure of turning his fantasy into reality. His band of assistants, chosen with infinite care, became celebrated in the annals of empire. They were all aware of having been so chosen, the public became aware of it, and the paradoxical effect of this careful selection was that they somehow came to be regarded as typical: they were the best that England could produce – but conversely only England could produce them. In this way, the emphasis on selection, which remained strong, in theory if not always in practice, and more in some places than in others, throughout the history of British imperial administration, reinforced the idea that of all the aspiring imperial powers only Britain had men of the right calibre for the job. The achievements of Henry Lawrence's young men were claimed immediately for the nation, and the judgement of the *Westminster Review* upon Henry Lawrence was applied to them all: they proved 'by how just a title we hold the place of the ancient Romans as the true *domini rerum*'.[38]

The glory days of the Punjab system were in the two years after the treaty of Byrowal and before annexation. Notwithstanding Henry Lawrence's supervisory inclinations, his assistants did indeed enjoy, in the words of Mrs Edwardes, 'Great power and great opportunities for accomplishing great good'. 'What days those were!' recalled one of them forty years on:

> How Henry Lawrence would send us off to great distances; Edwardes to Bunnoo, Nicholson to Peshâwur, Abbott to Hazâra, Lumsden somewhere else, etc., giving us a tract of country as big as half of England, and giving us no more helpful directions than these, 'Settle

the country; make the people happy; and take care there are no rows!'[39]

Edwardes himself was the most promising and the most favoured of them, brave, bold and evangelical, eventually to be the subject of an admiring essay ('A Knight's Faith') by his neighbour in retirement in England, John Ruskin. Edward Lake, Harry Lumsden, Reynell Taylor, George Macgregor, James Abbott, and John Nicholson all became, for a season, household names, and in the annals of the service their collective memory was eternal. Abbott, Henry Lawrence said, was 'a true knight-errant, gentle as a girl in thought and deed'.[40] Nicholson, too, received his share of knightly epithets, and indeed was capable of behaviour governed by standards of chivalry obsolete since the fourteenth century; his journey back to England from India in 1850 was enlivened by such episodes as an attempt to rescue Louis Kossuth from a Turkish prison, and the smuggling of a message from her husband to a woman incarcerated in an Austrian fortress.[41] But brave though he was, Nicholson was a brute. We first hear of him at the age of three, standing alone in a room, striking out with a knotted handkerchief at some invisible object: 'Oh! mamma dear', he is said to have explained to his mother, 'I am trying to get a blow at the devil. He is wanting me to be bad. If I could get him down I'd kill him.'[42] As a man he stamped on evil wherever he saw it, and in the intervals lamented his own shortcomings.

It was said of Nicholson as of so many others that he radiated force of personality, and in his case there seems no reason to doubt that it was true. Immensely tall with a long black beard, taciturn, tireless, careless of danger, and perfectly contemptuous of all legal restraint, he could scarcely have failed to create an impression. Sir Robert Montgomery, the Judicial Commissioner at Lahore, once received an official letter from him which read, in its entirety: 'Sir, I have the honour to inform you that I have just shot a man who came to kill me. Yours obediently, J.N.'[43] John Lawrence found it necessary to write to him: 'Don't send any more men to be hanged direct, unless the case is very urgent; and when you do, send an abstract of the case in English, and send it through the commissioner.'[44] Even Henry Lawrence, who loved him like a son, gently admonished him to curb his temper. Nicholson's idea of making the punishment fit the crime was to have a native who spat in his presence seized, held down, and made to lick up the spittle.[45] On another occasion he was riding through a Bannuchi village and noticed that the local mullah failed to salaam, as he was required to do when the great man passed by; he had the man's beard shaved off by the village barber.[46] These episodes were recounted by

Nicholson's contemporaries as if they were rather exuberant practical jokes. Perhaps his hatred – not too strong a word – of Indians owed something to the experience, early in his career, of finding the body of his brother Alexander in the Khyber pass, 'stripped of everything save a mere fragment of the shirt, and fearfully mutilated in true Afghan fashion about the base of the trunk'.[47]

John Nicholson also had the distinction of being an original of all those stories, so popular later in the nineteenth century, of the white man who was worshipped as a god. Around 1848 a Hindu holy man proclaimed him to be an avatar of Vishnu and founded a sect known to historians of British India as the Nikkulseynites, or, alternatively, the Nikalsainites. 'Flogging and imprisonment', however, 'were all the reward which Nicholson bestowed upon his intrusive worshippers.'[48] The more they worshipped him the more he flogged them; but they seem to have expected no less and came back for more. The end of the sect is variously recounted. One version is that the last of the disciples dug his own grave and was found dead in Hazara shortly after Nicholson's death in the siege of Delhi. Another version is that they decided the best way to show their devotion was to learn to worship the Christian god.[49] It was the first version which entered history; most authorities have preferred their Nikkulseynism undiluted by Christianity.

Nicholson liked nothing better than leading a punitive expedition, racing across the countryside at the head of a private army of wild Pathans. And in the end this was the image of the Punjab administration which stuck most vividly in the public mind – that of the fearless young man taking horse to chastise the wicked and uphold the righteous, supported enthusiastically by his personal retinue of devoted blackguards. The use of irregular Indian troops was not invented in the Punjab: John Jacob was already well known as the commander of the Scinde Irregular Horse, and James Skinner had formed Skinner's Horse, the famous Yellow Boys, as far back as 1803. But the leadership of irregular troops – sometimes very irregular – came to be regarded as a distinctively 'Punjabi' art. It was indeed a natural element of an administrative style which emphasized the personal rather than the institutional. The whole point of irregular troops, psychologically speaking, is that their loyalty is to the person of their officer rather than to the institutions of government which he represents – and conversely that such loyalty as they feel to anything as remote as a government is the result of purely personal attachment to its representative. The officers of irregular regiments were traditionally picked men, chosen, like

Henry Lawrence's assistants, for their capacity to inspire absolute devotion in the Indian mind; their work might be described as bloodless conquest in its highest form. In the Punjab, where the administration of a turbulent frontier required incessant but rather informal military activity, we can see how readily evangelical ideas of government through benign personal influence revealed their affinity with more ancient and aristocratic, and thus inevitably military, conceptions of leadership.

For an indication of what was involved emotionally for Henry Lawrence in the idea of irregular troops we can turn once again to that revealing work, *Adventures of an Officer in the Service of Runjeet Singh*. In one of its climactic scenes the hero Bellasis, who has been appointed by Ranjit Singh to the governorship of the Kangra fortress, deals with the discovery of a plot against his life by a rival Sikh commander, Nand Singh.[50] The scene opens with the villain and his accomplices being brought before the assembled Sikh garrison to hear their fate. Nand Singh is sentenced to death, and his accomplices to be branded, flogged, and set to hard labour in irons for the rest of their lives. Nand Singh curses Bellasis, who orders the executioner to cut off his right hand. Then Bellasis is struck by a shot fired from the ranks. It is Nand Singh's brother, and in a curious display of leniency Bellasis orders the troops to let him go. Before slipping into unconsciousness, he tells them that now they must choose between himself and Nand Singh. 'Did I choose to exercise my authority', he explains,

> I have ample means of enforcing it, but I purpose otherwise – the matter is now in your hands: you have a choice of commanders; a few minutes, and my unbandaged wound will end my career. Nand Singh's circumstances are the same; choose between us: run him up the block before you, or see me finish my career.

We discover Bellasis at the beginning of the next chapter being nursed back to health by the soldiery, Nand Singh having been duly despatched, with his own men lending a hand. We are never told what it is that accounts for Bellasis' triumph, what qualities he has that cause native troops to kill their commander for his sake. Henry Lawrence was an amateur in the craft of fiction, and he was content with the unexplained inevitability of obsession.

After the annexation of the Punjab a Punjab Frontier Force of 12,000 men was raised. This was an irregular army placed under the control of the civil officers and outside the jurisdiction of the British Commander-in-Chief. It was described with contempt by Sir Charles Napier as a body of 'independent auxiliaries'.[51] Two years earlier the corps of Guides had been raised, the fulfilment of an idea which had been in Henry Lawrence's mind since 1838.[52] Organized under a single English officer and spared the regular routine of discipline and drill, the Guides, whose dust-coloured uniforms contributed the word 'khaki' to the English language, were used primarily for the collection of intelligence. They rapidly acquired a highly romantic reputation, and it was an exploit of their first commanding officer, slightly amended, which Kipling immortalized forty years later in his 'Ballad of East and West'.[53] Kipling was always perfectly attuned to the meaning of the heroic in the imperial context, and in this instance he perfectly expressed it: 'But there is neither East nor West, Border nor Breed, nor Birth, / When two strong men stand face to face, though they come from the ends of the earth!'

It was the inevitable Edwardes who accomplished the prototypical Punjabi exercise in the leadership of irregular troops. Scarcely had he completed the conquest of Bannu, in the early months of 1848, when he was needed at Multan, where the flag of rebellion had been hoisted by Diwan Mulraj. Raising an army from the border tribes, he dashed across country, and though the fortress held out he won two important engagements, forcing Mulraj onto the defensive and checking the spread of the rebellion. His troops were Pathans who came in with their leaders in response to Edwardes' appeal for help. Why did they do this? In Edwardes' words:

> The army was raised by personal influence; such influence as it becomes every political officer to have in the country under his charge – such as I am proud to think every other Assistant to the Resident at Lahore had acquired in his own district. See how the Huzaruh tribes took James Abbott for their Khan. See how the Eusofzyes loved Lumsden. See how the men of Rawul Pindee followed Nicholson. When the Mooltan rebellion first broke out, I had been, off and on, about a year among the Trans-Indus people. I had gone to them at the head of great armies, on great errands, and met with great success. A master who had confidence in me, intrusted me with almost despotic power, for good or evil; and I trust the people never saw me wield it except for good.[54]

Or, as Ruskin, etherealizing a little further in summary, was to write, they were 'attached to him only by personal regard, by their knowledge of his justice, their experience of his kindness', and therefore – arriving at his essential point – 'to the English character he represented'.[55] From a careful reading of *A Year on the Punjab Frontier*, however, the more sober truth becomes apparent that the Pathan chiefs who came in did so because they owed their positions to Edwardes and the British power he represented. For the past two months the conqueror of Bannu had been on tour in the province of Dera Ishmael Khan. Rulers who made submission to the British had been confirmed in their authority with pledges of British support if they behaved and threats of British punishment if they did not. Petty tyrants had been deposed and 'rightful claimants' installed in their places. When the call for assistance came, it was these people who responded. As Edwardes grandiloquently put it:

> I found five different countries oppressed by one tyrant; and removed him. I found three chiefs in exile; and restored them. Those countries and those chiefs rallied round me in my hour of need, and were my army.[56]

At moments in Edwardes' narrative realism breaks through. 'It is a satisfaction to reflect', he observes after one particularly happy adjustment, 'that whatever country you march against, you have friends within the garrison, a party ready-made to your hand; the outs, who want lands, and castles, and titles, and thrones, that somebody else has taken away from them.'[57] And he is aware that in the unstable atmosphere of frontier politics, where petty warfare between people who are closely related is endemic, there are few inhibitions to overcome about Indian fighting Indian: 'You might put a quarrel', he writes, 'in any light you chose, and it would, in their opinion, be "a very pretty quarrel as it stands".'[58] In these conditions, after a convincing initial demonstration of British power, it was easy to exploit native awareness of it to interfere in local politics and create a system of alliances which could be brought into play as need arose.

This was a technique destined to be used extensively, and to devastating effect, in Africa later in the century. Many an African chief was tempted into a European alliance by the hope of dealing a rival a mortal blow, only to find himself at a later date, when the white man had been emboldened by success, contemplating his own political demise. In Uganda the rulers in alliance with the British were all men who owed their local ascendancy to British support; in the Punjab, Golab Singh was the pre-eminent example of methods described only inadequately by the expression 'divide and rule'.[59]

Henry Lawrence was in England, on sick leave, when the Multan rebellion broke out. His reaction was an explosion of confidence in his chosen representatives and their powers of command. 'I don't believe', he wrote to Sir John Kaye, 'that a British soldier will leave

Lahore, and I am sure they ought not to do so. The Sikhs and Politicals ought to have it all to themselves. . . .'[60] He could not know that one of them, acting on the highest principles of the Punjab creed, was about to apply the spark which fanned the local rising into a national revolt.

James Abbott of Hazara, a man devoted to Henry Lawrence and all he believed him to stand for[61], had come to believe that Chatur Singh, the governor of Hazara province, was organizing the Sikh notables in a conspiracy to eject the British from the Punjab. Inspired it appears by Edwardes' success in raising levies for Multan, he went off at the head of a Pathan army and besieged the provincial capital. The consequences were enormous. Chatur Singh was the father of Sher Singh, who was leading the Sikh contingent before Multan, and the humiliation inflicted on his father led Sher Singh to defect from the British cause and call the Sikhs to arms against the foreigner. The nation rose for what proved to be its last battle, and annexation shortly followed. As they were so frequently to do, the British had added another province to their empire by moving in to restore the order one of their own agents had disrupted.[62]

Henry Lawrence continued to serve in the Punjab after annexation, but now possessed supreme power only in name. John Lawrence was made head of the civil administration and Charles Mansel of the judicial system, with Henry remaining in charge of military and political work. Disagreements arose beween the two brothers, Henry favouring a form of indirect rule through the Sikh nobility, and John a system of direct rule under British officers, which he believed to be the only means of securing justice and prosperity to the peasant. Henry Lawrence, true evangelical that he was, placed his hope in regenerating the Sikh aristocracy. John regarded them as parasites requiring no special consideration.

In the end it was John, under the powerful patronage of the Governor-General, Lord Dalhousie, who emerged victorious, and Henry's resignation was accepted in an insulting letter from the Governor-General drawing attention to the fact that he was not 'a thoroughly trained and experienced civil officer'.[63] He retired in anguish to Rajputana, there to attempt as Resident to put into practice his theories of indirect rule through the native aristocracy: 'it is very easy, without offence', he wrote rather pathetically to Kaye, 'to give hints and help'.[64] The last act of his drama opened with his appointment to the Chief-Commissionership of Oudh, where he went down fighting in July 1857 in defence of the Lucknow Residency against 7,000 mutineers. The soldiers who carried him out for burial bent down one by one and silently kissed him.[65]

I have left until last an assessment of the real giant of the Punjab, John Lawrence. A man of the highest administrative ability, he left behind him by far the solidest achievement of any of the Punjabis. Building on what Henry had begun, he called into existence roads, railways, and canals; the Grand Trunk Road along which Kim was so memorably to travel was his creation. Trade flourished under his administration, and even the almost insoluble land and taxation problems were tackled, on the whole, creditably. Yet though he was greatly admired, he was never admired quite as extravagantly as his brother: he did not possess, as Henry was thought to do, the supreme quality of effortless dominion over native races. His achievements had no mystery. They were too evidently the result of intelligence, endurance, strong nerves, and hard work.

It was Henry who had the reputation of being fond of Indians, but a reader of their respective biographies, both generous with quotations in the Victorian fashion, might well conclude that it was John who showed the more authentic interest and affection. He approached getting to know Indians in the same way as he applied himself to mastering the intricacies of finance: patiently, without illusion, but with respect. After the Mutiny, when the evangelicals, led by Edwardes, were in full cry, he opposed their demand to introduce compulsory Bible classes into Indian schools. He took the position that instruction should be provided for those who desired it, and further than that he refused to go.[66]

His attitude towards the use of force was on the whole straightforward, and there was no trace in him of the sadistic fancy which revealed itself at times in Henry. Only in the period right after the Mutiny, when the battle was fought and the victory won, did he succumb momentarily to the illusion that Englishmen in India might be obeyed without it. In his relations with subordinates he was just as supervisory as his brother, but concerned more with bureaucratic procedures and legal restraints and less with loyalty to himself. He made a more effective effort than Henry to curb the excesses of John Nicholson, thereby so incurring Nicholson's dislike that he considered leaving the service[67]: Henry's fatherly admonishments had been easier to take than John's firm insistence that he sin no more. Yet John's administration left plenty of scope for personal initiative and exciting forays into untamed countryside. The Punjab was a Non-Regulation Province with a border occupied by unruly tribes; no less than twelve punitive expeditions were mounted against them between 1849 and 1856.[68] But in the day-to-day conduct of administration there was rather less summary justice than before.

John drove his assistants hard and expected them to live the spartan life he himself had led as a young Collector. Not all of them liked it, and of these some were winnowed out and others broken in. A civilian who brought a piano to the Punjab was moved five times in two years: 'I'll smash his piano for him', John Lawrence is reported to have said.[69] Those who throve were truly of the Punjab breed. One of them, Robert Cust, who worked for John in the early days in the Jallandhar *doab*, produced in old age what must surely be the definitive recollection of that time. He remembered with affection the long hours spent in the saddle,

> the rough-and-ready Justice: the words of sympathy and good fellowship: the living alone among the people without soldiers and policemen: the Court held under the green mangoe-trees in the presence of hundreds: the *right* man hanged *on the spot*, where he *committed* the murder.[70]

When the Indian Mutiny broke out on 10 May 1857 John Lawrence had been Chief Commissioner of the Punjab for the previous four years; he had made his mark as an administrator but he was not a famous man. By the end of 1857 he was known throughout the English-speaking world as the saviour of India. 'The Punjab held' were the words on everyone's lips, and John Lawrence was the man who had held it. Not only had the Punjab, though only recently subjugated and the home of not one but several martial peoples, failed to rise in revolt, it had provided the forces which accomplished the fall of Delhi and brought the Mutiny to an end.

The Punjab held for two reasons: the extreme rigour and promptness with which the administration put down any sign of revolt; and the traditional antipathy of the Sikhs towards the men of Hindustan. When the former had been accomplished, the British exploited the latter in creating the Punjab levies which marched on Delhi. They went to war inspired by the prophecy, assiduously revived, with embellishment, by the British, that one day the Sikhs would find the riches of the Mogul capital theirs for the taking.[71]

In this hour of crisis there was no nonsense about winning without firing a shot. The British were fighting for the existence of their empire. Within three days of receiving news of the outbreak at Meerut all native regiments of dubious allegiance had been disarmed, all forts and arsenals secured, and all treasure brought in from outlying districts and placed under guard. The disarmings were carried out in a manner which ensured their complete success. At Lahore on 13 May 3,000 sepoys found themselves lined up before five companies of European troops and a battery of guns with portfires lighted. They laid down their arms. Throughout the Punjab similar disarming parades took place, and they occurred with such suddenness that the initiative was lost forever to the mutineers. At the same time as the disarming was going on the first steps were being taken to ensure that unrest did not spread to the civilian population. Officials were given special powers to curb the first symptoms of disorder and they were used to the full. Anyone who talked treason, very liberally defined, was instantly hanged. The restraints which John Lawrence had struggled to impose on his wayward officers in time of peace were cast aside in time of war. Those sepoys who succeeded in breaking out from the cantonments were hunted down and destroyed without mercy. John Nicholson was unleashed on them at the head of a moveable column which was nothing less than a permanent punitive expedition. The number of mutineers personally despatched by him, cut down in flight or hanged upon capture, ran into hundreds, though the exact figure is unknown. A request from the civil authorities that he furnish them with a list was returned with the words 'The punishment of mutiny is death' written on the back.[72]

And if Nicholson was in his element, so were less likely characters. Herbert Edwardes, that sincere Christian, proved to have a stronger stomach for cold-blooded killing than Nicholson, who killed mostly in the heat of battle or shortly thereafter. In his anxiety to drive from the minds of the inhabitants of Peshawar any notion that the British would be easily got rid of, Edwardes proposed to blow away from guns all 120 of the prisoners taken from the mutinous 55th regiment at Peshawar. 'Five can be placed before each gun', he wrote, 'and two troops of artillery will throw sixty of them into the air at once. A second round will finish the matter; and, awful as such a scene will be, I must say my judgment approves it.' This seemed to John Lawrence 'horrible' and he persuaded Edwardes to be content with one-third of that number. He did not feel confident, he said, in the eyes of Almighty God in putting to death so large a number. 'If one-third or one-fourth were blown away it would answer every purpose, excite equal terror, and not the same horror.' And if no quarter were given, what inducement would there be to surrender?[73] But it was early days, and as the Mutiny dragged on and the loyal troops in the Punjab were siphoned off to Delhi, John Lawrence became less Solomonic in his judgements. At the end of August the 51st Native Infantry rose at Peshawar and this time he made no effort to restrain Edwardes' severity. 'Drumhead courts-martial going on now', Edwardes reported:

This simplifies matters greatly. One corps is got rid of, and we shall probably put another in irons. . . P.S. – James has just come back, nearly melted, followed the Pandies fifteen miles, killed every man, no prisoners taken by his party. Colonel Kyle with another pursuit has killed about one hundred, and prisonered sixty – great clearance.[74]

By the time Edwardes had finished, the 51st regiment, over 800 men, had ceased to exist.

If an explanation is sought for this surrender to wholesale slaughter on the part of a man who prided himself on conquering entire countries without firing a shot, it must surely be that his concern with the moral justification of violence was a highly subjective one, having more to do with the state of his own soul and the purity of his own intentions than with an appreciation of others' pain. In the circumstances of the Mutiny he could kill Indians with a clear conscience; and conscience, unallied with genuine human sympathy, is a poor guide to morality. In similar circumstances, Henry Lawrence would probably have done the same.

Looking back at those dreadful days in the Punjab, it becomes difficult to understand why one episode in particular was singled out for censure at the time. Frederic Cooper's execution of 237 captured sepoys at Ajnala was no greater a crime than some others but it was not found possible to excuse it in the same way. Cooper himself was inspired by Nicholson's example in dealing summarily with the mutineers at Sialkot a few days before and was well pleased with what he had done: he expected to be congratulated and he was. John Lawrence wrote immediately to tell him that he had performed a signal service to the state, and Robert Montgomery, the Judicial Commissioner, proclaimed: 'All honour to you for what you have done, and right well you did it. There was no hesitation or delay, or drawing back. It will be a feather in your cap as long as you live.'[75]

Cooper's chief offence against public decency apparently lay in publishing an account of the episode which showed too clearly his enthusiasm for his work. It was one thing for Herbert Edwardes to write brisk private epistles to his chief describing how whole regiments had been wiped off the face of the earth; it was quite another for Frederic Cooper to reveal all on the printed page. His offence was further aggravated by reproducing in his self-justifying book the two letters quoted above, noting with absolute correctness that they were highly characteristic of their authors, and that their perusal would 'sensibly diminish the wonder why the Punjab Government is so successful'.[76] But the Punjab government did not care for that kind of publicity, and nor, when it came down to it, did the British public, which was forming quite a different idea of the reasons for the Punjab government's success. Cooper had the poor taste furthermore to dedicate his book to Henry Lawrence – 'the patriot, the soldier, the statesman, the Christian, the victim of his own moral chivalry'. It could not be right to associate Sir Henry's exemplary death with this butcher's work: Cooper was condemned in India and England alike.

When Delhi fell the British troops who occupied the city gave themselves over to an orgy of killing and looting which the authorities at first did nothing to restrain. Blind vengeance was the order of the day. To his everlasting credit, John Lawrence succeeded in using his now very great influence to stop it. His reasoning was characteristic, or characteristic of him as he had been before the Mutiny and had ceased to be for a while in the midst of it. He saw that not only was a reign of terror morally repugnant, it was impolitic and ultimately impracticable. It would only unite the populace against the British and lead to a prolonged guerrilla resistance which would be beyond the capacity of British troops to put down.[77] His arguments prevailed and the administration of Delhi was transferred in February 1858 to the Punjab government. As his biographer, writing in 1863, clearly saw, by his moderation he had saved not only Britain's power in India but Britain's reputation, and the confidence of benignity it bestowed. Had the terror not been stopped,

> we should have ranked ourselves . . . with those earlier conquerors [of India]; not, as it is our hope that we have some right to do, above them. We should no longer have been able to boast that we have conquered India, to a great extent, by different methods, and held it for different objects from those of our predecessors. We should have been unable to flatter ourselves that our practice and our aim has been to preserve, to humanise, to elevate, not to persecute, to pillage, or to destroy.[78]

In March 1859 John Lawrence returned to England, broken down in health. A period of convalescence set him on the road to recovery and he was able to enjoy the experience of being a popular hero, for that is what he had become. But lionized though he was, it would nevertheless be true to say that John Lawrence's contribution to the preservation of their Eastern imperium was never fully appreciated by the British public, for he himself obscured the importance of his resourcefulness in the hour of crisis by the anxiety he now felt to advertise the virtues of the system he had presided over in the years of peace. Perhaps he was sick of blood and wished to think no longer about it; perhaps he was concerned by the public reaction to Cooper's book, which had appeared in the previous year. Whatever the reason, though he did not discount the part played by prompt military action, he was now concerned to stress that:

In times of peace, we had worked so as to be prepared for times of commotion and danger. We had laboured to introduce into a new country order, law, and system. Our object had been to improve the condition of the people, and obtain their goodwill and sympathies, and hence it happened that, by God's help, we were able to meet the storm which must otherwise have overwhelmed us.[79]

He lavished praise on his young assistants, pointing out to a fascinated public their quite exceptional personal qualities, and the general impression was left of a band of heroes who had ruled so wisely and well that millions of Indians had decided they would rather continue to be ruled by them than seize the opportunity to regain the independence so recently theirs. By a strange irony, it was John Lawrence, the supreme master of the calculated use of force, who taught the British public that all that really mattered was a few good men. Find them, he seemed to be saying, give them responsibility, and all would be well.

In fact, as the reports of his own officers show, the Punjab seethed with civil unrest in 1857.[80] There were many instances of civilians providing aid to the sepoys and there were outbreaks in a number of towns; 'dacoity' increased significantly, and some of the country gentry rallied the people and rose against the foreigner; a number of villages refused to pay taxes. But all these disturbances were easily put down. The British were in a strong position to deal with trouble: they had long ago disarmed the civilian population and all the identifiable troublemakers had been deported to other parts of India. The great nobles who remained in possession of their lands and titles knew well that they did so on British sufferance, and they noted the severity with which the administration responded to the first signs of disaffection. When they were ordered to supply troops for the assault on Delhi, they did so: 'I would not put up with any delay or hesitation on your part', John Lawrence told them, and they knew that he meant it.[81] Even then the Chief Commissioner was taking no chances. He made sure that the Punjab levies contained a healthy proportion of Pathans and Punjabi Muslims, men who had 'proved during the Second Punjab War and on previous occasions that they could be depended on to fight against the Sikhs'.[82] And when these troops had served their purpose he made sure they were disbanded before they had a chance to become dangerous.[83] There was nothing he did not think of, and so the Punjab, and India, remained in British hands.

While he was working at the India Office in the years between 1859 and 1863 John Lawrence argued for the extension of the Punjab system to the whole of India. As he saw it, this meant paying less attention to regulations and more to the quality of the officers administering them; it meant seeing that 'better men' were brought forward and given vastly more power to do as they thought best. In India, he argued, 'of all countries, the great object of the Government should be to secure the services of able, zealous, and high-principled officials. Almost any system of administration, with such instruments, will work well.'[84] At the end of 1863 he was appointed viceroy and given the opportunity to put his ideas into effect. He ended up attempting to govern India through, as he put it, 'one central authority . . . to which all other authorities . . . must entirely defer'.[85] Probably he saw his own life as a long series of triumphs over wrongheaded efforts to deflect him from faith in his own judgement, and he seems to have failed utterly to realize that the more discretionary powers he succeeded in attaching to himself at the top the fewer were left for those below. In the primitive conditions of the Punjab in the 1840s and '50s such centralizing tendencies had hardly mattered. But in the India of the 1860s, with the development of the telegraph and the railway system, the strong hand of the man at the top could be felt all over the country if he chose to apply it. Power cannot be successfully diffused through a system which is both hierarchical and anti-bureaucratic, unless communications are very imperfect. But these were not thoughts which troubled anyone in 1859. The Punjab system was assumed to operate through a mysterious concert of independent wills all working together for good – and what was good for the Punjab was self-evidently good for India. When John Lawrence was appointed viceroy it was not just a personal triumph, it was the triumph of his ideas.

The new importance attached to the personal qualities of the men who ruled India was reflected in the debate on the reorganization of the Indian army which began in 1858.[86] The most pressing issues were, of course, the size of the army and the proportions of British and Indian troops. It was evident to most of those concerned that more European troops were required, and it was decided to double the number. It was also evident that there should be more European troops in proportion to Indians, and the ratio finally settled on was approximately one to two; in 1856 there had been something like one British soldier for every nine Indian soldiers. There was no question of doing without any Indian troops at all; everyone recognized that Britain could never supply enough men to hold India with European troops alone. The next question was the controversial one. How should the army be organized, and in particular what should be the number of European officers in Indian regiments? The decision eventually taken was that henceforth native cavalry regiments, and the new infantry regiments of the mutinous Bengal army, should be run on irregular lines. What this meant was that there were fewer, not more, English officers than there had been before 1857. It also meant that they would be rigorously selected according to the principles developed in such famous units as the Guides and the Scinde Irregular Horse. The reason for the decision was the same as that which accounted for the sudden prestige of the Punjab system. During the Mutiny the irregular regiments had stood conspicuously firm – a point rammed home in a brilliant pamphlet campaign by John Jacob. Jacob himself had been in Persia when the Mutiny broke out, but his two regiments, the 1st and 2nd Scinde Irregular Horse, composed mostly of Hindustanis from the area around Delhi, remained loyal to a man.

In Jacob's system Indian officers were given a real measure of responsibility and were expected to be capable of rising to numerous military occasions without direct British supervision. They were often left in control of isolated outposts with no Englishman present. This was in accord with Jacob's express policy of stimulating loyalty by bestowing trust. But there was also in his regiments a terrific concentration of power in the hands of the European commanding officer, who ruled in the most informal and personal fashion. He recruited, promoted and punished, and against his decisions there was no appeal. His pre-eminent task was to inspire loyalty – by his irreproachable fairness, by his implacable devotion to the regiment, by his ability to show his men how much he valued their service, by his perfect condescension. The officer who managed all this, Jacob said, would be 'loved, respected, almost adored'.[87]

For Jacob these doctrines had long possessed implications extending far beyond the confines of the regiment. He believed that India could be held 'not by English bones and muscle, but by mind . . . a moderate number of cultivated English gentlemen, rather than . . . a multitude of rude soldiers'.[88] In the dying embers of the conflagration of 1857 these views fused with those of the Punjab school to produce heroic aspirations for the future government of India.

There was a darker side to the development of these aspirations which it would probably be too strong to describe as remorse but which could perhaps be defined as a sense of transgression. The Punjab had held and the war had been won, all of which tended to show that God had been on the British side. 'God put it into the hearts of our rulers to act with such energy and resolution', wrote Frederic Cooper[89], and many agreed with him: we had been granted heroes, the Indians had not. But people also wondered what had gone wrong, or rather, what they might have done wrong, to be so sorely tried. On this theme John Lawrence spoke in words which seemed divinely inspired. We must not forget, he said,

> that, if grievously sinned against, we may have to some extent sinned also; that we have to answer for our own shortcomings and defaults, whereby we placed sore temptation before a people who have no true religion, no true morality to sustain them; that while but too many have done that which can never be palliated or condoned, numbers have been guilty in various lesser degrees. There is a Judge over both them and us. Inasmuch as we have been preserved from impending destruction by His mercy alone, we should be merciful to others, reflecting that if He were to be extreme to mark what we have done, and still do amiss, we should forfeit that protection from on High which alone maintains us in India.[90]

Details were not gone into, but there was a sincere concern among the thoughtful and devout that the Mutiny might have involved some initial withdrawal of the divine favour as well as an ultimate affirmation of it. Now surely was the time to do something about this, thereby ensuring that God would have no further cause for displeasure. The solution was found in arriving at a firm and public intent to do right in India. The Company was deprived of what remained of its powers, and responsibility for the government of India was transferred to the British Crown, with daily control of affairs passing to a Secretary of State who sat in the Cabinet; the principle of rigorous selection for the civil service was fully accepted and acted upon. Henceforth, it appeared, India was to be governed according to the highest principles of government, and by the finest body of men. They would be benevolent, they would be disinterested – and they would be immovable: it would be inconceivable that Indians should ever wish to get rid of them again.

Statements of benevolent intention with respect to the government of India were, of course, nothing new. They had been produced routinely since the trial of Warren Hastings and had increased in fervour with the rising influence of the evangelical party in the state. What was new was their now implicitly propitiatory purpose. For one thing the Mutiny had done was to bring home to Englishmen the fact that they had no desire at all ever to leave India. The sentiment which had inspired Macaulay's great Charter speech of

1833, the exhilarating impulse to civilize India even if it meant ultimately paying the price of sovereignty, now faded rapidly away. In the fertile soil of the late 1850s an idea which had been floating in the air took root and began to grow: men, not institutions, were the true glory of the empire. A mystique of rule, infinitely corrupting in its detachment from any true sense of purpose, began to compete with the enthusiasm for reform which had inspired two generations of Indian administrators, including, let it not be forgotten, John and Henry Lawrence.

The attempt to organize Indian administration along Punjab lines failed for another reason besides the masterful personality of John Lawrence and the revolution in communications over which he presided. Government by personal fiat was unsuitable for areas which required complex codes of civil and criminal law; bureaucratic administration inevitably developed in India as the country settled down after the period of conquest. The heroes of the Punjab receded into the mists of time, their exploits taking on a more and more epic quality in the eyes of their successors. 'There is a size and force to them we lack', wrote one of them, Philip Mason, in his history of the Indian Civil Service[91]; he entitled his chapter on them 'The Titans of the Punjab'.

Nevertheless, Indian administrators continued to be expected to show qualities of character as well as of mind and the national fascination with the exercise of personal authority over natives showed no signs of withering away: it was constantly refreshed from other sources. As new frontiers opened up in other parts of Asia and in Africa, new heroes appeared upon the scene. Few achieved the fame of the Titans, who sprang to prominence in the spotlight of the Mutiny, but there was a public awareness of them and they were aware of each other; there was no shortage of material for *Blackwood's* even well into the present century. The British empire kept on expanding until shortly before it collapsed, so the frontier mentality never entirely disappeared. It died with the empire.

The myth of the few good men drew sustenance also from another source. When the British, ignoring the innumerable 'little wars' and police actions that were fought throughout the nineteenth century to extend or defend their empire[92], gloried in the exiguous nature of their control over native races, they were not entirely deceiving themselves. If nothing else, the parsimonious attitude to colonial affairs which most British governments deemed incumbent upon them, perhaps to show their imperviousness to romance, ensured that British imperial administration was carried on by far fewer people than that of other European powers as they began to come into the field. That familiar figure, the lone European ruling a million blacks, came closer to reality in the British empire than any other.[93] But a virtue was very much made of necessity. It was something to be proud of that Britain sent so few men to govern her ever-expanding dominions. They were the right men, if results counted for anything.

There were some colonies, particularly in Africa, which experienced a far more prolonged administrative infancy than India, mainly because they were so primitive to begin with. And there was one queer little colony which never grew up at all: Sarawak, which under the watchful eye of its white rajahs remained a frontier for a hundred years. For those imbued with the Punjab spirit, but content to do or die on a smaller scale, it was the perfect place.

Its first rajah, James Brooke, was, like the Punjabis, famous for his temperament as much as his achievements, and like them too was an inspiration to those who came after him. In the wilds of Borneo he carved out for himself a kingdom in which he sought to prove 'the influence to be acquired by conduct with small means'.[94] A true Prospero figure[95], incapable of getting on with his peers, with whom he habitually quarrelled, Brooke was happy and within certain limits successful when called upon to rule over a race of inferior beings. His methods of rule were simple and direct. Justice was administered from a room in his house, and he was accessible to all. It was his habit to see supplicants during dinner, when he would turn aside for a few moments from his guests to attend to the problems of a naked subject who had come to squat beside his chair. He intended at first to rule Sarawak without any European help – for this man who set himself up as absolute ruler of an oriental state believed that contact between Europeans and natives was invariably demoralizing, if not fatal, to the latter. Finding himself obliged eventually to find some Europeans to share the burdens of administration, he chose them as carefully as Henry Lawrence's assistants had been chosen a few years before. They acquired something of the same celebrity.

With magnificent inconsistency, Brooke aspired to rule his native subjects so as to enhance the reputation of his country in their eyes. 'I must always bear in mind', he wrote in a moment of financial despondence, 'that I am not acting for myself alone, and that my loss or gain is but a trifling consideration compared with my character for justice, and the impression of European conduct, generally, on the native mind.'[96] He could never decide whether he was a free agent in Sarawak or a representative of the British empire, and therefore got himself into the impossible position of expecting the British government to support him financially and with naval power, but wholly at his discretion. At bottom, he wanted recognition from those with whose opinions he affected to be unconcerned; like Henry Lawrence, he wished to do his duty without regard for the consequences, but hoped to be thought well of for it. He died a bitter man, convinced quite mistakenly that no one appreciated the great deeds he had done for his country.

Brooke established himself as a gentleman adventurer in the China seas in the late 1830s, and Sarawak more or less fell into his lap in 1841, when he was offered the government of the country in return for his help in suppressing a rebellion by the heir apparent to the sultanate of Brunei, Rajah Muda Hassim. Seeing everything in terms of the forces of light versus the forces of darkness, Brooke never realized how neatly he had been entangled in the power politics of the Malay archipelago, and Muda Hassim never realized what he had taken on in associating himself with Brooke.[97] His attempts in due course to fob off his new ally with the mere shadow of power met with the most determined resistance – for after years of vague hankering after fame and adventure Brooke had discovered his vocation. The man who had written

> I dreamed that honors decked my head,
> I dreamed of conquest hardly won.
> Welcome to the gory bed
> If brief and bright the course I run[98]

was not one to be easily put aside once he had a kingdom in his grasp.

Besides large visions of the good he could do, Brooke had a whimsical approach to it which must have contributed to his famous charm. 'I own that this development of the natives through their own exertions is a *hobby of mine*', he wrote, speaking for generations of District Officers yet unborn.[99] In high spirits he sent off for a magic lantern to begin their education. Other affairs of government were less easily accomplished, and money was usually the problem. Large supplies of it were required to transform the head-hunters of Sarawak into the contented peasantry he hoped to see them become at some distant date, and he abhorred the idea of turning to trade to get it: he was another completely uneconomic imperialist. '*I am averse to and incapable of all matters relating to commerce*', he wrote to his agent in London, whose hopeless task it was to find for him the steady source of income with no worries and no strings attached which would suffice for the governance of Sarawak. His mind, he said, was 'seriously disturbed and injured by the fluctuations, and even the *very discussion of commercial matters*'. They distracted his attention, he claimed, from higher things; and he was convinced that if his subjects saw him engage in trade his prestige in their eyes would suffer an irreversible decline.[100]

He was often discouraged. Reviewing the situation after his first three months as rajah, it seemed to him that he had accomplished little.

> Difficulty following upon difficulty; the dread of pecuniary failure; the doubt of receiving support or assistance: this and much more presents itself to my mind. But I have tied myself to the stake: I have heaped faggots around me. I stand upon a cask of gunpowder, and if others bring the torch I shall not shrink. I feel within me the firm, unchangeable conviction of doing right, which nothing can shake. I see the benefits I am conferring.

God willing, he would soldier on.[101] But in 1846 his fortunes changed. The publication of his journals, coinciding with a long-delayed visit to England, made him a popular hero. He received the freedom of the City of London and was invited to Windsor, where he was inspired to remark, in response to an inquiry from the Queen as to how he found it so easy to manage thousands of wild Borneans, that he found it easier to govern 30,000 Malays and Dyaks than to manage of dozen of Her Majesty's subjects.[102] Behind the neatly-turned compliment to British pugnacity there was, of course, nothing but the truth.

But though he now enjoyed an enormous reputation as the ruler of 30,000 adoring savages, it did not completely escape attention that in spite of all the good he did – and he did do good, abolishing forced trade, for instance, and the debt-slavery that went with it – his authority was not uncontested and his methods of asserting it were at times severe. The contradictions apparent in the career of Henry Lawrence were even more apparent in that of Brooke, and, being a freelance and a self-confessed adventurer, he did not enjoy the same immunity from public criticism. Few in number and truly unrepresentative of popular opinion, his critics gained in strength from his Prosperic inability to let any adverse comment on his actions pass unrebuked.

The trouble sprang from what he regarded as his efforts to extirpate piracy in the waters around Borneo and his critics regarded as, at best, an over-enthusiasm for battle, and, at worst, mere filibustering. The truth would appear to be that His Excellency did not distinguish very carefully among the various disturbers of the peace of the Malay archipelago. Seafaring Malay rivals for power, Dyaks who raided along the coast for heads and the antique Chinese

jars they rather touchingly cherished – they were all 'pirates' to
him.[103] Like Henry Lawrence hanging dacoits in the Punjab,
Brooke saw what needed to be done to establish his peaceable
kingdom, did it, and applied to the offenders a label which attracted
public support and satisfied that highly developed organ, his
conscience. There was probably no deliberate intention to deceive.

What made it particularly difficult for him to understand why he
was being criticized was that he had always been able to count on
support for his activities from the Royal Navy. Pirate-chasing had its
sporting aspect, and there were always officers stationed in Far
Eastern waters who were delighted to give him an unofficial hand
with it. It also had its remunerative aspect. Head-money was paid
by the British government for captured pirates and 'piratical
persons', and this created a substantial inducement to misidentifi-
cation which clouded the Royal Navy's otherwise splendid record in
the nineteenth century as the world's policeman. Brooke was not
eligible for navy bounty: whatever his motives were, they were not
financial. But they certainly included, as the publication of his
journals unfortunately made clear, a singular love of fighting for its
own sake. 'Wild fun' was his description of his first campaign.[104]
'Am I, then, really fond of war?' we find him asking as he planned a
later expedition:

> And I answer – 'Certainly' – for what man is not? And, indeed, what
> else makes among my countrymen so many sailors and soldiers? But if
> I ask myself whether I am *too fond* of war (meaning that I would
> sacrifice justice to gratify my pugnacious propensity), then my
> conscience and my entire conduct through life make me boldly reply
> with a magnificent 'No', for I truly feel that I am entitled to give this
> answer.[105]

The event which brought down the fury of the Radical party on
Brooke's uncomprehending head was his successful campaign of
1849 against the turbulent Saribas and Skrang Dyaks. Assisted by
ships of the Royal Navy, he struck a decisive blow. Nearly 500 of the
enemy were killed in the battle of Batang Maru, many of them cut to
pieces by the paddle-wheels of the steamer *Nemesis*, with about 500
more dying later of wounds and exposure in the jungle. Their
villages were burnt. British casualties in all this were nil, the only
losses on the side of right being '13 or 14 natives, killed and
wounded', according to the captain of the *Nemesis*.[106] The aged
Radical Joseph Hume, supported by Cobden, demanded an inquiry;
but the overwhelming sentiment of the House of Commons was that
it was very poor form indeed to question the integrity of a man

whom all decent people from the Queen on down knew to be a hero. Brooke's reputation protected him absolutely. Parliament averted its eyes before the dazzling clarity of his conscience, and a naval action undertaken at the behest of a private person and involving hundreds of casualties was not deemed worthy of investigation. It would be hard to think of a better example of how an accepted purity of intention could absolve Englishmen from a sense of moral responsibility for the bloodier side of their imperial affairs.

But the Radicals pressed their arguments, and a time came when the government of the day needed their support. An inquiry eventually took place in 1854 in Singapore, under the aegis of the Indian government. Brooke was exonerated of all the charges against him, but one of the commissioners, Charles Prinsep, wondered publicly if the pirates need have been dealt with quite so severely. The question which exercised his mind, he said, was whether Brooke's judgement had been corrupted by his prolonged exposure to the morality of savages.[107]

The answer to this appears to be 'No': Brooke's judgement had never been very reliable, by civilized standards, where matters of life and death were concerned. From the very beginning of his assumption of power in Sarawak he had depended for his fighting force on the head-hunting Dyaks. This often meant setting one group of Dyaks on to another, and the military encounters which resulted were not edifying. Shortly before he left Sarawak he founded the Sarawak Rangers, a predominantly Dyak force, which gave some semblance of regularity to the employment of these primitive warriors. But the essential Sarawak campaign, which went on more or less permanently as the country was never completely pacified, remained the rajah or local Resident setting off to war at the head of a crowd of enthusiastic natives bent on adding a few more skulls to the ones already decorating their longhouses. Rajah Charles Brooke, James Brooke's nephew and successor, was even more adept at this special form of warfare than his uncle; he led his last punitive expedition in 1903 at the age of seventy-three. The Dyaks were used to particular effect in 1857 to suppress a Chinese rising, pursuing the rebels through the forest where they had taken refuge and bringing back the heads of the fallen to be cooked in front of their relatives in the Kuching bazaar. A European trader, Mr Tidman, recorded his disgust at the spectacle of 'one set of savages [being] called in to punish another'. 'This feast of heads', he prophesied, 'will put off the civilisation of the Dyaks, and the prosperity of Sarawak, *sine die.*'[108] He was right: the Brookes never managed to distinguish very clearly between pacification, the object in view, and war, the means of achieving it.

Sarawak became a British protectorate in 1888, but, having little strategic and less economic significance, its internal affairs were largely ignored by the British government. The Sarawak administrative service became a sort of Lost Legion, gone permanently native, and indeed appeared in Kipling's poem of that name, written to celebrate the unsung path-breakers of empire. The paths broken in Sarawak led nowhere: there was never any serious attempt at economic or political development. Nevertheless, Sarawak officers had a high opinion of themselves and recalled with pride the origins of their service in James Brooke's few carefully chosen and risibly paid assistants. They took native mistresses, tattooed themselves *à la* Dyak, marched and counter-marched, and avoided other Europeans. They horrified the Colonial Office but inspired the Colonial Service, especially in Malaya.[109]

Only with the Second World War did those happy, wish-fulfilling days come to an end, first with the Japanese occupation and then with the cession of the country to the British Crown in 1946. The last rajah, Vyner Brooke, a man usually described as weak but perhaps only afflicted with a sense of the ridiculous, saw that the few good men of Sarawak had finally had their day.

Exciting as they were, the exploits of Brooke and his contemporaries in the Punjab were not perhaps enough in themselves to fix in the minds of Englishmen the belief that they were uniquely blessed with the capacity to overawe. What removed all doubts was the eccentric career of General Gordon, whose strange life and stranger death combined to provide the ultimate proof. In the event, Gordon failed spectacularly to display the invincibility with which, on the basis of his past achievements and striking personality, he was widely credited; but when he died the public found itself, against all reason, astonished, and instead of discarding the myth in the face of the facts revised the facts to fit the myth.

Gordon was a soldier of fortune who never in all his life held an important command in the British army. The troops he led to victory in out-of-the-way places were not British troops but Chinese, Egyptians, and Africans. Contrary to popular belief at the time, they were not irregulars but professional soldiers paid by the governments to whom Gordon lent his sword; their standards of discipline leaving something to be desired, it was assumed by Gordon's admirers that they fought only because he inspired them to do so. Gordon did not fight for money, to which he was truly indifferent. Much of what he earned was spent on his numerous private charities. Like Henry Lawrence, though, he was not indifferent to honours, at least not big ones. Most people thought the Chinese had had to press upon him the high distinction of the Yellow Jacket, but in fact he told them at the end of his term of service that it was the Yellow Jacket or nothing.[110] On the other hand, when he was in command of the Royal Engineers in Mauritius in one of his periods of wilful oblivion, he made a point of covering up his medals with his hat when he went to church. Everyone knew his aversion to praise – 'I had rather be dead than praised' was one of his most quoted *mots* – but few noticed the passage in his published journals in which he declared:

> What a fearful infliction hero-worship is to its victim. I think it a great impertinence to praise a man to his face. It implies you are his superior, for the greater praises the smaller; and though that may be the case, it is not necessary to announce it to the smaller.[111]

Well-known also was his aversion to society: he was denouncing dinner parties almost to the last. Friends who invited him to pass an evening at their table were liable to be accused of luring him into frivolity. People concluded therefore that he lived by a higher standard of seriousness than ordinary mortals. He did, but this was not the only reason why dinner parties were a trial to him. He confided to his sister that 'you are certain to say something you regret'; it was 'a different thing with one's brothers and sisters; they know you are a "tuppenny" and full of faults, and do not pick at you like strangers'.[112]

Gordon's religious beliefs were peculiar in the extreme and came as a nasty shock to politicians who first became acquainted with them when they were published shortly after he was sent to Khartoum. His belief that Mauritius was the Garden of Eden, based on the vulval contours of a certain Mauritian fruit, leaves one wondering if he was entirely sane. Probably not, but at least he possessed the proverbial lucidity of the maniac, often seeing the obvious solutions which failed to reveal themselves to more encumbered minds.

He was not a conventional imperialist and disapproved of India as a drag on policy and a corrupter of morals, a fatal place which enveloped Europeans in a delusive grandeur.[113] His instinctive conception of empire was as a roving commission to set the world to rights. Only frontiers interested him.

His reputation was made by the campaign he fought in China in 1863–4, leading a brigade of government troops known as the Ever-Victorious Army against the Taiping rebels. His exploits earned him the sobriquet 'Chinese Gordon', by which he was known to his countrymen until he entered history as Gordon of Khartoum. These adventures, consisting as they did of assaults on mysterious walled cities defended by Eastern fanatics, had the appeal of high romance, but what seems to have struck people most about them was that they were accomplished without Gordon himself resorting to the use of force. The story which is found in all the biographies – and which seems to have made its first appearance in Andrew Wilson's *The 'Ever-Victorious Army'*, published by Blackwood's in 1868 – is that Gordon, though always in the thick of the battle, never carried any weapon other than a little cane, which he used to direct his troops. The Chinese called this cane Gordon's 'magic wand of victory'.[114]

This is so much a part of the Gordon legend, so much associated with Gordon's distinctive personality, that it comes as something of a surprise to learn that it was not a particularly original thing to do. His predecessor in command of the Ever-Victorious Army, an American by the name of Frederick Ward, led his troops brandishing a riding crop[115], and at this period it was by no means uncommon for regular British officers to go into battle unarmed or very lightly armed: Lord Cardigan led the charge of the Light Brigade equipped only with a cigar. Assuming the British public to be ignorant of Ward's demeanour on the battlefield, it would appear that Gordon's behaviour was notable to them because he was serving in a foreign army and leading troops who supposedly felt no institutionalized compulsion to obey him. By disdaining to arm himself he was showing them what true leadership was all about, and it was their awe of him which caught the public's attention.

The public also concluded that bloodshed was a thing abhorrent to Gordon and that he somehow won his battles without it, a theme which is implicit throughout the vast hagiographical literature which sprang up after his death. This literature is notable for, among other things, the way in which the profession of soldiering seems reduced in it to the leadership of men – a wilful misapprehension perhaps only possible where the battlefield is too distant and too unpeopled with bodies like one's own to matter very much. But Gordon knew – though he never doubted his own ability to inspire disorderly troops to feats of valour inconceivable without him[116] – that his battles were won not by waving his magic wand of victory but by efficiently deploying his heavy artillery. He carried on his conscience for the rest of his days the slaughter inflicted at Quinsan, where over 4,000 fleeing Taipings were killed at the cost of only two men on his own side.

This apparent ability to win battles without fighting argued for remarkable powers of personality, and the public were unwilling to set a limit to what Gordon might thereby accomplish. Like Henry Lawrence he was credited with the ability, purely by force of example, to make the evil do good. He supposedly cast his spell upon Li Hung Chang, the governor of Kiangsu province and official commander of the Ever-Victorious Army, who came by degrees 'to understand that what this man cared for supremely, or only, was truth and justice and mercy', and thereby received 'a new revelation . . . of what goodness is' – 'the conquest of "Governor Li" himself', as this contemporary admirer put, 'by Gordon's character'.[117] Gordon would have been amused at the idea that he revealed to Li Hung Chang the true nature of goodness; by the end of the campaign he had come to feel a reluctant admiration for Li's imperturbable realism.[118]

His motives for going into battle unarmed are unknown, this being one topic – there are very few – on which Gordon chose to remain silent. The military historian John Keegan has suggested that such behaviour on the part of British officers at this time arose from a desire to dissociate themselves from the plebeian work of killing and define themselves as candidates for honourable wounds.[119] This may have formed part of Gordon's thinking: honour was very dear to him. But it is hard to overlook the element of bravado in behaviour of this sort. Frederick Ward was clearly not in search of honourable wounds; he was simply showing off. Perhaps he was Gordon's immediate inspiration. Be this as it may, it is apparent from everything that is known about him that Gordon had a great liking for danger – so marked indeed that one biographer, Anthony Nutting, has explained it by the existence of a longing for extinction. It would seem more plausible, however, to attribute it to an addiction to outwitting death. Though Gordon at times expressed a wish to be gathered home to the Friend (his name for Jesus), he otherwise displayed no suicidal preoccupations and was the least passive of men. We may presume that when he came through another action unharmed, or saw the dawn break over Khartoum after a night spent sitting at a lighted window for all the world to see and take aim at, he felt the surge of adrenalin known to players of Russian roulette. God – or something – had protected him again! The likelihood is that his numerous survivals gave him a sense of power, and confirmed his belief that he was preserved to be the instrument of divine purpose in the world. The public sensed, and to an extraordinary extent accepted, this assumption of invincibility.

The next significant stage in Gordon's career was his employment by the Egyptian government to suppress the slave trade in the Sudan. The task was too big for him, as it would have been for any single man: the slave trade was the life-blood of the Sudanese economy. Nevertheless, the years in the Sudan, from 1874 to 1879, added justifiably to his reputation, for though his achievements were ephemeral they were genuinely the result of daring and resource, which was usually all he had to draw on. With very little force at his disposal, he faced down rebellious tribesmen, Abyssinian free-booters, and grandees of the slave trade. He loved to set out on immense camel journeys, outdistance his escort, and burst unaccompanied upon some lonely outpost or nest of robbers. Of civil administration he knew nothing and he evinced no desire to learn: its complexities overwhelmed him.

This, then, was the man selected by acclamation for the fateful mission to Khartoum in 1884. To this day, historians argue over just what it was that the British government intended him to do towards solving the problems created by the Mahdist rebellion in the Sudan, but there can be no doubt what the public expected of him. 'We cannot send a regiment to Khartum', wrote W.T. Stead in the celebrated editorial which inspired the clamour for Gordon's appointment,

> but we can send a man who on more than one occasion has proved himself more valuable in similar circumstances than an entire army. Why not send Chinese Gordon with full powers to Khartum, to assume absolute control of the territory, to treat with the Mahdi, to relieve the garrisons, and to do what he can to save what can be saved from the wreck of the Sudan?[120]

In an inspired phrase, Stead urged the government to 'Sarawak the Sudan', meaning to get someone like Gordon to set himself up as a benevolent and semi-independent ruler on the cheap: the white rajah was by then an established figure in the imperial landscape.[121] Gladstone and the Liberal government, deeply reluctant to commit themselves to an imperial war, may have thought they were sending Gordon out to evacuate the beleaguered Egyptian garrisons, but everyone else knew he was going out singlehanded to put things straight.

It seems inconceivable that Gordon's reputation as a miracle-worker failed to play any part in the Cabinet's deliberations. His task, by almost any definition, was a superhuman one, and the risk involved in sending anyone less than extraordinary into the Sudan at that time must have been obvious. Gladstone was a ruthless man but few have supposed him to be so ruthless as to send someone to certain death for the sake of momentarily appeasing public opinion: he must at least have believed that Gordon was unlikely to come to harm. It is worth recalling that as a younger man he had been briefly under the spell of James Brooke; perhaps even in old age he was not immune to the dragonslayer's fatal charm. There is evidence, furthermore, that at least one member of the Cabinet had enough belief in Gordon's prestige with the natives to suppose that he might actually be able unassisted to provide a cheap, popular and Liberal solution to the problem of the Sudan. 'Do you see any objection to using Gordon in some way?' Granville asked Gladstone in November 1883, over a month before Stead unleashed his press campaign: 'He has an immense name in Egypt – he is popular at home. He is a strong, but sensible, opponent of slavery. He has a small bee in his bonnet.' The tone is hardheaded – Granville no doubt intended it to be – but the faith implicitly revealed is as simple as that of the man-in-the-street. How far it was shared by his colleagues we do not know; but Gladstone did agree to ask Baring, the British Agent in Egypt, if Gordon would be 'of any use to you or to the Egyptian government, and if so, in what capacity'.[122] And thus it seems to have come about that a Cabinet professedly averse to imperial adventures of any kind found itself embarking on what was in a sense the ultimate imperial adventure – sending a single man on a mission which by all logical calculation required an army to carry out.

The scene of Gordon's departure for the Sudan remains one of the most haunting in the history of the empire, so saturated is it with the imperial imagery of the day. Alone, Gordon took a taxi to Charing Cross, where he was met by a cabinet minister (Lord Granville), the Adjutant-General (Lord Wolseley), and the Commander-in-Chief of the army (the royal Duke of Cambridge). Granville bought his ticket, Wolseley carried his bag, and the Duke of Cambridge opened the carriage door for him. Gordon had forgotten his uniform, and his money. At the last moment his nephew arrived with the uniform, and Wolseley pressed upon him his gold watch and chain and all the loose cash he had in his pocket. There is no need to suppose, as has often been supposed by historians unwilling to imagine senior officials of the British government sharing the passions of the mob, that these dignitaries turned up at Charing Cross out of embarrassment – animated, as it were, by a guilty desire to give the condemned man a hearty breakfast. They came, as all admirers of Gordon have instinctively known, to do him homage. And Gordon himself, arriving at the station with nothing at all to suggest that he was other than a private individual, and a singularly unworldly one at that, played his part to perfection.

Once let loose, he was off like a rocket, his optimism and enthusiasm knowing no bounds. 'Do not be panic-stricken. We are men, not women. I am coming', he telegraphed to Khartoum from Cairo.[123] Arrival at the scene of danger quickened all his fighting instincts, and before long he was talking about 'smashing up the Mahdi'. But he underestimated the enemy, and he was soon forced on to the defensive. Being unwilling to save his own neck at the expense of those for whose welfare he believed himself to be responsible, he ended up marooned in the besieged garrison of Khartoum, the recipient of strangely beseeching messages from the Mahdi, who seems to have recognized in him a fellow seeker after truth.[124] When his plight became known at home the public which had clamoured for him to be sent unassisted to the Sudan to turn back the tide of rebellion now displayed a remarkable lack of faith in his powers and clamoured for an expedition to relieve him. The government then found itself after all under irresistible pressure to put an army into the field. The relief expedition, as everyone knows, arrived too late. Khartoum had fallen and Gordon was dead.

As she was so often to do, Queen Victoria led the nation in giving expression to the prevailing sentiment of the day, which was a profound shock at the sudden rude disproof of Gordon's supposedly superhuman mastery of events. Like her subjects, the Queen blamed her ministers for Gordon's death; but this surely was to some extent a displacement of a deeper and less expressible rage directed against the savages who had so disrespectfully murdered England's hero. It was believed for a long time that Khartoum had fallen through treachery[125]: it was an explanation which allowed Gordon to retain some shreds of invincibility.

As time passed, and Gordon's letters to his sister and Khartoum journals were published, a need seems to have been felt to visualize for him a fitting end. In the absence of any reliable evidence as to the manner of his death, it was an overwhelming temptation to deduce the facts from what was known about his character, and this was what happened.[126] The first reports from Khartoum suggested that Gordon had died fighting, but after a few years the accepted version came to be that he had met his end unresisting, standing at the top of the palace stairs dressed in his official uniform and surveying with perfect calm the mob of dervishes below. Details differ, but most accounts have him turning away from his attackers after receiving the first blow. Reports that he had defended himself with a revolver were rejected as implausible, for

> A revolver would better suit one who is swift to shed blood, which Gordon never was; and we cannot suppose that, when once he saw the city was lost, he would wish to destroy life needlessly. Gordon, therefore, in all probability carried either his sword, as several witnesses aver, or if not his sword, then no arms at all, but only that little cane which constantly went with him into battle.

The writer was prepared to allow Gordon his sword on the grounds that it was part of his official uniform, but it is apparent that he would have preferred to think of him, even in that desperate hour, facing his attackers with his wand of victory.[127]

The interpretation of all this is open to some question. There can be no doubt that the passive version of Gordon's death satisfied a need to see him as morally superior to his enemies.[128] The reluctance to imagine him shedding blood, the specifically Christian nature of much of the literature, the curious belief that he was the one Christian who was prayed for at Mecca[129] – all are evidence that this was so. But the gesture of turning away from his attackers also carries with it an unmistakable implication of contempt. It was so interpreted in the earliest complete description we have of Gordon's death, the account of Ibrahim Bey al-Burdayni. Gordon, according to al-Burdayni, was speared through the body, and then, 'it is said, made a gesture of scorn [what was it, one would like to know?] with his right hand, and turned his back, where he received another spear wound, which caused him to fall forward, and was most likely his mortal wound'.[130]

It would be a mistake to impose logical consistency on the public reaction to Gordon's death. But rage was surely as important as sorrow, and if his death was seen as a kind of victory, it was not just as a moral victory but as a victory of the will. He died with a sublime gesture of contempt, supremely confident to the last. There was, of course, no way in which the public expectations of Gordon could be fully reconciled with the fact of failure, but at least it was heartening to know that in the end his daemon had been unbetrayed. Consoling also was the belief, which is supported by the historical evidence, that Gordon was killed in disobedience of the Mahdi's orders.[131] His death could thus be seen as in some sense an accident, the chance work of a person of no account: his aura had remained intact. It was possible therefore, in spite of everything, for Gordon's biographer to write six years after his death that

> it was not so much by force of arms, or skill in the great art of war, that Gordon vanquished his enemies, quelled his own mutinous troops, mastered the slave hunters, and moulded to his will the dusky tribes of the Sudan. No, it was by sheer force of personality. His whole career, in fact, is one long triumph of individuality; and, looked at from this point of view, must have an abiding interest for all people and all time.[132]

Where Gordon had gone, others followed. Once the Sudan had been reconquered, in 1898, and the fact of British dominance unequivocally established, a corps of British administrators set out to rule it in a style which bore a close resemblance to that of Gordon himself. The men of the Sudan Political Service were recruited not by competitive examination, as had become the case with the Indian Civil Service, but by interview with a selection board whose members were looking for brilliance of temperament rather than brilliance of mind. In the words of the founder of the service, Lord Cromer, they were required to be 'active young men, endowed with good health, high character, and fair abilities . . . not the mediocre by-products of the race, but the flower of those who are turned out from schools and colleges'.[133] They ruled over vast and tumultuous provinces with few troops to support them, like Gordon always in motion, exercising initiative to the limits of their individual capacity. They regarded themselves as the elite of British African administrations and retained their tradition of local independence even after the development of communications brought the outlying districts into regular contact with Khartoum. Had Gordon's imagination been able to encompass the thought of a regular administration, the Sudan Political Service would have been what he wanted.

Gone were the days when the Collector of Boggley Wollah, 'lazy, peevish, and a *bon-vivant*', could be presented to an English audience as a plausible imperial type: he would never have got through the interview. By the time Gordon went to Khartoum there was an established tradition of high imperial behaviour which was perfectly understood by actors and public alike. What Brooke had done in Sarawak, Gordon could do in Khartoum; and Gordon himself in his last days drew inspiration from the memory of Henry Lawrence, beleaguered in his Residency at Lucknow, fighting the good fight as he himself was fighting it at Khartoum. 'P.S.,' ended his last letter to his sister, 'I am quite happy, thank God, & like Lawrence, I have *"tried* to do my duty".'[134] It was as an imperial hero, of a recognizable mould and stamp, that this most individual and unorthodox of men prepared to meet his end. It was as an imperial hero, superior yet representative, that he was honoured after his death.

2

Frederick Courtenay Selous, Adventurer

When the news of Gordon's death reached Cecil Rhodes, at that time an obscure colonial politician, he repeated over and over again, 'I am sorry I was not with him'. So, of course, were thousands of others who persuaded themselves momentarily that they had the stuff of martyrs in them. But Rhodes' was no mere rhetorical statement. Difficult though it is to imagine the Cecil Rhodes known to history falling before the spears of the Mahdi at Khartoum, the event almost took place, and did not only because in Rhodes Gordon encountered someone with a sense of personal destiny equal to his own.

The two men met during one of the less celebrated episodes in Gordon's career, his brief visit to South Africa to sort out the Basuto problem in 1882.[1] By this point in his life Gordon's consciousness of glory was getting the better of him. He treated the instructions of his employers, the Cape authorities, with the contempt due to the utterances of the unenlightened. He reviewed his troops – he was Commandant-General of the colony's forces – dressed in a shabby frock coat and top hat, yet deplored their insubordination. Invited to South Africa in the expectation that he would squash the Basutos as he had the Taipings, he decided he liked them and advocated prayer and reconciliation instead. The inevitable flaming row and ultimate resignation followed and he left the Cape disgusted with almost everybody except Rhodes, with whom he was deeply taken. Rhodes was only twenty-nine at the time and unknown outside South Africa, but he had a strong enough sense of his own indwelling importance to decline the offer of the world-famous older man to 'stay with me and we will work together', an offer made in the confident expectation that it would be accepted. Gordon spurned could not resist remarking that: 'There are very few men in the world to whom I would make such an offer, but of course you *will* have your way. I

48

have never met a man so strong for his own opinion; you think your views are always right.' This was comical coming from Gordon, but after the first pique he seems to have borne Rhodes no ill will. On the eve of his departure for the Sudan he remembered him and telegraphed him to join him. Rhodes, on the verge of acquiring cabinet office in the Cape Parliament, thought about it and then refused. He was spared to become the Colossus. Such conjunctions of men and events incline one to think of God as an ironist.

Gordon appealed to a side of Rhodes' character which most modern students of his life feel unable to take seriously and which strained the credulity even of many of his contemporaries, some of them his admirers. He claimed to be driven by an ideal vision of a world dominated for its own good by the Anglo-Saxon race, a world in which wars would cease and decency prevail in the public life of nations. Such a conception seems so at odds with the squalor of his methods, which was widely suspected if not definitely known, except to a few, during his lifetime, that it is hard to believe he meant it. In the very country to which he gave his name it was put about at the time of his death that his last words were not, as in the official version, 'So little done, so much to do', but 'So few done, so many left to do'. Yet a glance at the fantastic document which was his will is enough to show that he thought passionately, and with a sense of original revelation, about the empire as the practical expression of an ideal of personality. It was for this reason that he was able to attract into his orbit men who set out to live such an ideal – like Gordon; and like the subject of this chapter, Frederick Selous. The interest of Selous' life lies in the attempt of a self-consciously exemplary man to come to terms with the imperialism whose baser nature Rhodes eventually laid bare to him.

The document which Rhodes called his Confession of Faith was written in 1877 while he was at Oxford, and remained throughout his life the basis of his will. It was such an embarrassment to his biographers that none of them reproduced it unexpurgated until John Flint in 1974.[2] Rhodes would have been amazed and annoyed at this for he regarded the composition of the Confession as an epoch-making event in human history and showed it with pride to those deemed worthy of a peep into his soul. The mistakes of grammar and punctuation, the crudities of thought and expression which discomfited those wishing to raise a dignified biographical monument to his memory, were nothing to Rhodes, who was unaware of them.

The premise from which Rhodes starts out is that 'we are the finest race in the world and that the more of it we inhabit the better it is for the human race'. 'Just fancy', he says, 'those parts that are at present inhabited by the most despicable specimens of human beings what an alteration there would be if they were brought under Anglo-Saxon influence. . .' Just fancy, too, he goes on, what a difference it would have made to America to have remained an English colony: 'great as they have become how infinitely greater they would have been with the softening and elevating influences of English rule. . .' But he consoles himself with the thought that there remains, awaiting benign Anglo-Saxon attention, the rest of the world. 'We know the size of the world,' he writes,

> we know the total extent. Africa is still lying ready for us. It is our duty to take it. It is our duty to seize every opportunity of acquiring more territory and we should keep this one idea steadily before our eyes that more territory simply means more of the Anglo-Saxon race more of the best the most human, most honourable race the world possesses.

In Rhodes' mind the simple lust for territory co-existed in full consciousness with the belief that the empire justified itself by the moral uplift it produced: unlike a great many others he saw no need to deny the one to make more credible the other. Nor did he ever make the mistake, so tempting to Englishmen brought up on the heroic legends of the Punjab and Rajah Brooke, of supposing that empire could be acquired by moral influence alone. In his apparent simplicity Rhodes understood that the process of expansion itself was essentially amoral.

The heart of the will was a proposal for a secret society, to be organized by the executor with Rhodes' money. Pondering on the Jesuits and the Masons and what they had been able to accomplish, Rhodes had experienced a moment of illumination. In his own words:

> The idea gleaming and dangling before one's eyes like a will-of-the-wisp at last frames itself into a plan. Why should we not form a secret society with but one object the furtherance of the British Empire and the bringing of the whole uncivilised world under British rule for the recovery of the United States for the making the Anglo-Saxon race but one Empire. What a dream, but yet it is probable, it is possible.

In the hands of advisers such as Lord Rothschild the secret society transformed itself eventually into the Rhodes scholarship scheme, but even in the final and most conventional version of the will it is clear that Rhodes himself never abandoned the earlier plan.[3] It remained 'the idea' which was to transform the history of the world, the idea which in Rhodes' mind was like something an inventor might register at the Patent Office.[4] Nor was Rhodes the only person to take it seriously. We do not know to whom exactly he unburdened himself – Gordon, probably, was one – but they were not all eccentrics and outsiders. A letter survives from Reginald Brett, later Lord Esher and one of the sturdiest pillars of the Edwardian establishment, betraying considerable excitement over 'the idea' as it had been unveiled to him by Rhodes, and suggesting to him that the society be organized along the lines of a snowball subscription.[5]

A curious feature of the society as described in the Confession is Rhodes' conception of the types of people who might be approached about membership. First he makes the obvious suggestion that promising schoolboys and university men should be watched for signs of suitability to his purpose; but the other recruits are all imagined by him as people who lack a sense of purpose in life – a rich man tired of what money can buy, a younger son compelled to earn a living in a dreary job, even 'a man of great wealth, who is bereft of his children perhaps having his mind soured by some bitter disappointment who shuts himself up separate from his neighbours and makes up his mind to a miserable existence'. Underneath the heroic ideal of empire by which Rhodes professedly was inspired there was, it seems, another, very different, ideal which he could not directly express: an ideal of community in the most radical sense – as an escape from existential loneliness and despair. A man who can clothe such a prospect with the appearance of reality will find recruits to his banner in any age. There is never a shortage of people whose need for community remains unsatisfied by ordinary human relationships, and some of them seek their satisfaction in amorphous brotherhoods whose demands on them appear greater but are actually less.

Though Rhodes himself no doubt felt such stirrings, they were, of course, only one element in his complicated character. Unlike most people who fantasize about finding meaning in life through devotion to a cause, he loved money, was very good at making it, and had so clear an appreciation of its usefulness that, though he was a gentleman by birth, few people in England thought of him as one. He was aghast when Gordon told him he had refused a roomful of Chinese gold: there was no use, Rhodes reminded him, in having big ideas if you had not the cash to carry them out.[6] Nor did he ever feel restrained by his belief in the moral superiority of the Anglo-Saxon race from treating his fellow Englishmen as though every man had his price, as indeed he had good reason to suppose that they did. His personal life was unorthodox but by no means pathologically so. He never married and would have preferred Rhodes scholars to be celibate[7], but he was capable of friendship and occasionally of deep attachment. When his friend and secretary Neville Pickering lay dying his grief was such that he was unable to attend to business – a prostration which seems the more remarkable when we consider that this was at a critical time in the race for control of the Rand. He may have been, like Winston Churchil, a chronic depressive who stimulated himself by activity.[8] Certainly, he showed some depressive characteristics. Like Churchill, he spent a great deal of time lying in bed, 'a favourite thinking and scheming place of his', as one of his associates perceptively observed.[9] And he showed a genuine elation in the face of mortal danger – the ultimate occasion to which depressives are prone to rise.

Sordid as his activities often were, Rhodes possessed a personal charm which excited and bewildered people and made them temporarily oblivious of the tremendous contradictions in his nature. Even so devoted an enemy as the radical Henry Labouchere was enchanted by him when he finally met him. But he could not enchant everybody, only those who came within the range of personal contact, and his too evident regard for money, not to mention his assumption that everyone shared it, ruled him out as a true imperial hero for the British people. His readiness to spend his private fortune to expand the British empire endeared him to politicians who wanted territory without public expense; but it never quite succeeded in endearing him to a public already accustomed to see its men of empire in a more ethereal light. Admired he was, but more as a natural phenomenon whose manifestations seemed in harmony with the right design of the universe than as a man: there are no memorials to him in the Abbey or St Paul's.

Frederick Courtenay Selous was such an obvious candidate for Rhodes' secret brotherhood – intelligent, athletic, patriotic, and at the time of his critical encounter with Rhodes, unattached and sadly in need of a purpose in life – that it was tempting at times while doing the research for this chapter to assume that at some point he had been enlisted to the cause. But there is no evidence that any approach was made, and though Selous became an important agent of Rhodes' plans the two men seem never to have been really close. Relations between them were complicated by Selous' own ambition, which in his innocence he imagined could be pitted against that of Rhodes, and, though it was sorely tried and often proved wanting, ultimately by the honesty for which he was famous. These two things kept Selous an agent rather than a collaborator, and an unpredictable one at that.

The two men first met in 1879[10], when Rhodes was on his way to acquiring the fortune which had only existed in aspiration when he wrote the Confession of Faith and Selous had just completed his eighth unprofitable year in the bush. Misled by the romantic accounts of William Charles Baldwin and Gordon Cumming, Selous arrived in South Africa too late to make a living, as he had hoped to do, out of ivory hunting. Most of the elephants south of the Zambesi were already accounted for and those which remained were in the 'fly' country, where horses could not be used, and therefore had to be hunted on foot – a difficult, dangerous, and unremunerative pursuit. Selous never had the success under these conditions enjoyed by some of the famous Boer hunters of the day. As a hunter, he perhaps had more courage than skill: he was three years in Africa before he shot his first lion, and he was never considered a first-class shot by those qualified to judge.[11]

After the first excitement of Africa had worn off he was chronically distraught about money; he even considered suicide, though not, apparently, returning to England.[12] England he loved in theory but abhorred in practice. After the age of seventeen, he never spent more than a few months at a time there if he could help it. He was probably another depressive, looking for change and excitement to keep the vital juices flowing. His sister remembered him as not having had 'the love of life that would have seemed so natural – though there seemed to be so much in his life to live for'.[13] The year 1879 was a particularly desolating one, though Selous was not in fact to touch bottom until ten years later, at which point Rhodes turned up in his life again, this time with critical results. In 1879 two of his best friends died, and he himself was seriously ill for months with recurrent attacks of malaria which he barely survived. In his weakened state the death of his friend French, lost in the bush and overcome by thirst, affected him horribly. 'For several nights', he wrote, 'I never slept, as the vision of my lost friend . . . wandering about and dying by inches, continually haunted me.'[14] He himself, a year after his arrival in Africa, had survived being lost for three days and four nights[15], but French's miserable end, coming at a time when Africa seemed neither so wonderful nor so new, appears to have made dreadfully plain to him what his own future might very well contain: an inglorious death at the end of a brief and unremembered life.

It was at this point that he decided to be a writer, and thus began not only to earn a living but also to establish the reputation for physical and moral prowess which eventually was to make him so valuable an asset to Cecil Rhodes, and to confuse him in his encounters with him. 'I hope to be in England by the end of the year', he wrote to his family in March 1880:

I shall then go in for writing a book, for which I may get a little money. I know that people have got good sums for writing bad books on Africa, full of lies, though I do not know if a true book will sell well. My book at any rate will command a large sale out here, as I am so well known, and have a reputation for speaking nothing but the truth.[16]

The result was *A Hunter's Wanderings in Africa* (1881), a narrative of thrilling adventure which enjoyed an immediate and long-lasting success.

With remarkable skill for a novice writer Selous managed to make his communicated personality the guarantee of his veracity. *A Hunter's Wanderings* was written in an intimate, conversational, and self-deprecating style which was at that time unknown in books on big game hunting, though it had become fairly common in other types of travel writing since Alexander Kinglake's *Eothen* in 1844. Selous' inspiration was to apply this technique to a traditionally vainglorious subject, thereby automatically increasing the plausibility of his narrative and also drawing the reader empathetically into it; in *A Hunter's Wanderings*, the reader is given hope that he, too, might acquit himself decently if he encountered a charging elephant. We discover that Selous was at first such 'a tyro in forest lore' that when he was lost in the bush he went cold and hungry because he had no idea how to start a fire without matches. We learn, too, that his aim was not unerring: 'I fired at her first,' he writes of a lioness shot by a companion, 'but missed her most disgracefully, though I was very close to her.' Running through heavy sand under a tropical sun, he tells us, 'is no joke', and he describes a working costume as informal as his prose – a hat, a shirt, and a leather belt. Curiously enough, he had himself photographed in this scanty outfit, and the photograph appears in J.G. Millais' biography, with 'shorts' whited in on the bare legs.

A sense of humour, grim on occasion, contributed to the charm of the book. We learn, for example, that when an elephant stamps on someone, 'persons thus operated upon are seldom known to complain of their treatment after it is over'. When an elephant tries the treatment on the author he wriggles free and beats 'a hasty retreat, having had rather more than enough of elephants for the time being'. Everything in the jungle is very cosy – so cosy indeed that one almost forgets that the experience which the reader is invited to share remains the despatch to the nether regions, for no compelling reason, of large numbers of harmless animals. Selous was aware of some incongruity here. The book may appear, he admits, 'a dreadful record of slaughter, but it must be remembered, that I was often accompanied by a crowd of hungry savages, exclusive of the men in my employ, all of whom were entirely dependent upon me for their daily food'. There were times, he says, when he had wished the shots unfired that laid some lovely creature low, as when a cow giraffe, dying by his hand, 'reared her lofty head once more, and gazed reproachfully at me with her large soft dark eyes' – but his hungry Kafirs were on the scent, so 'stifling all remorseful feelings, I again raised my rifle and put an end to the miseries of my victim, whose head, pierced with a heavy bullet, fell with a thud upon the ground, never to be raised again'. Selous often denied shooting animals for sport – a singular claim for a big game hunter to make – but the thrill of the chase permeated everything he wrote.

He denied, too, being especially brave, but his narrative told its own story, and his self-deprecating commentary on it demonstrated that he was modest as well. Once he shot an elephant cow with a calf, and he describes how the calf, which was 'quite large enough to pound one to a jelly', charged everyone who approached the dead mother. Trying to distract its attention, he

> let it come on to close quarters, and then dashing a heavy assegai into its face, sprang past it at the same time. This feat, which after all required nothing but a little presence of mind and judgment, seemed greatly to astonish the Kafirs, who declared that 'to-day we have seen that the white man's heart is hard'.

In such relatively unarmed encounters Selous established his claim to be not a butcher of harmless animals but a brave and honourable fellow: courage, not killing, was indicated to be the point of the book. In his concluding comments on the elephant calf he managed to suggest both a soldierly respect for a valorous enemy and a friendly concern for baby animals bereft by unfortunate necessity of parental care. 'I was very glad', he writes, 'he had at last made up his mind to decamp, as it would have been a thousand pities to shoot such a plucky little beast, and I had really begun to think I should be obliged to do so before I could take possession of his mother's carcass.'[17]

The book began with a disarming preface, a model of how to seem modest while asserting firmly the claims one intends to make. His views on the behaviour of wild animals may be different, Selous admits, from those of 'other men equally competent to give an opinion; but, at all events, they are the result of long personal experience of the beasts themselves . . .' He has visited, he says, areas hitherto unknown to Europeans, but as the expeditions were not undertaken for a scientific object but in search of game, 'I do not claim any credit to myself for their results'. He will try, he concludes, to express himself in plain English, and he trusts that the shortcomings of the book 'will be leniently judged when it is remembered that the last nine years of my life have been passed amongst savages, during which time I have not undergone the best training for a literary effort'.[18]

The authorial personality so vividly conveyed in *A Hunter's Wanderings* – honest, modest, brave, and enlivened by an innocent love of mischief – was one which was thoroughly familiar to English readers. It was that of Tom Brown and his successors in innumerable annals of schoolboy adventure. The resemblance does not seem to have been coincidental. Selous entered Rugby seven years after *Tom Brown's School Days* made its immensely successful appearance on the literary scene, and his adventures at school bore so close a resemblance, both in style and in substance, to those of the celebrated Thomas that one can assume a powerful influence to have been at work.[19] Like Henry Lawrence, Selous, it seems, set out to create himself in his own image, and, despite a disfiguring self-consciousness, he enjoyed a certain degree of success. On his courage it would be impertinent to comment. Of his modesty, it may be said that though everyone remarked on his reluctance to talk about himself it is not recorded that anyone ever failed to get him to do so. His honesty, as will become clear, was of a complex kind, but the aspiration to be honest was one which never entirely left him, and honesty was what he sought most strenuously to suggest about himself. At Rugby, even long after the death of Dr Arnold, lying was the sin against the Holy Ghost, and of Selous it could perhaps be said that he cherished a lifelong fantasy of being an honest man.

I have quoted liberally from *A Hunter's Wanderings* partly to show why it seems certain that Rider Haggard based the character of Allan Quatermain upon Selous. Haggard always denied this, saying he had conceived the character of Quatermain before meeting Selous.[20] Perhaps so, but the narrator of *A Hunter's Wanderings* (1881) and the narrator of *King Solomon's Mines* (1885) might easily, except for the difference in age (Quatermain is older), be one and the same person. Not only are their professions and attributes of character the same, but they speak with the same voice. Quatermain's style is more polished than Selous', with the professional storyteller's trick of hinting that there is more to be told than space permits, and as is appropriate for an older man, he loves to take the long view; but the similarities are nevertheless striking. Quatermain's 'Introduction' to *King Solomon's Mines*, for example, is a more titillating version of Selous' preface to *A Hunter's Wanderings*, ending up in exactly the same way with an apology for the book's shortcomings which is at the same time an assertion of the author's qualifications for writing it. 'And now', Quatermain concludes, 'it only remains for me to offer apologies for my blunt way of writing. I can but say in excuse of it that I am more accustomed to handle a rifle than a pen, and do not make any pretence to the grand literary flights and flourishes which I see in novels . . .'[21] Like Selous also, Quatermain hunts trouserless and fortifies himself with cold tea; and he and his companions strike out into the unknown from Sitanda's Kraal, the furthest point reached by Selous in his wanderings up to 1880. An African servant in *King Solomon's Mines* meets the same gruesome end as an African servant in *A Hunter's Wanderings*, torn to pieces by an elephant who holds him down with his foot while taking him apart with his trunk. The only difference is that in *King Solomon's Mines* the man dies in an attempt to save his white master – a quite usual end for servants in imperial fiction.[22]

Selous unwittingly provided the point of connection between two literary creations – Tom Brown and Allan Quatermain – which were virtual archetypes of the Victorian world view. But the interconnection between his life and literature did not stop there. Through the medium of romance, his personality came to represent for a vast audience a quintessential imperial type, and that he was conscious of this there can be no doubt. He became in time a friend of Haggard's and was accustomed to seeing himself referred to in print as the original of one of the most popular fictional characters of the day. What seems to have happened then is that life imitated art once again. With each succeeding book, until the sudden loss of verve in *Sport and Travel, East and West*, published in 1900, Selous sounded more and more like Quatermain. The *faux* clumsy style, the conspicuous diffidence in asserting opinions, the little touches of humour, the rough-hewn philosophizing – they are Quatermain to the life, if that is the term; the only thing missing is the *Ingoldsby Legends*. The effect of all this is rather ambiguous. Read as fiction, Selous' books are a delight, and may be recommended to children; read as fact, they are very much less attractive. This is because in the one case – Quatermain – we have art imitating the naturalness and spontaneity of life; but in the other – Selous – we suspect that we have life lived with the self-consciousness of art.

One rhetorical habit which Selous noticeably picked up from Quatermain was that of claiming to be a timid man. There is barely a hint of this in *A Hunter's Wanderings*, but it appears in full flower in the later books, and as all fans of Quatermain know, it was, to quote Sir Henry Curtis recalling his dead friend in *Allan Quatermain*, 'a favourite trick of his to talk of himself as a timid man, whereas really, though very cautious, he possessed a most intrepid spirit'.[23]

Haggard's readers – and Selous' – required, of course, no prompting to understand these professions of timidity as a form of modesty.

As time passed Selous seems to have begun to think of his personality as something he might bequeath to the nation. In 1895 he sat to J.G. Millais' father, Sir John Millais, for his last drawing, which shows a white man (Selous, though he is not identified) lying dead on the veldt while his black servants sit nearby in attitudes of desolation. It has the very Victorian title, 'The last "trek"'. In 1914 the younger Millais came upon him one day composing a memoir of his school days in the form of a story for a boy's magazine. In this story Selous appears under the name of 'John Leroux', whose 'features, if not very handsome or regular, were good enough and never failed to give the impression of an open and honest nature', and who 'was not only a general favourite with all his school-fellows, but was also beloved by all the masters in spite of the fact that his adventurous disposition was constantly leading him to transgress all the rules of the school'. 'All prevarication', Selous assures us, 'was foreign to John Leroux's nature', and, like Arthur in *Tom Brown's School Days*, young John never uses a crib for his translations.[24] Millais, the dutiful memorialist, printed it all, noting without irony that in the course of his existence Selous had become 'a type and an influence in our national life'.[25]

Selous' death in battle in 1917 at the age of sixty-five, in an obscure action against the Germans in Tanganyika, released a flood of eulogy, all of which dwelt on his supreme conformity to a national type. He was, said *The Times*, 'an example of the very qualities which the Germans hold most in contempt'.[26] Rhodesian settlers recalled with especial admiration the respect he inspired in natives. 'The natives around my farm all remembered him', wrote one,

> though it is well over twenty-five years since he was last here; and it is a pretty good testimony of his character, that wherever he travelled amongst natives, many of whom I have talked to about him, he was greatly respected and esteemed as a just man. We, settlers of Rhodesia, will always have this legacy from him, that he instilled into these natives a very good idea of British justice and fairness.[27]

'Fearless for the right', another recalled, 'and dauntless in the face of danger, he won the hearts of all men, black and white, Englishmen and Boers.'[28] And in the words of another: 'Anything mean or sordid literally shrivelled up in his presence . . . no one has ever left me with the impression of being a "whiter" man . . .'[29] As late as 1960 Selous was still functioning for white Rhodesians as a powerful totem of the tribe. He was, one wrote, of the type of Christian English gentleman who knew how to make friends with backward and coloured peoples, and who consequently were able to gain their respect and obedience. This was the spirit that created the pax Britannica and gave that order, safety and happiness to millions of helpless people in the British Empire, which modern education and so-called democracy strains every nerve to destroy.[30]

It seems only fair to add that, if he did not in fact inspire their reverent awe, Selous seems to have been liked by Africans well enough. The Zimbabwean writer Lawrence Vambe says that his grandparents remembered him as a charming man who won their confidence. And indeed, he had a number of African descendants. One of them, a son, lived in a house in Salisbury bequeathed to him by Selous, and when an attempt was made in the 1960s to evict the family for some project of urban renewal, the authorities were embarrassed to discover that he had in a too literal sense been one of the fathers of his country.[31]

Before 1889 Selous had nothing to do with the formal extension of empire, but was proud to consider himself one of a select group of enterprising Britains who blazed the trail for the flag to follow.[32] The elephant hunters and traders of the not-yet-British interior were, to him, not the unfortunate commercial prelude to the advent of disinterested administration, but the unsung heroes of empire, who by their honesty and plain dealing advertised, as it were, the coming attractions of formal British rule. These men, he wrote in *A Hunter's Wanderings*, had done more

to raise the name of Englishmen among the natives, than all the pamphlets of the stay-at-home aborigines protectionists, who, comfortably seated in the depth of their arm-chairs before a blazing fire, are continually thundering forth denunciations against the rapacious British colonist, and the "low immoral trader", who exerts such a baneful influence upon the chaste and guileless savages of the interior. I speak feelingly, as I am proud to rank myself as one of that little body of English and Scotchmen, who as traders and elephant-hunters in Central South Africa, have certainly, whatever may be their failings in other respects, kept up the name of Englishmen among the natives for all that is upright and honest. In the words of Buckle, we are neither monks nor saints, but only men. However, a Kafir who is owed money by one Englishman, perhaps the wages for a year's work, will take a letter without a murmur, to another Englishman hundreds of miles away, if he is told by his master that, upon delivering the letter, he will receive his payment. This fact speaks volumes to anyone who knows the crafty, suspicious character of the natives. There are, perhaps, a few Boer hunters in the interior to whose word the Kafirs would trust, but very few; whereas on the lower Zambesi near Zumbo, you cannot get a native who has been in the habit of dealing with the Portuguese to stir hand or foot in your service unless you pay him all or part of his wages in advance.[33]

To Selous, this augured well for British prospects of expansion beyond the Limpopo. At this point in his life he believed that Africans would be content without coercion to allow their lives to come under the direction of Europeans they felt they could trust. In a letter to *The Times* in January 1890, written to dispute the claims of Portugal, he even suggested that the British claim to Mashonaland rested in part on 'the implicit trust that the Mashunas now have in the honour, truth and justice of the white man', a trust arising from 'their dealings with Englishmen and South Africans' who had gone there to hunt and trade.[34]

When Selous returned to South Africa at the end of 1881 it was with the intention of settling down in the ostrich-farming business. But the bottom had fallen out of the ostrich-feather market and he had to find something else to do. It was not long before he set off again for the interior, hoping this time to make a living acquiring natural history specimens for museums. This was his main source of income throughout the 1880s, but, as with elephant-hunting, it did not constitute a living and he soon found himself once more in debt and often depressed. During these years he generally travelled alone, except for a few African employees, and one imagines that this contributed to his depression. In 1887 he was employed as a guide to a group of gentlemen hunters, and with the earnings he accumulated he decided to embark on a project on which he had long set his heart – a journey of exploration across the Zambesi.

From the beginning, everything went wrong. First he was obliged to change his route upon hearing that the country north of the Zambesi was in the throes of tribal warfare. Then his wagon-driver became ill with fever and died. Then his other African employees deserted. He took on some locals and pressed on but soon found himself confronted by a small Batonga army demanding payment before he could proceed. He paid up, his heart 'almost bursting with rage and indignation'.[35] From here, things rapidly went from bad to worse. At every Batonga village along the Zambesi he had to submit to armed extortion; ruin, or worse, stared him in the face. This was a most unpleasant surprise, because he had traversed the same country eleven years before, and met with the friendliest reception, receiving presents of goats and food at every village. After some thought, he concluded that the Batonga had welcomed him on his first visit because they had been afraid.

No white man had been through their country since Drs. Livingstone, Kirk and Charles Livingstone had passed up the Zambesi on their way to Linyanti, many years before, and they had a superstitious dread of the white stranger who, with his breech-loading rifle, killed game afar off, and travelled among them without fear that they could harm him. Since then numbers of them had been to the diamond fields, and found out that white men are mortals like themselves.[36]

The moment of insight passed, however, or proved indigestible, and in 1894 he was telling the Royal Colonial Institute that in twenty years of travelling in Africa he personally had always got along well with the black race: 'I have been in many parts of the country where they had never seen a white man before, and I always managed to win their friendship . . .'[37]

Eventually he succeeded in striking out north from the Zambesi into Mashukulumbwe country.[38] Here the natives were even less friendly. 'You will live two days more', he was warned at the first town he stopped at, 'but on the third day your head will lie in a different place from your body.' This almost came to pass. He was attacked in the dead of night at a Mashukulumbwe village and only by the greatest good fortune escaped with his life. Lying in the long grass where he had taken shelter, he 'had time to realize', he later recorded, 'the full horror of my position. A solitary Englishman, alone in Central Africa, in the middle of a hostile country, without blankets or anything else but what he stood in, and a rifle with four cartridges.' He had left behind £400 worth of property – all he possessed – in the village where he was attacked.

Now began an incredible journey through hundreds of miles of bush with only his own resource and experience to guide him. After further adventures he reached the Zambesi. Here he took a few days' rest and then set off across the river again, hoping to trade and hunt in the Barotse country. At first all went well, but then his canoe was capsized by a hippo and once again he lost everything he had – trading goods, ammunition, ivory, and a collection of butterflies he had made for the Cape Town Museum. Stuck in the Zambesi valley waiting for the weather to change so that he could get back to Bamangwato and the known world, he had word that his old friend George Westbeech, the trader, was dead – worn out by the rigours of frontier life. The news was infinitely depressing. 'That is the end of every one who remains long in the terrible climate of this part of Africa', he wrote to a friend; 'If I live through next year I shall come home, though I do not know what I am to do for a living in England.'[39] After seventeen years in Africa, he was forced to confess complete defeat.

Had he but know it, salvation was awaiting him in Bamangwato – not, as yet, in the person of Cecil Rhodes, but in that of Frank Johnson, a young man in a hurry who was to lead him into the heart of the struggle for power and gold in central Africa. In January 1889 Johnson was in Bamangwato gloating over a mining concession he had recently extracted from the Portuguese government and wondering how to put it to use.[40] This concession was in the Mazoe river valley in northern Mashonaland, an area over which Portugal claimed a vague but ancient jurisdiction, and Johnson saw it as the key to his eventual control of the whole of central Africa, if only the British government would give him its support.[41] Johnson was only twenty-two at the time and no one of importance in the British government had ever heard of him, but these considerations did not deter him. Like Rhodes and many others he had looked at the blank space on the map north of the Limpopo and dreamed the dream of immense dominion.

He and Selous had known each other since 1887, when Johnson had spent some time prospecting in Mashonaland on behalf of his Great Northern Trade and Gold Exploration Company, the first of many companies to be floated by him in the course of a long and enterprising life. Nothing had come of this earlier venture but he was now back in the field with his concession from Portugal and Selous struck him as the ideal person to lead an expedition to the Mazoe and stake out the claim on the ground. Selous needed little persuading. He was destitute, and his belief in the gold-bearing potential of that part of Africa was equal to Johnson's.[42] The Selous Exploration Syndicate was formed with funds supplied by a group of Cape Town businessmen, and plans were made for Selous to go out to the Mazoe, via the Zambesi, later on in the year when the rainy season would be over.

Selous filled in the time before the expedition could start with a trip to England. Here he was active in the interests of his syndicate, and this brought him inevitably into contact with Rhodes, who was in London in 1889 negotiating with the British government for the grant of the Royal Charter. It was at this point that Selous embarked on the intricate series of ethical adjustments which were to preoccupy him until his final rupture with Rhodes in 1896.

Sometime in the 1880s Rhodes had decided that the best hope for achieving his dream of founding a great British colony in central Africa was the formation of a chartered company, along the lines of the old East India Company. For this a legal pretext was required, and in October 1888 Rhodes acquired it in the form of a mining agreement obtained by his agent Charles Rudd from Lobengula, chief of the Matabele. In this agreement Lobengula granted exclusive mining rights throughout his dominions to Rudd and his associates but made no mention of rights to land. Apparently he was given verbal assurances – worthless, but how was he to know? – that only ten white men would enter the country and they would be subject to Matabele laws. By the time he realized that he had, in effect, signed away his kingdom, it was too late: the British government had already decided to grant the charter and had no further interest in his opinion.

The important fact to note so far as Selous is concerned is that the Rudd concession applied to all the territory controlled by Lobengula – 'my kingdoms, principalities and dominions' were the precise words of the document to which he put his mark. Lobengula claimed sovereignty over the Mashona people to the north and east of Matabeleland, so the concession was interpreted by Rhodes as applying to Mashonaland as well – and this, in fact, was the whole point of it in his eyes. Rhodes' schemes for gold mining and colonization were directed at this stage not at Matabeleland itself but at Mashonaland, for this was where he believed the gold and the colonizable land to be. The Selous Syndicate's concession, also obtained in October 1888, was in Mashonaland: if the British government recognized both the Rudd concession and Lobengula's sovereignty over the Mashona, it was worthless; if Mashonaland, or at least the relevant part of it, could be shown to be independent of Lobengula, then it might be worth a lot, if only through a deal that might be struck with Rhodes.

Selous knew of the Rudd concession before he arrived in England, though he may not have known its exact wording; he probably also knew that a charter was in the offing. He later claimed to have discussed the charter with Rhodes in London in January 1889. The date must be wrong – Selous did not arrive in England till the end of February – but he does appear to have met Rhodes and talked about Mashonaland some time in the early part of 1889. His actions after this must be understood in the light of his two dominating interests at the time: his desire to set himself up financially, and his desire – equally real if not equally urgent – to see the British empire extended into central Africa.

It appears that at this meeting with Rhodes Selous was offered the job of leading the projected pioneer expedition to Mashonaland should Rhodes get the charter.[43] Rhodes had no intention simply of throwing the country open to all comers. His plan was for it to be occupied at a time of his own choosing, with due ceremony, by a carefully selected body of men possessing to as high a degree as possible those characteristics he so deeply admired in the British race.[44] Selous was a natural person to think of in such a connection. He replied, however, to Rhodes' offer that he was under contract to prospect on the Mazoe, and Rhodes told him in that case to see him when he got back.

The atmosphere of high politics and high finance, not to mention high personal desirability, in which he so abruptly found himself then seems to have gone to Selous' head. His next move was to publish in the *Fortnightly Review* an article whose contents can only be explained on the supposition that he imagined it to be a masterly effort to promote simultaneously the interests of the empire, Cecil Rhodes, and himself. This article, 'Mashunaland and the Mashunas', appeared in May 1889.

In 'Mashunaland and the Mashunas' Selous drew an entrancing picture of a fertile and temperate land 'where European children would grow up strong and healthy, and our English fruits retain their flavour'. Fortunately for the British race, most of it was uninhabited and so could be colonized, as Selous was at pains to point out, 'without wronging any human being'. This area, which comprised all of the high plateau of Mashonaland over 4,000 feet, had once been thickly populated by peaceful and industrious Mashonas, but around the middle of the nineteenth century the Matabele had entered the area and massacred the inhabitants. It was now 'an utterly deserted country, roamed over at will by herds of elands and other antelopes'. The Mashonas who survived had fled to the broken country to the south and east of the high plateau, where they lived in a state of terror but not, it was emphasized, of subjugation to the Matabele. A few communities of Mashona paid tribute to Lobengula, but many were 'in no wise subject' to him. These Mashonas, Selous asserted, would welcome the colonization of the now empty high plateau by Europeans for they would thereby acquire protection. The British government should therefore, he concluded, give full support to all those Englishmen who had concessions in Matabeleland and Mashonaland, for if mining communities were established farmers would soon follow, 'and the richest country in South Africa will be, in fact as well as in name, within the sphere of British influence'.[45]

Coming from someone with Selous' reputation as an African traveller, the assertion that large numbers of Mashona were independent of Lobengula was potentially very damaging to Rhodes in his quest for a charter giving him administrative powers in Mashonaland. But nothing came of it. The reason probably was that the British government had already, in February 1888, concluded a treaty with Lobengula, 'Ruler of the tribe known as the Amandabele, together with the Mashuna and Makalaka, tributaries of the same',[46] in which Lobengula bound himself to make no agreements with any foreign government without British consent. This was used as the basis for the proclamation of a British sphere of influence – that mentioned in Selous' article – up to the Zambesi, in accordance with Lord Salisbury's policy of fending off Portuguese intrusions into this area. Rhodes' interests and the interests of the British government coincided where the Mashonas were concerned: neither party wished to know that they were independent of the Matabele. Selous was thus from the beginning spitting into the wind – an indication perhaps of how intoxicated he had become by his sudden proximity to wealth and power.

Nevertheless, it was not in Rhodes' interests to have the issue of Mashona independence raised publicly, and when he learned of the article before publication he was beside himself with irritation and concern. Steps were therefore taken before it went to press to render it less dangerous and several pages of particularly inflammatory matter were excised by the assistant editor of the *Fortnightly Review*, who fortunately was the Reverend John Verschoyle, one of a number of well-placed people who had been persuaded in the early months of 1889 to exert themselves in promoting the Rhodes point of view. Why Verschoyle allowed any of Selous' assertions of Mashona independence to appear in print is unclear. Probably he did so because Selous insisted on it as the price of giving him the article, which in other respects was a valuable puff for Rhodes' scheme of colonization beyond the Limpopo. 'I have not without difficulty', Verschoyle reported, 'got rid of the pages of dangerous matter in S's article... He is still sore about the omissions I have insisted on making.'[47] Verschoyle may have been responsible for inserting the sentence: 'However, they [the Mashonas] are within the limits of the country raided on by Lobengula's warriors, and therefore are within the British sphere of influence', which appears awkwardly at the end of Selous' emphatic remarks on Mashona independence.[48]

Selous was correct in asserting that many Mashonas did not acknowledge Matabele sovereignty over them; modern authorities on Shona history all concur in this.[49] The Matabele reached the zenith of their power, which was never as extensive or as absolute as the owners of the Rudd concession would have liked everyone to believe, in the middle of the 1870s, and after that the Mashona steadily revived in strength. What was not correct, however, in Selous' article was the statement that all the Mashona highlands over 4,000 feet – an area of well over a thousand square miles – had been depopulated by Matabele raids. There were depopulated areas, but they were far smaller than was suggested. Selous was not speaking from ignorance in this matter. In 1882 he travelled in the high country and reported to the Royal Geographical Society that: 'The whole of the country travelled through was more or less thickly populated by Mashunas or allied tribes.'[50] In 1883 he was on the high plateau between the Hanyani and Mazoe rivers and reported that: 'The very best parts of the Transvaal are not to be compared to it; it is splendidly watered, droughts and famines are unknown and nowhere do the natives get such abundant and diversified crops as here; rice especially is grown in large quantities.' It was, he said, the perfect place for a European colony, but he feared the Boers would get there first.[51]

Selous, then, indulged in a deliberate deception. Why? It seems he lied to promote the cause of empire. In 1889 he knew the occupation of Mashonaland, which for some years he had regarded as desirable, to be imminent, and wanted to forestall criticism of it by assuring the public, and the ever-censorious and increasingly vocal aborigines' protectionists, that no one's land would be stolen because no one was there. But what of the Mashonas who were repining at the lower altitudes? Were they then to remain unmolested? Selous had not forgotten them. Their country, too, he wrote in 'Mashunaland and the Mashunas', 'in time to come will probably be occupied by Europeans' – but that would only be after all the empty land had been colonized. 'By that time', he added, 'there will be a settled form of government, which will be capable of controlling individual Europeans, and which ought to be capable of protecting the rights of the natives at least as well as they are protected in any other of our colonies' – meaning, of course, very well. Anyone who was inclined to be taken in by this scenario for orderly and virtuous occupation might profitably have reflected on Selous' concluding remarks:

> One hears the gentlemen who have got concessions to exploit the Matabele and Mashuna countries stigmatised as adventurers ... "Adventurers!" Yes, and not, after all, a term of reproach to an Englishman, for surely Clive and Warren Hastings were adventurers, and adventurers have made the British empire what it is.[52]

At some point, it appears, Selous had decided to make a supreme sacrifice – that of his honesty on the altar of a greater, imperial, good. It is clear, however, from everything that we know about him subsequently, that he intended it to be a highly discriminating and occasional sort of sacrifice: he might announce to the world that central Mashonaland was empty, but he expected to remain as committed as ever to truthfulness in matters where the fate of empire was not seen to be in the balance; and he seems to have trusted to the power of his intelligence, and his command over his pen, to keep

him from lying any more than was necessary, and to enable him to
lie to effect. Read carefully, his *Travel and Adventure in South-East
Africa*, which he published in 1893, provides abundant clues to the
true nature of the situation in Mashonaland and of Rhodes' dealings
with Lobengula, and it is difficult not to conclude that these were
planted there by Selous as a sort of esoteric record for those who care
to read. By such means he preserved his sense of himself as a
fundamentally truthful man, though, needless to say, he failed
ultimately to exercise the degree of control over his fabrications to
which he aspired: if nothing else, his love of assuming a dramatic
persona would have ensured that he was on occasion carried away.
In matters not affecting the immediate practical interests of empire
he was fearless for the right. He was the first to recognize and tell the
shocking truth about Zimbabwe – that it was built by Africans and
not some mysterious Semitic visitors[53]; and later on he was one of
the few Englishmen who could bring himself to acknowledge the
fighting qualities of German officers and their black troops in Africa
in the First World War.[54] His deliberate and selective sacrifice of his
honesty was made in full consciousness of its value.

His conscience seems further to have been beguiled by a growing
suspicion during the 1880s that conscience was biologically irrelevant to the conflict between the races in Africa. He succumbed,
in other words, to an intellectual temptation which had never
presented itself to the strong men of the Punjab, who had had to rely
for self-justification wholly on a reiterated purity of intention – that
of Social Darwinism. A gifted naturalist, Selous accepted without
reservation Darwin's theory of natural selection and recognized its
revolutionary implications; in 1889 he named a mountain after 'that
illustrious Englishman whose far-reaching theories ... have ...
destroyed for ever many old beliefs that had held men's minds in
thrall for centuries'.[55] In time, he embraced the full Social
Darwinist doctrine of the survival of the fittest.[56] This enabled him
to accept, like Rhodes, who arrived at the same position without
recourse to scientific logic, the fundamental amorality of imperial
expansion. Like a devout Leninist, this devout Darwinist realized he
could bend the truth a bit to assist history on its inevitable course.

He was never, however, as serenely committed to amorality as
Rhodes. He preferred wherever possible to proceed by force of
character, whereas to Rhodes force of character merely justified the
acquisition of territory after the fact. Selous more judiciously
supposed it wanting in scientific realism to think that evolutionary
objectives would always be achieved by strict adherence to the
conventional rules of morality. Hence his admiration for 'adventurers'; and hence, for example, his approving remark in *Travel and*

Adventure in South-East Africa that, though the British South Africa Company had been anxious to acquire a certain territory claimed by the Portuguese 'legally . . . under the rights acquired by a treaty' with its chief, 'possibly, had no such treaty existed, the British flag would still have waved over the hills of Manica'.[57]

His admiration for adventure actually stood in little need of encouragement or sanction from scientific theory: the revelations of Social Darwinism fell in Selous' case on fertile ground. The schoolboy love of mischief enshrined for him in the personality of Tom Brown, and encompassing, if we are to judge from Thomas Hughes' deeply moralizing but also deeply indulgent book, and from certain episodes in Selous' own schoolboy career, such by no means harmless peccadilloes as stealing from farmers and assaulting the lower orders, had already predisposed him towards a rather flexible conception of what was right and what was wrong with respect to the gratification of personal impulses: 'we are neither monks nor saints', he had felt it necessary to remark as early as 1881, 'but only men'. 'Adventure' was a notion he found it easy to admire, and in pursuit of it in its imperial form he found perhaps the most persuasive justification for his occasional abandonment of that highest good, the truth.

By the time the *Fortnightly Review* article, his maiden effort in propaganda, was published Selous was on his way back to Africa. Accounts differ as to whether his syndicate still had the Portuguese concession; possibly, in the now very strained atmosphere of Anglo-Portuguese relations the Portuguese had cancelled it. Be that as it may, Selous pushed on up the Mazoe, accompanied by two other Englishmen, until he lighted upon a Mashona chief who appeared to be independent of both the Portuguese and the Matabele. This man, Nigomo, did not give Selous the concession he requested, but two of his headmen – later promoted by Selous to chiefs[58] – put their marks on 25 September 1889 to a concession which covered a large area of the Mazoe valley. This document emphasised the signatories' complete independence of everybody. In high excitement Selous wrote back to his associates in Cape Town on 2 October 1889,

> Here you have a concession embracing probably the richest little piece of country in all Africa . . . This concession is perfectly square, fair and genuine and nothing can upset it . . . If there is really any payable gold in Africa, much of it must lie in your concession. The Matabele claim to the country is utterly preposterous and cannot hold water for a moment. Should the matter at some future time be inquired into by a Commission, I am and shall be prepared with

evidence . . . in the face of which the Matabele claim could never be allowed . . . It rests entirely on the strength of a raid made in 1868, for the two subsequent raids made respectively in 1880 and 1883 did not touch the country.[59]

The enthusiasm expressed here is unmistakably for money, but a few weeks later Selous was thinking imperially again and writing to his syndicate that, should 'Mr Cecil Rhodes have got the charter' (which he did the day after this letter was written), the true course for him to follow in occupying the country was to avoid Matabeleland, where there was sure to be trouble, and go straight up to Mashonaland by a southern and easterly route from Bechuanaland which would 'not pass within the territory of a single chief who owns allegiance or pays tribute to Lo Bengula . . . Once get a footing in Eastern Mashonaland, and the country will quickly be settled up westwards, and before very long', he added significantly, 'the Matabili question will settle itself.'[60] This was the exact opposite of the programme of settlement he had outlined for the tender-minded readers of the *Fortnightly Review*.

When Selous arrived back in Cape Town in December 1889 he found a letter from Rhodes telling him to come and see him at Kimberley.[61] What happened when he got there is, as usual, far from clear. We have Rhodes' account and the accounts of other interested parties, and they all differ. According to Rhodes, in a letter written by him on 31 March 1890 to the Duke of Abercorn, the illustrious nonentity who was chairman of the board of the British South Africa Company, Selous arrived in Kimberley with his Mazoe concession and told him he was about to write a series of articles showing that Mashonaland was independent of Lobengula.[62] Rhodes then went to work and persuaded Selous that 'the only hope for the country was the success of the Charter' and, seeing the reason of this, Selous abandoned his concession and agreed to come into the British South Africa Company's service as leader of the pioneer expedition. Rhodes gave him £2,000 out of his own pocket 'for the time and labour he had spent'. This implied no recognition, Rhodes said, of the validity of the concession and was merely 'a personal gift' inspired by the consideration that Selous might put 'his able pen' to work to the chartered company's disadvantage. In other words, it was a bribe. Rhodes' lack of compunction about showing himself in this unsavoury light to the Duke of Abercorn, and to the Colonial Office officials to whom he knew the letter would be passed on, reveals how arrogant he had become after many months of 'squaring' – his word – people in England and elsewhere who might be useful to him or who stood in his way.

There is, however, no particular reason to accept Rhodes' version of the story and at least one good reason not to. Though it was at this time of the utmost importance to Rhodes to suggest that he had done nothing which implied recognition of the validity of the Selous Exploration Syndicate's concession, there is evidence to indicate that, in fact, he had.

A Mr William Lippert, a leading member of the syndicate, had been in touch with the Colonial Office asking for official recognition of their claim, and in support of his contention that the concession was outside the area of Matabele hegemony – and therefore not superseded by the Rudd concession – had quoted Selous' letters of October 1889. He had also told the Colonial Office that Rhodes bought 'from Selous and other members more than one-third of the total Syndicate's interests' and had offered a hundred square miles of land in exchange for the remainder.[63] This was bad news for Rhodes and he was at pains to call Lippert a liar. '. . . I believe a Mr Lippert, who was the head of the syndicate, has been home stating that I recognised the concession and had offered them 100 square miles,' he wrote to Abercorn. 'The above facts [about the payment to Selous] will show you how fallacious these statements are . . .' Lippert was not exactly the soul of integrity – he had later to flee the country to avoid arrest for bank forgery[64] – but it does appear that he and not Rhodes was telling the truth about Selous. Selous' two companions on the Mazoe journey were Edward Burnett and Stephen Thomas. They also received payments from Rhodes, which Rhodes described to Abercorn as £750 each for their 'time and labour'. But there exists a letter from Frank Johnson to Rhodes, written in January 1892, which states clearly that the payments to Burnett and Thomas were 'for their interest in the "Selous Syndicate"'. Johnson asks Rhodes in this letter to reimburse him for 'the £1,500 I paid Burnett & Thomas, on yr a/c . . . At the time I sent you a letter showing the interest you acquired in the Selous Syd. together with Burnetts and Thomas' receipts.' A note is enclosed signed 'E. Burnett', stating receipt of payment in 'about January' 1890.[65] If Rhodes lied about the payments to Burnett and Thomas, it seems probable that he lied about the money he gave to Selous. The £2,000 would then have to be seen not as a bribe but as a simple payment for Selous' share in the syndicate. For what it is worth, this is how Selous himself described the transaction. 'This concession the South African Chartered Company has taken over', he told his mother in December 1889, 'and altogether I have made more than £2,000 cash this year . . .'[66]

Most writers on the period have accepted Rhodes' version of *l'affaire Selous* and have therefore been at a loss to reconcile Selous' behaviour with his reputation. Allan Quatermain selling his soul for £2,000! In fact, Selous sold his soul for much more. As leader of the pioneer expedition he received a high salary, a hundred De Beers shares, and a grant of 10,000 morgen (about 21,000 acres) of land in Mashonaland. He also received shares in the chartered company.[67] The land was not actually Rhodes' to give – he did not acquire any rights to land in the country until February 1892 – but Selous seems not to have been any more concerned about this than anyone else. After he entered the Company's service no more was heard in public about independent Mashona chiefs. In his *Travel and Adventure in South-East Africa* he described the Mazoe journey, and the concession, but made no mention of Mashona independence from the Matabele, stressing instead their independence from the Portuguese.

It is not obvious, however, that Selous threw in his lot with Rhodes just for the money. Money he most certainly wanted, after nearly twenty years of insolvency, but he also wanted to see Britain in Mashonaland. Rhodes' statement, therefore, that he had agreed that 'the only hope for the country was the success of the charter' was probably not without foundation. As an independent operator, Selous had shot his bolt. He now accepted that, Rhodes having got the charter, the hope of empire in Central Africa was vested exclusively in his person. In nailing his colours to the chartered company's mast he got himself a good job and a position in the vanguard of imperial expansion. As for Rhodes, he got himself an expedition leader who knew the country better than anyone living, and who enjoyed a reputation for good character which could do his venture no harm in the public eye – though by now he might have been entertaining some private doubts about that character.

Rhodes accepted Selous' contention that it would be prudent to enter Mashonaland by a south-easterly route. Rudd concession and Royal Charter notwithstanding, Lobengula, Rhodes knew, would not accept with equanimity the arrival of a small army of prospectors and colonists in what was indisputably his domain. Once the basic route was decided on Frank Johnson – who, with his usual resilience, had already jumped aboard the company band-wagon – was put in charge, on a contract basis, of the practical organization of the expedition, a task he accomplished with despatch. The proposed size of the pioneer column had increased far beyond Rhodes' original conception of a small but immaculate company, but principles of selection were still enforced. Less than a tenth of those who applied were chosen. Even so, they were a mixed lot. Aristocrats and out-of-work gold miners mingled together, sometimes in the same person. Selous busied himself with cutting the road and, to Rhodes' annoyance, with a flying visit to Bulawayo to ascertain Lobengula's attitude to the expedition, which unsurprisingly turned out to be negative. Rhodes' friend Dr Jameson, who enjoyed high favour with Lobengula, had to be sent to Bulawayo to smooth things over. Selous remained concerned throughout most of the journey to Mount Hampden, the expedition's point of destination on the Mashona plateau, about the likelihood of a Matabele attack. The fact that this never materialized was attributable mainly to the existence of an armed escort for the pioneers of 500 British South Africa Company 'police', and the stationing on the southwestern border of Matabeland of another 500 men of the Bechuanaland Border Police. Legend was later to have it, however, that it was Selous' 'influence with the great chief of the Matabele' which 'enabled him to guide the expedition through the territories of that powerful potentate'.[68]

The pioneer column set off from Kimberley on 6 May 1890. On 14 June it arrived at the Macloutsie river and was there inspected for military efficiency by Major-General Methuen, Deputy Adjutant-General in South Africa. Under the able direction of Johnson, whose paramilitary tendencies had burst into full flower, they passed with flying colours. The general then addressed the officers as follows:

'Gentlemen, have you got maps?'
'Yes, sir.'
'And pencils?'
'Yes, sir.'
'Well, gentlemen, your destiny is Mount Hampden. You go to a place called Siboutsi. I do not know whether Siboutsi is a man or a mountain. Mr Selous, I understand, is of the opinion that it is a man; but we will pass that by. Then you get to Mount Hampden. Mr Selous is of opinion that Mount Hampden is placed ten miles too far to the west. You had better correct that: but perhaps on second thoughts, better not. Because you might be placing it ten miles too far to the east. Now good-morning, gentlemen.'[69]

The pioneers then marched off into the relatively unknown.

On 13 September they reached what was later to become Salisbury. A parade was held, prayers offered by the chaplain, the Union Jack hoisted up a pole, and the country annexed, with no legal authority at all, to the British empire.

Selous was not present at this historic moment. He was off treaty-making in Portuguese-claimed territory, for Rhodes was now preparing for a confrontation with the Portuguese. This confrontation came at the end of 1890, and resulted only in a partial victory for Rhodes. He went to extraordinary lengths to embroil the British government in a war which would drive the Portuguese into the sea, but the British government was not, in the event, to be so easily embroiled, even by such an arch-embroiler as Rhodes, and Lord Salisbury contented himself with negotiating a treaty which left Portugal in possession of the coast while giving the Company control over much of the highlands and guaranteeing it access to the sea. It is entertaining to note that at one point the Portuguese supported their claim to Mashonaland with a quotation from Selous – the very sentences in his *Fortnightly Review* article which had given such offence to Rhodes by their assertion of Mashona independence from the Matabele.[70] Selous himself shed no tears over the eclipse of 'this feeble nerveless power'.[71]

From the moment when he accepts employment with the British South Africa Company, Selous' statements on Central African matters become increasingly difficult for the historian to assess. There are any number of instances where one's first thought is, he lied in every word, but inquiry reveals this to be uncertain. What he more often seems to have done was to mislead by omission, though he stuck through thick and thin to the outright lie that Mashonaland was depopulated: this he apparently regarded as essential to the cause.

His self-conscious belief in himself as an honest man continually complicated his rational intention to be dishonest. Though he ceased after 1889 to refer publicly to Mashona independence from the Matabele, he continued to worry about it in private, and he persuaded Rhodes' official representative with the pioneer column, Archibald Colquhoun, that in order to secure the Company's rights in Mashonaland agreements had to be arrived at with independent Mashona chiefs. Colquhoun therefore sent him off in early August to secure a treaty with one Chibi, the most independent-looking of the chiefs. Selous wrote the journey up in *Travel and Adventure in South-East Africa* as reconnaissance of the route, which was indeed one purpose of it, but not, of course, the only purpose.[72] Throughout 1890 he irritated the hard cases in the Company's employ by what Jameson described as his 'mania as to the limit of Loben's authority, and his impolitic way of blurting it out'.[73] These men were happy to relegate unfortunate facts to some grey area where they might conveniently be forgotten, but Selous had to have it all sorted out. Sometimes one gets the impression that he was not so much truthful as tidy-minded.

After he had served his purpose as leader of the pioneer expedition he was promptly consigned to that oblivion reserved in corporate enterprises for those who fail to appreciate the importance of being a team player. Throughout 1891 he was employed in making roads, and in May 1892 he terminated his agreement with the Company, 'there being no more work for me to do',[74] and returned to England. He could afford to give up his salary, for his De Beers shares produced enough income for him to live on, and there was the prospect of remuneration from his land holdings in Mashonaland, once the country developed, and from his shares in the chartered company. The chartered company never paid a dividend in its entire existence, so if Selous made any money from his shares, it must have been from selling them. His land holdings do not appear to have proved spectacularly profitable. In the early 1900s we find him selling off bits of his Mashonaland farm to raise cash, and in 1911 he sold off what remained of it to repay a loan made to him by the Natural History Museum.[75]

But in the early 1890s it was Rhodesia's – for this was now the country's name – rosy dawn, and Selous and many others believed that a glorious future awaited those who went to seek their fortune there. There was gold, there was agricultural land, and there was capital to develop these resources: 'If Mashonaland is not worth this experiment', Selous had written in 1889, 'then there is no country in the interior of Africa that it will pay any company to spend money upon.'[77] He himself had no interest in settling down to the uneventful life of a colonist; he planned to use his new-found affluence to travel in America and Japan and watch his assets grow.

These plans were changed when news reached England, in July 1893, of the Matabele raid on the Victoria district of Mashonaland. Sensing that the collision with the Matabele he had long hoped for and expected – in 1888 he had told the missionary bishop, Dr Knight-Bruce, that nothing could be done with the Matabele short of war[78] – had at last arrived, Selous took ship for South Africa, arriving in September in time to join the chartered company's forces at Fort Tuli.

Since the arrival of the whites, Lobengula had kept his young warriors on a tight leash. But he had begun to lose his grip, and the raid on Victoria district was to prove his utter undoing. Throwing restraint to the winds, a Matabele impi slaughtered the Mashona in the streets of Fort Victoria, under the very noses of the whites, not scrupling even to put their personal servants to the sword. Such impudence was not be borne, and the settlers demanded war. Dr Jameson was the Administrator of Mashonaland at the time, and if a war seemed winnable, he was not averse to fighting it. Like everyone else connected with the Company, he assumed that some day there would have to be a showdown with the Matabele, and on (very brief) reflection he decided this might as well be it. Rhodes gave him his support, and from then on Lobengula was doomed. His efforts to preserve the peace were futile; Jameson proved to be a master of disinformation and soon had the imperial authorities in Cape Town believing that the Matabele were ready to descend *en masse* on the white settlements. He was given permission to deploy the Company's forces, and the war which came to be known, quite inappropriately, as 'the first Matabele rising' began. The campaign was a brief one and ended in a rout for the Matabele, who got a taste of what the Maxim gun could do. Lobengula fled north and died, probably by his own hand.

Selous' exhilaration at taking part in these events was extreme. He got himself wounded, entered Bulawayo with Colonel Goold-Adams' column, and informed his mother on this occasion that 'the campaign is virtually over, and the fair-haired descendants of the northern pirates are in possession of the Great King's kraal . . .'[79] He then returned to England, to get married – he had become engaged early in the year – and to justify the war.

Some justification had become necessary, for the accomplished controversialist Henry Labouchere had been attacking the war and the way it was conducted in the columns of his newspaper *Truth*. Labouchere had got hold of the notorious 'Victoria Agreement', whereby the settlers had been promised loot – Matabele land and cattle – when the war was over, in return for their presence on the battlefield; and he had information that villages had been burned and prisoners and wounded shot in the Company's headlong rush to Bulawayo. Appointing himself spokesman for white interests in Rhodesia, and thus, by extension in his eyes, for the interests of the white race, Selous responded to these charges. He did so enthusiastically but contradictorily, denying specific accusations[80] but arguing also that normal moral standards could not be applied to the all-important task of establishing 'the absolute supremacy of the numerically small white race over the aboriginal blacks. Savages do not understand leniency', he pointed out; 'they take it for fear, and at once take advantage of it.'[81]

The terms in which Selous defended the war when he felt he had a sympathetic audience, make it plain that he was now well launched along the slippery slope which leads from reluctantly accepting the amoral to positively rejoicing in the immoral. Evolutionary imperatives were now held to justify, not mere lying and land-grabbing, but an admittedly aggressive war. Reverting to his Viking imagery, he told the members of the Royal Colonial Institute that:

> It may be wrong to occupy the waste places of the earth, to extend the British Empire, and to come into contact with savage races at all. On

that point I will not offer an opinion[!]; but, right or wrong, it is a British characteristic to take possession of any country we think is worth having, and this piratical or Viking instinct is, I suppose, an hereditary virtue that has come down to us in the blood of our northern ancestors. All other nations would like to do the same, and do so when they can; but we have been more enterprising than they, and, so far, have had the lion's share.[82]

In a chapter which he wrote for a book at the same time he described himself as 'one of those who think that the war was an absolute necessity, and the crushing of the Matabeli power at any cost the only possible means of maintaining the supremacy of our race on the plateau of Central South Africa'.[83]

Rhodes and Jameson, buccaneers that they were, would never have allowed themselves such public candour. Selous, however, seems to have succumbed to the excitement of being swept up in the tide of history. Finding himself once again at the centre of events, he was now emboldened to tell the (essential) truth as he saw it to as many people as would listen. And on the whole, he did not mistake his audience. His speech at the Royal Colonial Institute was received with cheers, and the chairman of the meeting, the Marquis of Lorne, observed that: 'It is a satisfaction to listen to a man who can hold so straight, ride so straight, and talk so straight, and we are very grateful to him.'[84] Coming from Selous, the brutal opinions he expressed acquired an odour if not of sanctity at least of respectability. Rhodes should perhaps have been grateful to him, but one wonders how pleased he was when and if he heard that Selous had told the Royal Colonial Institute that

> Mr Rhodes has never posed as a champion of the Mashunas or any other black race; his object, I take it, is to extend the dominion of the British race, and to secure for Englishmen any country worth having on the plateaux of Central South Africa. Therefore for what he has done and is doing unborn generations revere his memory, let the enemies of Imperial England snarl as they may.[85]

Whatever reservations Rhodes may have had about Selous, he was not ungenerous in rewarding him for his services; the records of the British South Africa Company show that a grant of 22,012 morgen of land (about 45,000 acres) was given to 'C.T. Rhodes; F.C. Selous' in July 1894.[86]

At this point a voice from the imperial past was raised against Selous and all who sought to justify the Company's war against the Matabele. Robert Cust, in retirement after his career in the Punjab, where he had rejoiced, we may remember (Chapter 1, page 25), in 'the *right* man hanged *on the spot*, where he *committed* the murder', produced a pamphlet entitled *The Matabéle-Scandal and its Consequences: By one who (1) Remembers the Punishment Which Fell upon Cain for Killing his Brother, and (2) is Jealous of the Honour of Great Britain*. 'Imperial nations', Cust wrote, 'must have Imperial instincts; the highest self-control, an entire absence of greed and lust for gold, a pity for the wounded and slain.' The old East India Company, he claimed, had never dispossessed anyone; they wanted only 'the Government of the country'. And even now, in these evil days, the British administrator in India

> acts from Imperial motives, according to his orders, and for the good – as far as he can see – the *real good*, of the great Native population, whose interests are in his hands; he *detests slaughter*; he has no slaughterers of mankind under his *own* orders; he invites no shooters of big game to help him: and he has to answer to the Government, if he call out the Military forces without due cause, and to God, if he misuses his power: he has a permanent interest in the welfare of his people.

Rhodes was a sinner, Cust pronounced, and his sin would bring down ruin on the British nation, whose great good fortune in the world required it 'to evidence a much greater amount of self-restraint, noble abstention from blood and rapine. Can we do such great wickedness and sin against God? Some humiliation would be the just punishment for this National sin.'[87] The evangelical conscience could not more clearly have expressed itself, though Cust was oppressed, as well he might have been, by a sense of resonating in the void.[88]

Selous was not a Christian[89] and seems to have had no sense of a divine will at work in the world. Yet in spite of his appeals to evolutionary inevitability he did still feel the need to justify the war in moral terms. Whether this was the result of a fundamental confusion in his thinking, or of a cynical intention to obtain support by any available means, is scarcely possible to say. At the very least, however, he sensed a public unwillingness to discard completely the moral fig-leaves he had been accustomed to provide. Though he had not been present at the time the outrage took place, he assured the world that the Matabele had killed over 400 Mashonas in the Victoria raid (a far higher number than anyone else thought probable[90]), thereby justifying the severity of the Company's response. And he eulogized the white men who had fallen in the war. They were mirrors of chivalry whose 'splendid spirit of comradeship and true nobility of character have embalmed their memory in every true man's heart wherever the English language is spoken'; men such as Gwynyth Williams, 'beloved by all who knew him and as gentle and kind and brave as any Bayard', and Captain Lendy – whose notorious behaviour it was that Selous had excused on the grounds that 'Savages do not understand leniency' – who was 'soldierlike and handsome, and as kind-hearted as he was brave'.[91] We are back in the moral atmosphere of the Punjab: whatever the imperial process was, Selous seemed to be saying, it was being carried on by men whose essential goodness remained unaffected by it.

So exercised was he with the desire to defend his fellow Rhodesians from calumny that he unwisely issued a writ for libel against Henry Labouchere, a man who in the course of a long muckraking career was never once successfully sued. Labouchere had accused Selous of clothing a filibustering expedition in the language of heroism[92], and Selous decided it was incumbent upon him to rescue the reputations of himself and his associates from a man he described as a 'dirty old bird that has fouled its own nest'.[93] He repudiated all Labouchere's accusations, including the one that there had been scenes of drunken debauchery when the triumphant settlers entered Bulawayo. Selous' Vikings were not now allowed even a manly weakness for drink.[94] For several weeks an enthusiastic correspondence ensued in the columns of *The Times*. In spite of the editorial backing of the newspaper, Selous emerged from this looking much the worse for wear. The libel suit appears to have been quietly dropped.

In masterly fashion, Labouchere attacked Selous on two points on which he could not offer a convincing defence. The first was his financial connection with the Company, which Labouchere deduced from odd scraps of information and from the careful wording of Selous' statement that 'I hold no interets in Mashonaland that it is reasonable to suppose would be prejudiced in any way if the charter were revoked and the Imperial or Cape Government was to supersede the British South Africa Company'.[95] Labouchere concluded correctly that Selous probably had land or mining claims in Mashonaland and Chartered shares, and that his testimony therefore deserved to be regarded 'with the suspicion that I always feel for that of an interested party'.[96] But Labouchere's second point was potentially far more damaging, and after he spelled it out, the correspondence ceased.

This concerned Selous' involvement in one of the most shameful episodes of the war, the shooting of Lobengula's envoys at Tati on 18 October 1893.

In a final attempt to avert war, Lobengula had sent three envoys to the High Commissioner in Cape Town, carrying a message which denied that the Matabele were preparing to attack the whites. The trader James Dawson, a friend of Selous', was sent with them from Bulawayo as guarantor of their authenticity. Dawson arrived with them at Tati and was surprised to find soldiers under Goold-Adams encamped there. He did not, as might have been expected, report himself immediately to Goold-Adams but left the envoys to be taken care of by an employee of the Tati Concession Company, got himself a drink and then, according to his own testimony, went off with Selous to give him the latest information on what was happening in Matabeleland. He and Selous then had dinner with the manager of the Tati Company, and only after dinner did Dawson bestir himself to go over to the camp and report to Goold-Adams. On the way over, he and Selous discovered that the envoys had been put in detention and that two of them had been killed while resisting arrest.[97]

This is a very peculiar story indeed, and even historians sympathetic to the British South Africa Company have found it difficult to swallow. The inquiry which was performed at the time by the High Commissioner's military secretary was of an only too evidently partial nature, and some of the statements by the principal characters were taken down by none other than Rhodes himself before being forwarded to the High Commissioner.[98] Selous made no official statement and was not called to give evidence for the inquiry – an amazing omission, as he must almost certainly have been the first to know, from Dawson, who the three Matabele were, and it would in this case have been his duty as an officer to see that their business was carried forward without delay. Selous gave his own version of what happened in an interview which appeared in *The Times* on 6 February 1894. In this interview he claimed that Dawson only told him during dinner that the Matabele were envoys. But Dawson, though he does not say explicitly that he told Selous who the men were, is at pains in both his accounts of the incident to say that immediately on arrival he briefed Selous on events in Matabeleland. In his second account he says that Selous took him aside, just out of sight of the Matabele, for this specific purpose.[99] It defies belief that he omitted to tell Selous what he was doing at Tati, or that Selous omitted to inquire.

Labouchere found the behaviour of all concerned, including Selous, quite inexplicable. It seemed to him astonishing

that no inquiry was made of Mr Dawson respecting these men, and that, if Mr Dawson had forgotten their existence, Mr Selous did not remind him of it. This is called a misunderstanding! What would it have been called had it occurred in a Prussian or French camp during the last Franco-German war? The fact that it did occur throws a considerable light on the mode in which hostilities were conducted in Matabeleland.[100]

To this there was no reply and Selous prudently did not attempt to make one.

Labouchere, almost alone of Selous' contemporaries, had the impudence to laugh at him. How absurd, he said, that Selous should make himself responsible for everything done in Mashonaland and Matabeleland! And how absurd, too, that people should believe every word that came out of his mouth: 'One would really suppose', he observed, 'that Mr Selous has, in some special way, proved his veracity above all other human beings.'[101] Of course, in the eyes of his admirers, he had.

Though Selous intended now to settle down in England, it was not long before the need for money and the call of the wild began to exert their accustomed pressure on his soul. In 1894 he had married, bought a house, and indulged in expensive travel with his bride. When his old friend Maurice Heany asked him in 1895 to go out to Matabeleland and assist him in the management of a land and gold-mining company of which both men were directors he accepted and left for Africa, taking his wife with him. In Cape Town they stayed with Rhodes, who, Selous later recalled, 'wd sit meditating for 2 hrs after dinner with his guests around, then slap his knees & go off to bed without saying a word'.[102]

Rhodes had good reason to look pensive. His hopes that the goldfields of Mashonaland and Matabeleland would prove to be a 'second Rand' had been disappointed – though he was careful not to let the public become aware of the fact – and his new country's chief engine of development was therefore in danger of grinding to a halt. 'I shall have a good deal of worry in developing Mashonaland', he had written to W.T. Stead in 1891, 'I quite appreciate the enormous difficulties of opening up a new country but still if Providence will permit a few paying gold reefs I think it will be all right.'[103] Providence had not so far permitted this and it thus became imperative to Rhodes to ensure that nothing impeded his access to the gold deposits of the Rand. He already had vast holdings there, but in the unpredictable political conditions of the Transvaal he could not assume them to be secure. He therefore hatched the plan for armed intervention in the Boer republic which was to materialize

at the end of 1895 as the Jameson raid. It was not love of money
which brought Rhodes to the point of committing this immense folly,
but love of power and consciousness of approaching death. Already
he was ill with heart disease and knew he would never make old
bones. The time was short in which to make his name immortal.

Selous presumably knew nothing of this plan. He may have known
that Rhodesian gold was not all that had been hoped, but he had
been loyally boosting it all the same. His interests in the country
were now considerable. The company of which he and Heany were
directors and joint managers, Matabele Gold Reefs and Estates, held
221,000 acres of land and 488 gold claims in Matabeleland when it
was floated in 1894; a further 285 claims were soon acquired.[104]
Much of this land was close to Bulawayo and supported a large
native population, as Labouchere was not slow to publicize in
Truth.[105] He was wasting his breath. No one seriously supposed
any longer that Rhodes was confining his attention to the 'waste
places of the earth'.

The farm on which Selous and his wife made their home was
Essexvale near Bulawayo. Twelve hundred head of cattle were run
on this farm, distributed among the native population who herded
them in return for milk. Selous attempted to develop the cultivation
of fruit trees, gum trees and maize, and appears to have been happy
there. The natives were friendly and it seemed that he and his wife
were well liked. It was therefore a great shock to him when the
Matabele rose in March 1896 and one of the chief instigators of the
rebellion turned out to have been Umlugulu, a prominent local
native with whom he had hit it off particularly well.[106]

The war of 1896 was a much more serious affair than the war of
1893.[107] The Matabele had learned how to avoid pitched battles
with artillery; they were organized; and in June the Mashona rose to
join them in revolt. In 1893 the Mashona had paid off old scores by
helping the whites to hunt down the Matabele; now they perceived
where their true interests lay. Both sides in the war saw themselves
as fighting for their homes, and the rules of civilized warfare were
consequently discarded. White families on outlying farms were
clubbed to death by Africans, and their mutilated remains inspired
those who saw them to swear horrible vengeance. Quarter was
neither expected nor given. The balance of force was on the
Company side, but nevertheless the war went slowly. Rhodes began
to fear that a prolonged campaign would either strain the
Company's finances to the breaking point or else bring on what he
perhaps dreaded even more – the intervention of the imperial
government in his private kingdom. He therefore boldly decided to
make peace with the Matabele.

The peace settlement hammered out in the Matopos hills in August 1896 came to be regarded in Rhodesia as one of Rhodes' finest achievements, but it received little support from settlers at the time. They were in an exterminating mood. Rhodes, however, was in a gambling mood, and ready to risk all on one more throw of the dice. The Jameson raid had failed; his political career was in ruins; all that remained was one last chance of eternal remembrance.

Even at this desperate hour, however, he remained enough of a politician to seize the opportunity presented by the rising to evade the reckoning demanded of him at home. When Chamberlain asked for his resignation from the board of the chartered company he sent from the field the superb reply, 'Let resignation wait – we fight Matabele tomorrow'. But he also grasped with both hands the chance to show the world he was of no common clay. A degree of physical courage no one had suspected manifested itself within him and he proved himself a warrior in the best imperial style. In the attack on Taba Zi Ka Mambo he was to the fore, 'riding unarmed, switch in hand, leading the hunt'.[108] Perhaps as he spurred his horse forward he thought of Gordon. The peace negotiations in the Matopos were also undertaken at great personal danger to himself. With only three companions, one a journalist, he rode into what could easily have been a trap. There was an uneasy moment while the white men waited for the Matabele to appear, but when they did, Rhodes' face broke out into a 'wonderful smile' and he exclaimed, 'This is one of those moments in life that make it worth living!'[109] With extreme and no doubt fully experienced composure he listened to the recitation of Matabele grievances – the confiscation of cattle, forced labour, the brutal behaviour of the native police – and responded to them, as Terence Ranger has said, as though he was hearing these things for the first time.[110] He had become the Great White Father, above the fray, who deals out justice to his people: he was the embodiment of that Anglo-Saxon character he had for so many years only abstractly revered. After the first meeting he wrote to his Administrator, Albert Grey: 'I have been sitting with the rebel chiefs in the hills for about four hours, and the war is over so far as this part is concerned'.[111] There were to be further meetings, some of them stormier than the first, but in essence Rhodes was right. It was a great triumph of personality.

Rhodes made no effort to exercise his magic on the Mashona. They had not the martial reputation of the Matabele, and he did not compromise his grandeur by sitting down to treat with them. Their rebellion lasted for another year and was suppressed eventually by the dreadful method of dynamiting the caves in which they lived. One of their leaders, the chief Makoni, was induced to surrender by a promise of his life and then shot. Even Selous would have been hard put to present the Mashona campaign to the public in a heroic light. Fortunately, he did not attempt to do so. He wrote his account in August, before the dynamiting began.

This account, *Sunshine and Storm in Rhodesia* (1896), was presented with the usual apologies for the author's plain and homely style, which now seems intended not only to establish his credentials as an honest man but to render rather more acceptable the horrific nature of what he has to say. While Rhodes was discovering within himself the qualities of an English gentleman, Selous was fashioning his apologia for abandoning them completely. Essentially, he denies nothing. Yes, it is true that unresisting Africans have been shot down; and yes, it is also true that Africans have been hanged as spies after trials of 'a somewhat rough-and-ready' nature. But all this, he says, is a natural response to the murder of white women and children. He himself, activated by 'a desire for vengeance, which could only be satisfied by a personal and active participation in the killing of the murderers', has shot down fleeing Africans 'with as little compunction as though they were a pack of wild dogs'. At such times, he writes, man reveals his innate savagery – 'the cruel instinct which, given sufficient provocation, prompts the meekest nature to kill his enemy – the instinct which forms the connecting link between the nature of man and that of the beast'.

All this instinctual activity is conceived as taking place within the framework of evolutionary inevitability – 'the inexorable law which Darwin has aptly termed the "Survival of the Fittest"' – but also, for Selous is still not prepared, even at this point, to abandon entirely the moral element in his imperial thinking, as leading to the establishment of a civilization which is 'orderly and humane'.[112] One senses a need to explain after the event the impulses which took hold of him during the war. One senses also a need to explain the rebellion, which, as he admits, took him by surprise. The evolutionary approach allows him to suggest that it was a predictable stage in the struggle for dominance between the races.

Selous, like many other settlers, was rendered particularly distraught by the fact that some of the dead whites had been killed by their own servants. Distancing himself slightly from the feelings he describes, though clearly they are his own, he finds it not surprising that the average settler would conclude that

> beings who are capable of such deeds, who can lick your hand and fawn upon you for eighteen months and then one day turn and murder you, and afterwards perhaps mutilate your senseless corpse, are not men and brothers, but monsters in human shape, that ought

to be shot down mercilessly like wild dogs or hyaenas, until they are reduced to a state of abject submission to the white man's rule.[113]

Could the problem be that the hand-licking and fawning, now so properly despised, had formerly been taken at face value – as evidence of a perfectly natural devotion?

In 1896 the whites in Rhodesia believed the country had settled down and the natives were learning to be grateful for the blessings of white rule. Immigrants were flooding in and no one expected trouble, particularly from the Mashona, who after all were being protected by the European government from their old enemies, the Matabele. The degree of confidence which was felt is indicated by the fact that shortly before the rising the police force had been withdrawn from Matabeleland for use in the Jameson raid. When the Africans rose in rebellion they showed how little they in fact cared for the British or their rule. And the treachery of servants was especially wounding because it expressed this in concentrated and unambiguous form. Servants are the eternal recipients of kindnesses which cost nothing; when they give notice it deeply offends us.

Sunshine and Storm in Rhodesia must be read not as a defence of the Company but of the great cause which it now only imperfectly represented. Selous' loyalty had been profoundly strained by the Jameson raid, which he described in *Sunshine and Storm* as a 'deplorable invasion . . . in defiance of all international law, to accomplish I still fail to understand what'.[114] He liked the Boers and was shocked to see applied to them the Viking spirit he had extolled heretofore. It seems not to have occurred to him that *furor imperialis* knew no natural limits; he had always thought of the Boers as friendly rivals. The raid brought about great changes in his thinking.

He began to speak more honestly in public about the prospects for Rhodesian gold, announcing to the press upon his return to England in 1896 that he now expected only a very small proportion of the gold properties in Rhodesia to prove remunerative.[115] Disillusion proceeded apace and in 1897 he was criticizing the calibre of British settlers in Rhodesia. If there turned out to be no paying gold in the country, he wrote, the British would desert it, leaving it to be colonized by South-African born British and Boers: 'the British Isles can no longer produce', he wrote, 'a plodding, unambitious peasantry or yeomanry that would be content to settle and live in a poor country where there was no prospect of growing rich'.[116] He also modified his assessment of Rhodesia's agricultural prospects.

The country was not a granary, he now asserted, and never would be, but a man could make a very pleasant homesteading life there for himself and his family, if his attitude was right.[117]

Attitude, of course, was the problem, and Selous' doubts on the subject became even deeper after he visited the American West in the autumn of 1897. There land with far less agricultural potential than Rhodesia was rapidly being settled, by men 'of a stamp such as one does not encounter in South Africa, as one cannot hope to see I imagine in any country where there is a large native black population, and where consequently, in the matter of manual labour, white men usually act only as overseers over black labourers'.[118] 'I am not surprised', wrote one of Rhodes' critics at the time, 'that Mr Selous is in bad odour with the Chartered Company.'[119]

Selous had not become an anti-imperialist. He still hoped to see Britain supreme in Africa, but believed now that success depended 'more upon the settlement of her sons upon the land than upon the building of cities upon a gold or diamond mine, which must sooner or later cease to exist'.[120] The piratical instinct he had got into the habit of exalting was now being revealed to him for the squalid thing it was, and he went in search of the simpler virtues he had abandoned somewhere along the way: he was like a man sobering up after a very long drinking bout. For some years he became immensely prosaic, and only came to life again as a writer when the events of 1896 were long past.

As he had foreseen, the Jameson raid led to war between the British and the Dutch in South Africa, and when the war came he found himself among those in opposition to it. He became vice-president of the South Africa Conciliation Committee and wrote letters to the newspapers deploring the war hysteria which now possessed the British public.[121] The first of these was written in response to Swinburne's poem, 'The Transvaal', in which the great pervert, carried away with imperial enthusiasm, exhorted Britons to 'scourge these dogs, agape with jaws afoam / Down out of life'; this outburst was printed in *The Times*.[122] So rancid did the atmosphere become that Selous thought of emigrating to America.[123] One of his crimes was that he refused to underestimate the Boers. Jameson had set off on his raid believing that 'anyone could take the Transvaal with half-a-dozen revolvers'.[124] Selous knew the Boers for the fighters they were. Publicly he never uttered a direct word of criticism of Cecil Rhodes, but privately he denounced the war as the result of 'dirty work done by the cpaitalists'.[125]

Not everyone who was a pro-Boer in 1899 sympathized with the Boer approach to the 'native problem' – always, in South Africa, to be distinguished from the 'race problem', which meant Anglo-Dutch relations – but Selous did. He had written in *Travel and Adventure in South-East Africa* that:

> The greater part of the Boers I have known have been kind masters to their servants, though they are severe with them if they offend. They treat the natives, as do all colonists, as an inferior race, not as equals, and there can be no doubt that they are perfectly right in doing so. Granted that certain Kafirs are better men than certain white men, the fact remains that as a whole the Kafirs are an inferior people, and in their present state of development are with some few exceptions only fit to be hewers of wood and drawers of water. However, this is a difficult question, and one which I am not competent to discuss. . .[126]

This view accords with that expressed as the collective opinion of the South Africa Conciliation Committee in their pamphlet entitled *The Treatment of the Natives in South Africa*.[127]

The Committee was Selous' last foray into politics. His life settled down into a pattern of hunting and egg-collecting trips alternating with brief spells at home. Though he had a wife and two children, they do not seem to have detained him unduly. Egg-collecting became a passion and took him far afield. In April 1906 he went all the way to Bosnia to take the nest and eggs of the nutcracker. He produced some impressive works of natural history, one of which – *African Nature Notes and Reminiscences* – had a foreword by his friend Theodore Roosevelt. But he was not a happy man. He travelled because he was melancholy at home and sought happiness in the thrill of the chase. When success in the field eluded him, he became even more melancholy; when he had a good day he was briefly his old self again. 'Did I feel sorry for what I had done . . .?' he asked himself after bagging a magnificent caribou.

> Well! no, I did not. Ten thousand years of superficial and unsatisfying civilization have not altered the fundamental nature of man, and the successful hunter of to-day becomes a primeval savage, remorseless, triumphant, full of a wild exultant joy, which none but those who have lived in the wilderness and depended on their success as hunters for their daily food, can ever know or comprehend.[128]

As the years passed, away from the intoxicating influence of Cecil Rhodes and the opportunities he provided for putting morality to the test of action, Selous seems to have drifted into an easy belief in the compatibility of violent behaviour with essential decency. Gone were the days when it required strenuous argument to reconcile the two.

He accepted himself as a folk hero and sat down to compose the memoir Millais found him writing in 1914.

It is an innocent piece of work: Selous had the knack of resuming his virginity. Yet it has its nasty side. John Leroux's practical jokes can be cruel, and though he never lies he does a great deal of refraining from telling the truth. The creation of a sixty-three-year-old man, he too vividly has the moral sense of a twelve-year-old boy.

Selous' reputation never seriously suffered by his over-enthusiastic defence of greed, cruelty and murder in the 1890s. It did suffer for a while as a result of his position on the Boer War, when his opinions were out of step with those of the majority. But that was forgotten, and when he died in action in 1917 the floodgates of adulation opened up. Perhaps the most curious claim for his virtue was made by his biographer, Millais, when he wrote that Selous 'never shot a native except purely in self-defence'; possibly he was confusing him with another hero of romance, Allan Quatermain, who had written: 'I have killed many men in my time, yet I have never slain wantonly or stained my hand in innocent blood, but only in self-defence.'[129] The confusion was understandable, for it reflected Selous' own.

And what of Rhodes? He, too, expired in the odour of sanctity. The war he had caused gave him the opportunity to indulge his new-found taste for action and he got himself heroically besieged in Kimberley. When he died in 1902 his funeral in the Matopos was a state occasion. The white population of Cape Town turned out *en masse* for it. But more surprisingly, the Africans turned out for it, too. In 1896 Rhodes had discovered in himself a talent for fatherly concern for native well-being. He liked displaying it and made a point in later years of personally receiving African delegations and hearing their complaints: in his heart of hearts, he may have been a District Officer. Two thousand five hundred Africans are said to have attended his funeral, and when the gun-carriage carrying his coffin went past they rose to their feet and gave him the royal salute. A few weeks later his brother met the principal Matabele chiefs at the grave and entrusted it to their keeping.

3

Hugh Clifford, Administrator

Hugh Clifford was never a popular hero like Selous. Though his early adventures were equal to anything reluctantly recounted by the great white hunter, as a civil servant Clifford had to be content with the esteem of the establishment. This he enjoyed in full, becoming one of the most admired colonial governors of the day and ending up doyen of the Colonial Service. He came to the notice of the public mostly as a writer of short stories about native life, and in this capacity produced a large amount of semi-fictional material, now forgotten, which stands as a fascinating record of the thinking of a gifted imperialist.

There is a difficulty in writing about Clifford which must be admitted at the outset: towards the end of his career it became apparent that he was not always sane. He suffered from a manic-depressive illness which had periods of remission but eventually cut short his career. Since we do not know at exactly what point in his life these episodes of insanity began – it has been suggested that he may have contracted syphilis from an early liaison with a native woman[1] – it is not easy to be sure in any given instance whether eccentricities of thought or behaviour should be regarded simply as such, or whether they reflect the presence of an undiagnosed pathology.[2] How do we know, especially in a life as unconventional as Clifford's, where eccentricity ends and an essentially organic impairment begins? We do not. But for the purposes of this chapter, it will perhaps suffice to note that, almost to the end of his career, Clifford's official mind was a powerfully rational one. His despatches remained formidable even as he crumbled within. They deserve to be granted a certain autonomy, and they will be.

The career which ended tragically with enforced retirement in 1929 began in the jungles of Malaya in 1883. Unlike most colonial civil

servants, Clifford actually was that stereotypical figure, the sprig of
an impoverished aristocratic family who was shipped off to the
outposts to earn his living without losing too much caste. Of the
ancient and once powerful Catholic family of Clifford, which for
generations, under the stress of religious disability, had sequestered
itself on its West Country estates, Hugh Clifford was to rediscover
through imperial service his hereditary vocation for government.
Over a long career he slowly emancipated himself from the narrow
world of the aristocratic estate and entered the world of public life,
shedding in the process some of the romantic attachment to tradition
bred in him as a boy. In colonial government, for those able to see it
in that light, there was a sense of infinite possibility for good, and it
was by this that Hugh Clifford was ultimately beguiled.

At the age of seventeen Clifford took up a position in the Malayan
Civil Service offered to him by his father's cousin, Sir Frederick
Weld, who was at that time governor of the Straits Settlements. He
had expected to follow his father, Sir Henry Clifford, VC, into the
army; but his recently widowed mother pressed him to take the
Malayan appointment.[3] In those days an officer in a fashionable
regiment was not self-supporting, and the large Clifford family had
been living exiguously for some years. Henry Clifford had gone
abroad on half-pay after compromising himself with a servant girl in
1875[4], and his early death only four years after being recalled to
active service in 1879 left his dependants not well off. Hugh Clifford
was therefore induced to begin what at times he regarded as his
lifelong exile among the middle classes.[5]

He arrived in Malaya at a time when a series of activist
governors in Singapore, anxious to promote trade and tranquillity in
the hinterland, were extending British authority discreetly but
inexorably into the independent Malay states of the peninsula.[6]
Discretion was required to avoid alarming the British government,
which had no desire for expensive and potentially disruptive
entanglements in Malaya; Singapore, with its strategic position on
the Far Eastern sea routes, was what mattered in London. The
Malay states were therefore never annexed, but were controlled
informally through Residents appointed by and responsible to the
governor of the Straits Settlements. Most governors were able to see
the beauty of this arrangement: the Colonial Office's reluctance to be
directly involved gave them in effect a free hand.

Sir Frederick Weld was governor from 1880 to 1887. Most of his
life up to that point had been spent in New Zealand, where he
settled as a young man and rose to be prime minister. His
premiership was remembered for its gentlemanly tone, though his
first act in office was to confiscate three millions acres of Maori land,

an act aptly described by a modern New Zealand historian as a crime.[7] Where natives were concerned Weld believed in the iron fist in the velvet glove – 'wholesome severity and well-timed kindness', as he put it[8] – and he piqued himself on the affection he inspired in all those who knew he had their interests at heart. He was forever telling people what was good for them and then recording their undying gratitude: once he was kind enough to show Tennyson how to read one of his poems.[9] During his term of office in Singapore he directed most of his attention to the Malay states, to whose rulers he could give unsolicited advice whenever he felt like it and count on receiving what he supposed to be their heartfelt thanks in return. 'Maharajah of Johore called today', we find him recording in his diary:

I had a long and satisfactory conversation with him. One of his remarks struck me. He said: 'If I saw a thing as clearly as the sun in the heavens, and you saw differently, I would yield (my opinion) to you. You are my Father, and I wish always to take advice from you.' Very oriental, but I think he meant it.[10]

There are many such entries in Weld's diaries, but behind the fatuous belief in the light of his own countenance there was a firm grasp of the realities of power. In a despatch shortly after arriving in Malaya he wrote that:

Nothing we have done so far has taught [the Malays] to govern themselves, we are merely teaching them to co-operate with us and govern under our guidance. To teach men to govern themselves you must throw them on their own resources. We are necessarily doing the very reverse. Moreover, I doubt if Asiatics can ever be taught to govern themselves; it is contrary to the genius of their race, to what we know of their past history, and to tendencies created by their religious systems. What suits them is a mild and equitable despotism; that *we* can give them, but in the present circumstances, having regard to the discordant elements existing in the Malay Peninsula, they would be unable to give *themselves*.[11]

Weld was opposed to annexation, believing that Malays required 'personal government', and fearing that 'annexation means increased red-tapeism and an increase of technicality. Without annexation you rely more upon good officers.'[12] He included among them, of course, himself.

This was the man from whom Hugh Clifford imbibed his earliest notions of the government of subject races. He spent his first few months in Malaya under Weld in Singapore, and then was sent to Perak to be secretary to the Resident, Hugh Low.

Low's regime in Perak was exactly what Weld had in mind when he wrote of the virtues of 'personal government'. Now an old man, Low had been in his youth a protégé of Rajah Brooke and had spent many years in Labuan in North Borneo applying the Brooke philosophy of government, which might be summarized in its mature form as 'Make haste slowly'. So slow was he in Perak that it seemed at times doubtful that the day would ever dawn when he considered it advisable to abolish slavery. But all accounts agree that he was the most benevolent of despots. He had had a Malay wife and lived like a Malay aristocrat, taking a personal interest in all classes of his subjects, among whom he strolled about unarmed and unattended.[13]

The Residents were theoretically mere advisers to the independent Malay sultans, but the Pangkor Engagement of 1874 had in practice given them control of revenues and general administration in their various states. Advice under these circumstances was of an imperative nature, but Hugh Low knew how to sweeten it with tact and jocularity and so was accounted an outstandingly successful Resident. The French traveller Brau de St Pol Lias has left us an account of a Perak Council meeting during his tenure of office: 'He [Low] introduced the agenda, explained situations and opened the discussion, which usually consisted of agreement with his position, or a response prompted by the form of the motion. Opposition was met by persuasion, explanation, and finally by a joke which made everyone laugh and closed the subject.'[14] As secretary to the Resident Hugh Clifford was well placed to observe the great man's technique. He conceived a lifelong admiration for him.[15] Brought up to believe in the virtues of aristocracy, he was profoundly receptive to Low's view that British rule over native races should take, wherever possible, the form of endeavouring to guide their traditional rulers towards a more responsible conception of their position.

Clifford's great opportunity came in 1887 when Sir Frederick Weld decided that it was time to enfold yet another Malay state, Pahang on the east coast, in the Residential embrace. He chose his twenty-year-old nephew to undertake the task of persuading the sultan of Pahang to sign a treaty allowing for the installation of a permanent British representative at his court. Clifford was not an unreasonable choice. He had a talent for the Malay language, and young men such as he were often sent to blaze the trail. Besides,

Sir Frederick Weld thought he had 'a remarkable power of gaining the confidence of the Malays'.[16] He accepted his selection with 'very great content'[17], and was sent up to Pahang with instructions to obtain a letter from the sultan requesting British intervention in his affairs.

The mission to Pahang was the formative experience of Clifford's life, and to understand why we need only turn to his published recollections of it in old age. They describe an experience which was part adventure, part idyll: a little youth, a little ambition, a little love of the unknown, suffice completely to explain its fatal charm.

Getting there involved a two-month journey across the Malay peninsula, the last two weeks of which were spent floating slowly down the wide Pahang river on an enormous raft. 'It was often possible', Clifford recalled

> without delaying our progress, to go ashore and walk through the villages for a dozen miles or so; to shoot snipe in the rice-fields and grazing-grounds that lay behind them, from which the virgin forest stood back in veritable cliffs of vegetation; and thereafter to rejoin the Râkit Bâlai Gambang, as these huge house-rafts are called in Pahang. In this fashion I contrived to see a great deal of the country through which the river loafed along; to learn something of the people, by sitting on the threshold-beams in the doorways of their raised houses chewing betel-quids and listening to their comments on men and things, and little by little, to form a general idea of their condition and mode of life and of some of the eccentricities of unadulterated Malayan rule. Morning and afternoon a running header from the punting-platform forward was the prelude to a glorious swim – a romp and rag in the cool, olive-green waters, in which practically every Malay on board the raft took his light-hearted part. And it was all new, all wonderful, all a tremendous lark, for a boy of whom the late Lord Knutsford – then Sir Henry Holland and Secretary of State for the Colonies – somewhat exaggerating my youthfulness, later spoke to Sir Fred Weld as being of 'an age when he ought to be being switched at Eton.'[18]

Once in Pekan, Clifford spent three weeks persuading Sultan Ahmad of the benefits of British advice. The sultan's habits were nocturnal, and as befitted an autocrat, he was unpredictable. Sometimes Clifford found himself waiting hours, even days, for an audience which suddenly materialized in the middle of the night. But he was young and there was

> food to be had – excellent Malayan curries; the river close to hand in

which to swim; hosts of amused and amusing Malays with whom to gossip, chaff and chatter; chess and a kind of Mah-jongh to play with little Chinese paper cards; a host of new and interesting things to learn; and, it may have been, a book in my pockets to fill up the chinks of time.[19]

And on Easter Day 1887 the sultan emerged from his seraglio with the long-awaited letter. Clifford departed that night for the mouth of the Pahang river, where a yacht belonging to the sultan of Johore lay at anchor. Two days later he arrived in Singapore and surprised Sir Frederick Weld with the news that he had, in effect, added another province to the empire. His reward was to be sent back to Pahang, first to negotiate the details of the treaty, and then to take up the position of British Political Agent at the sultan's court. Weld wished to break the sultan in gently to the idea of British control; a full Residential appointment would come later. Pahang was to be Clifford's home, apart from periods of leave and a spell as governor of North Borneo, for the next fourteen years, and after he left Malaya in 1901 it was to become the lost Eden to which he longed always to return.

During the early part of his sojourn in Pahang he lived almost wholly among Malays and rarely saw another white man. The experience formed the basis of the sketch called 'Up Country' which he wrote in 1895 and described in 1927 as his *'Apologia pro vita mea'*.[20] 'Up Country' was an extended meditation on the pleasures and pains of immersion in native life, and not the least remarkable thing about it was the degree of honesty with which it was written. The outcome – complete insight into the native mind – is never seriously in doubt, but the miseries of isolation among people to whom one is a queer and unwelcome stranger are vividly and affectingly described. Clifford makes no attempt to deny the longing for civilized companionship and trivial civilized pleasures which overwhelms the expatriate in a simpler society, nor does he disguise the fact that, initially at least, the white man is in many respects an object of revulsion to the *indigènes* – even if he does add that though he is 'hated for his airs of superiority, pitied for his ignorance of many things, feared for what he represents, laughed at for his eccentric habits and customs, despised for his infidelity to the Faith, abhorred for his want of beauty, according to native standards, and loved not at all', he is nevertheless 'respected for his wisdom'. He describes how 'old women snarl at him as he passes' and 'mothers snatch up their little ones and carry them hurriedly away' and how he begins to give up hope that he will ever be accepted. But there is a way out of this impasse, and it is provided by the white man's superior capacity for knowledge of what is outside himself. 'Almost unconsciously', Clifford observes, 'he begins to perceive that he is sundered from the people of the land by a gulf which *they* can never hope to bridge over. If he is ever to gain their confidence the work must be of his own doing. They cannot come up to his level, he must go down to the plains in which they dwell.' He therefore conquers his pride and abandons his prejudices, tries not to think what his compatriots would say if they saw him, and is 'content to be merely a native Chief among natives'. Gradually, he learns that there is 'a great and marvellous book lying beneath his hand', the 'Great Book of Human Nature', and the chapter which deals with natives 'engrosses his attention and, touching the greyness of his life, like the rising sun, turns it into gold and purple'.

The rewards of study are many, but the chief of them is that the white man comes 'to instinctively feel the native Point of View', which is 'really the whole secret of governing natives'. He becomes their protector and friend, at one with them in their joys and sorrows: 'Above all, he understands, and in a manner, they love him.'[21]

It would be hard to find a more articulate statement of what might be called the District Officer ideal – or a clearer intimation of how fine could be the line between helpless submersion in native society and a controlled descent into it to acquire the tools for governing it. If Clifford was not yet consciously aware of how easily the one could be confounded with the other, he soon was, for his first novel, '*Since the Beginning*' (1898), was about a young Englishmen morally destroyed by his obsession with the mysteries of Malay life, and it was a theme to which he would often return. The hero of '*Since the Beginning*' takes a Malay mistress, tires of her, marries a pure-hearted English girl, and then shoots himself after the discarded mistress murders his wife and unborn child. The moral of the story is explicitly drawn: only a strong man can live the life of a Malay and emerge from the experience none the worse for it.[22] Clifford was never one to suppose that all Englishmen were born with a capacity for productive intimacy with native races.

Yet though he thought of Malay life as full of temptations, he also felt for it a deep and passionate attachment quite apart from the interest it presented as an object of study. He loved its boldness and colour, its shameless exaltation of leisure, its ceremoniousness. He felt the novelist's attraction to a life given over wholly to the joys and sorrows of human relations. He contrasted the instinctual life he thought he saw around him with the duty-ridden littleness of civilized existence. Nostalgia makes its appearance early in his writings: on the first page of his first book he is deploring 'the boot of the ubiquitous white man' which 'tramples on the growths of nature and the works of primitive man, reducing all things to that dead level of conventionality, which we call civilization'.[23] From the beginning he was caught between a rock and a hard place, the agent of civilization and yet its enemy.

Clifford's period of seclusion among the Malays came to an end late in 1888. Sir Cecil Clementi Smith had succeeded Sir Frederick Weld as governor in Singapore and he was impatient to bring Pahang under closer British control. The ambiguous position occupied by a mere Political Agent, who had no control over revenue or appointments, had no appeal to Clementi Smith's active and unmystical mind, and when the sultan of Pahang decided to dispose of a Hong Kong Chinese whose wife he coveted, he got the excuse he needed to demand the appointment of a full Resident.[24] Sultan Ahmad briefly considered resistance, but capitulated when the sultan of Johore reminded him of the successful British military expedition against Perak in 1876.[25] Clifford was too junior to be made a Resident and was in any case in no fit state to remain in Pahang, having become seriously ill with a mysterious intestinal disorder in July. J.P. Rodger became the first British Resident in Pahang, and Clifford sailed for England and a year's sick leave in October 1888.

Clifford's published version of the events leading up to the appointment of a Resident – the story 'At the Court of Pělěsu', in which he appears as the hero Jack Norris, 'with a mouth that shut like a trap, and the dogged strength of a dominant race in every hard line which early responsibility and an eastern climate had drawn upon his ugly face'[26] – has him single-handedly facing down the sultan and preparing the ground for the British takeover of Pahang. But his correspondence at the time shows him in a less masterly and farseeing frame of mind; he was writing to Clementi Smith in June advising him to let the matter of the murdered Chinaman drop for 'I don't want to irritate my Sultan more than I can help'.[27] 'At the Court of Pělěsu' was published in 1899 at a time when Clifford had come to believe with almost religious intensity in the sanctity of the political officer's calling, and perhaps this explains what appears to be a lapse of memory. No doubt his experiences at the time in Pahang, alone, and as he truthfully states, 'totally unsupported by any show of force'[28], were exciting enough even if he was not quite the superman he later imagined.

He returned to Pahang early in 1890 to serve under John Rodger, taking over as acting Resident in 1891. He soon had an opportunity to show his mettle when in December of that year some of the disaffected chiefs rose in rebellion. Once again, there is a discrepancy between Clifford's published remembrance of things past and his recorded statements at the time. He remembered himself returning to Pahang, immediately scenting trouble, and finding his repeated warnings to higher authority falling on deaf ears – he assumed, he says, on account of his 'absurd youthfulness'.[29] Yet the records show him writing just before the rebellion broke out:

> The past year has been one of unbroken peace, and although from time to time rumours of intended risings among the Malays in Pahang have been originated and circulated by the Natives of neighbouring States, I am happy to be able to report, possessing as I do a somewhat intimate knowledge of all the important Natives in Pahang, and after having had many opportunities of gauging the feeling of all classes of natives, that these reports have been entirely without foundation . . . an increased confidence and goodwill between the Natives and the European officers is noticeable throughout the country . . .[30]

The Pahang rebellion continued on and off till 1895 and Clifford was deeply involved in its suppression. He assumed the role of military leader with a certain ambivalence, both regretting the necessity for a resort to force, which was difficult to reconcile with his conception of himself as a loved and loving father to his people[31], and relishing the opportunity to perform feats of valour in the field. He had taken with him on his return to Pahang in 1887 'a couple of dozen Malays – friends of mine, from the western side of the Peninsula, who had elected to follow my fortunes', 'men who had seen some good, honest bloodshed in their time, and who were to prove themselves during the next two years some of the best and most loyal ruffians in the Peninsula'.[32] These men had not yet been required to fight, only to display a conspicuous loyalty, but in the years of the rebellion Clifford had the chance to lead these and other Malay irregulars into battle – thereby proving simultaneously his courage, his devotion to his imperial duty of suppressing disaffection, and his ability, through the art of leadership, to exercise a personal ascendancy over at least some of those he was supposed to rule. He did well enough as a warrior for the Malay chronicler of the *Hikayat Pahang* to record that 'Men as valiant as *Tuan* Clifford are seldom met with'; and he had the satisfaction of reporting to his superiors that the Pahang Malays who accompanied him on his rebel-hunting expedition in Kelantan and Trengganu had done so without payment and purely for his *beaux yeux*.[33] There is a photograph of him at this period, taken amid the artificial greenery of a studio in Singapore, which shows him dressed in bush-clothes and an enormous hat, with a Malay dagger at his waist and a sword on his lap. He just fails to look like a bandit chief. No one could mistake the expression of civilized self-consciousness which appears upon his face.

The episode in which Clifford truly distinguished himself, and which was respectfully recorded in the *Hikayat Pahang*, formed the basis of one of his best-known stories, 'One Who had Eaten my Rice'. On this occasion, he had to deal with some Malay chiefs who arrived at his camp with uncertain intentions and an armed force which vastly outnumbered his own. He went out to meet them alone except for an old Malay retainer, Ûmat, whom he employed as a punkah-puller, and who refused to be left behind; he had eaten, he said, Clifford's rice, and where Clifford went, he would go. Together they faced the chiefs, and while Clifford explained to them that if they killed him the vengeance of Her Majesty's Government would surely follow, 'the knowledge that Ûmat's great, fleshy body was wedged in securely between my enemies and the small of my back' gave him 'an added confidence which was worth many points in my favour'.[34] The chiefs dispersed, and the rebellion subsided – for the time being.

In 1899, after three years of being full Resident of Pahang, Clifford was appointed governor of North Borneo, a tiny colony which was technically under the jurisdiction of the British High Commissioner in Singapore, but was in practice run by a chartered company, the British North Borneo Company. He spent eight months in Borneo discovering what should have been obvious from the start – that he was not designed by nature to be the instrument of economic imperialism. When he realized that the governor was expected to be the mere agent of company policy, his letter of resignation, breathing contempt for his employers' indifference to good government[35], followed in due course. Most of his time in Borneo was spent putting down a revolt sparked off by the violation of native treaty rights for the sake of building a railway; when he made his views on this known to the board of directors he was rebuked for scaring off investors. After the inevitable parting of the ways he was welcomed back to Malaya and reappointed Resident of Pahang. His passage of arms with the North Borneo Company had done his reputation no harm in the eyes of the Colonial Office.

The return to Pahang, and presumably happiness, was of short duration. In 1901 he was once again seriously ill and he spent the next two years in England, struggling to regain his health on half-pay. This time the cause of the illness was known but not publicly disclosed: ground glass was found in his stomach, introduced there, it was asumed, by an ill-wisher in Pahang.[36]

During his long convalescence, Clifford had plenty of time to think about the meaning of his life and work hitherto, and one can assume that his reflections were influenced by the nature of his injury. Sent to Pahang because he had 'a remarkable power of gaining the confidence of the Malays', he had found himself engaged in protracted jungle warfare with the populace, and now was laid low by attempted murder in a particularly cruel and deliberate form. It required some working out. The process of assessment began before his illness, as can be seen from the articles and stories he published between 1896 and the early part of 1901, but the need to earn money and fill the idle hours stimulated him to produce a large amount of printed matter before his return to active employment at the end of 1903.

It would be wrong to expect too high a degree of philosophical consistency from a young man of such essentially ambivalent character and actively empathetic imagination as Clifford, a young man who, furthermore, had been pitched at the age of seventeen into a life for which he had no preparation and of which he can have had very little preconception. But though the opinions he uttered – always with the judiciousness and urbanity of the born writer of minutes – were often contradictory, certain recurrent themes can nevertheless be discerned. Clifford believed that the British empire was justified by the good which it did; he believed that it should be permanent; and he believed that, without the right men to run it, it could be neither permanent nor good.

Clifford had discovered from experience that imperial expansion had its own dynamic, and that this had nothing to do with morality. He was a man of the frontier and had felt that 'restlessness, which under Elizabeth drove men Westward Ho!' and 'sets our fellows itching to cross the borders of the King in this later day, there to seek new countries, to see new things, to experience new dangers, excitements, privations'. He knew that: 'If the matter were left in the hands of the frontier-men, the expansion of the empire would proceed at a rate positively terrific, and England would have more little wars on her hands than she owns men to fight them.'[37] All this he accepted, while at the same time continuously worrying about how the process could be justified morally. He made a far more strenuous effort to resolve this problem than Selous, whose exaltation of evolutionary prerogatives would have been unthinkable to Clifford, partly because he was so much more kindly disposed to begin with towards the societies whose destruction he was encompassing, and partly because the doctrines of Social Darwinism, with their implicit ethic of struggle, held no attraction for him. To satisfy his conscience he had to prove that the white man made 'the lives of those of whose destiny he has taken charge better, cleaner and happier than they would have been but for his coming'[38], and given the reservations on the subject he had already expressed, this was no easy task. The obvious solution was to draw attention to the evils of pre-colonial society. As a result, Clifford's portrait of Malaya was rather like that ambiguous drawing once used by psychologists to study the mechanisms of perception, which at one moment looks like a beautiful young bride and at the next is metamorphosed into a hideous old mother-in-law.

Clifford's concern to convince himself and others that the British empire was a force for good led him greatly to exaggerate the horror of what had gone before. In a talk given at the Royal Colonial Institute in 1899 on 'Life in the Malay Peninsula; As it was and is' he described in harrowing detail traditional Malay methods of execution, traditional Malay methods of incarceration, and all the abuses customarily practised by corrupt and unfeeling rajahs upon their uncomplaining subjects.[39] So lurid was this account of Malaya 'as it was' that Hugh Low, who was in the audience, was moved to comment that: 'The Malays themselves, notwithstanding the dreadful accounts we hear of them, confirmed to some extent by Mr Clifford in his Paper, are not such an unamiable set of people as you might suppose'. W.H. Treacher, who had succeeded Low as Resident of Perak, also felt obliged to sound a cautionary note, and asked the audience 'to be careful of how you digest the exciting fare that has been presented to you, I do not want you to go away with the idea that life in the unprotected Malay States is entirely unendurable . . .'[40] He noted the failure of attempts to get Malays from other parts of the peninsula to settle in the British protected states. Abashed, Clifford replied that Malays had not 'sufficient intellectual energy' to 'realise their own misery'.[41]

There was, of course, nothing unusual in equating the advance of empire with the shedding of light upon primeval darkness, and in recent years the opening up of Africa, where cruelty seemed all the more shocking to the Victorians for being practised by the unclothed, had offered strong support for this assumption. The sight which met the eyes of the British expeditionary force which entered Benin in 1897 was one not easily to be forgotten, nor was it: the piles of twitching corpses, freshly slaughtered in the hope of averting catastrophe, were worth a million pamphlets to the imperial cause. But Clifford jumped, one feels, a little too enthusiastically on to this particular bandwagon, and unfortunately one must conclude that he did so in part because he enjoyed the view. Violence stimulated his imagination, to a degree which ought indeed to have concerned his employers, though there is no evidence that it did.

From the beginning of his career as a writer Clifford was given to describing bloodshed and pain in an extremely graphic fashion. Someone is always running amok in his stories, and his characters regularly meet gruesome ends gruesomely described. In 'The Flight of Chêp the Bird', a cuckolded husband despatches his wife's lover with an ancient matchlock, leaving him 'dead upon the sward with his skull shattered to atoms, and the bloody, mucous strings of brain flecking the fresh green grass'.[42] In 'His Little Bill', a Chinese coolie murders an employer who has failed to pay his wages and: 'With cries of horrible satisfaction, he rubbed his blood, which ran still warm from the gaping wounds that the *pârang* had made, over his face and chest; then scooped up a double handful in his reddened palms and drank of it; he grovelled about the dead body in a hideous revel of satisfied revenge . . .'[43] In 'The Vigil of Pa'Tûa, the Thief', a fisherman is trapped in a cave and dies after five minutely depicted days of agony, eaten alive by ants attracted to the grease smeared on him by his friends in their attempts to pull him out.[44] And so on. Clifford seems incapable of leaving such things to the imagination. When his stories began to appear before an English public (they were published at first in Singapore by the *Straits Times* newspaper) he appears to have felt a slightly embarrassed consciousness of this. In the preface to *Studies in Brown Humanity* (1898) he apologized for the 'ugly depths' which he was about to reveal to the reader, his strange excuse being the inadequacy of his powers of describing the peaceful commonplaces of everyday life.[45] Compared with the Malayan sketches being published at the same time by his friend and colleague Frank Swettenham[46], Clifford's fiction was definitely X-rated. It may be that this fascination with the painful and ugly sides of human experience was an early symptom of the insanity which later overwhelmed him. Whatever its cause – and there is nothing discoverable in his background or early life which seems psychologically relevant – it was a constant element in his writing.

In the earliest stories the violence had no discernible pattern with respect to type of victim, motives, or circumstances. At this stage it seems to have been simply violence itself which fascinated Clifford. But around 1900 a change occurred. In the 1890s he wrote about natives killing other natives, or succumbing to painful accidents; in the early 1900s he wrote in addition, and equally graphically, about whites killing natives.

One story in particular, published in 1900 and reprinted on a number of occasions, contains sadistic fantasies of such a startling kind that one wonders how its author could ever have been passed fit for employment in the Colonial Service. This story, 'In the Heart of Kalamantan', arose from Clifford's experience in Borneo, which seems to have released in him feelings of anger towards natives that could not quite rise to consciousness, given his passion for Malays, in Malaya.

Gervase Fornier, 'a very sensitive and imaginative young Englishman'[47] with literary leanings, of good but poor family, is stationed alone in a remote Borneo valley among the wild Mûruts, 'an unclean branch of the human family, whose members squatted like a foul parasitic growth on the rich alluvial soil'.[48] They are head-hunters of the most avid sort, partial to home-brewed alcohol and meat in an advanced state of putrefaction, and they were not, be it noted, a figment of Clifford's imagination. He met them in Borneo and reported to the directors of the chartered company that they were 'amongst the lowest types of human beings whom I have yet encountered'.[49] In his isolation, Gervase becomes possessed by the fear that one day his skull will join those hanging from the roof-beam of a Mûrut hut. His only solace is his daily telephone conversation with his nearest European neighbour, Burnaby, who is in charge of an even remoter valley sixty miles away. Burnaby is made of sterner stuff than Gervase: he rules his Mûruts 'with blended sympathy and firmness', and they in turn think 'all the world of him'. One day Burnaby goes off to quell some tribal wars, leaving Gervase temporarily alone with his imagination, and returns with a spear wound whose seriousness he disguises from his weaker colleague. He remains at his post out of a sense of duty to Gervase, listening to him night after night pouring out his troubles and allowing him to relieve his mind. Suddenly Gervase finds himself giving orders to his men with a new air of authority and is delighted to see them instantly obeyed. 'He was trying to be more like Burnaby.' In due course, Burnaby dies, and Gervase, realizing now that his friend has sacrificed his life for him, is overcome with self-disgust. He sets out for Burnaby's station, which is being threatened by rebellious natives, determined now to do the right thing. Attacked by Mûruts, he flings himself into the midst of them with his little force of Dyak police. Soon:

Marred bodies lay around him, sprawling grotesquely among the rank growths of the clearing, and from three of these he had torn the souls with his own hand, fighting for his life with an intoxication of joy in his heart such as he had never before experienced. And in that instant it flashed across his mind that never again would it be possible for him to feel afraid of Mûruts or of any other natives. The consciousness of the racial superiority of the white man over the brown had come to him with the force of absolute conviction. Gervase Fornier's new-born manhood had been baptized in blood.

The Dyaks crowd admiringly round, and their recognition in him 'of the one virtue that all men prize more than aught else' thrills Gervase strangely and sends the blood 'pulsing through his veins and flushing his cheek'. He sets off on a punitive expedition into the interior, brings back 300 prisoners, and becomes a legend in the eyes of the Mûruts, who 'drunk or sober, swear by the very toe-nails of Tûan Fornier'. His superiors marvel at the change in him: 'He has got a grip', they say, 'on the people that is worth all the theories of administration in the world'.[50] Gervase knows it was Burnaby who made a man of him, and he sits by his grave every evening in silent thankfulness.

There is not a trace of irony in any of this. We must suppose that Clifford meant what he said. As if to prove it, he published another Mûrut story, of similar import, in 1903. This story, 'The Quest of the Golden Fleece', was about two men, an Englishman and an Irishman, who set out on a private expedition to avenge the death of an explorer killed by the Mûruts. The Irishman, O'Hara, is captured by Mûruts and tortured. Rescued at the point of death, he returns the next day with his Dyaks to the Mûrut village and wipes it out. The story concludes with the ambiguous suggestion that O'Hara, who claims to have no recollection of anything that happened after his rescue, may have known perfectly well what he was about. The Mûruts he massacres turn out to be the very ones who killed the explorer.[51]

'A Dying Kingdom', an article about Brunei published in *Macmillan's Magazine* in 1902, reveals even more explicitly the murderous feelings which seem at this period in his life to have welled up uncontrollably in Clifford's breast. Unprepossessing as it was, the seedy little sultanate of Brunei can hardly have deserved this response. 'We all know', writes Clifford,

> the sick horror which seizes us when we see some hideous creature, maimed and mangled, twisting under foot in a detestable impotence of pain, dying, but dying with the slowness which prolongs and intensifies the acuteness of its misery. We all know with what a frenzied haste we strike, and strike, and strike again to end the horror, to put the writhing thing beyond the reach of pain. Much the same feeling possesses the man who looks upon a dying Asiatic kingdom during the last disgraceful moments of its repulsive existence. He longs to make it cease; to cleanse the world of this stain upon its fair

fame; to wipe out hurriedly the mildew whose foulness seems to degrade humanity since it has spread its leprosy over a portion of our kind.[52]

Much more follows in the same vein. Even the vegetation, even the very houses, seem rotten in Brunei, and Clifford himself cannot escape a feeling of uncleanness: 'Disgust, horror, contempt, repulsion, and an unreasoning feeling of contamination, all held me in their grip . . .' Meeting the sultan's son, he experiences 'a sensation of physical nausea, . . . a violent desire to destroy a creature whose very existence seemed, for the moment, to make the whole earth filthy'. And yet, and yet: 'behind all this passion of disgust there lurks another feeling, a certain tenderness and regret, born of that unreasoning love of ancient things, things with a glorious past, which all men know in greater or lesser measure'. Even in Borneo Clifford was not released entirely from the Orient's spell, and his 'unreasoning feeling of contamination' was the unreasoned acknowledgement of that fact.

Clifford wrote one substantial piece of fiction during his convalescence, the novel *A Free Lance of To-day*. Most of his conflicting impulses found expression in it, and an attempt was made to resolve them.

The hero of *A Free Lance of To-day* was another of Clifford's alter egos, Maurice Curzon, 'a white man of the white men – a masterful son of the dominant race', who nevertheless has come close to being 'denationalized' through his fascination with the Malays, an affliction which is at first sympathetically described. At the opening of the novel Maurice is contemplating a little gun-running to Sumatra, where the natives of Acheh are holding out against the incursions of the Dutch. Despising Dutch colonialism, sympathizing with resistance to it, and looking forward to tasting again 'the free life of the jungle, with that added spice which would come, he thought, from the lust of battle, himself in the forefront of the fight!', he allows himself to be seduced by the romantic fascination of the Achehnese past. He hopes to find in Acheh, which has never known European control, a primordial Malay utopia, bold and free yet 'a State wherein strength and power existed only for the protection of the weak, and wrong and oppression were dead'. Naturally, he is disappointed. The Achehnese, he soon discovers, are vicious, indolent, and incompetent.

Maurice's most instructive encounter in Acheh is with an Englishman who has been enslaved by the Achehnese, and who clearly represents what Maurice, if he persists in error, might become. This man, formerly a private in the Dutch army, has betrayed his officers to the Achehnese and then seen them tortured to death. Broken by the experience, he is now, in the eyes of the natives, an object of contempt. He inspires in Maurice the same impulse the prince of Brunei inspired in Clifford, a passionate desire 'to kill the creature before him – to put it out of its pain, to cleanse the world from the infinite pollution of its presence'. In the end Maurice does kill him – accidentally! By this time he has had enough of the Achehnese and no longer cares whether their ancient culture is trampled under the boot of the white man or not. Even his experience of battle, to which he had looked forward so much, is spoiled by finding the body of a Dutchman mutilated by his comrades-in-arms.

> The whiteness of that awful corpse made the dead man akin to him – it was as though this vile outrage had been perpetrated upon the body of one dear as a lifelong friend. A fierce hatred of the brown man who had done this thing, a passion of indignation, surged up in his heart. They were devils, not men – devils, cruel, bestial, infinitely degraded who had conceived and executed this unspeakable mutilation; and he, of his own will, by his own actions, had identified himself with them! The realization of the full horror which this fact held maddened him.

He swears an oath never to 'strike another blow for brown men against Europeans'[53], and the novel draws to a close with his carrying a letter from an Achehnese chief to the governor of the Straits Settlements, begging the British to annexe Acheh and save it from the Dutch.

Maurice's disillusion is clearly Clifford's, though Clifford in real life never returned so unambiguously to the fold. The conflict between passionate attachment to the Malays and passionate hatred of them was one he never resolved. Sometimes rage was uppermost in his heart, sometimes love. Clearly, love came first, though this does not mean that Clifford ever felt for the Malays anything like unequivocal approval. It means that he saw their faults but was drawn to them all the same. In one of his early stories he writes of a wicked old sultan: 'He was an exceptionally unpleasant person, but for some reason, which I can never explain, and which I dimly feel was undoubtedly to my discredit, he and I were on very friendly terms'. The discredit need not be taken too seriously: we learn on the next page that 'courage was the one and only virtue which relieved the Egyptian darkness of the king's character'.[54] The problem was that though he had loved Malaya, and loved it still, on the whole there was no denying it had not loved him. What was the devotion of a few bravos and an old servant beside the rising of whole provinces

and the ground glass which reposed in his stomach? Not, it must
have seemed at times, very much. But perhaps it was just as well.
Worse dangers, he knew, lay in wait for the man who succumbed to
the charm of what was after all an unlovely condition of society. The
more unlovely it seemed the more justifiable was his rage against it,
and the easier it was to disguise from himself that the origin of his
rage lay in rejection. Clifford continued all his life to look for
evidence that his conduct inspired affection in native peoples, and
some of his later ebullitions against nationalism arose quite clearly
from his sense of having being denied it. A modern historian of
Ceylon has observed how seriously Clifford took the formal
expressions of regret emitted by the Ceylonese when he left that
country, at the end of a singularly alienating governorship, in
1927.[55]

All in all, it was no wonder that Clifford so appreciated Conrad,
sought him out, became his friend, and took an almost proprietary
interest in him – he had travelled, at least in imagination, to the
heart of darkness himself. Conrad observed of *A Free Lance of To-day*
that he found the character of Maurice implausible – 'terribly
unscrupulous' but 'as nervous as a cat in his disappointment, in his
disenchantment, in his horror', coolly shooting at Dutchmen one
minute 'and then directly afterwards beside himself with horror at
the mutilation of the dead bodies'.[56] Conrad was right to conclude
that as a fictional creation Maurice was not a success; as a writer of
fiction Clifford never rose above the status of the talented amateur.
But sometimes the empathetic power of the novelist carried him
along to insights for which the reader is quite unprepared, and
which read strangely indeed coming from the pen of a colonial civil
servant. In *A Free Lance of To-day* a village headman reveals to
Maurice Curzon the deceptions to which the Achehnese must resort
in their struggle against the Dutch.

> Maurice lay thinking. He saw how inevitable it was that in a struggle
> such as this between white men and a brown race the former's notions
> concerning loyalty and good faith should become warped and
> perverted. Lacking that saving grace of imagination which alone
> enables a white man to appreciate the point of view of the native, the
> average European who partakes in such a contest cannot understand
> that what he names loyalty – that is, loyalty to the invaders, is really
> treachery of the blackest, the ugly crime of the paid renegade. And
> thus it comes to pass that a grotesquely distorted standard of morality
> is set up by the white men, an inverted code of conduct whereby the
> intruders judge their new subjects. Maurice who by virtue of his birth,
> could gauge the sentiments of the Dutch, and through his sympathy

with the natives could understand their view, thought that he could mark the widespread demoralization which cruel circumstances must render inevitable. Even the passionate patriotism of the Achehnese rooted honour in dishonour. It bred a low cunning, a bewildering duplicity; it taught men to look upon the telling of truth as a crime, and made a tongue that lied glibly and plausibly a possession of which a man felt that he did well to be proud. For the moment it seemed to Maurice that this was the most bitter wrong of all that Dutch aggression had inflicted upon the Achehnese.[57]

Clifford had 'that saving grace of imagination'.

It should be noted here that Clifford was not in practice a particularly violent man: his darker impulses were worked out upon the printed page. During the Mat Saleh revolt in Borneo he put a stop to the summary shooting of prisoners, and in 'Bush-whacking' he recalls his fictionalized self as feeling painfully ambivalent about such usual punitive techniques as village-burning and the shelling of civilians: 'A man to go bush-whacking with a light heart should have no insight, no sympathy, no imagination.'[58] By the standards of the time, there was nothing in Clifford's actual conduct towards the natives for which his superiors could have reproached him. Nevertheless, it seems strange that the Colonial Office's only concern about his writing appears to have been that it might take too much time from his official duties.[59] Perhaps no one in the Colonial Office read what he wrote, which seems unlikely considering that it was published in *Blackwood's* and other popular magazines; or it may be that the feelings he articulated were more common than one would like to suppose.

But if his employers did not reproach him, it seems that at some level of consciousness Clifford reproached himself. In 1903 he described the officers of the Malayan Civil Service as men

who are prepared to devote their energies exclusively to the task of improving the conditions of those around them, who [are] guided by a deep sympathy with the natives and by the understanding which sympathy alone can give; men who are completely free from any selfish motives, and who have at their command an unlimited stock of patience and forbearance.[60]

Coming from the exterminating angel who was the author of 'A Dying Kingdom', such visions of benignity have a distinctly expiatory look. They are common in Clifford's writings. Though he well knew how little resemblance the heroes described above bore to the ordinary human agents of imperial rule, including himself[61], he loved to write of empire as though it were nothing but an exercise in unexampled benevolence – moving imperceptibly from the argument that the British empire was justifiable only if it did good to the assertion that, whatever the results might be, British intentions were completely pure. As if to compensate for all his bad thoughts and misgivings, he embraced an imperial philosophy of exceptional high-mindedness. On the whole it liberated and ennobled him.

In this philosophy there was, of course, no place for profits. Though Clifford had quite conventional notions about the development of the imperial estate as a young man[62], his increasing preoccupation with the idea of empire as good government, and his spell in Borneo, turned him into another very uneconomic imperialist. He despised the Dutch for wanting to make money out of the natives, and – one of the stranger consequences of his concern not to exploit – was an extreme advocate of the policy of importing Chinese labourers into Malaya in order to spare the Malays the necessity of having to work in European enterprises.[63] There would be tin mines, there would be rubber plantations; but they would operate in a separate sphere from that in which the work of good government of the natives was carried on. Then Clifford could claim that: 'From the first, the Native States of British Malaya have been regarded by their English rulers as countries held in trust for their native inhabitants'.[64] Certainly, there is no evidence that he himself ever profited personally from the empire, beyond drawing his salary. He had a clean record with respect to land speculation in Malaya, a weakness in which some of his most eminent colleagues indulged very profitably.[65]

He was not, as has been noted, a Social Darwinist. When he tried on one occasion to defend a policy by appealing to natural selection, he tied himself up in knots: he had no aptitude for that kind of analysis.[66] He instinctively thought of the empire as frozen in time at around 1900, the point by which, according to his personal interpretation of history as revealed in *Further India* (1904) and elsewhere, the British had purged themselves of the grosser imperial impulses and settled down to the serious business of government. 'The age of frank brutality had passed away for ever', he wrote in *Further India*, 'and has been replaced by an age of philanthropy and humanitarianism.'[67] His conception of empire was essentially one of permanent administration. He did not think of natives learning to govern themselves, or of whites teaching them: President Roosevelt's statement that, under American tutelage, the Filipinos could be

expected to make steady progress towards self-government, struck
him as the most dangerous and inexplicable twaddle. In his view,
the history of the brown races showed that self-government was not
an art to which they could aspire. Left to themselves, they murdered
and oppressed one another, and there was no reason to think that,
unsupervised, they would ever cease to do so.[68]

On this point Clifford was pessimistic to a degree far exceeding
many of his contemporaries, who at least acknowledged in theory the
prospect of eventual independence from British rule. But what else
could he say after investing so much energy in demonstrating the
moral inferiority of the Malays? He had no alternative, emotionally,
but to suppose it ineradicable. When W.H. Treacher pointed out to
him after his lecture on 'Life in the Malay Peninsula; As it was and
is', that it was not long ago that men had been hanged for stealing
sheep in Britain, and that slavery had 'existed under our flag, with
all its horrors, to an extent unknown to the Malays', Clifford simply
refused to entertain the argument.[69] So far as he was concerned,
there was no comparison to be made: the white races were capable
of moral development, the brown races were not.

He published two novellas demonstrating this point in 1904 and
1908 – 'Sally: a Study' and *Saleh: A Sequel*. Together they tell the tale of
a young Malay prince who spends five years living in England with
an English family, receiving the finest moral training the ruling race
can offer. At first the boy seems to have become the perfect
gentleman; but soon an occasion arises when the essential baseness
of his nature reveals itself. In a fall from grace very much of the
period, he strikes a woman – and then there is nothing left for him to
do but return to Malaya, go to the dogs, raise a revolt against the
English, and die in a suicidal *amôk* after realizing, too late, that white
rule is the only hope for peace and prosperity in his country.

How little relation Clifford's fantasies on this subject bore to the
facts can be seen from the recollections of Mary Smith, the wife of
Arthur Smith, a tutor of Balliol in whose household the Rajah Alang
Iskander of Perak resided for five years as a boy, having been
consigned there in 1899 by none other than Hugh Clifford himself.
Far from embarking on a career of crime, Rajah Alang Iskander
grew up to be a model sultan of Perak and a man for whose
character Mrs Smith had nothing but praise: 'no pupil', she wrote,
'has ever repaid us better for all the trouble we took with him'.[70]
Clifford could not wait to see the outcome of the moral experiment
he had begun. Instead he yielded to a disgraceful but apparently
irresistible impulse to predict publicly what it would be. Fictionally,
Rajah Alang Iskander never stood a chance: his allotted task was to
show why it was that brown people could look forward indefinitely

to being ruled by 'a white race which, acting unselfishly and with a paternal care for the welfare of all classes of the community – orders the destiny of all more wisely than the natives are capable of doing on their own account'.[71]

In *Saleh: A Sequel*, Saleh's revolt is crushed by Jack Norris, the least ambiguous of all Clifford's fictional selves, a man who lets 'the oriental half of him' have an airing for an hour before breakfast, when he customarily puts on native dress and enjoys a quiet cigarette before getting down to the business of the day.[72] He turns the tide against Saleh by the sheer power of his reputation as 'a good man to deal with and a bad man to cross'. When Norris arrives on the scene Saleh knows his cause is lost: 'Mentally he contrasted the grip and the grit, the calm, keen force of the man, with the feeble qualities of those about him'. In what must have been for Clifford a supremely wish-fulfilling moment, Saleh writes Norris a note, shortly before his final *amôk*, apologizing for all the trouble he has been.[73]

For Clifford, such men as Norris were the very foundation of the empire, the rock on which the whole edifice stood. At the heart of all his thinking was the same faith in a few good men, their utility and availability, which had inspired John and Henry Lawrence – though in Clifford's case the inspiration was not the evangelical ethos but a now established imperial tradition, which he interpreted in a distinctly aristocratic fashion. All his official life he proudly inscribed the letters 'MCS' – Malayan Civil Service – after his name, and when he rose to gubernatorial eminence he took infinite pains over bush postings, watching carefully to see which of the young men proving themselves in the outposts might be groomed to follow in his own footsteps. He believed that the highest appointments in the imperial service should be reserved for those who had shown a personal capacity for ascendancy over native races, proposing to the Colonial Office in 1917 that they now desist from offering governorships to outsiders and recruit solely from within the service.[74] His fiction abounds in prodigious District Officers, performing their feats of influence unknown and, according to Clifford, hitherto unsung. There is the sad figure of Simon Strange in '"Cast"' (1902), who destroys his health ruling his jungle fastness and is invalided home to an obscure and unappreciated existence on a paltry pension; there is the Indian administrator who single-handedly keeps the peace in his district during the Mutiny and gets no thanks for it: 'Oh dear, no!' he says, 'You see, mine was one of the districts which had no Mutiny history, and there were heaps of them – heaps of them!'[75]

Clifford was much given to lecturing America on the inferior quality of her administrative personnel in the Philippines, and had little good to say of the French, Dutch, Spanish and Portuguese either; in resources of character he found their representatives sadly deficient. In spite of his affection for the term 'white race', he was not, when it came down to it, a race patriot but a British patriot who enjoyed crowing a little over his country's rivals. It was an obvious delight to him to wonder aloud why other nations required so many more men than the British to keep their natives down. If Britain, for instance, only needed 500 men to rule India, with its population of 300 million, why were the French unable to get by with less than 200 *fonctionnaires* for one and a half million Cambodians?[76] The question answered itself. But, boasting aside, the issue of quality was one which Clifford pondered extremely seriously. Lurking never very far from the surface of his mind was the idea that the empire which did not have the right type of men suffering unrewarded exile in its outposts was doomed. Though he seems to have had the greatest difficulty imagining the British voluntarily relinquishing power, he had no difficulty at all imagining it being wrested from them. He thought the Portuguese had lost their colonies to other European nations because they had treated their natives cruelly and without honour, and had therefore failed to instill in them a binding 'consciousness of benefits received'[77]; and he warned America that she would lose the Philippines unless she managed to find men who could by their character and conduct secure the active consent of the Filipinos to alien rule. He could not resist adding that these would have to be 'men of a stamp similar to that of the officers who did the early work among the Malays of the peninsula' – a requirement which he implied rendered the outlook for America hopeless indeed.[78] For Clifford British Malaya as he had known it in the 1880s and '90s remained the sum and measure of things imperial.

When he finally resumed employment in the Colonial Service at the end of 1903 it was not to Malaya that he was sent but to, of all places, Trinidad – the very epitome of the colonial slum, a country whose native inhabitants, far from being cherished, had long ago been exterminated to make way for a servile population devoted to the profitable production of sugar. No one had ever supposed that this colony existed for any other purpose than to make money. It was a place which made lofty notions of imperial purpose very difficult to sustain, but Clifford did his best.

Trinidadian society at the turn of the century consisted of a small white population, some Chinese shopkeepers, a sizeable but so far politically quiescent group of East Indians originally brought to the island as indentured labourers, and a coloured middle class which placed itself at the head of the agitation for political reform. At the top of this combustible heap of human material sat a governor and a Colonial Secretary appointed by the Colonial Office. It was the latter position which Clifford reluctantly accepted in September 1903. The political situation in Trinidad was at that time even less appetizing than usual. Port of Spain had recently been convulsed by a riot in which nine people had been killed and the central government offices burned to the ground by an angry mob. The government had drifted into a state of paralysis, and a commission of inquiry had issued a report deploring the governor's lack of grip. At this point, the Colonial Office had decided that Hugh Clifford, with his reputation for firm but sympathetic handling of subject races, was the man to take charge until the discredited governor, Sir Alfred Moloney, could be discreetly removed from the scene.[79] There is something touching about the British government's selection for this task of a man whose career up to that point had been spent struggling to impose British rule on a backward Asiatic society. It suggests, to say the least, an all-purpose view of imperial ability.

Clifford's immediate instinct was to apply the emollient techniques he had first learned at the feet of Hugh Low of Perak, and to begin with they worked. The riot's proximate cause had been a proposed new Water Works Ordinance which, unexciting as it sounds, had inflamed the passions of the community by raising certain tender issues of local representation on public bodies. Summoning all his charm, Clifford persuaded the contending parties to agree to a new bill which in essentials differed not at all from the previous one, but whose details were the product of extremely well-managed public consultation. Unaccustomed as they were to having their opinion solicited on anything, let alone listened to with every appearance of respect, the agitating classes of the colony found themelves momentarily disarmed by the shock of Clifford's benign attentiveness. It was a notable success for him, and a clear vindication of the faith in his powers entertained by the Colonial Office. He felt he could congratulate himself on 'removing from the public mind the impression that their voices were persistently ignored that unquestionably prevailed until recently'.[80] The era of good feelings did not last long. As it became clear that though he liked to hear suggestions Clifford had no interest in conceding power, public opinion turned against him, and he left Trinidad in 1907 unregretted by those who had once detected auguries of democracy in his emphatically announced commitment to the public weal. To Clifford, representation really meant being allowed the privilege of consultation. With his conception of the high calling of government, and the qualifications required for it, it could hardly be otherwise.

By his own lights, he was prepared to go a long way to meet what he regarded as justified complaints by the non-white population of inadequate representation. He advocated changing the composition of the Legislative Council to include a large number of coloureds and an East Indian member, seeing this both as a necessary reform and as a means of foiling the political ambitions of the irresponsible opposition. The new members would be nominated by the governor, who would be careful to choose 'the men of moderation, of judgment and of discretion who are the true representatives of their people'.[81] This proposal was over-ruled by the Colonial Office, but another one, to introduce a mixed elected and nominated Municipal Council for Port of Spain, was supported, and then came to grief when the members of the committee appointed to consider it split irreconcilably between those who wanted a wholly nominated council and those who wanted a wholly elected one. Forced to take sides, Clifford instinctively went for nomination, thereby finding himself embarrassingly at cross-purposes with the new governor, Sir Henry Jackson, who proposed a scheme whereby an initially nominated council would be transformed over a period of five years into a wholly elected one. In the subsequent exchange of correspondence with the Colonial Office it became clear that Clifford's commitment to the elective principle was tentative indeed.[82] The idea of a council without any nominated members at all was one he found difficult to comprehend, and he was determined that the elective process should be of such a nature as to make it very hard indeed for irresponsibles to slip through the hallowed portals of government. He proposed, for instance, that if an insufficient proportion of people cast their vote in a municipal election, the government should be empowered to nominate someone to the vacant seat.

Not the least interesting aspect of this episode was the indulgence shown by the Colonial Office to Clifford, who received no reproof for involving his superior, the governor, in what had become a public difference of opinion. He was, of course, the coming man, whereas Jackson was obviously destined to circulate for ever in the gubernatorial second division; but the gentle handling Clifford received was due in part to the sheer brilliancy of his despatches. He was actually thanked by the Secretary of State 'for the frank and able manner in which you have placed your views before me'.[83] One wonders sometimes how much of Clifford's high standing in Whitehall was due to his, by bureaucratic standards, positively Proustian fluency and elegance of self-expression, as opposed to his actual accomplishments.

During his leave in England in 1905 Clifford produced at the request of the Colonial Office a 'Memorandum on the Existing

Condition of Race-Feeling in the Island of Trinidad'.[84] In it he sought to harmonize his views on empire with the ugly fact of Trinidad's existence. He started from the observation that the blacks hated the whites with a hatred which appeared to be ineradicable. This must have been a painful admission. Nevertheless, he made it, and saw that the feelings of the blacks were understandable if not, in his view, entirely justified. As slaves they had never known justice, and the loathing which they therefore felt for their masters had passed down from generation to generation. Here once again Clifford showed that 'saving grace of imagination' which set him apart from many of his colleagues. Passing from the negro, long-suffering and perhaps more sinned against than sinning, he considered the coloureds, and here his powers of empathy failed him a little, as they were apt to do with those who were serious rivals for power. He understood that the coloureds, excluded by the island's colour bar from the society of those who had sired them, had their justified resentments, but nevertheless he judged them contemptible. They had Latin blood in their veins and liked to read Rousseau. As for the Europeans, words for once almost failed him as he sought to convey the extent to which they had let down the white race: 'the white man in Trinidad, and indeed in all the West Indies', he noted in painfully understated prose, 'has never maintained his position in relation to the coloured and black peoples in the way that has kept up the white man's reputation and authority in the East'. Morally and physically degenerate, they cut a poor figure in the eyes of those it was essential for them to impress. Some of them had even sunk to menial occupations. How different, Clifford remarked, things were in the East, where white men who started to go under were shipped home before they could bring discredit to the race. But perhaps the worst failing of the whites was their want of moral courage. They feared the coloureds and blacks and lacked the nerve to stand up to them in an emergency. This was because they were money-minded, and would never risk financial loss for the sake of principle. They had no sense that the honour of the race was in their keeping.

Having constructed a political impasse, Clifford suggested a way out of it. As there was no one in Trinidad to whom political power could safely be entrusted, the only reasonable course was to hand over the government of the colony to 'men who are free from all local ties and interests'.

Government by selected white officials, who are instructed to acquaint themselves in the most painstaking fashion with local needs and requirements, to give a sympathetic hearing to all parties, and to decide every question to the best of their ability for the good of the community as a whole, without fear and without favour, without affection and without ill-will, is, I venture to think, the only form of government in the least suited to the conditions which prevail in this Colony.

It was the Malayan solution, served up on this occasion with a quite breath-taking want of realism. There was no prospect at all of pure Colonial Service rule being adopted or succeeding in Trinidad at this date. 'We only hope', remarked the editor of a local newspaper in 1907, shortly before Clifford's term of office drew to a close, 'by this time he has realised that there are vast differences between West Indians and Malayans, and that the same treatment will not do for both.'[85] Apparently in 1905 he had not, though he made a concession of sorts to reality at the end of his memorandum by suggesting that a force of white men, not less than 100 strong, should be recruited in Britain and stationed in Trinidad for the purpose of maintaining order; in the dangerous circumstances of Trinidad, his proposed administration of selfless bureaucrats would, he divined, require 'at its back something more solid than moral force'.

The solution proposed by Clifford to Trinidad's problems was his attempt to reconcile empire with honour in that unhappy place. His solution does not appear to have satisfied him for long, however. By 1906 he is doubtful about the whole idea of white colonization of the tropics; experience, he says, has shown that colonists tend to become either indolent or oligarchical, and can never in any case possess the detachment which provides 'the best security for the altruism of British rule in the East'.[86] By 1907 he has reached the point where he would like to wash his hands of places like Trinidad altogether. In an article published pseudonymously in the *Fortnightly Review* he proposed exchanging the West Indies for the Philippines, by which happy arrangement America would gain a convenient source of sugar and Britain would add the final link to the chain of her Eastern possessions.[87] America, accustomed to dealing with ex-slaves, might not do too badly administering the West Indies, and Britain could put to good use in the Philippines her unquestionable expertise in the governance of Asiatics.

The experience of Trinidad raised questions about the fundamental nature of empire which in the end Clifford did not seriously attempt to answer. Repelled by the reality of what his countrymen had wrought over a century of undisputed ascendancy, he retreated into a fantasy of empire as a clean and cloistered world of disinterested administration where everything was done with the best intentions and was therefore defensible. 'How can we have an empire without sacrificing our moral integrity?' was the question which seems to have formulated itself in his mind, rather than 'Why should we have an empire at all?' For a man who demonstrably possessed the saving grace of imagination, this was a serious failure.

The next stop was Ceylon. Here, as in Trinidad, Clifford won the battle and lost the war. As Colonial Secretary to a weak and blustering governor – the same position of power behind the throne that he had occupied in Trinidad – he was instrumental in persuading the Colonial Office to reject the very modest proposals for constitutional reform put forward by the leaders of the Ceylonese middle class, thus unintentionally acting as midwife to the emerging nationalist movement. The dissatisfaction provoked by Clifford's policies among the educated Ceylonese, and the resentment they felt at his all too evident contempt for their aspirations, contributed mightily to the radicalization of their ideas.[88] Just how contemptuous his attitude was can be gauged from the fact that Winston Churchill, then Parliamentary Under-Secretary at the Colonial Office, found a despatch from Clifford dismissing criticism of the government by the Ceylon Labour Union too reactionary in tone.[89] Once again, however, it seems that the superior quality of his written communications helped to carry the day. The Colonial Office had in fact been prepared to consider favourably the reforms proposed by the Ceylonese National Association in 1909, but the despatches from Ceylon, which went out under the governor's name but were drafted by Clifford, changed the official mind. It was deemed inadvisable to make any significant concessions to people who were, in the well-argued opinion of the men-on-the-spot, denationalized politicians representative of no one but themselves. Clifford had just completed *Saleh: A Sequel* and was in good form for an exposition of this topic.

Ceylon and it peoples did not inspire him to any significant literary production, but he found inspiration in Cambodia which he visited while on leave in 1910.

In Pnom Penh two decrepit Brahmans in a temple shrine, descendants of the builders of Angkor, set him thinking of 'the intolerable fate of gods and empires' and stimulated his imagination to 'fearful probings of the Future', which the sight of Angkor itself did nothing to dispel.[90] Like most Europeans at that time, Clifford supposed Angkor to have been built by Indian invaders – it was as difficult, apparently, to imagine Angkor built by Cambodians as it was to imagine Zimbabwe built by Africans – but then his version of its history took an idiosyncratic turn. He surmised that the alien rulers, cruel and arrogant as they had become, yet had an 'uneasy sense that retribution threatened' from above, and he recorded his conviction that 'rightly understood, all these colossal monuments are one immense act of faith and propitiation, one eternal prayer and supplication to the Powers Invisible'.[91] Sitting amid the ruins one evening, watching the stones acquire an aspect of putrescence in the fading light, Clifford asked himself if this was, indeed, the fate of all empires.[92] The fact that the possibility of propitiation had occurred to him suggests that, deep down, he thought it was not.

He was rewarded for his services in Ceylon by a KCMG, bestowed on him in 1909 at the early age of forty-three, before he had even held the governorship which usually accompanied this honour. It was a sign of how much the Colonial Office appreciated him. But Clifford felt that he had not been appreciated enough; the governorship for which he believed himself qualified – North Borneo did not really count – was in his opinion long overdue.[93] The mantle of governorship, however, was about to descend upon him. In 1912 the Colonial Office decided that the Gold Coast administration needed shaking up, and Clifford was promoted from a trouble-shooting Colonial Secretary to a trouble-shooting governor. It was in the Gold Coast that his high sense of governance at last came into its own.

The history of the Gold Coast, alas, reflected no greater glory on the British empire than that of Trinidad, but Clifford accepted this and concentrated on the hope of redemption in the present day. The opportunity which presented itself to him there was an unexpected one. He found himself, for the first time in his career, responding with fascinated enthusiasm to the idea of economic development. His beliefs on the subject of the economic exploitation of colonies had not changed, but what he saw in the Gold Coast revealed to him that government could be involved in economic activities without thereby sullying its honour, and his active mind responded eagerly to this new challenge.

In 1911 the Gold Coast had become the world's leading producer of cocoa, and this had come about, not through plantations controlled by Europeans, but through small family farms operated by Africans who had seen the economic potential of the crop. Clifford was deeply impressed by this development and held opinions on it which were far ahead of his time. Unlike many Europeans in the Gold Coast, including those in the Department of Agriculture, who could not quite bring themelves to believe that an agricultural miracle had been wrought by illiterate peasants who paid no heed to their advice, Clifford accepted the essential rationality of the African farmer, and saw in him the key to the future prosperity of the colony. When the Agriculture Department pressed him to approve stiff penalties, including imprisonment, for cocoa farmers who were guilty of what received opinion held to be insanitary cultivation practices, Clifford pointed out that some of these practices were in fact the result of long experience in dealing with cocoa diseases and produced good results.[94] His percipience was remarkable, considering the contempt in which African agriculture was held at the time, and for many years afterwards.

He was also astute enough to understand that heavy-handed official interference in traditional methods of farming could have undesirable political results.[95] African nationalism acquired its mass organizational base partly as a result of precisely this kind of interference, which produced a whole set of comprehensible grievances for agitators to agitate about. Clifford grasped this possibility and moved to forestall it.

As soon as he had recognized the nature and magnitude of the African farmer's achievement, Clifford appointed himself his champion. He did everything he could to see that the native producer received the full financial reward of his labours, and did not seem to mind whom he offended in the process: he had found a new field for the exercise of good government. In 1915 he took the extraordinary and most ungubernatorial step of calling a meeting of farmers to advise them to withhold their stocks of cocoa until better prices could be obtained from the local European merchants. In 1916 he advocated the formation of farmers' associations – co-operatives in all but name – to enable the farmers to get a better deal for their product. In 1918 he granted cocoa export licences forfeited by enemy firms to native growers, thus further assisting them to circumvent the middle man. The London and Liverpool Chambers of Commerce complained to the Colonial Office, but to no avail.[96] Perhaps Clifford's greatest service to the cocoa industry was his road construction programme, which dramatically improved the farmer's access to his markets. The lightweight Ford truck had been introduced into the colony in 1913 and Clifford soon saw that this, and not the railway, was the solution to the farmer's transportation problem. During his tenure in office, 165 miles of hard-surface roads, and over 650 miles of secondary roads, were constructed.[97]

In contrast to his apprehensions about Malaya, he seems to have felt little anxiety about the social and economic revolution which was occurring, with his assistance, in the Gold Coast. He even looked forward with equanimity to the political changes which he saw would come in its wake. This was in part because the traditional society of the Gold Coast struck him as not worth preserving[98]; but it was also because he had arrived at such a large conception of imperial rule that he was able to be rather dispassionate about what could be seen from a very great height to be mere details of local administration. Putting it another way, the broad oak of Colonial Service rule could shelter all sorts of exotic shrubbery in its shade.

The units of 'native administration' in the Gold Coast were the tribal councils, in which chiefs and elders, under the supervisory eye of European District Officers, deliberated the local issues of the day. Clifford proposed in 1916 that the young men who had made money out of cocoa farming, and who were becoming impatient with traditional authority, should be given seats on these councils. This was such a radical proposal that it was not implemented for another thirty-five years.[99] Clifford made it because, though he believed throughout his career that government should be carried on wherever possible through existing hierarchies, his commitment to good government took precedence over his commitment to chiefly government; and he thought that good government required giving the new social forces in the colony an adequate means of political expression.

He did not contemplate, of course, any redistribution of power at the very top. Indeed, he believed that in the period of rapid change which was before them, 'chiefs and people alike will stand in greater need than ever before of the assistance and guidance of the Government . . .': the broad oak would always have a vital role to play in the colonial ecology.[100]

His response to the embryonic nationalist movement was inevitably hostile. But he knew that to put the ideal of good government into practice it was necessary to be in touch with all classes of the community, and so he increased substantially, in the face of Colonial Office opposition, the number of African representatives on the Legislative Council.[101] From 1916 there were six Africans on the Council – three paramount chiefs and three educated men, all of them nominated by the governor, elective representation being out of the question 'for a long time to come'.[102] Their function was not to exercise influence but simply to be available for formal consultation. 'Officials have not the advantage of being omniscient', Clifford wrote.[103] The representative principle was strictly adhered to; that is, the paramount chiefs represented the people in their districts, and the educated men represented the educated population of the coast – and no one else. Their claims to speak for 'the people' were not entertained; that privilege fell, by default and by superior competence, to the colonial government. In appointing men who happened to be nationalists – Casely-Hayford, Hutton-Mills and E.J.B. Brown – to the Legislative Council Clifford was not making any concessions to nationalist ideas.

His priestly view of colonial administration also enabled him to take a paradoxically generous view, for the time, of the role Africans could play in the Gold Coast civil service. So long as the inner sanctum of the political service was left inviolate, Clifford saw no reason to refuse positions of responsibility to qualified natives of the country. He argued successfully for the admission of African doctors to the public service, and he was instrumental in securing the appointment of the Ga lawyer, E.C. Quist, as the first African Crown Counsel. He made short work of a proposal by the government medical service to introduce residential segregation of Africans from Europeans, observing characteristically that the maintenance of the health of Europeans was not 'the sole aim for which British rule is established in this country'.[104] Equally characteristically, he was unable to appreciate the desirability of providing secondary education for Africans; that would be rushing things. Like many people even today, he found it difficult to believe that the transition from illiterate savage to something indistinguishable from the average educated European could be made in a single lifetime. This was one petty prejudice he failed to rise above.

From 1914 the war occupied much of Clifford's attention. There was fighting in Togo and the Cameroons and he concerned himself enthusiastically with the management of the war in West Africa and with recruiting for the Gold Coast Regiment, which distinguished itself in the East African campaign. In 1920 he published an affectionate book about its exploits.[105] Shortly after war broke out French and British troops occupied the German colony of Togo. This added a further administrative responsibility to those Clifford already had, but also gave him an opportunity to reflect on the subject of German imperialism. The result was *German Colonies: A Plea for the Native Races*, which was published in 1918.

In *German Colonies* Clifford returned once again to the problem of the moral justification of empire and arrived once again at the same conclusion. Empires were only justified by the good which they did to native races, and by this standard Clifford pronounced Germany's imperial enterprise clearly to be immoral. The Germans, he said, had revived the spirit of the conquistadors, and, now that the war was over, the only decent thing for them to do was to give their colonies to the British. Their unforgivable sin was that they had, as he put it, 'besmirched the escutcheon of Europe in Africa' – thus thoughtlessly endangering the reputation for disinterested beneficence which was vital to the continuation of white rule over brown races. Unfortunately, though there was, of course, no indication of this in *German Colonies*, it was a problem which Clifford had only recently, to his immense and justified chagrin, had to deal with in his own backyard.

In July 1916, fifty-seven Africans living near Zoutugu in the

Northern Territories of the Gold Coast were despatched to a better world by a force of native constabulary under the command of the local District Officer. The reasons for their deaths were never satisfactorily explained. It seems that there had been disturbances, they had got worse, a native policeman had been killed, something had to be done, and the District Officer, a Mr Castellain, had been rather casually supplied by the Provincial Commissioner, Captain C.H. Armitage, with thirty constables and two Maxim guns and left to get on with it. An expedition had set off which encountered a mob of Africans yelling abuse; thirty-four of them were shot. After lunch, the column moved on and encountered another group of natives, who 'attempted to creep within bowshot'; more were shot. Two days later, there was another encounter, and this brought the total number of dead to fifty-seven. Castellain informed his superior that 'a few more expeditions like this one and I think the native will once more realize that the white man still lives'. Armitage found Castellain's action 'very reassuring' and passed on his good opinion of him to the governor, who promptly exploded.[107]

Clifford then embarked on one of the few battles with the Colonial Office which he ever lost. Ignoring the dictates of the Punjab creed, which his erring subordinates clearly assumed, in wartime, would apply, he asked for Armitage's head and was not only refused it but eventually made to suffer the spectacle of Armitage's being appointed governor of the Gambia. Clifford believed that the honour of the Colonial Service, which, as he informed the Colonial Office, was 'to me, personally . . . the most precious and the most sacred thing on earth'[108], was at stake, and could only be saved by conspicuously expunging from its ranks the man who had disgraced it. (What he actually proposed was a transfer to Barbados, which amounted to the same thing.) But the officials at the Colonial Office did not agree. Less sensitive to the stench of impurity than Clifford, they were determined to sweep the whole affair under the rug: it was German, not British, atrocities they wanted to hear about in 1916. Unfortunately, Clifford provided them with an excuse for doing so. His despatches on the Armitage affair were disorganized and even incoherent: for once, his lucidity deserted him. This may have been a symptom of incipient mental decline, or it may have been a result of the strain he was under at the time: his son and his brother were both killed in action on the Western front in the summer of 1916. In any case, his obviously distressed state of mind gave the Colonial Office the opportunity to put aside while pardoning his 'over-reaction'.

Clifford's intention had been to take the whole Northern Territories administration in hand once Armitage had been got rid of. For the first time since leaving Malaya he had a frontier to run, and he had intended to demonstrate to the Colonial Office how to do it. Under Armitage things had been very slack. Officers had loafed at headquarters instead of going out on trek – Clifford himself, despite his advancing years and eminence, had bicycled all over Ashanti in 1914 – and far too much latitude had been allowed to native subordinates, with deplorable results in the form of overbearing behaviour. This was a particularly sensitive point with Clifford. Years ago, in one of his stories, he had described how the white man's reputation for justice suffered in the hands of ignorant and over-mighty native helpers: 'Our motto is Justice', he had written, 'and from end to end of Asia our name is a proverb for that virtue in its highest expression; but, alas! our understrappers' reputation is a byword in quite another sense.'[109] It was gall to him to be denied the opportunity to put things right.

At about the time he got his governorship of the Gold Coast Clifford acquired a new fictional persona – Sir Philip Hanbury-Erskine, GCB, GCMG, who, like himself, had left his soul on the frontier though his body was in Government House. The story in which he made his debut – '"Our Trusty and Well-Beloved"' (1913) – was one of the most illuminating products of Clifford's ready pen.

Briefly, Sir Philip Hanbury-Erskine returns as governor to the colony – not named, but obviously Malaya – where he spent his apprenticeship. Surveying the scene one night from his verandah, he yields to an impulse to taste once more the pleasures of his youth. 'For years – such long, long weary years – he had not been suffered to be natural, to be himself – even to be a Man. Instead, he had been only an Official, only the temporary holder of a given post . . .' He slips into native dress and finds his way through the back alleys to an inner room where a group of natives are playing cards. Two of them are known to him – Raja Sulong, a mighty warrior who of old had loved him as a brother; and Bedah, once a dancing girl, now, alas, a hag, who too had loved him. Thinking him one of themselves, they reveal to him the details of a rising which is about to take place. Raja Sulong, it transpires, is to go to the new governor and, trading on their old friendship, deceive him as to the direction from which the attack will come. At this point, Sir Philip Hanbury-Erskine, instead of retiring prudently to the safety of Government House, reveals to the assembled company who he is.

Prudence had bidden him depart as he had come, undetected; but prudence he had thrown to the winds. He knew that he had but to follow her wise counsels, and presently he would find himself within the walls of Government House, where, armed with the authority that belongs to rulers, he would be able to baffle utterly the paltry schemes that had been laid bare for his inspection. But to-night, for a little space, he had promised himself, he would put off the things of his authority and would pass down, for the only, for the last time, into the world of men, to be there just a man among his fellows. If he were to defeat Raja Sulong and his conspiracies, he would compass his end unaided by powers external to himself.

A *mêlée* ensues and he finds a sword thrust into his hand – by Bedah. As the police demand entry she leads him away, and then dies warding off a blow aimed at him by Raja Sulong. Freeing himself from her dying grip, he despatches Raja Sulong with a single stroke, cleaving, inevitably, his head to the cheek-bones. The next day finds Sir Philip Hanbury-Erskine 'clothed and in his right mind', writing the famous minute on the native rising 'upon which rests the almost superstitious belief of his subordinates in his prescience and understanding of native character'. Duty is done, but 'in the dead unhappy night, he told himself that old age had come upon him in the space of a single hour'.[110]

The familiar motifs are all there – the uncertainty of love between the white man and the brown, the ultimate necessity of hate, the white man's ambiguous knowledge: all the contradictions which inevitably arose from Clifford's early experience of the imperial relationship as a human relationship. But what the story is most vividly about is the experience of power. Sir Philip Hanbury-Erskine wants to defeat Raja Sulong 'unaided by powers external to himself'. As governor he has institutional power – the power which attends his office; what he wants to know again is personal power – the power which he assumed he had as a young District Officer with his back to the wall. To experience this, he must reduce the distance between himself and the natives and ask to be judged as a man. This he accomplishes by disguise, which makes him, not 'just a man', but supremely a man. The *dénouement* is ambiguous. He wins through, but only by killing. Is this why old age comes upon him in the space of a single hour? Or is it because of Raja Sulong's treacherous presumption on his friendship? The reader is left uncertain, but he knows that Sir Philip Hanbury-Erskine's victory is incomplete. The power of personality has not after all quite prevailed.

By all accounts Clifford enjoyed the ceremonial trappings of gubernatorial office and was if anything a shade too insistent on them. In Lagos, when he was governor, he used to go to the local Catholic church in full dress uniform and have the priest and acolytes meet him at the door.[111] Clearly, he enjoyed power in whatever form it fell to him. But, like Simon Strange, the crocked-up D.O. in "'Cast'", he had known that special kind of power, that intimate, immediate and absolute authority, which is one of the most addictive of human experiences – "'a strong drink which, once tasted, you cannot do without'".[112] Enthroned in Government House, surrounded by yea-sayers and adorers of the King's Majesty, could he ever be sure that he still had what it took to quell treason with a glance? He might dominate the Leg. Co., but it was officially given to him so to do, and he had to appoint people to tell him what the masses thought, instead of sensing it unerringly, as once long ago he had surely done. Afflicted with a sense of power leaking away from him, he consoled himself with thoughts of better days. Perhaps some of the unresolved tension in the story arises from the apprehension that he was consoling himself with an illusion: there never had been a time when he was obeyed for himself alone.

When Clifford departed from the Gold Coast to take up the governorship of Nigeria in 1919 he was, for once, succeeding a man who enjoyed a reputation greater than his own – Sir Frederick Lugard, conqueror of Nigeria and administrator *extraordinaire*. Lugard's standing with the Colonial Office had been so high that for six months of the year he had been permitted to abandon his post in Lagos and govern Nigeria from a desk in Whitehall. Clifford soon discovered, however, that though Lugard's administration had indeed been extraordinary it had been far from efficient. In the north, the Muslim emirates were festering in the advanced state of corruption later described so vividly in Joyce Cary's novels. In the south, there was uproar brought on by Lugard's attempts to reorganize local government and introduce taxation. A rebellion at Abeokuta in 1918 had been suppressed with an official estimate of 564 Africans dead. In Lagos there was no coherent system of central administration at all. The great man had made all the decisions himself, down to the purchase of lavatory supplies.

All this was grist to Clifford's mill. Among his many talents was the supremely bureaucratic one of organization, and he soon developed an efficient secretariat in Lagos and took steps to make provincial officers responsible to it. Lugard had been a trial to the Colonial Office in his last two years as governor, but Clifford's proposal to make a public admission of the government's mistakes in Southern Nigeria, in the interests of making a fresh start towards developing a system of administration more acceptable to the people, did not sit well.[113] It was one thing to criticize an imperial hero privately, quite another to expose his sins to public view. So Clifford was handicapped from the start in his efforts to make the British yoke easy for the peoples of the south. All he could do was drag his feet in imposing the system of direct taxation with which the Colonial Office, appalled at the thought of visibly repudiating Lugard's ideas, wished to press on regardless. Like everyone else, Clifford refrained from personal criticism of Lugard in public. In private he described him as 'blood-stained to the collar-stud with slaughtered Hadeijas and Egbas' and 'a crashing bore'.[114]

His suggestions for reform of the northern administration, which he felt exceptionally well qualified to make in view of his long years of experience with primitive Muslim kingdoms in Malaya, also alarmed the Lugardians in the Colonial Office, though they were far from extreme. He accepted in principle Lugard's method of ruling the northern provinces through the emirs, whose claim to political legitimacy he accepted and whose support for the administration he wished to enlist; but, mindful of the empire's sacred mission for improvement, he deplored what seemed to him to be the deliberate fossilization of the northern provinces.[115] After nearly twenty years of ruling the north the British had yet to train a single native clerk: these necessary functionaries were imported from the south or from other colonies. Clifford wanted to see primary education made available to children from all social classes in the north. He also wished to reverse the policy of discouraging immigration into the emirates. But the greatest change he wished to make was in introducing much closer supervision of the emirs by the British political officers; remembering the Malayan rajahs who were the companions of his youth, he took it as axiomatic that the undiluted rule of native potentates would never conform to acceptable standards of justice and humanity. None of these proposals was adopted.

Failing to make his mark on the substance of northern administration, Clifford set out to improve its style. On his visits to the north he had not been impressed by the rather casual approach to their work evident in some of the younger officers; and in 1922 he produced a celebrated minute summarizing for their benefit the fundamental principles he believed should be their guide.[116]

The first and never-to-be-forgotten rule, Clifford observed, was courtesy, which in the exotic context of a Nigerian emirate could only be the product of long and patient study to be kind. Subject peoples, he pointed out, were not in a position to resent openly the affronts intentionally or unintentionally delivered to them by their rulers, and responded to them by silently withholding the confidence which it was the task of the political officer to inspire. Without this confidence, the political officer could never hope to achieve that which ought to be his aim: the complete and perfect knowledge of the people which alone would enable him to carry out the great work entrusted to him by his country. At this point, Clifford permitted himself a long quotation from 'Up Country', now rescued from oblivion for the enlightenment of a new generation.

He then turned in his minute to the necessity of making allowances for the relatively untutored state of the native mind and conscience. The people of Northern Nigeria, he reminded his readers, had had the benefit of British influence for only two decades, and it would scarcely be fair to hold them too rigidly to standards of conduct which they as yet hardly understood. Nevertheless, he went on, the political officer's job was to effect a moral revolution in the conduct of government, and this end he must undeviatingly pursue, seeing to it always that the people suffered no extortion or oppression at the hands of their rulers. But, at the same time, remembering that the emir and his officers constituted the *de facto* government of the country, he must be careful to avoid undermining their authority. 'The Political Officer', Clifford concluded, 'should be the Whisper behind the Throne, but never for an instant the Throne itself.'

He did his best to see that this impossible advice was carried out. Officers who involved themselves too blatantly in the affairs of their emirates were reprimanded or removed. Emirs who too blatantly abused their authority were dealt with likewise, though not, it must be admitted, with quite the same degree of peremptoriness. In his minute Clifford warned his young officers not to be seduced by 'the glamour of age, of simplicity, of the unmoral and of the picturesque', but, even as he wrote, the old Adam of delight in the vividness of unregenerate native life stirred within him. His first response to the allegations against the emir of Zaria, whose misconduct included child-raiding for his harem, was that the emir's harem was his own business; but eventually the emir was removed.[117] On a visit to Sokoto in 1922 he found the sultan being exposed to public insolence from an underling with whom the acting Resident had allied himself. Out went the acting Resident – but at the same time an investigation was begun into the charges of misconduct brought by this officer against the sultan.[118]

As he had in Trinidad and the Gold Coast, Clifford moved to broaden native representation in the central councils of government. He recreated the Legislative Council abolished by Lugard and introduced into it four African members – and this time the means of selection was not to be nomination by the governor, but election. The basis of the franchise was very limited, but the action was none the less extraordinarily important, in that it was the first recognition of the elective principle at this level of government in British colonial Africa.

Most commentators on Clifford's career in Nigeria have found this part of it very puzzling, for at the same time that he was fashioning his radical new Legislative Council he was firing off rhetorical salvos against the nationalists. Early in 1920 the National Congress of British West Africa convened in Accra, and Clifford poured elaborate scorn on its 'ridiculous claims and pretensions'.[119] But in the light of his notions of good government and concern for the permanence of the British empire the decision to provide for elective representation was not incomprehensible. As in Trinidad, Clifford was anxious to seize the initiative from the opposition by granting what seemed to be their more reasonable demands[120]; and he still saw native representation, whether elected or nominated, as simply a means of more effectively supplying the rulers with the information they needed to govern in the best interests of the ruled. The unofficial representatives were heavily outnumbered in the Legislative Council, and it is unlikely that Clifford supposed it would ever be otherwise.

Able as he was, Clifford left out of his calculations what in retrospect appears to be the most obvious consequence of his actions. The reform in Nigeria operated as a precedent for the enactment of similar reforms in the Gold Coast and Sierra Leone, and in no case did the nationalists, who invariably captured the available elective seats, regard their position in the Legislative Councils simply as an opportunity for self-expression. Power was what they wanted and power was what they supposed they were getting; and in due course the supposition became fact. Clifford's boldness in setting this process in motion arose from a fundamental confidence that, so long as matters were well managed, Britain would continue to occupy the commanding heights of the Nigerian political system.

He left behind in Nigeria one indisputable achievement. In 1924 Lord Leverhulme moved to establish palm oil plantations in Southern Nigeria, and in a battle of wills widely reported at the time Clifford succeeded in preventing him. The lines of combat were clearly drawn. Leverhulme argued that the business of empire was to encourage trade; Clifford replied that, on the contrary, it was to establish the rule of law. Leverhulme declared that 'the African native will be happier, produce the best and live under the larger conditions of prosperity when his labour is directed and organized by his white brother who has had all these million years start of him'; Clifford pointed out to him the success of native cocoa-growers in the Gold Coast.[121]

He had in fact already made his position clear on plantation agriculture in a memorandum written in 1920, in response to a proposal to establish cotton plantations in northern Nigeria. This memorandum summed up with impressive authority the arguments in favour of peasant production.[122] Drawing on his experience in Trinidad, Malaya and Ceylon, Clifford noted that plantation agriculture depended everywhere for its labour supply on some organized system of immigration, or, failing that, on 'some form of more or less open compulsion'; either way, the existing social system was endangered or destroyed. Peasant production, on the other hand, being firmly rooted in traditional forms of social organization, involved no problems of labour supply. It was also cheaper, because overhead expenses were lower, and it was highly flexible in its response to the market; experience had shown that the peasant proprietor was able to expand or reduce his output with relative ease. His record of expansion in fact put that of European planters to shame.

On this occasion Clifford enjoyed the support of the Colonial Office for his views, and Leverhulme was denied the concessions of land he was seeking in Nigeria. The passage of time has shown that not all Clifford's arguments in favour of peasant production apply to the palm oil industry[123], but on the larger issue he was right. 'A plantation system', he once said, 'is not a society'[124]; and for his clear perception of this Nigerians surely have reason to be thankful.

The victory over Leverhulme and the threat to imperial morality which in Clifford's mind he undoubtedly represented was perhaps his finest hour: few governors can have demonstrated a more genuine or timely appreciation of the African way of doing things. And no matter how subterranean was the route by which Clifford arrived at this appreciative state of mind, he should be given credit all the same for getting there. Unfortunately, this victory for good government was to be his last. His remaining governorships presented him with problems undreamed of in his philosophy, and his mind, though brilliant on occasion, was becoming increasingly incapable of dealing with them.

On 6 February 1925, he gave his valedictory address to the Nigerian Legislative Council. Buoyed up by his battle with Leverhulme, which was then drawing to a satisfactory close, he expressed himself expansively on the role of the colonial governor, declaring it vaingloriously to be 'the leadership of all work and of every movement of moment in the country entrusted to his charge'.[125] The cat had leapt out of the bag and Clifford immediately wished that he could put it back in again. Convinced that he had made himself a laughing-stock, he fell into a deep depression which lasted for over two months. Adding to his misery was the belief that he had made a fool of himself over the preparations for the Prince of Wales' coming visit to Nigeria in April, and the apparently sudden realization that his fondness for the company of women had made him, at the age of sixty, an object of scandal and derision.[126] The success of the prince's visit buoyed him up again, but his behaviour now became distinctly manic. In his last two weeks in Nigeria, before departing to take up the governorship of Ceylon, he threw himself into a frantic round of activity; and on the morning of 7 May he turned up at the house of Daphne Moore, the wife of one of his secretariat officers, with the news that an old mistress who had committed suicide many years before had spoken to him on the telephone in the middle of the night.[127]

Daphne Moore saw to it that the Colonial Office was informed of this behaviour, and no less a person than the Prince of Wales also took it upon himself to write to the Secretary of State recording his opinion that Clifford's nerves were 'all gone to pieces'.[128] The Colonial Office, however, chose not to take these warnings too seriously and contented itself with giving him an extra few months' leave before proceeding to Ceylon.

Here Clifford found a situation quite different from any he had known before. Since 1920 the Legislative Council of Ceylon had had an unofficial majority, and since 1923 thirty-four out of the thirty-seven non-officials had been elected. The governor was left only with powers of veto which were politically dangerous to use. Clifford's response to the situation was to stage an elaborately expressive silence on all substantive issues relating to the government of Ceylon. He did not break this silence until he received the news that he had been appointed governor of Malaya, and then, as if to show the Ceylonese what they had been missing, made a characteristically incisive contribution to the discussion of the land problem.[129] His final act before his departure was to announce the appointment of the Donoughmore Commission to investigate the, to him, impossible constitutional situation. While he and the members of the Legislative Council were waiting for reporters to arrive at the dinner at which this announcement was to be made, he entertained the company by reading from a volume of Kipling's poems which he produced from his pocket.[130]

The appointment to Malaya was the fulfilment of his greatest desire; but with a tragic aptness not often encountered in the lives of real people, the land which he had always regarded as his spiritual home turned out to be the scene not of his greatest triumphs but of his final decline. At first all went well. He created a sensation by replying to speeches of welcome in fluent Malay. He embarked on tours of the peninsula in which his reception was all that could be desired. In Pahang he had a hero's welcome. In Kelantan the widow and child of Ûmat the punkah-puller were there to greet him. He was moved almost beyond endurance and decided that his life had not been lived in vain.[131] But his behaviour was becoming odder and odder[132], and there were frequent periods of depression. Under these circumstances there seems little point in subjecting his political record to analytical scrutiny. Yet in his official pronouncements he remained remarkably the same. One might say that as the waters of despair closed over him he went down waving a perfectly argued minute. Magnificently opposing himself to the forces of disruption and change, he produced what was immediately recognized to be the classic statement of traditional British policy towards the Malay states. There must be no truckling, he said, to those forces – meaning the nationalists and the now very vocal Chinese – which sought to undermine the special relationship between His Majesty's Government and the Malay rulers; Britain's responsibility in Malaya was, and would always remain, the protection and purification of the Malay way of life.[133] In administrative matters he displayed his perennial concern for the quality of the British presence in the field, giving orders in January 1928 that new recruits were to be posted to outstations, where alone, in his unalterable opinion, the essence of administration was to be learned.[134]

In the summer of 1928 he underwent a complete collapse in health and was shipped home to England and retirement. He remained at large for some time, being in the habit, it is said, of putting on Malay dress and going to sit on the steps of the Colonial Office, where he gave colleagues passing in and out of the building his advice on the imperial problems of the day.[135] From 1930 till his death in December 1941 he was confined in a private nursing home in Roehampton. He lost all interest in the world and so was presumably unaware that in his last days the Japanese army was overrunning his beloved Malaya. On 18 December, the day he died, his compatriots were engaged in evacuating themselves – and only themselves – from Penang. Their abandonment on this occasion of those whom it had been their pride to protect destroyed at a stroke such loyalty to them as remained. Everywhere the Malays silently defected from the British cause; even the Malay rulers, the objects of such avowedly special concern, declined at this critical moment to identify their fortunes with those of the British empire.[136] When the British came back at the end of the war, nothing was the same.

4

Kenya: White Man's Country

You Europeans are nothing but robbers, though you pretended you came to lead us. Go away, go away you Europeans, the years that are past have been more than enough for us.

Verse from K.A.U. Song[1]

In 1894 the British government, in thrall to the geopolitical fantasy that an unfriendly power on Lake Victoria might divert the course of the Nile, and thus, by an unhappy chain of events, bring about the collapse of the British empire in India, declared a protectorate over Uganda.[2] The declaration of a protectorate over East Africa – the area between Mombasa and Uganda as it was then defined – followed a year later, and in December 1895 construction was begun, at great expense to the British taxpayer, of a railway linking Lake Victoria to the coast. With that practicality after the fact which characterized Britain's lunges into the unknown at the end of the nineteenth century, the government decided to recoup the cost of the railway by attracting to the territory settlers who would provide it with freight. By chance, one of the first of these was Hugh Cholmondely, third Baron Delamere. Almost single-handedly, by his untiring activity and influence, he succeeded in bringing into existence what no one had hitherto suspected lay concealed in the highlands of East Africa: a colony fit for gentlemen to live in. Known after 1920 as Kenya, the new colony was incomparably the most aristocratic of Britain's outposts overseas; it was not long before one of its few hotels was known as 'the House of Lords'. That its creation should have been the result of Lord Salisbury's aristocratic conception of empire as diplomacy by other means seems entirely fitting.

Though Delamere first set foot in Kenya in 1897, he did not

return to settle until 1903, the year in which settlement in Kenya can properly be said to have begun. He arrived to find in place not only a railway but a whole apparatus of government. Administration preceded settlement in Kenya, with important consequences for the nature of the political dramas enacted therein. Because government was established independently of settlement and intended at least implicitly to effect the just administration of backward races, the stage was set for a mighty conflict between two opposing schools of imperialist thought: that which held that the colonies existed for the benefit of the master race, and that which held that they existed as a God-sent opportunity for the export of good government. That this conflict turned out to be less mighty than could have been expected was due largely to the fact that the leading landowners of Kenya were noblemen endowed with the natural persuasiveness of rank, and possessing a long corporate experience in identifying their own interests with the common good. Nevertheless, conflicts did occur, and of an illuminating kind.

The priority of government in the field meant that the pacification of the country was essentially completed before the settlers arrived, or at least preceded them into the interior. There was thus a tendency for the settlers to forget that pacification had occurred at all, and to believe that the occupation of the country had been peaceful and consensual. Kenya in fact was conquered the way much of the rest of the British empire was conquered: without spectacle, bit by bit, and using irregular native troops out for booty, adventure, or revenge.[3] But the records of conquest lay gathering dust, unread, in ancient files, and this had an important influence on the settlers' perception of themselves. It encouraged, in their new inter-racial context, their natural tendency, as English gentlemen, to believe that their inferiors thought well of them. Never having had to defend their homes from natives expressing their hostility in terms impossible to misunderstand, they could see themselves as not unwelcome bearers of intellectual enlightenment and moral re-generation to the African.

Their arrival too late on the scene to do any fighting meant also that, though the settlers in Kenya enjoyed the illusion of welcome, they were deprived by circumstances of the heroic myth of the frontier enjoyed by South Africans and Rhodesians. They seem to have hankered after inspiring tales to tell around the hearth fires; and the material for these was found in the process of farming itself. Much was made in later years of the tribulations of agricultural experiment in a new country, and these were endowed with an epic quality – notably by Elspeth Huxley in her biography of Lord Delamere, though memoirs of Kenya in this vein are abundant. 'So the settlers came', wrote Huxley in one of the letters she exchanged with Margery Perham in the 1940s,

> and found forest, bush and veld. The forest and bush had to be cleared, the veld improved and fenced; land had to be ploughed, game driven back, water supplies discovered and harnessed, buildings erected, and Africans taught the elements of farm skill; cattle and sheep imported and bred, roads made, transport organized, everything built up from nothing.
>
> That was the first stage. Then came the second: a long, often heart-breaking stage. Crops that had at first done well grew poorly: unsuspected plant pests had appeared. Pastures that seemed rich failed to nourish stock. Cattle died of unknown diseases. Game broke down fences and trampled crops. Droughts and locusts spread devastation. African labour proved unreliable and slipshod. Markets fluctuated and slumped.
>
> Gradually most of these things were overcome. Experiments showed which crops were suited to each varying district. Fungi and insects were studied and fought. Cattle dips were built everywhere, inoculations started. New plants were imported, new methods introduced; fertilizers, rotations, soil conservation practices all became part of the farming routine. Labour was trained, mechanization started, co-operative marketing organized, the search for markets begun. And so on. Again, all this was due to the enterprise of settlers, assisted to some extent by the government, mainly through the work of scientists.
>
> The African had no part in the initiation of all this . . .[4]

This was all true. But, as Margery Perham pointed out, and the early settlers knew, their effort 'was not so strenuous as the taming of the wilderness in Canada, for example, where the pioneers had no native labour to ease their task on the farm and in the house'.[5] 'I do not believe', wrote Lord Cranworth, who farmed in Kenya in the early days,

> that a man [i.e. an Englishman] could, for instance, go on ploughing or digging all day and day after day [in an equatorial climate] without being in danger of falling a victim to nervous collapse . . . Luckily, in East Africa there is no need for man [sic] himself to do the actual work on a farm. It is essentially an overseer's country.[6]

To Huxley, the 'training' of native labour was yet another obstacle for the settlers to overcome.

Delamere himself, unlike Cranworth and others looking for, to quote the title of Cranworth's first book, *Profit and Sport in British East Africa*, was a genuine colonist. Rude, ruthless and egotistical though he was – everyone from the governor down felt the rough side of his tongue, and no one was safe who got in his way – he was nevertheless a man with a vision, and he gave it all he had. In pursuit of his dream of a great white dominion in East Africa he spent several fortunes, experimenting indefatigably with new crops and different kinds of stock, and living, until his second marriage late in life, an utterly spartan existence. His homes were a series of mud huts, adorned by his long-suffering first wife with china and silver brought out from England, and his days on the farm were packed with activity from dawn till dusk.[7] He was no verandah farmer, watching the grass grow from a seat in the shade and bestirring himself now and then to pick up a rifle and shoot something to hang on the wall. His hunger for land was insatiable, and he was not above speculation, but it was a genuine land hunger in that he had a real attachment to the soil.

He was a far more appealing character than that other 'Grand Old Man' of Kenya politics, Ewart Grogan, who seems scarcely to have done a hand's turn, but made rather than lost several fortunes in Kenya. In 1918 Grogan acquired a grant of land on the shoreline at Mombasa, made some rudimentary improvements to it, and sold it back to the government as harbour facilities in 1925 at a profit of nearly £300,000, the wharf which he built from soft podocarpus wood from his timber concession on the Mau collapsing shortly thereafter.[8] In Nairobi he purchased for a nominal sum a 120-acre swamp, which he named after his wife ('Gertrude Swamp'). He had some canals dug and then let it out to Indians for allotments and a bazaar. By and by, under the eyes of its indifferent owner, it became a centre of disease and filth, and the city fathers made efforts to buy it back for re-development. But Grogan's price was too high, and he eventually sold it privately in 1948 for £180,000.[9] By comparison, the career of Delamere was a model of selfless service.

Many settlers' most heroic struggles were with their banks. The speculative boom in land prices in the early 1900s meant that settlers who were not of the Mayflower class paid high prices for their farms and then had to finance day-to-day operations through bank loans, often accumulating a considerable burden of indebtedness because it was difficult to make their over-extensive holdings productive.[10] A large number of those who settled in Kenya had no experience of farming, and this combined with their expectation of a high income – high enough to pay for a car, trips home and boarding school in England for the children – was the undoing of many an ex-officer lured to Kenya by assurances such as those of Lord Cranworth that 'the amount of money made and owned per head of the white population and landowners is very high indeed'.[11] Those who made it through the Depression, however, when many farms were abandoned, recouped their fortunes in the Second World War, which was a bonanza to the Kenya farmer. During that happy time, agricultural prices were fixed at astronomical levels to stimulate the patriotic production of food, Africans and Italian prisoners of war were assigned to farms as labourers, and the Royal Navy brought bird droppings from the Seychelles for use as fertilizer.[12]

Under pressure of need, many a Kenya settler in the 1920s and '30s developed an ungentlemanly talent for turning an honest penny through trade. Those with cars, for instance, rented them out to those without[13]: there was a great deal, economically speaking, of taking in each other's washing. But even those who had relatively little need to do so turned apparently without embarrassment to ways of making money which would have been beneath them at home. Cranworth himself was involved in a multitude of activities, including a hotel and a motor transport service from Nairobi. The legendary Denys Finch Hatton, whose feet one would have supposed from Karen Blixen's *Out of Africa* and other memoirs scarcely to have touched the ground, apparently received a large part of his income from trading in the native reserves.[14] Derek Erskine, an old Etonian and guards officer who became a prominent man in Kenya, started out running a grocery store in Nairobi.[15] The task of building a new country seems to have liberated a talent, or at least a taste (Cranworth's ventures were rarely remunerative), for enterprise. Away from the convolutions of the English class system, and the particularly inhibiting effect within it of the watchful presence of their immediate inferiors, Kenya's gentlemen settlers often found within themselves resources of which they had not been aware.

Small-scale farming was not something normally attempted by Kenya Europeans. Indeed, it was severely deprecated by the leaders of the settler community as conducing to the development of a population of poor whites. The poor and huddled masses, and even the not sufficiently affluent classes, were never welcome in Kenya. Cranworth firmly discouraged the man with £500 in the bank from taking ship for East Africa: 'By himself he is not likely to make good, and the indigent white in a country peopled by a black race is a sorry sight indeed, and one for which I should be ashamed to be responsible.'[16] In *Profit and Sport in British East Africa* Cranworth stated without subtlety his preference for the public school man as the agent of civilization. East Africa being, as he ventured again 'to affirm, in the face of inevitable criticism, essentially an overseer's country', what better raw material could there be than the public schoolboy, whose entire education fitted him, not to work, but to supervise the work of others? His ignorance of farming was no drawback in a country where so much had to be learnt anew; and then

those virtues which furnish the hall-mark of his caste – honour, scrupulous fairness, temper well held in check but not dead, and, last but far from least, a sense of humour – endear him [to the natives] most of all, and enable many a man to obtain and hold labour for which his neighbour, perhaps in many respects the better man, offers in vain a higher wage.[17]

The ideal Kenya farmer was not a magnate – there was not enough room for many of those – but a man of decent social standing with a few thousand acres of well-tended land. On this land ideally stood a house of stone or cedar logs, furnished with plenty of books, a piano, a gramophone, a mixture of good furniture brought out from home and pieces made by the local carpenter, a few animal skins, and some Persian rugs from the dhows which put in at Mombasa. Outside spread a garden remarkable for its blend of temperate and tropical delights. Such places existed everywhere in Kenya, and their claim to represent a high degree of civilization, if not perhaps the very highest, cannot be ignored. It was the Cotswold ideal, transplanted to the equator, inflated in scale, and without the servant problem.

The inhabitants of this earthly paradise were always very few. It was clear by 1910 that, with the prevailing notions of the desirable size of land holdings, there was only room in the highlands for a few thousand settlers.[18] By 1937, when little available land was left for sale, there were about 1,500 European farms.[19] Nevertheless, by 1907, when they still numbered well under a thousand, the settlers had demanded and obtained a Legislative Council, and were confidently looking forward, under the leadership of Delamere, to the day when self-government would be theirs. This was an ideal destined never to be realized. Bend and sway as it might before the mighty wind of organized complaint which blew from Kenya, the British government was unable entirely to forget that its imperial purpose in Africa supposedly transcended the interests of its race. The fate of 4 million Africans[20] was in the end a responsibility which could not be ignored.

Up to 1923, however, when the Devonshire White Paper produced an unexpected check to their ambitions, the settlers seemed to be having it all their own way in their tussles with the

Colonial Office. Having accepted the economic argument for a
settler presence in Kenya, the British government rarely found the
will to obstruct developments which might lead to the colony paying
its way.

The Colonial Office early developed the habit of avoiding
responsibility for the settler-inspired excesses of Kenya policy by
conceding very wide discretionary powers to its man-on-the-spot, the
governor. Governors were often sent out with instructions to do right
by the African, but these instructions remained confidential, and no
public declaration was ever made of Colonial Office determination to
see that they were carried out.[21] Once in the notoriously exciting
altitudes of East Africa, governors almost invariably succumbed to
the affable beseechings of the colony's noble politicians. Most
governors were of worthy but undistinguished bourgeois stock; had
there been a governor like Clifford, of aristocratic credentials and
exalted commitment to the ideals of the Colonial Service, the history
of Kenya might have been very different. As it was, there rapidly
grew up the system described by Delamere as 'government by
agreement', whereby bills were introduced only after consultation
with elected members of the Legislative Council.[22] The settler
politicians were naturally inclined to adulate themselves. They
strode like giants across the pages of each other's newspaper articles.

On the land issue[23], the British government made its first
concession to settlerdom before it even existed except as a bright
idea for recovering the money spent on the railway. In order to make
settlement possible at all, certain legal difficulties had first to be
resolved concerning the right of the British Crown to alienate land in
a protectorate, which in theory had the status of a foreign country.
The speed with which the legal mists cleared on this subject boded
ill for the future of African interests. By 1899 the British
government's position was that land occupied by 'savage tribes' with
no settled form of government could be declared Crown land and
disposed of as Her Majesty's Government saw fit, it being left to
British officials in the territories concerned to decide what land met
this criterion of availability. There speedily followed the eviction
from land they were industriously and fruitfully occupying of large
numbers of East African natives, notably the Kikuyu from their land
near Nairobi and the Masai from their grazing grounds in the Rift
Valley. The Masai indeed were moved twice – once in 1904 to the
Laikipia plateau, and again in 1911 from Laikipia to a poorly
watered area on the border with German East Africa. Delamere and
his brother-in-law, Galbraith Cole, had observed the land on
Laikipia and seen that it was good.

The settlers' great triumph in the sphere of land policy was the creation of the White Highlands – the area in which only Europeans were allowed to own land. In the early 1900s racial discrimination in land grants was contrary to British colonial policy and had been refused when requested by Australia and Natal. Nevertheless, in 1903 the governor of Kenya, Sir Charles Eliot, in response to settler pressure, announced that applications for land by Indians in the fertile upland area between Machakos and Fort Ternan would be refused. In 1906 the Colonial Office allayed further settler anxieties on the subject by announcing that, though it was not 'in accordance with the policy of His Majesty's Government to exclude any class of his subjects from holding land in any part of a British protectorate', 'a reasonable discretion' would be exercised in dealing with applications from non-Europeans for land in the highlands. Two years later it was determined more explicitly that though it was

> not consonant with the views of His Majesty's Government to impose *legal* restriction on any particular section of the community, . . .as a matter of administrative convenience grants in the upland area should not be made to Indians.[24]

For another thirty years the White Highlands, from which Africans as well as Indians were of course excluded, remained a purely administrative rather than a legal entity, saving the British government the embarrassment of having to define in law what it agreed to in practice.

The structure of racial discrimination which evolved in Kenya was indeed in almost every respect administrative rather than legal in form. Segregation in housing, for example, was enforced not by law but by restrictive covenants on leases.[25] Africans were excluded from hotels not by law but by custom. When an Indian member of the Legislative Council requested a list of discriminatory laws in 1953 he was surprised to find that hardly any such laws existed.[26] This way of doing things, or rather not doing things, was what chiefly distinguished Kenya from South Africa.

The British government made some attempt to restrict the size of landholdings in Kenya, but its efforts were unaggressive and unsuccessful. Some of Kenya's most venerated pioneers, including Galbraith and Berkeley Cole, the sons of the Earl of Enniskillen, amassed land in excess of the legal limits by 'dummying', the practice of applying for land in the name of another person.[27] During the First World War, when there was officially a freeze on land alienation, over 300,000 acres somehow found their way into the hands of the Kenya magnates: by 1919 much of it had been sold for speculative gain.[28]

The issue of taxation need not detain us long. Briefly, the settlers were against it except on Africans as a stimulus to labour, and their views carried the day. As a result, Africans yielded up a large part of their cash income to taxation while Europeans were taxed hardly at all. It has been estimated that in the period 1920–23 Africans contributed nearly 70 per cent of tax revenue in the colony.[29] Most of this money went on providing the services and economic infrastructure required by the Europeans; almost nothing was spent on developing the native reserves.

The labour issue was the one where the British government made its most serious effort to intervene on behalf of the African: labour was a subject which attracted the attention of those do-gooders and aborigines protectionists who had so exercised Selous, and whose views were aired regularly in Parliament at question time.

The average settler arrived in Kenya expecting to find a plentiful supply of cheap labour – waiting, as it were, in the wings of history to take up mattocks for the cultivation of his private demesne. Africans, however, proved generally uninterested in working for whites[30], and forced labour was early perceived to be the only solution to the problem. After a few scandals arising from private labour recruitment practices, the administration found itself pressed to provide a discreet but efficient system of organized coercion. The practice grew up of 'encouragement', whereby administrative officers exerted pressure on the local chief to provide an orderly supply of labour to the adjacent European districts. When this system was given explicit sanction in the Labour Circulars issued by the Northey administration in 1919 humanitarian opinion in Britain was aroused, and instructions eventually emanated from the Colonial Office that officials were 'to take no part in recruiting labour for private employment'.[31] But such instructions were not easily enforced. Informal co-operation between settlers and officials with regard to labour remained a permanent feature of the Kenya scene.

Many District Officers appear to have disliked being labour recruiters and dragged their feet when they could. But their scope for action was limited not only by settler influence but by the exceptionally close system of administration which developed in Kenya. Because real practical demands were made on them, beyond keeping the peace and looking good, Kenya's administrators were far more numerous and ruled more directly than in other British African colonies. There were four times as many British administrators, in proportion to the African population, as there were in Nigeria.[32] The District Officer's potential for autonomy was correspondingly diluted.

The official who interpreted too literally his service's proud tradition of standing up for the humble native found as a rule that the support of his superiors was not something he could count on.[33] A posting to Wajir – roughly the world's end so far as a career in the Kenya administrative service was concerned – was the reward of the young Shirley Victor Cooke when he resisted, and ultimately exposed to public view, the labour recruiting practices of a local farmer in the 1920s.[34] Other administrators wrestled with their consciences privately, or resigned themselves to a career as a 'native's man' in primitive or unhealthy districts where Europeans did not settle. One 'native's man' who did manage to rise high in the service was John Ainsworth, who became Chief Native Commissioner in 1918; but his career shows how hard it was to do this and remain on the moral high ground where the governance of natives was concerned. As Provincial Commissioner of Nyanza in western Kenya from 1907 to 1917 Ainsworth promoted African production of commercial crops like cotton and sesame, entertained such visionary notions as universal primary education for Africans and the formation of mixed European-African Provincial Councils, and publicly deplored the conditions of labour on European farms.[35] But the rest of his career was a series of first agonizing and then cynical capitulations to European interests. As Sub-Commissioner of Nairobi district he acquiesced, after only a few squeaks of protest, in the dispossession of both the Kikuyu and the Masai.[36] As Commissioner for Labour during the latter part of the First World War he presided over the mass press-ganging of 150,000 Africans to serve as porters in the East African campaign, in which roughly one in three of them died of disease. After the war the Northey Labour Circulars went out under his name, and though he is said to have deplored them, he did not oppose them.[37] Inevitably, he became a proponent of the view that the only solution to the conflict of black and white interests in Kenya was segregation of the one from the other on land reserved for the exclusive use of each. Eventually, the native areas would become 'civilised black states under white control'.[38] It was his version of Clifford's administrative Eden, where the apple of discord, in the form of settlers, need never be eaten.

As for the settlers, their views on labour and other topics followed naturally from their views on Africans in general. The much-admired Grogan, stirred by an encounter with cannibals on his early travels, believed that a good dose of slavery was the best thing for them.[39] He himself, in a famous incident, publicly flogged three Kikuyu in Nairobi in 1907. For this he received a month's imprisonment, served in a private house where he was looked after by the ladies of Nairobi, and upon his release he was re-elected to the presidency of the Colonists' Association.[40] Kenya magistrates and juries were notoriously reluctant to convict a white man of criminal assault upon a black man, even when the facts of the case were not in dispute. When Galbraith Cole shot and killed an escaping stock thief in 1911 he was acquitted of murder though he did not deny the shooting. Criticism of the verdict in England led eventually to his deportation, but he returned after the war, 'welcomed', Lord Cranworth records, 'by his many white friends, and perhaps even more by the natives among whom he had lived'.[41] Settlers who got carried away inflicting chastisement on Africans enjoyed a remarkable degree of public sympathy and support. In 1920 a European who flogged a native to death, and ordered the flogging of a pregnant woman who miscarried the next day, found subscription lists opened on his account in several districts.[42] Flogging, with the hippo-hide whip known as the kiboko, seems to have been considered no more eccentric as a disciplinary measure than the canings many settlers had endured at school: Cranworth's memoirs are full of the most casual references to it, and at the hearings of the Labour Commission of 1907 several Europeans freely admitted to its use.[43] As late as 1935, a white hunter resident in Kenya published a book in which he described without shame his own recent application of the kiboko to various natives in his employ.[44] In this atmosphere of contempt the existence of forced labour was inevitable.

Probably the most horrible case of European violence against Africans was one which received little publicity. In 1902 Delamere's great friend Dr Atkinson resolved a dispute with some Rendille tribesmen over the price of ivory by attaching a slow fuse to a keg of gunpowder, summoning them over to look at it, and going off to relieve himself in the bush. Though there was no lack of evidence to hang him, the European jury refused to convict and he retired unscathed to his estate at Karura. The following year, during the agitation over a proposal to allow Zionist immigration into Kenya, he declared himself opposed to it on the grounds that 'Jews rendered themselves obnoxious to the people of every country they went to'.[45] This was the invincible self-regard which saw the settlers through the many crises of the years ahead.

In 1919 the settlers, not content with having the Highlands to themselves, sought a prohibition on Indian immigration. The fury into which they worked themselves on this issue was in the end to destroy their chance of obtaining the self-government which from the earliest days had been their goal.[46]

Though at first it seemed as though the settlers, pulling the customary wires of kinship and acquaintance in the House of Commons and the House of Lords, would get their way, the Colonial and India Offices published in 1922 a joint report advocating free Indian immigration, the ending of residential segregation, and the institution of a common electoral roll with voting qualifications so designed that 10 per cent of the electorate would be Indian. Gandhi had just conducted his first mass civil disobedience campaign, and at that moment assuaging nationalist feeling in India seemed to the British government to possess a more urgent claim on its attention than calming the fears of Kenya's perennially choleric settlers.

Professing, as they always did in moments of extreme sedition, unshakeable loyalty to the British Crown, the settlers then took to arms. Their plans were thorough, and included one for kidnapping the governor and sequestering him at a highland farm where the trout fishing was said to be good. Faced with this challenge, the British government instantly caved in: then as later it was inconceivable to British politicians to send troops to put down a white rebellion in Africa.[47] The principals of the Kenya dispute were summoned to London for negotiations, and in July 1923 the Devonshire White Paper emerged. This famous document established the framework of political debate in Kenya for the next fifteen years, and enjoyed a shaping influence long thereafter. In it the settlers were told that there would be no common roll and there would be no hope for the Indians of ever gaining admission to the Highlands. But – it being necessary for the British government to offset the extent of its capitulation by a re-assertion of its authority – there would be no prospect of self-government either. In timely fashion the Colonial Office had rediscovered the existence of several million Africans and it declared that for their welfare it deemed itself responsible: henceforth, in Kenya, 'the interests of the African natives must be paramount'.

This was a trap the settlers had helped to dig for themselves. In their public pronouncements, if not their private lives, they had rushed to embrace the responsibility of white civilization to protect the poor African from the corrupting influences of the East and to show him the better way. A Mr Powys Cobb, who in 1914 had acquired a farm containing a large part of the Masai's dry season grazing which he had done nothing either to demarcate or develop[48], announced to the press that:

> Western civilization, no matter what error it had made, stood for Christianity, openness and above-board dealings. . . What was there to put against this on the other side of the ledger? The corrupt, cheating, hidden ways of the semi-civilization of the East. . .[49]

And in the time of crisis before the publication of the White Paper, Africans were produced to state publicly that they would prefer to be ruled by Europeans rather than Asiatics.[50]

From then on until the Second World War, when the interests of the race could once again be unabashedly brought forward, the debate over the degree of settler control in Kenya was couched largely in terms of the degree of settler fitness to preside over the destiny of the African. 'Trusteeship' was the magic word, and the administration, whose professional ethic trusteeship was, found itself in ideological competition with those whose baser instincts it was supposed to control. The settlers in their pursuit of power simply took over the rhetoric of colonial administration, asserting as members of the traditional governing class their prior claim to it, and discovering anew the legitimizing force of good intentions. The irony was that they were trying to show themselves worthy of a trust which the Colonial Office had in fact, if not in theory, abandoned.

Some candidates in the 1924 elections for the Legislative Council explicitly dissociated themselves from the trusteeship line – 'otherwise', as Berkeley Cole was reported to have said, 'we should find ourselves without labour and a mass of Africans ruined by becoming over-burdened with riches which they neither desired nor knew how to make use of'[51] – but Delamere was remarkably successful in the years which remained before his death in 1931 in controlling the ebullience of the rank and file and setting Kenya politics on its new course. The 1920s and '30s saw a series of public relations triumphs for the settlers. Commission after commission sent out to inquire into the affairs of Kenya came back persuaded that the destiny of the Africans could be in no better hands than those of the magnates whose hospitality they had so delightfully enjoyed. The Ormsby-Gore Commission of 1924 announced upon its return to London that trusteeship over native interests should no longer be considered 'the special function of the agents of the Imperial Government' but should be exercised by the settlers as well.[52] The British government adopted what came to be known as the 'Dual Policy' – meaning the complementary development of both European and native interests – and increasingly in its pronouncements associated the settlers with itself in the great task of bringing the natives forward. The sentiment of the day was perhaps most perfectly expressed by Sir Robert Coryndon, a South African and former protégé of Cecil Rhodes who was governor from 1922 to 1925, when he said that, in the context of East Africa as a whole, the settlers were

a central nerve ganglion – a power house – of exceptionally high class and capable Europeans to leaven, control, guide and encourage the immense dormant native energy. It is a fine, and a true conception of the real point, the 'ten thousand' whose mission it is to galvanise and control the ten million willing workers for whom they are trustees. Times and views have changed these last two years or so [since 1922]. The 'settlers' should not now be regarded as merely a turbulent wayward colony of wayward children, but a group of strong men very determined to maintain their duty to their race and colour, very sensible of their responsibilities to the native population, and always striving upwards.[53]

The most substantial achievement of the new rhetoric was Elspeth Huxley's biography of Lord Delamere, appropriately entitled *White Man's Country*, which appeared in two volumes in 1935 and rapidly became a standard reference for the early history of Kenya. This extremely able piece of work was critical in establishing in the public mind not only the stirring and romantic nature of white settlement but the pure and chivalrous intentions of white settlers towards Africans.

The daughter of settlers and the possessor of a university degree in agriculture, Elspeth Huxley was ideally qualified to expound the ideas and record the tireless agricultural experimentation of Kenya's foremost settler politician. She also had the popularizer's great gift of judiciousness, which made her an effective spokesman for the cause of white settlement. The administration's case is always given its due in *White Man's Country*, but the settlers' case is stated with a sympathetic amplitude which leaves the reader in no doubt that it is the writer's own.

The tone throughout is one of conspicuous moderation. No one, Elspeth Huxley writes in discussing the labour crisis of 1907–9, has ever been *forced* to work in Kenya, nor have the settlers ever demanded any system of forced labour, and there are no laws on the books to that effect. But the settlers' view has always been that it was 'impossible . . . for a district officer to be entirely impartial towards the labour question, because a negative attitude was equivalent to official discouragement'.

Every administrative officer thus bore a special responsibility which he could not shirk. If he checked the flow of labour by doing nothing to stimulate it he would be at once retarding the economic progress of the country, depleting the revenue upon which the native, like everyone else, depended for future benefits (such as education, hospitals and agricultural instruction) and allowing habits of idleness to take hold of the young men.

Seven pages are then devoted to canvassing the question: 'How far does an obligation rest on every able-bodied man who enjoys some of the advantages of civilisation to contribute, through some form of work, towards the upkeep of the system from which he benefits?' To questions like this, answers are superfluous.

Only occasionally does Elspeth Huxley spoil her case by over-emphasis, as when she adds to the standard arguments on the African land issue the one that in any case no harm has been done because

> regions most favoured by Europeans may be those least suited to Africans. Europeans instinctively select a country where the climate, vegetation and temperature most resemble those of the cold north. They make, therefore, for the mountain-tops. Natives, on the whole, thrive best in hotter, lower, wetter places.

The relation of the settlers to the administration is depicted as one of heroic antagonism – the individualist pitted against the soulless bureaucrat, the pioneer fighting in the tradition of the American colonist for his rights as a free-born Englishman. This is of a piece with the author's contention, implicit throughout the book and stated occasionally with her usual circumspection, that the colonization of Kenya was by 'the best'. 'It is generally agreed,' she writes,

> that if the colonisation of Africa is to be a success, from the point of view of immigrants and aborigines alike, it must be entrusted to the best among the colonising race, not the remittance men and the indentured coolie. Although it may be impossible to select the best, at least it is feasible to eliminate the illiterate and the beggar

– these being, presumably, self-evidently the worst.

Of 'the best', Delamere is the *nonpareil*. He appears as a rather irascible but delightful Cincinnatus living in Arcadian simplicity and devoting himself to the interests of his fellow men. All his faults are amiable ones, such as a fondness for locking hotel managers in meat safes and giving unhelpful Indian stationmasters a kick in the rear – behaviour apparently pardonable in the best and in no way reducing respect in its victims. Other stars in the Kenya firmament are treated with a discretion amounting to deception. Delamere's friend Dr Atkinson – '"the Doctor" to all who remember East Africa in its pioneer days' – appears as just another enterprising settler: his encounter with the Rendille and subsequent trial for murder are nowhere mentioned. The Grogan flogging incident is likewise omitted, though Grogan himself appears in his capacity of maverick

politician. Galbraith Cole's shooting of the stock thief is recounted
without ever mentioning his name: he appears as a pioneer in the
raising of sheep.[54] In *White Man's Country*, these buccaneers become
plausible candidates for trusteeship, men to whom the Colonial
Office could have handed over African destinies without a qualm.

White Man's Country was followed up ten years later by *Race and
Politics in Kenya*, Elspeth Huxley's published controversy with
Margery Perham, the leading academic authority of the day on
British colonial administration, and also a leading lay admirer of the
Colonial Service. The battle lines were thus clearly drawn, and sins
of omission made correspondingly harder to commit. Pressed by the
well-informed Perham, the calm apologist of *White Man's Country*
found herself transformed into a breezy exponent of *Realpolitik*.
'That's human nature' and 'What's done can't be undone' become
the standard refrains, and they sit very oddly with the continued
assertions of settler qualifications for trusteeship – many of which are
in any case founded on odd bits of decency perpetrated not by the
settlers but by the administration in the teeth of settler opposition, or
by missionaries, as Perham was at pains to point out. Huxley's
citation of the distinguished record of Alliance High School in
support of her claims for Kenya's prowess in the field of native
education invited and received the obvious rejoinder that that
excellent school was the creation of the Protestant missions.[55]

But though Perham seemed to win on points, the result of the
encounter was in fact more like a draw, for Perham's advocacy of
imperial control as a necessary counterweight to settler self-interest
was fatally compromised by her failure to face up to the fact that
imperial control was ultimately only as good as the government
which exercised it. 'That's human nature' is a dictum which applies
just as much to the behaviour of governments as to the behaviour of
individuals – for it is of individuals, after all, that governments are
composed. But the imperial moralist uttering remonstrances from
her desk in Oxford seems unable to come to terms with this, and
holds steadfastly to a vision of a colonial state enjoying perfect moral
autonomy and perfect moral authority, in spite of all the evidence
from the sorry history of Kenya suggesting that such a state –
supposing that it could exist at all, given that men love power for its
own sake – could never exist under conditions involving direct
pressure from interested members of the ruling race. One of the
fascinations of *Race and Politics in Kenya* is to see the Colonial Service
point of view presented it its purest form.

It is apparent from Margery Perham's letters to Elspeth Huxley
that the British government's suppleness in the face of settler
pressure never ceased to puzzle and embarrass her. The Colonial

Secretary's refusal in 1938 to give the Highlands the official title of the 'European Highlands' (as requested by the settlers in recognition of the *status quo*), because discrimination while permissible in practice was deplorable in law, struck her as 'a subterfuge which seems unworthy of a great Empire'. She did not pursue the implications for her advocacy of Colonial Office control of the fact – which she fully recognized – that the Kenya Land Commission of 1932–4 was prevented at the start from doing justice to African claims because it was part of its terms of reference to 'define the area generally known as the European Highlands in which persons of European descent are to have a privileged position in accordance with the White Paper of 1923'. She was evasive about the fact that the official report on the Mombasa dock strike of 1939 revealed the Kenya government to be one of the worst employers, paying wages which were derisory and breaking its own rules about the provision of housing. 'Kenya', she wrote in one of her letters to Huxley, 'offers a test of our political art and our sense of justice . . .'[56] It took the Mau Mau Emergency to make her understand that it was a 'test' that 'we' had failed.

It is to the sense of justice that Margery Perham constantly appeals in *Race and Politics in Kenya*, implicitly opposing it to the settlers' concern with their own self-interest and appearing at times to regard it as the moral property of the Colonial Office. But the settlers had their notion of justice, too, albeit a rather primitive one, and it was not in fact so very different from that prevailing among the rank and file of her beloved Colonial Service. Settlers on lonely farms shared with District Officers in lonely *bomas* a tendency to believe that the man of good character was *ipso facto* a just man, and that good character was essentially all that was needed to do justice to the backward races.[57] The problem was not that the settlers possessed no sense of justice; it was that their idea of justice was so limited to the personal. They confused the just man with the just society, assuming, when pressed, a wholly untenable aggregate equivalence between the two. Lord Cranworth thought it was all right for Africans to be made to work for Europeans, 'provided always that the conditions of employment are good and just'.[58]

The greatest public relations success of the 1930s, however, was in the nature of a windfall – the work of a woman who had no political purpose but wrote simply for her own pleasure and reputation, and who actually disliked most of the English she knew in Kenya. In 1937 the Danish writer 'Isak Dinesen', who as Karen Blixen grew coffee at Ngong from 1914 to 1931, until the farm failed and she had to return to Denmark, published that perfect example of the memoir as a work of imaginative literature, *Out of Africa*. A critical and popular success, *Out of Africa* was, to use a word of which its author was inordinately fond, a noble work, and Kenya was established in it as a noble place. No other British colony had the good fortune to find itself re-created in print as the lost paradise of a world-famous writer.

In Karen Blixen's Africa, finer spirits breathe a purer air. To the farm at Ngong, 'a little too high for coffee', come the choicest personalities of the colony – Denys Finch Hatton, Berkeley Cole, Lord Delamere, Hugh Martin, 'Uncle Charles' Bulpett, and others who refresh themselves in the shade of the author's hospitality. She presides amid her household familiars: Juma, the major-domo; Kamante, the cook; and Farah, the Somali servant whose duties are undefined but whose presence contributes essentially to the *karma* of the house. All these people, including the servants, are of a quite extraordinary distinction. 'Uncle Charles' has swum the Hellespont, climbed the Matterhorn, and ruined himself for love: 'It was to me', Karen Blixen says, 'as if I were sitting down to dinner with Armand Duval or the Chevalier des Grieux themselves.' Kamante, the lame child taken in and cured of his affliction, performs untaught prodigies in the kitchen, possessing 'in the culinary world . . . all the attributes of genius, even to that doom of genius, – the individual's powerlessness in the face of his own powers'. Berkeley Cole sets 'a standard of gallantry' for the whole colony: 'soon after his death people began to talk of their troubles'. On his visits to the farm he enjoys a bottle of champagne 'out in the forest every morning at eleven o'clock'. Denys Finch Hatton, coming back from his safaris starved for talk, lingers long at the author's table, and the talk is so incandescent that 'We . . . kept up the theory that the wild Masai tribe, in their manyatta under the hills, would see the house all afire, like a star in the night, as the peasants of Umbria saw the house wherein Saint Francis and Saint Clare were entertaining one another upon theology'.[59] This is dressing for dinner in the jungle with a vengeance.

The effect achieved is one of perfect unconstraint – of people being supremely themselves in an environment at once alien and accepting. And of no one is this more true than of Denys Finch Hatton, who moves through the book and the African landscape with a magical lightness and unconcern. Just by being himself he inspires universal admiration and affection, particularly in the natives, for whom his death in a plane crash is 'a bereavement'.[60] If the Kenyans could have chosen their own iconographer, they would surely have chosen 'Isak Dinesen', for she endowed them with largeness of soul.

Karen Blixen was a fabulist, and it is as the work of a fabulist that

Out of Africa should be read. In life as in her tales she saw people in their representative capacity and enlarged upon that representativeness when she wrote about them. Her friends in Kenya, adventurous and well-born, represented to her the aristocratic values which, according to her biographer[61], throughout her life she struggled to identify as legitimately her own. Denys and Berkeley, with their immaculate pedigrees – Denys was the son of the Earl of Winchelsea – and their uncompromising standards of behaviour and sensibility, embodied that aristocratic ideal with a finality and completeness arising from their untimely deaths and her own departure from Kenya shortly thereafter. She wrote a book to immortalize them and her own association with them, and the result was an unintended affirmation of the notion that Kenya was ruled, benignly and effortlessly, by 'the best' – unintended because it is clear from her letters[62] that though Karen Blixen idolized her small circle she felt for the average settler nothing but contempt.

Denys Finch Hatton and Berkeley Cole had no lack of other admirers among their contemporaries besides Karen Blixen. Berkeley raised and led a troop of Somali irregulars during the First World War, very much in the Punjab tradition, and for this in particular he was greatly esteemed. The Somalis mutinied and had to be disbanded, but only Lord Cranworth, who was liable to fits of candour, sees fit to mention this in print.[63] Denys seems to have represented to many people a personally unattainable but quintessentially English ideal. Though he died without achieving anything of note, from his days at Eton to the end of his life he suggested by his bearing immense reserves of character and intellectuality: many who met him claimed to have divined his 'greatness' on sight.[64] He was the epitome of 'promise', of personal attractiveness forever uncompromised by action, and in reality a permanent adolescent who feared growing old, wore a hat all the time to disguise his baldness, and visited his old school with inordinate frequency.[65] The secret of his charm, alas, has vanished with time; the extracts from his letters to Karen Blixen quoted by her biographer are very dull. Possessing apparently a superiority so evident it compelled recognition and was not required to be tested, he was an appropriate colonial hero.

There was another side to Kenya's public image in the 1920s and '30s which was less welcome to those hoping to steer the fortunes of the country in the direction of greater settler control. This was its reputation as a haven for refugees from the London gossip columns – 'Are you married or do you live in Kenya?' was one of the witticisms of the day. The Happy Valley set, led by the ultimately five times married Lady Idina Sackville and her third husband, the ultimately murdered Lord Erroll, acquired international notoriety by indulging, before a splendid backdrop of big game and blue sky, in all the vices popular among the idle rich in that or any other day. They stood in unfortunate juxtaposition to the picture so carefully painted in *White Man's Country* of ungrudging and heroic toil. They were not, as was often claimed, entirely peripheral to the life of the settler community. In the early thirties Erroll was encouraged by Lord Francis Scott, who succeeded Delamere as leader of the settlers, to enter politics, and in 1935 he was elected president of the principal settler organization, the Convention of Associations. This was shortly after he dropped his membership of the British Union of Fascists, of which, until Mussolini's invasion of Abyssinia, he had been an enthusiastic supporter. Lady Eileen Scott, who along with her husband Lord Francis Scott had at one time vastly disapproved of Happy Valley and all its works, expressed her 'surprise and delight' at Erroll's election: 'Nearly everyone expected a Bolshie to be elected.'[66] At the time of his death in 1941, apparently the victim of a *crime passionel*, he was Military Secretary of the colony.

And there was another side of settler life which was equally uninspiring but which rarely appeared in print, at least not in any detail; usually it was alluded to only to have a veil quickly drawn over it. This was the experience of the small undercapitalized and underconnected white farmer who went unlamented to the wall. We have one description of such an experience by a Swiss woman, Alyse Simpson, whose husband farmed an arid valley for six years in the 1930s and then sold up and went home. *The Land that Never Was* (1937) is a bitter and disillusioned book, reminiscent of Emily Innes' description of life as the wife of a junior official in the Malayan Civil Service in the 1870s and '80s, *The Chersonese with the Gilding Off* (1885); perhaps there is a woman's eye view of empire which, if the sources could be assembled, would repay study. In Alyse Simpson's world there are tribulations aplenty, but they are unredeemed by any practical consciousness of a great shared endeavour. 'Until one had lived in these parts', she writes,

> one fondly imagined that such misdemeanours as cheating or trying to get the better of one's neighbour were not done in these outposts of Empire where there was, according to one's preconceived ideas, a sort of bond between exiled brothers! It was, alas, the very opposite. Neighbours had a habit of sending offensive notes about trifling matters and imaginary happenings, accusing some innocent, for instance, of allowing his men or cattle or mules to wander on to their farms. One fellow actually shot his own mule which he found wandering amongst his corn, thinking that it belonged to his neighbours . . .

White men coolly cut off one's water-supply, if they happened to live nearer to the source of the stream and wanted to irrigate their dying crops. One could of course go to law about it but there were those preliminary notes oozing misery and hatred, whilst in any case the damage had been done to one's own crops. The unwritten law of helpfulness in exiled places that one read about in pre-war novels existed only in story-books![67]

Llewellyn Powys, too, gives us a glimpse of such a world in his strange book *Black Laughter* (1925), a semi-fictional account of his sojourn on a 'remote Rift Valley farm where we lived lives devoid of love, devoid of religion'.[68] How many farmers lived such lives is impossible to say, but clearly there were some, and for them the experience of empire was not one of expansion into a suddenly larger and less resistant context but of contraction into a smaller and more pressing one.

Though the nature of the political argument changed significantly in Kenya after 1923, the nature of the political situation did not. The settlers continued to enjoy the informal co-operation of the administration, and through membership of the boards set up to regulate various aspects of Kenya's economic life, they steadily increased their power.

For the Africans, little changed, and in one respect at least their position deteriorated. The old system of employing as farm labour squatters who worked in return for rights of residence and cultivation, which at least gave Africans an opportunity to preserve a normal family life when they went to work for the white man, began to disappear. Squatters were evicted from many farms beginning in the early 1930s, when Europeans were switching from maize culture to mixed farming and needed for their livestock the land taken up by squatters and their cattle.[69] The hated *kipande*, or labour registration certificate, which had been introduced after the First World War, and which Africans wore in a metal container around their necks, remained in use; an attempt to substitute universal fingerprinting for this dog-like contrivance foundered in the late 1940s on the opposition of a section of the European community. The colour bar continued in operation, and as more Africans became educated it became an ever greater irritant. As late as 1955, the exclusion of Africans from hotels was defended on the grounds of 'the impossibility of distinguishing between the truly civilized Africans and the many who merely ape our standards'.[70] Africans who returned from study abroad with credentials in their pockets found that they had not thereby achieved equality in European eyes. When Peter Mbiyu Koinange, the son of the Kikuyu chief Koinange, came back in 1938 with a degree from Columbia and a teaching diploma from London he was offered a job as principal of a government school at £10 a month; the previous incumbent had received £1,000 a year.[71] And back on the farm, unevolved but enterprising Africans found their efforts to move into the lucrative coffee market frustrated by settlers who feared they could produce a high quality crop more cheaply than themselves. The Chagga in Tanganyika were already growing coffee which fetched higher prices on the London market than their settler neighbours. Naturally, the Kenya government never enacted any law preventing Africans from growing the crop: those Africans who had the temerity to plant it were 'persuaded' to destroy it, and the rest learned by example. A few token experiments in native coffee-growing were eventually permitted for the sake of decency.[72]

This state of affairs eventually took its toll on the patience of the African, although this remained remarkable in spite of the government's clumsy and authoritarian handling of any attempt at organized political activity. Natives indeed were allowed to have views – but only within the system which provided for their expert supervision by administrative officers, that is, within the Local Native Councils. At the outbreak of the Second World War the Kenya government, acting in the name of wartime security, took the opportunity to proscribe the Kikuyu Central Association, and intern the Kikuyu and Kamba political leaders.

At the end of the war the settlers were more firmly entrenched in positions of influence within the Kenya government than ever and, undeterred apparently by imperial reverses in India and Burma, looked forward to an indefinite stay. Immigration was encouraged and settlement schemes developed. The Electors' Union – successor to the now defunct Convention of Associations – published in 1949 its ambitious *Kenya Plan*, which, though preserving the language of trusteeship, laid out in effect a framework for permanent settler domination. The aim of the Union was stated to be 'The greatest possible executive control by the European community'[73] – the boldest statement of settler aspirations to be found in a public document for many a year. Flushed by victory against enemies within and without, the settlers were beginning to come out of the closet constructed for them by the White Paper of 1923.

But a mere three years later, in October 1952, this atmosphere of buoyant confidence in the future was shattered by the declaration of a State of Emergency; and fourteen years later, after the British and Kenya governments had spent a total of £55 million on military operations, and over 10,000 Africans had been killed and 80,000 detained, Kenya received its independence under an African government.

The usual explanation of these events, espoused naturally by the current Kenya government, is that the people of Kenya took up arms against the oppressor and won. But it has for some time been clear to historians at any rate that the Mau Mau Emergency was nothing so simple as a war of liberation. The surprising facts are that not a single European was killed before the State of Emergency was declared, and that during the entire period of the Emergency, which lasted from October 1952 to January 1960, there were only thirty-two European civilian deaths which could plausibly be attributed to insurgents. There were no significant acts of sabotage against government installations, though the railway offered an easy target, no disruption of supplies to Nairobi, and no interference with the coffee crop, though the European growing of coffee on land which had formerly belonged to Africans was an especial object of resentment.[74] There was indeed a Kikuyu secret society, to which Europeans gave the name 'Mau Mau', and it certainly included elements which were preparing for military action, but the evidence is overwhelming that it was not organized for an armed rising at the time the State of Emergency was declared.[75]

Neither is it apparent that it ever became so organized. The political leadership of the Kikuyu was interned *en bloc* at the outset of the Emergency, and there is no reliable evidence that anti-government activity after that date was under any effective form of central direction. Furthermore, the memoirs of retired insurgents which began to appear in the 1960s[76] make one thing entirely if inadvertently clear: the so-called 'war in the forest', which produced the guerrilla heroes of independent Kenya, was no war at all. Rather it was a very large government operation against roving bands of outlaws, most of whom had taken up residence in the Aberdare mountains, not with any positive intention to do battle, but in order to avoid being picked up by the security forces and deposited in a detention camp.

In the forest, these men preoccupied themselves almost entirely with survival. They were supplied with, or stole, food from the Kikuyu reserve, and made off with cattle from European farms. They developed their bushcraft in hopes of staying out of the way of enemy patrols and aerial bombing attacks. They augmented their meagre supply of weapons by raiding the odd Home Guard post. Leaders arose who whiled away the hours arranging the disposition of forces and deciding who could be a general and who could be a field marshal but who rarely ventured outside the forest. Dedan Kimathi was the most prominent of these.[77] Of all the Mau Mau generals only General Kago, who operated in the Fort Hall district, posed a serious threat to the administration.[78] He did not live to write his memoirs, but General China did, and these reveal that, by the end of 1953, he was in despair about his men's military prospects. Morale was at rock-bottom in the face of the tremendous force arrayed against them, and they were unwilling, he writes, to attack European farms because the Africans living on them had made known their fear of reprisals.[79] China was captured early in 1954 and entered into abortive negotiations with the government.

The most spectacular Mau Mau military operation of the Emergency was the raid on the Naivasha police station of March 1953, when eighty men drove into the township under cover of darkness, attacked the post, released the prisoners, and departed with a supply of weapons – a notable success, but hardly the Tet offensive. There was some urban terrorism, mostly directed against African policemen, but this was pretty well over by the middle of 1954, after 'Operation Anvil', a massive police search of Nairobi, resulted in the removal from the city of all suspicious-looking Kikuyu – a total of some 60,000.

European civilian casualties were, as noted above, very few, and the significance of the relatively large number of African civilian casualties (1,819 according to the official estimate) is extremely difficult to assess. It was believed at the time that these people died because they were government loyalists, and of a certain proportion of them this was in one way or another undoubtedly true. There were Kikuyu Christians who preferred to die rather than live in bondage to pagan oaths; there were Kikuyu kulaks who staked their future on the continuation of European rule; there were Kikuyu unfortunates who found themselves forced by the circumstances of the Emergency to choose between the devil and the deep blue sea and made what turned out, for them, to be the wrong choice; and there may even have been Kikuyu idealists who were genuinely inspired to die for the European cause.[80] But there is evidence that a substantial number of these African deaths were due to individual disputes over land.[81] Thousands of Kikuyu were forcibly repatriated to the reserve during the early months of the Emergency, and many more followed voluntarily in the first half of 1953. This movement revived many ancient conflicts, and in the turbulent atmosphere of the time some of them were settled by recourse to violence. Such attacks were almost invariably reported as Mau Mau atrocities, but near the end of 1953 the District Commissioner at Kiambu admitted that half the murders in his district during the past year had been due to land cases. Indeed, the most notorious 'Mau Mau atrocity' of the Emergency, the Lari massacre in which 97 Kikuyu villagers were killed, was not, as was announced at the time, a deliberate attack on government loyalists but the outcome of a long-standing dispute about land.

All in all, it hardly seems to have been much of a rebellion. What, then, drove the government first of all to declare a State of Emergency, and then to keep on pounding away at the Kikuyu long after it should have become obvious that no serious resistance was being offered? Dedan Kimathi, the last of the forest chieftains, was captured in October 1956 and the army was withdrawn from operations at the end of that year. But the rate of committal to the detention camps did not diminish until 1959 – although the average length of stay in them seems to have become shorter – and the rate of committal to prison for offences under the Emergency regulations declined only a little: 7,276 in 1956, 6,924 in 1957, 6,059 in 1958.[82] Conditions in the camps steadily deteriorated and in 1959 became the object of international scandal after eleven detainees at Hola camp were beaten to death by warders. The rate of releases was speeded up, but none the less many of those held in the camps were not released until after the official end of the State of Emergency in January 1960.[83] As it went on, the Emergency looked less and less like a counter-insurgency operation, and more and more like a pogrom.

Space does not permit a detailed discussion of these fascinating questions, and they cannot in any case be pronounced upon with certainty. Though much has been written on the subject, a definitive history of the Emergency remains to be produced, and may in fact never appear: the absence of critical documents – many were lost in a fire in the Nairobi archives – and the inevitably undocumented nature of much that went on create formidable obstacles. Nevertheless, some suggestions may be offered.

There was evidence in 1952 of considerable disaffection from government among the Kikuyu. The Kikuyu-dominated Kenya African Union was becoming more aggressive in its political demands and there was sporadic agrarian violence at the grassroots level throughout the year, including arson and hamstringing of cattle on European farms. It was known to the police that an anti-government oath was being taken among the Kikuyu, and by mid-1952 it was estimated that about a quarter of the Kikuyu had taken it. (This estimate suddenly rose to 80–90 per cent shortly after the State of Emergency was declared.[84]) There was increasing unease among the provincial administration[85], but this was discounted, to his everlasting execration, by the governor, Sir Philip Mitchell, who concluded on the basis of his forty years' experience in the Colonial

Service that Mau Mau was just another in the long series of anti-
European cults he had seen come and seen go. He may well have
been right. Nevertheless, there can be no doubt that the alarm felt
by the administration was genuine, and it was probably accounted
for by three factors in the situation which Mitchell failed to
appreciate.

The first was the provincial administration's suspicion that the
local acts of violence were occurring under the central direction of
the leaders of the KAU. This was a horrible prospect, not only
because it seemed to invest the violence in Kikuyuland with a
national significance, but also because it suggested that control of
the Kikuyu had passed away from their administrators and into the
hands of those 'agitators' whom all good District Officers devoutly
believed had no authentic basis of popular support.[86] Mitchell
seems not to have appreciated these fears very keenly. He was in his
third colonial governship by then (the others had been Uganda
and Fiji) and was strongly committed to a multiracial approach to
Kenyan politics, involving not repression but co-optation of African
évolués.[87] The second factor was the presence of settlers in the area
where disturbances were occurring. It was inevitable, given the long
record of Kikuyu grievance over lost land, that Kikuyu disaffection
would at times take the form of direct action against European
farmers, even if this was only lighting a few grass fires; and,
historically, action against settlers, who are not the professional
agents of control but the race made flesh, has always inspired greater
outrage than action against administrators. It seems reasonable to
assume that in Kenya, where for many years administrators had
been allowed to become settlers and settlers administrators, there
was a more than usual capacity on the part of the administration for
a strong response to anti-settler manifestations. Mitchell, on the
other hand, had spent most of his career outside Kenya, and, though
he planned to retire there, he was a Colonial Service man to his
fingertips; for a Kenya governor, his powers of empathy with
settlerdom were unusually undeveloped.

There was probably also a third factor contributing both to the
administration's alarm and Mitchell's relative indifference to it. In
Mitchell's youth 'unrest' of the type now occurring among the
Kikuyu would have been dealt with either 'administratively' by
switching chiefs or, if that had failed to get results, by a quick, quiet
punitive expedition. That day had passed, but, short of these time-
hallowed measures, it was difficult to know what to do about the
situation in Kikuyuland. When the provincial administration began
to press for emergency powers during the first half of 1952[88],
Mitchell, who had served his apprenticeship in the imperial service

as a bush DO in Tanganyika and Nyasaland, may have disregarded their pleas in the belief that an officer worth his salt knew how to finesse these little local difficulties till they blew over.

Mitchell retired in June 1952 and there was then a three-month interregnum before his successor, Evelyn Baring, arrived to take up his duties. Three weeks after Baring arrived a State of Emergency was declared. Jomo Kenyatta, the leader of the KAU and the presumed evil genius of Mau Mau, was arrested along with 82 other African politicians; police and magistrates were given special powers to deal with suspected insurgents; and a battalion of British troops was flown in from the Canal Zone to assist in the restoration of law and order.

The decision to declare a State of Emergency owed a great deal to the character of the new governor.[89] Essentially an indecisive man, Baring shared with many indecisive men a taste for decision. Though he was apt to take a long time making up his mind, inclining first to the views of one party and then of another, once his mind was made up it was closed to all further discussion, and it could at that point display 'an extraordinary ruthlessness'.[90] When he arrived in Kenya in September 1952 he was confronted, not with conflicting assessments of the situation, but with a single point of view. Settlers and administrators alike were united in the opinion that Something Must Be Done. Under these circumstances Baring's mind was soon made up. Any lingering doubts he may have entertained – there is evidence that at one point he thought of making contact with Kenyatta[91] – were dispelled by the gangster-style murder on 7 October of the loyalist Kikuyu chief Waruhiu, which in the charged atmosphere of the time was instantly assumed, though never proved, to have been the work of Mau Mau. On 9 October Baring telegraphed to the Secretary of State proposing the declaration of a State of Emergency and the simultaneous arrest of Kenyatta and his associates.

It is important to realize that Baring saw the declaration of the State of Emergency as a way of avoiding bloodshed. The immediate aim was to take the ringleaders out of circulation, and this was to be done under emergency powers so that the government would have the authority to nip in the bud an anticipated violent reaction to the arrest of Kenyatta. Baring also believed that once the troublemakers were removed the State of Emergency would last no more than a few weeks, his reasoning being that if the government took decisive action at this time waverers would come over to its side and the situation would be contained. 'I believe', he wrote to the Secretary of State, 'that the risk of trouble is very great and we should be too strong rather than too weak.'[92]

One is reminded at this point that not only was Baring an indecisive man whose mind was relieved to the point of ecstasy by the actual taking of a decision, but that he had been in his youth, in the late 1920s, a District Officer on the North West Frontier of India. Was he influenced in his mind by the recollection that the Punjab 'held' in 1857 thanks to the timely action of a few bold men – men who believed it was better to be 'too strong rather than too weak'? The Punjab creed was alive and well on the North West Frontier in the 1920s, and Baring himself once strikingly applied its principles in single-handedly putting down a prison riot at Dera Ishmael Khan[93] – an achievement which would have surprised many who knew him later as the perfect Secretariat man. It is tempting to suggest that Baring and Mitchell learned the same lesson from their early experiences in imperial government, but because of differences in temperament and assessment of the situation – Baring believed in a conspiracy masterminded by the KAU; Mitchell did not – applied it differently. Certainly throughout his stay in Kenya Baring proved highly susceptible to the views of the provincial administration, and placed the upkeep of their morale high on his list of priorities.

The arrest of the KAU leadership was followed immediately by the arrest and 'screening' of many thousands of Kikuyu. In the first three weeks of the Emergency over 30,000 people were picked up for screening and 8,500 subsequently detained. By the beginning of December another 4,500 had been detained.[94] At the end of November the first compulsory moves began, with the expulsion from the Leshau Ward near Thomson's Falls of 3,500 Kikuyu squatters and their families.[95] Collective punishments – usually stock levies – were instituted for dealing with the 'passive wing' of Mau Mau, that is, villagers who were suspected of supporting insurgents but against whom nothing could be proved, and Mombasa enjoyed a meat boom.[96] A public gallows was put up on the golf course at Nyeri, and a travelling gallows was constructed by the Public Works Department; the object of striking fear into the hearts of the population was presumably achieved in spite of the ignominious difficulties experienced in getting the latter under railway bridges.[97]

To get all this in perspective, it has to be pointed out that during the early months of the Emergency – from 20 October to 31 December 1952 – the total number of settlers murdered by insurgents was two. Two more were killed on New Year's Day 1953, swelling the numbers to four. By no stretch of the imagination had the dreaded 'night of the long knives' materialized in Kenya, yet the settlers and the government behaved as though it had.

In the middle of January, in response to settler demands for summary justice against those who had laid hands on some of their number, the death penalty was introduced for the administration of oaths binding the recipient to commit murder. Then, after the murder of the Ruck family on the night of 24 January 1953, capital punishment was introduced for a series of other offences, including unlawful possession of arms and ammunition, consent to the administration of unlawful oaths, consorting with terrorists, and providing supplies to terrorists.[98] It was some months before the courts could cope with the flood of capital cases, but by the end of 1953, 162 Africans had been hanged for offences under the Emergency Regulations, and by the end of 1954 another 605.[99] Altogether, over 1,000 Africans were executed during the Emergency: a further 221 in 1955, 72 in 1956, 14 in 1957, and 8 in 1958. Of these, only about a third were executed for murder, and in the latter half of 1954, when the Emergency assizes were in full swing, the proportion was far less. Between 5 July and 12 November 1954 there were 243 executions in Kenya for offences under the Emergency Regulations, and only 17 of them were for murder.

At the same time, a military campaign was going on against Mau Mau. If this was not at first felt to be entirely successful, it certainly was not for want of trying. By the beginning of July 1954 there had been 6,189 'known casualties to Mau Mau adherents', of which 5,567 had been killed and 622 wounded – a truly remarkable ratio. Casualties to the security forces in the same period were 422 killed and 367 wounded.[100] RAF planes went into battle with 'kills' emblazoned on the fuselage and British battalions kept scoreboards of insurgents accounted for, with few questions asked as to how they got that way.[101] The Colonial Secretary announced in the House of Commons on 29 April 1953 that since the beginning of the Emergency 430 people had been 'shot while resisting arrest or after being challenged to stop'.[102] The conduct of the military improved greatly after General Erskine arrived to take command of operations in June 1953, but there continued to be scandals arising from the behaviour of the Kenya Regiment and the Kenya Police Reserve, both of which were composed of settlers.[103] The case of Brian Hayward of the KPR, who was sentenced to three months' hard labour for burning suspects' eardrums with cigarettes, led to the formation by local Europeans of the Young Settlers Defence Fund: Hayward spent his sentence in a hotel doing clerical work.

Police brutality against Africans was often passed off as the work of native policemen, over whose crude impulses it was impossible to exercise perfect control – an interesting inversion of Hugh Clifford's concern that the doings of such people brought the whole imperial enterprise into disrepute. How deeply the tolerance of police malpractice took root in Kenya was shown in the dispute leading to the resignation of Colonel Arthur Young, the Commissioner of Police for the City of London, whose efforts on secondment to reform the Kenya Police led him to conclude that until they were removed from the control of the administration and made directly responsible to the law their behaviour would never approximate to civilized standards.[104] The administration did not agree that civilized standards were required and Young departed. His report was never published.

The level of verbal violence also increased notably in Kenya during the Emergency. There were suggestions that 50,000 Kikuyu should be shot, that 100,000 Kikuyu should be put to work in a swill tub, that a government worth its salt would see that a hundred Kikuyu were hanged for every European killed.[105] Colonel Grogan, now seventy-seven, rose in the Legislative Assembly to propose that a hundred suspected insurgents should be 'popped . . . up to the Northern Frontier', charged with treason, found innocent or guilty, and then either hanged in the presence of the others or given fifty pounds of cornmeal and a compass and told to find their way home.[106] Reports of bestial oaths revived his ancient memories of cannibals and in jocular fashion he accused the African member of Leg. Co., the very *évolué* Eliud Mathu, of casting a roving eye over the front bench 'for a succulent morsel'.[107] At a public dinner in Nairobi, in April 1953, a prominent settler, Sir Richard Woodly, gave it as his opinion that:

> Three years of slavery from dawn to dusk, on a ration sufficient to keep him alive and working but no more – powers to prison officials in charge to cut rations, and inflict corporal punishment of a severe nature for misdemeanour – are more likely to be an effective deterrent than ten or twenty years of an ordinary sentence.[108]

It has been suggested by some authorities that the proclamation of a State of Emergency radicalized the African population of Kenya and created a rebellion where none had existed before.[109] The existence of any kind of rebellion before or after October 1952 seems open to doubt, but what is not open to doubt is that the Emergency radicalized the Europeans. The realization that, as it appeared, the Kikuyu were conspiring for their obliteration destroyed at a stroke the proud pretence that white rule was based on black acceptance of white superiority, and released with explosive force the fear and hate accumulated within.

The Ruck murder in particular was a terrible blow to European complacency. Quite apart from the intrinsic horror of the killings – a young farmer, his wife, and six-year-old son were hacked to death at their lonely farmhouse – there were elements in the situation which aroused the most furious sense of betrayal. The Rucks represented to many settlers the Kenya ideal: a rugged, hard-working young husband known as an exemplary employer, a doctor wife who ran a free clinic for the natives, a manly little boy to whom one day the fruits of his parents' labour would be passed on. If anyone had what it took to hold Africans in willing subjection, it was the Rucks – yet they had been destroyed. There was no accounting for it except by the innate depravity of the African, and lashing out in all directions was the natural response.

Certain circumstances of the crime added fuel to the flame. The chief accomplices in the murder were the family's groom and tractor driver; and it was reported that bloody strands of Mrs Ruck's long fair hair were found scattered across the lawn where she had tried to run from her assailants[110] – a detail which exerted a powerful appeal both to racial identity and the European ideal of defenceless womanhood. It was all extremely reminiscent of the Matabeleland murders of 1896, and the effect on the Europeans was the same: instant legitimation of blind rage. Fifteen hundred of them marched on Government House in Nairobi to demand they knew not exactly what, other than that restraint should be abandoned. Though Baring was careful to make no immediate concessions, from then on the gloves were off.

But the Europeans had not entirely convinced themselves of the futility of being good. Side by side with the vengeful pursuit of the Kikuyu there existed an extraordinary attempt to reclaim them. With enthusiastic settler participation and support, 'rehabilitation' programmes were set up in the detention camps, and, under the guidance of a new government department created for the purpose, detainees were processed through a series of reformative experiences until rehabilitation was declared complete and they were allowed to return home. The aim of these programmes was to bring the Kikuyu back to an appreciation of the virtues of loyalty to the European.[111] What had been destroyed was to be re-created, what had been lost was to be regained.

The intellectual rationale of rehabilitation was derived from the explanations proffered for the Mau Mau phenomenon by various European authorities, including a psychiatrist, J.C. Carothers, and the anthropologist Louis Leakey.[112] All these explanations were based on the assumption that Mau Mau was a mental pathology of which the Kikuyu had to be 'cleansed'. That it might be a political phenomenon was not seriously entertained, even by Leakey, who was relatively sympathetic to Kikuyu grievances and had long advocated palliation of them[113]: it seems to have been difficult for Europeans to grasp the possibility that Africans might be rationally disaffected to the point of actual rebellion. As with American counter-insurgency theories of a later date[114], the trouble was laid at the door of excessively rapid modernization: Mau Mau arose, wrote Dr Carothers, 'from the development of an anxious conflictual situation in people who, from contact with the alien culture, had lost the supportive and constraining influences of their own culture, yet had not lost their "magic" modes of thinking'.[115] 'Too much change, too quickly: that has been the trouble', said Elspeth Huxley in her downright way.[116] Maladaptive behaviour such as oath-taking, arson and murder was the inevitable result of these stresses and strains on the Kikuyu psyche. This was the view which was eventually enshrined in the Corfield report as the official European explanation of the Emergency.

Clad though it was in impresively medical language, Dr Carothers' judgement on Mau Mau represented in reality nothing more than the conventional settler wisdom that civilization ruined the African: this is presumably why it was universally regarded in Kenya as brilliantly insightful. It might be argued indeed that it was not so much the Kikuyu who had trouble handling their entry into the modern world as the British. Surely it is no less maladaptive to vituperate against Africans who go to school and wear shoes than it is to swear horrible oaths with goat penises when these aspirations appear to be denied.

All this theorizing was taken very seriously, and a programme of 'cleansing' was instituted upon what was believed to be the best scientific advice – as it happened, that of Leakey. As early as April 1952 loyal Kikuyu headmen were travelling round the country at government expense sacrificing goats and pronouncing ritual absolutions in the infected areas. When it was revealed in the press that the goats were bludgeoned to death the Kenya Society for the Prevention of Cruelty to Animals considered prosecuting the offending headmen in the courts, but this proposal was turned aside by the administration in the national interest.[117]

As the work of reclaiming the Kikuyu was developed and elaborated it began to acquire a more pragmatic and less theoretical aspect. Apart from the mediaeval emphasis on confession, which continued, being said by its advocates to transfigure those who experienced it[118], much as confessed heretics in sixteenth-century Spain were supposedly transfigured *en route* to the *auto da fé*, the routine in the camps settled down for the most part into the kind of activities which District Officers had believed for many years to be good for the African soul.

Literary education is given and instruction in civics, which includes the political and economic history of Kenya. They are told in clear language of the vast benefits brought by the British Government to Kenya, and not least to its Kikuyu inhabitants, and the prosperity before the Emergency contrasted with the miseries of pre-Government days. In addition, technical training is given by an ex P.W.D. instructor. Recreation such as football, physical training for the young men, two hours of propaganda broadcasting each day, which includes religious instruction, cinema performances showing films of an instructional nature, complete the programme.[119]

Work was deemed to be 'an essential ingredient of rehabilitation' and inmates were employed on the familiar tasks of bush clearing, bridge building, road making and terracing. Leaders were encouraged to emerge 'on the lines of the Patrol Leader and Prefect Systems'. And the healing power of mirth was not forgotten.

Plays allowed steam to be let off harmlessly in laughter. Songs so long as they did not extol Jomo Kenyatta were encouraged. Ngomas [traditional dance gatherings] were equally valuable. The hilarious sports meeting such as those organised at school sports and on ships had a great appeal to youths and even grown men.[120]

Though T.G. Askwith, the director of the Department of Community Development and Rehabilitation, was sent to Malaya to glean what he could from detention camp procedures there, the chief influence on the rehabilitation programme was clearly the traditional Colonial Service philosophy of regeneration and reform. The Emergency provided an opportunity for putting this into practice on a mass scale, unhampered by any Cliffordian regrets for a supposedly more vital native past.

In some camps a more intensely ethical onslaught was attempted, especially at the Athi River camp where the commandant, Colonel Alan Knight, and some of the staff were members of the Moral Re-Armament movement. MRA had obtained something of a foothold among Kenya settlers in the early 1950s, its principles of Absolute Honesty, Absolute Purity, Absolute Unselfishness and Absolute Love appearing as a heaven-sent recipe for solving the knotty racial problems with which Kenya was beset. The only thing missing, of course, was Absolute Justice[121], but this was not a disadvantage in Kenya: MRA offered the magical promise of getting everyone on better terms without demanding any fundamental alteration in the *status quo*; in its emphasis on the moral power of the 'changed' personality in the fundamentally unchanged society it was the twentieth-century heir to evangelicalism. In England the Movement threw itself into the task of improving industrial relations, exhorting workers to ask for less and employers to give a little more; in Kenya it went to work on the problem of rehabilitation, hammering home the message that white and black could live harmoniously together if only they abandoned their selfish preconceptions and learned to respect each other's different, but equal, contributions to society – trusteeship perhaps once again redefined. Athi River was acclaimed by the Movement as one of its great success stories, Colonel Knight being accorded the honour of speaking at the funeral of Frank Buchman, MRA's founder, in 1961.[122] The emphasis on confession in the rehabilitation programme as a whole probably owed something to the Moral Re-Armers' insistence on confession of sins as the first step to salvation. But their colour-blind application of this principle inevitably provoked official resistance. One of the plays they put on in the camps showed a settler repenting of exploiting labour; this play was rapidly withdrawn.[123]

The confusion and ambivalence of the white response to Mau Mau cannot be overstated. Colonel Knight himself, though kind and understanding to those who felt the urge to confess, was, by all accounts, a scourge to those who did not.[124] Conditions in the camps deteriorated even as the rehabilitation programme went ever more frantically forward, for rehabilitation, it was believed, could not begin without confession and confession was not easy to obtain. Faced with an enormous camp population of unconfessed insurgents, the lawyers in the Attorney General's office racked their brains to decide what was a legitimate degree of force to be applied in obtaining the vital admission of guilt. 'Compelling' force, it was decided, was legal, and this included moving detainees against their wishes, cutting their hair, shaving them, forcibly feeding them, and dressing them in a camp uniform. 'Overwhelming' force was illegal, and this was defined as applying force to a detainee to break his moral resistance to a lawful order. Thus, it was legal to use force to take one set of clothes off a detainee and put on another, but illegal to hit the same detainee with a baton in order to make him change his clothes. A system was evolved in some camps whereby, if a detainee refused the initial request to confess, he was given a lawful order such as being told to put on a camp uniform. If he refused, 'compelling' force was then applied and was continued until he confessed.[125]

This kind of hair-splitting, so indicative of the crisis of self-perception the whites were going through – were they leaders, marching ahead of the Africans to a new dawn, or were they merely rulers, keeping them down as best they could? – led directly to the tragedy and scandal of Hola. On the advice of J.B.T. Cowan, a Senior Superintendent of Prisons regarded as the foremost authority on detention camp procedure, a plan was adopted in the early part of 1959 for halting a reported decline in discipline among the hardcore detainees interned at Hola camp. Cowan's plan was for detainees to be taken out and set to work under conditions which he envisaged as strictly controlled.[126] Weeding was the chosen task, and recalcitrants were to be carried to the work site by warders, who would then take their hands, entwine them around the weeds, grasp firmly, and pull. Their psychological resistance to authority would then be broken and the road to confession and eventual rehabilitation opened. At no point were blows to be administered; Cowan believed corporal punishment to be 'completely ineffective'.[127]

Unfortunately, as this ridiculous plan filtered down through the camp hierarchy, its fine distinctions were completely lost. On 3 March a group of detainees, guarded by warders instructed by the camp commandant to apply light taps on the legs with batons in the event of recalcitrance, were marched to the work site and set upon when they refused to work, with eleven deaths resulting. At first it was announced that the men had died through drinking contaminated water, and the facts of the case emerged only slowly, mainly because of Baring's reluctance to face them: he had thrown himself mind and soul into the task of Kikuyu rehabilitation and could not bear to see it jeopardized by scandal.[128] In spite of the tremendous outcry which ensued, no one resigned over Hola, the excuse of honourable misunderstanding being allowed to prevail all round.

The imminence of a general election had no doubt a great deal to do with this – resignations would have been embarrassing to the Conservative party – but the extent to which good intentions genuinely existed and were accepted as such must not be underestimated. Cowan himself was completely confused about the difference between what he repeatedly referred to as 'moral compulsion'[129] and plain old physical compulsion. He imagined his plan being carried out in an atmosphere of high moral purpose, putting on record at the outset his belief that 'firmness . . . does not imply a brutal and harsh regime but a high standard of personal example and insistence always on immediate obedience'.[130] It must have taken a truly desperate ambivalence about the use of force in the restoration of imperial authority, and a sincere belief that that authority was, in a very individualized sense, ultimately moral, to suppose that a high and compelling standard of personal example might be achieved in the conditions of Hola camp.

The Emergency, it should be noted, generated its own loyalty myths, some of which may be found celebrated in Robert Ruark's best-selling novel, *Something of Value*. The use of 'pseudo-gangs' – patrols composed of captured insurgents, sometimes with a European in black face at the head – encouraged the belief that, in a fair fight for hearts and minds, the European would ultimately prevail. Brands plucked from the burning, these men seemed a supreme example of that long procession of irregular native troops conjured into existence by the leadership qualities of the European. The pseudo-gang phenomenon was later explained by its leading practitioners, Captain Frank Kitson and Police Superintendent Ian Henderson[131], as the result of apprehension of imminent defeat or immediate execution in men who had either never been very fanatical about Mau Mau, or had been disaffected from it by the savagery of the forest leaders; pseudo-gang candidates were carefully selected. But perhaps Henderson and Kitson were too modest. Both men come across in their memoirs as actually possessing that calm authority and nerve to which loyalty would have been a plausible response. None other than General China has paid tribute to Henderson's integrity and courage.[132]

Loyalty is only this important to people whose ultimate concern is personal, rather than political or economic, power. Africans had come to mean much, much more to Europeans than just cheap labour, important as that was: they were one half of an intimate equation – emotional, at bottom, rather than moral – in which x was the legitimate assertion of authority by one human being over another. To a remarkable degree, over long years of advertising to the Colonial Office their qualifications for trusteeship, the settlers had come to share this essentially Colonial Service approach to the African.

The Emergency threw all assumptions about loyalty dramatically into question and revealed their importance. Hence the energy with which the Europeans set about reclaiming the Kikuyu. Hence also the belief, in spite of all the evidence to the contrary from decades of misrule by the most self-consciously superior people ever exported by Britain overseas, that the case for government by 'the best' had only been strengthened by the events of 1952. Dr Carothers advised, shortly after the onset of the Emergency, that henceforth, if the 'moral lead' of Europeans were to be retained in Kenya, aspiring immigrants should go through a selection process to 'assess their qualifications for living in a land where their every act will have much wider repercussions than is the case in the land they aim to leave'.[133] There was no thought of giving up, only of how best to hang on.

This concern with their own personal radiance, and loyalty as the proof of it, provides the key to understanding not only the apparent contradictions in the European response to the Emergency, but the route taken, thereafter, to independence.

The British government was appalled by the turn taken by events in Kenya in 1952. Out of what seemed to be a clear blue sky – no one in London had thought it worthwhile hurrying along Baring's departure for Kenya – a full-scale colonial rebellion had materialized. At least, this was the only conclusion which could logically be drawn from the new governor's declaration of a State of Emergency. The Colonial Secretary, Oliver Lyttelton, went out immediately to survey the scene. He concluded that, though 'it was first imperative to put down the rebellion', the future of European settlement in Kenya could only be secured if 'the confidence of the Africans was gained by giving them, gradually, a share in government'. The only alternative to that was 'government by force', and this was impossible because 'on the lowest level of argument we did not have the force, on the highest level we did not believe in it as a method of government'.[134] Accordingly, he spoke with 'brutal candour' to the settlers, upbraiding them for provoking an explosion with which the British government had now to deal militarily, and warning them that 'besides force, which must now be used and which we will furnish, you must turn your minds to political reform, and to measures which will gradually engage the consent and help of the governed'.[135] The declaration of a State of Emergency had brought in the 'imperial factor' that Cecil Rhodes had so rightly dreaded, and as the 'rebellion' proved apparently more and more difficult to contain, and was more and more expensive to fight, it asserted itself ever more insistently. Blazing away at phantoms in the forest, the settlers ended up, politically speaking, shooting themselves in the foot.

In its programme of reform the British government was able to enlist the support of the settler politician Michael Blundell, who gradually mobilized around himself those elements of European opinion disposed to tolerate the 'multiracial' constitutions which the Colonial Office tried out in Kenya in the 1950s. Under his leadership they steadily increased in size and importance, gathering strength from the appeal that multiracialism came to possess for people whose political opinions were rather diverse but who had in common a willingness to attempt the preservation of European influence by informal rather than formal means.[136]

In practical terms, multiracialism meant ultimate parity of representation among the three races of Kenya, the whites, Africans and Indians each having the same number of unofficial representatives on the Executive and Legislative Councils, and, in a ministerial system, the same number of ministers: the Lyttelton Constitution of 1954, with one African minister, was the first step in this direction. Multiracialism, it is important to note, was viewed not as a precursor to majority rule but as an alternative to it, its intellectual rationale being that *all* the races had their essential and permanent contribution to make to Kenya's progress. Its intellectual roots were in the Dual Policy of the 1920s, in particular that version of it, associated in blessed memory with Sir Robert Coryndon, which saw the settlers as the great leaven in the East African lump. Mervyn Hill, for many years the editor of the settler newspaper, *The Kenya Weekly News*, made the transition from Coryndonian trusteeship to Blundellian multiracialism without dropping a stitch. 'I believe', he wrote in *The Dual Policy in Kenya*, in 1944,

> that the European community of Kenya will only achieve political advance by making it very clear that they accept the white man's role of leading the African towards a better life, and by taking the lead in all matters affecting native policy. It is the very essence of the Dual Policy that the interests of the European and the African are complementary; and that the advance of either is for the good of both. It is utterly fallacious to assume that native advance means European stagnation or retrogression: or that white settlement can only survive or advance at the expense of native interests.[137]

Substitute 'multiracialism' for 'Dual Policy' and you have Hill's views of the 1950s. The connecting link was his belief in the European capacity for 'leadership'.

Everyone who was serious about multiracialism in the 1950s believed that the future of white settlement could be staked on this capacity for leadership. Given minimum conditions of representation, it was assumed, the natural intellectual, ethical and temperamental superiority of the European would manifest itself sufficiently to guarantee him a place in the East African sun for an indefinite period, just acceptably short, perhaps, of eternity. The exhilaration which comes across so strongly in the multiracialist pamphleteering and speechmaking of the time can be explained by this sense of rising to a challenge. Multiracialism, its adherents seem to be saying, is a risk worth taking – if you believe in yourself.

Blundell himself, though ever the practical politician, was at heart a believer. When the right-winger Cavendish-Bentinck demurred at accepting the Lyttelton Constitution, Blundell explained to him that, in the face of a vast African majority in the population, 'the European contribution to East Africa' – otherwise known as white settlement – could only continue if 'we were able to capture the support of the African and secure his acceptance of our position'. When the Lancaster House conference of 1960 opened the way to independence under an African, not a multiracial, government, destroying, it appeared, all Blundell's political ambitions at a stroke, he found the impetus to go on in the faith that there was 'a place for the white man in our new African country as an individual of ability and energy', finding 'his security in the fact that Africa needs him as an individual but does not want nor will tolerate his race thrust down her throat'.[138] He put his faith into practice and stayed on in Kenya after independence. When the author of this book was living there from 1979–80 he was writing a regular newspaper column which gently admonished the Kenya government to conduct itself in a civilized manner – the last manifestation, one imagines, of that influence for good the multiracialists always hoped to exercise.

The appeal to white self-confidence, which the Emergency had not shattered but only shaken, ensured that it was a motley band of individuals that was attracted to the multiracialist banner. Certain luminaries who had no democratic instincts at all, but who thought they could handle a few Africans in the Leg. Co., drifted into Blundell's orbit. Sir Charles Markham, who throughout the Emergency attended Legislative Council meetings in his Kenya Police Reserve uniform, was one of these.[139] The Earl of Portsmouth was another.[140] Portsmouth was an admirer of 'the new spiritual awakening in Germany' in the 1930s, and was active, before coming to Kenya, in a variety of blood-and-soil groups advocating a return to Merrie England and the craft tradition. Even Grogan, though opposed to political multiracialism, wandered into paths of multiracial behaviour, taking up African politicians, and advocating that educated natives should be invited to dinner and Jomo Kenyatta released.[141] With typical bravado he refused to carry a gun during the Emergency. Had it not been for his inveterate hatred of Indians, he might have seen the theatrical possibilities inherent in a multiracial legislature.[142]

Elspeth Huxley supported multiracial government because its adoption proved that unofficial as well as official whites could be benevolent towards blacks. Her old adversary, Margery Perham, supported it for the same reason, hoping thereby to ensure that Kenya Africans would 'freely choose to remain in association with Britain'.[143] Huxley began work in the 1950s on her highly successful childhood memoirs of Kenya, *The Flame Trees of Thika* (1959) and *The Mottled Lizard* (1962). They painted a charming picture of a land peopled with whites guilty of nothing worse than eccentricity and blacks who obligingly materialized out of the ground to work for them.

The most ardent multiracialists were supporters (as was Margery Perham) of the Capricorn Africa Society, an organization whose name became synonymous during this period with the promotion of inter-racial goodwill. Its energy in the field of human relations helped to obscure the fact that its chief political objective was the maintenance of the integrity of the White Highlands. Founded in Rhodesia by Colonel David Stirling – former commando and future amateur *condottiere* – in 1949, it advocated in its *Declarations* of 1952 a political system which was virtually indistinguishable from apartheid. The Society responded to this accusation by pointing out that in the so-called 'Open' areas – that is, areas of European settlement in which Africans could live but not own land – the franchise would be granted on the basis of a common citizenship to all those, regardless of race, who were 'capable of achieving the requisite standards'. Only Africans, however, would be required to prove their suitability, Europeans automatically having the vote. The Society's great dream was of Central African – and even, it was hinted, of East and Central African – federation, and it was revealingly its opinion that 'European leadership will not endure in Africa' unless it obtained African support for this project. Concluding the *Declarations* was a tribute to the British Colonial Service and an appeal to the British public to recognize that the settler, too, was 'a worthy and indeed indispensable vehicle of responsibility in Africa'.[144]

In Kenya, the leading personalities of the Capricorn Africa Society were Michael and Susan Wood, and Susan Wood's book *Kenya: The Tensions of Progress*, published just befor the Lancaster House conference, was a comprehensive statement of evolved multiracialist doctrine. Europeans, she wrote, must realize that they would have to come down from their pedestal and compete in the political arena on more equal terms:

> It is probable that . . . European influence cannot survive as such [i.e., formally] in the political revolution that is taking place. That it can and should survive with even greater influence within a national rather than a racial setting is an important point which many Europeans find it difficult to appreciate and accept. It is a step of faith which needs to be taken.[145]

Lancaster House did not quench Susan Wood's faith, but made it more exalted. 'A situation such as faces the European to-day in Kenya', she wrote in the expanded edition of 1962, requires of the individual the deepest understanding, a heroic patience, devotion to a vision of a future which he may never see, and the finest courage. Such a combination of virtues is seldom found in ordinary men. There are sound arguments why it is important that the European should have them all, and should continue, through thick and thin, to stay in Africa, exert his influence how he may, and create, here and there, the standards of civilization which will produce the creative stimulus essential to the success of the great African experiment.[146]

In this vision of the future, all Europeans are expected to conform to the standards of 'the best' – the only logical solution, in the context of multiracial thinking, to the problem of their survival as a community.

Multiracialist ideas were reflected in the content of the Mau Mau rehabilitation programme. The programme's director, T.G. Askwith, was noted for his many social contacts with members of other races, and was one of the founders of Kenya's first racially integrated club, the United Kenya Club, in 1948. His booklet, *The Story of Kenya's Progress* (1953), which was the source book for political re-education in the camps, has been aptly described as a 'multi-racial primer'.[147] Nevertheless, his aim in political re-education was stated by him, confidentially, to be the eradication from the Kikuyu mind of 'the crazy notion that they could manage their affairs without the European'.[148] The rehabilitation programme was where the connection between European leadership and African loyalty was made practically explicit.

It had been a magnificent effort, but the triumph of multiracialism was not to be. No sooner had the Lennox-Boyd Constitution, which seemed to Europeans the last word in generosity, come into being in 1958 than African politicians began to demand majority rule. They were not mollified by European concessions but inspired by them to ask for more. The British government, reluctant at first to abandon its leisurely constitution-mongering, suddenly decided to accede to African demands for formal political ascendancy and announced that Kenya would receive its independence in 1963. The unexpected force of the nationalist onslaught, the scandal of Hola, the last-ditch hysteria of the diehard Europeans over the abolition of the White Highlands in 1959, and Harold Macmillan's fundamental lack of sympathy with settler colonialism[149], all appear to have made their contribution to this decision.

However disappointing it was in the end to its progenitors, multiracialism served a useful purpose in making possible for the

European farmers a peaceful and profitable transition to independence. By softening to some degree the atmosphere of confrontation it set the stage for the hard bargaining over land which took place between 1960 and 1965 and which enabled Europeans either to depart with a golden handshake or remain on their farms in relative security from any immediate prospect of takeover or division. It was the leaders of the multiracialist movement who took the lead in this bargaining, for it was they who had established the essential contacts and political habits.[150] When the freedom fighters came out of the forests to claim at last their just reward, many of them found it already spoken for.

'Gentlemen', said Kenyatta at a famous meeting with settlers at Nakuru on the eve of independence, 'let us forgive and forget.' A sigh of relief audible all over the area of European settlement went up from Nakuru, and, it is said, £1 million worth of farm equipment was ordered the next day. Overnight, hard-bitten settlers switched from loathing Kenyatta to loving him. He had given them that which, with his keen political instincts, he had divined they most wanted – the chance to stay on in their own little fiefdoms, kings of their own castles if not ministers of the Crown. What they had fought for in the end was not a political or an economic system, but a way of life, and it seemed that they were going to be allowed to keep it. Though some departed, many stayed.

The statue of Delamere in Nairobi was taken down and replaced, with appropriate ceremony, by one of Kenyatta. Delamere's monument had shown him dressed informally in open-necked shirt and cardigan, seated comfortably with his hand in his pocket. Kenyatta's shows him installed on what appears to be a throne, equipped with assorted ceremonial insignia: the resemblance to statues of Queen Victoria is striking. Iconographically, the messages are clear. Delamere dominates the scene with nothing but his own personality; Kenyatta is the great chief once in exile, come at last to the glory of office.

5

The Masai and their Masters

'Do you love me, Master? No?'
'Dearly, my delicate Ariel.'

This book would not be complete without a glance at a place where, more than any other, the ideals of colonial administration and administrative reality appeared to exist in harmony together – those rolling grasslands of the Great Rift Valley, on either side of the border between Kenya and Tanganyika, where lived the people who more than any other fascinated the Europeans who came to East Africa: the Masai. If there was a paradise in the Colonial Service, it was here, it was here, it was here.

After 1914 no further large-scale attempts were made in Kenya to take land away from the Masai, and their administrators settled down relatively undisturbed to pursue the arts of government. No one expected the pastoral Masai to go out to work *en masse* as agricultural labourers for the Europeans, and so their officers were spared the necessity of acting as labour recruiters – in itself enough to lighten the heart of any administrative officer in Kenya. In Tanganyika there were few settlers in the country, no evident injuries had been done, and the Masai, with their conspicuous but unbelligerent attachment to their traditional way of life, were perceived from the start simply as a rather interesting problem in administration. The League of Nations mandate under which Britain held Tanganyika after 1920 decreed that native interests should come first. The only question with the Masai seemed to be how best to translate benevolent intentions into administrative actuality.

There was a widespread belief in colonial East Africa that men posted to Masailand succumbed to a disease called 'Masai-itis', an emotional obsession with the Masai which destroyed their desire to

172

rule. Certainly there was the occasional spectacular apostasy from civilized values, as in the case of Jack Driberg, a Kenya Masai official who went native and then proceeded to a distinguished career as a lecturer in anthropology at Cambridge[1]; but on the whole the records, in so far as they can be relied on in such matters, do not support this view. It was not unknown for men to become peculiar, or even on occasion completely to lose their reason, in the vast spaces of Masailand, but there is no evidence that this was more likely to happen there than in other lonely postings. Nor does it seem to be the case that the notorious reluctance of the Masai to accommodate themselves to the modern world was to any significant extent the result of administrative protection from it. Social scientists who have considered the phenomenon have all agreed that there are more important reasons for it than the attitudes of administrators.[2] The Kenya administration in particular included a number of vigorous reformers, most prominent among them R.W. Hemsted and C.E.V. Buxton – both completely wrapped up in the Masai and both determined to bring them, under British supervision, into the twentieth century. Such reformers usually saw themselves as making it possible for the Masai to survive as a race: getting obsessed with the Masai was not inherently a passive occupation.

What was it exactly that made Masailand such a pleasant place for members of the British Colonial Service to be? First, and most simply, though it was not at all uncommon for administrators to feel exasperated by Masai obduracy, or disapproving of certain aspects of the Masai way of life (such as collective fornication throughout the years of early manhood), it was rare indeed for one in close contact with them to conceive a personal dislike for them. 'All Europeans who deal with the Masai inevitably, after a short period, appreciate that the Masai have certain characteristics which we, the British, deeply applaud', wrote the District Commissioner in charge of Narok in 1955.[3] He did not enumerate them, but it is not hard to reconstruct them from the records of over half a century of Masai administration.

Most administrators agreed with D. Storrs-Fox that the Masai were 'more intelligent than, and of a type superior to, the other native tribes around them'.[4] They were also admired for their military prowess, it being widely assumed that before the arrival of the British the Masai had been paramount among the tribes of East Africa; they were 'aristocrats and formerly conquered east central Africa'.[5] The British have always been prepared to give a measure of recognition to the imperial qualities of other races, especially when these races have been absorbed into their own dominions; for obvious reasons of self-esteem, conquerors especially enjoy the subjection of those who were formerly paramount. The courage of the Masai was also extolled, indeed was legendary among the British. A Masai who acquitted himself well in hand-to-hand fighting in Burma during the Second World War was allowed to keep the samurai sword he captured: 'Please do not take this sword away from this soldier', the man's commanding officer wrote on the wound tag around his neck, 'He is a Masai.'[6] The Masai furthermore had the looks which went with reckless courage and a consciousness of superior worth. Their athletic form and delicate features, reminiscent of classical heroes, were much admired. The British, of course, have not been alone in this; there is something in human nature which responds worshipfully to the sheer splendour of the Masai physical presence.

The stoicism with which the Masai endured the harsh circumstances of their lives made a deep impression on the British, and the opportunity to share that hard life and thus to display to some extent their own possession of this admirable quality was part of Masailand's attraction for many Englishmen. An officer who was not himself thus inclined complained that his predecessor (and friend) had 'considered that the man in charge of the northern area of Masailand should place himself in an atmosphere of utter discomfort; in short should become a wild man of the west and suffer privations of all kinds. If he did not follow this code then he was not a Bwana Shauri of the Masai tribe.'[7] Under these circumstances it was not surprising that Masailand developed a tradition of preternaturally forceful District Officers – men as tough and independent as the Masai themselves. In Masailand, cut off from all civilized amenities, and, if he conscientiously followed the herds instead of trying to rule the country from his office, beyond the reach even of the telegraph, a DO could enjoy as much autonomy as he liked.

Perhaps the most admirable characteristics of the Masai in the eyes of the men whose job it was to administer them were their honesty, directness, and highly developed sense of justice. They had an '*Eric, or Little by Little* schoolboy sense of honour' and were 'completely straight'.[8] Administrative reports abound with comments on the infrequency of corruption in Masai Native Councils and the amazing way in which Masai cattle thieves, once apprehended, would confess their guilt of their own free will and proudly take their medicine. It is recorded that a Masai once killed a cattle robber and then came into the district office to report the murder.[9]

Last, but definitely not least, the Masai were much esteemed by the British for their beautiful manners, especially the dignified courtesy which marked their behaviour towards Europeans. Joseph Thomson, the first European to explore Masailand, noted that 'they indulged in none of the obtrusive, vulgar inquisitiveness or aggressive impertinence which makes the traveller's life a burden to him among other native tribes'. He and his party were 'not a bit inconvenienced by crowding or annoyed by rude remarks'.[10] Fifty years later an administrative officer found the Masai to be perfect hosts: 'they do respect your privacy; men of other tribes rather fuss round you, always sure there is something they have omitted to do as hosts, thus making a nuisance of themselves – but the Masai leave you alone'.[11] English people, relying as they do on the creation of an invisible but supposedly recognizable barrier of reserve to ensure personal privacy in public places, have always been particularly appreciative of this form of tact.[12] The Masai's famous 'aloofness' contributed substantially to Englishmen's enjoyment of their company.

But the social tact of the Masai was most impressively demonstrated by the fact that they rarely asked for anything. They were never importunate, never servile; they never tried to lure Europeans into the kind of patron-client relationship which is often assumed to be vital to the functioning of the colonial psyche but which many Englishmen in fact found more annoying than gratifying. 'People in England say we slave-drive the Africans', a white Kenyan once told the journalist Richard West, 'but, my God, it's the other way round. You come back dog-tired in the evening, and they start coming up to you: somebody's stolen my wife, somebody's raped my daughter, my eyes hurt, I want a new pair of trousers . . .'[13] There was no danger of this with the Masai, who preferred to solve their problems in their own way, without the assistance of Europeans. Throughout the colonial period they made little use of the judicial system set up by the British and made few requests of their administrators. 'They are a people who ask for little but who are enormously and genuinely grateful for any help', wrote one official who witnesed a terrible drought in Masailand in the early 1960s: 'They live a hard life uncomplainingly.'[14]

The personal qualities of the Masai made them not only attractive to the British but 'attractive . . . to administer'.[15] Their officers might experience at times a tension between enjoyment of these qualities and impatience at their collective unco-operativeness, but few of them seem to have become so downhearted that they ceased to enjoy their work. The Masai, so strikingly undegraded by their encounter with imperial authority, possessed the great virtue of allowing Englishmen to exercise that authority without regret. After thirty years of British rule, observed the distinguished scholar-administrator Henry Fosbrooke, they displayed none of the distressing symptoms of that 'soul erosion', defined by him as a 'deterioration in obedience to existing moral standards, a falling off in observance of organized religion, a lack of purpose in life'[16], which seemed so often to be the result of British efforts to bring civilization to the African. When a Masai owned up to cattle raiding and invited punishment he did so in a spirit, not of insolent defiance, but of self-respect. One could assume no harm was done.

Because their demands were nil, the Masai could be approached in a way which came close to the Colonial Service's proclaimed ideal of disinterested benevolence. It seemed easier to do right by a people who wanted nothing than by peoples who clamoured for what you were not at all sure you wanted to give them. But before good government could actually begin, government in the most basic sense had to be recognizably established. The Masai were elusive, even when constantly told they had nothing to fear, and consequently the British administration found itself engaged for fifty years in a ceaseless struggle to impose on them some measure of control.

Almost everything done by the administration in Masailand had as one of its objects greater control over the Masai. Even when that object was not consciously in view most proposals for Masai development tended in practice towards that end, their essential ingredient being some measure designed to move the Masai away from the semi-nomadism they had immemorially practised towards a way of living which would make it easier for administrators to keep a benevolent eye on them. At the top of the list of reasons for developing communal ranches in Tanganyika Masailand given in the 1955 Annual Report was 'Closer control of the Masai'.[17] And the Kenya Masai Annual Report for 1927 contains a summary of policy which nicely illustrates the extent to which economic development and administrative control were associated in the official mind. Policy, the report said, was to include 'the improvement of the water supplies of the province in order to conserve the pasture, make more grazing available in dry seasons and thus make possible for the tribe a more settled and less migratory life'.[18] The association of water conservation measures with improved administrative control was apparent from the earliest days of Masai administration, and though it became fashionable in later years to talk about 'anchoring' the Masai for development purposes, administrative convenience was always a powerful interest: 'the Masai have, in my view, two outstanding needs', wrote the Provincial Commissioner of the Northern Province of Tanganyika in 1950 – 'water and discipline'.[19]

A less drastic measure often proposed for improving administrative surveillance of the Masai was the institution of regular cattle auctions. As Henry Fosbrooke of the Tanganyika administration pointed out, these would serve the dual purpose of providing an outlet for excess Masai stock and an opportunity for the transaction of administrative business; courts, for instance, could be held at cattle auctions.[20] Kenya administrators also discovered the 'importance and usefulness of [cattle] sales as a meeting place for the transaction of official business'[21], but except in wartime, when the army needed meat, veterinary quarantines imposed in response to pressure from representatives of the European livestock industry meant that such sales were not a prominent feature of life in Kenya Masai District.

The first British administrator of Tanganyika Masailand was Colonel E.D. Browne, who had been Assistant District Commissioner at Laikipia at the time of the second Masai move in 1911–13, and who came down to Tanganyika convinced that the Kenya Masai had had a rotten deal and determined to see that the Tanganyika Masai got a better one.[22] It was said of him that he would have given the Masai Africa had he been able.[23] Nevertheless, it was his firm conviction that the Masai needed 'all the administrative control we can give them'[24], and the many waterworks he constructed were designed in part to curtail their wanderings. His goal was to make the reserve habitable throughout the year and thus deprive the Masai of any excuse for straying beyond his jurisdiction.[25] During his long administration, little else was attempted. He had a poor opinion of the utility of book-learning to the Masai[26], and it was no doubt in part due to his influence that nothing was done in Tanganyika to bring education to them till the 1930s, whereas the first government school was opened in Kenya Masailand in 1921. There was always an air of mystery about Browne, and he departed in 1926 amid hints of unsavouriness. He held court during his years of office in Arusha, known to the Europeans as 'Masai' Browne and to the Africans, on account of his toping habits, as 'Bilauri' (Swahili for glass) Browne. His successor, H.C. (also 'Masai') Murrells complained that Browne depended on force of personality alone to administer the Masai rather than, as was proper, 'custom, procedure and authority ... *supported* by "personality"'.[27] He was right; Browne was a proto-DO of purest frontier type to whom rules and procedures and administrative directives were so much dustbin fodder. He got away with being what many others could only secretly aspire to be.

Browne administered the Tanganyika Masai through Swahili-speaking Masai agents whom he brought down from Kenya and deployed in ineffable ways. He responded unenthusiastically to directives issuing from Sir Donald Cameron after 1924 that some system should be found for governing the Masai through their legitimate traditional authorities. But he did rather cynically produce a proposal that the laibon (or chief religious authority) of the Tanganyika Masai, and his 'chosen men', the laigwenak, should be constituted a Masai Native Authority.[28] Browne knew the Masai well and understood how alien such a proposal was to their consensual system of politics, but nevertheless this was the beginning of a long and unavailing effort by the British to set up the laibon as chief of the Tanganyika Masai, until at last in 1933 the current occupant asked to be relieved of his office.[29]

When H.C. Murrells came to power after the departure of Browne in 1927 he attempted to devise a system of administration more in keeping with the realities of Masai political life. Like Browne, he knew that the real locus of power in the tribe was the informal councils of elders, and he proposed that government sanction be given to their authority.[30] But in his innocence – and Murrells was, administratively speaking, an innocent – he had forgotten that the first prerequisite of British control was to identify the men who would function as British agents, so that they could, in the event of unsatisfactory performance, be replaced. The Provincial Commissioner, Philip Mitchell, then near the beginning of the career which was to culminate in the governorships of Uganda and Kenya, complimented Murrells on his anthropological acumen – and advised him that the local councils of elders should 'consist where possible of one man, with three or more advisers, rather than a Committee because of the notorious weakness of Committees as executive instruments'.[31] Mitchell then forwarded to Cameron in Dar es Salaam a quite unrecognizable version of the Murrells scheme which was nothing more than a vastly elaborated edition of the existing system of administration through the laibon and laigwenak.[32] Cameron, impressed but evidently rather baffled, minuted that he approved of the proposals and found them 'entirely in accord with what we wanted and what I thought was being practised'.[33]

Reorganization followed reorganization in Masailand with indifferent results. 'We all "reorganize" the Masai when we first meet them', observed Mitchell in 1933, 'but they continue to function as they please.'[34] He knew what he was talking about: he too had put in a stint as a junior officer in the reserve in the early 1920s. Masai on the government payroll contentedly drew their salaries and accepted whatever titles were bestowed upon them, but either did nothing or interpreted their duty to be that of spokesmen for their compatriots labouring under some inconvenience inflicted on them by the government.

Though incapable of grasping the subtleties of indirect administration, Murrells was not wanting in the ambition to control. There survives a report by him of a meeting of the Masai Tribal Council – an invention of the British – at which he addressed those present in a most autocratic manner, to the point of publicly reprimanding the laibon for neglecting his duties.[35] The Masai were given 'a full and complete lecture' on the subject of forest fires, another on their 'apathetic attitude' towards water conservation, and yet another on overstocking. Missionaries were brought in to address the meeting on the advantages of a mission education. Murrells concluded by announcing the appointment of three new headmen chosen by himself and asking if there were any complaints. On this occasion there were none.

Murrells' great dream, to which he dedicated himself entirely, was to turn the Masai into a productive peasantry. To this end, he spent much of his time personally constructing dams and pipelines. His idea was that, as the Masai acquired more and more permanent waters, they would at first acquire more and more cattle; indeed, the prospect of doing so would be the incentive required to get them to pay for the water in the first place. But once a group of Masai had a permanent water supply, paid for by themselves, they would develop a sense of ownership and settle down. Then, being prevented from moving into other grazing areas by groups which had developed similar ideas of ownership, and realizing that there were limits to the carrying capacity of the land, they would sell off surplus cattle until they arrived at a perfect balance between the land and the stock residing upon it. And then – then they would take up the hoe and become farmers.[36] Thus water conservation was the solution to 'the Masai problem', which was nomadism.[37]

Like Browne before him, Murrells conducted his business mainly through Masai agents; he liked to refer cryptically in his reports to mysterious private sources of information. His superiors had complete confidence in his ability to control single-handedly 22,000 square miles of territory with virtually no roads and no telephones. When the laibon Parit died in mysterious circumstances in 1928, the Provincial Commissioner cabled Dar es Salaam that disturbances could be expected 'but Murrells will keep situation under control'.[38] Margery Perham wrote of Murrells and the Masai in 1930 that he was 'reputed to be the only man they trust'.[39] Murrells spent ten years in the reserve, kept there for the last few years against his will because Mitchell considered him indispensable.[40] In 1933 he suffered a complete 'moral and mental collapse'[41] and departed the Colonial Service. No one was ever left in Masailand for so long again.

The enthusiasm felt by British officials for Masai development, of course, far transcended the mere desire for control, urgent as this was. Control was merely the essential prerequisite to constructive administration. But few of their efforts in the field of development were blessed with success, and this contributed to the erroneous impression that nothing was attempted.

One or two of Murrells' water conservation projects were spectacularly successful, but most were failures and in the end proved an embarrassment to the administration – particularly as the method of financing he selected was an unlucky one.[42] In the name of self-help, the Masai were asked to pay for the waterworks by selling cattle. The cost was calculated in terms of the current price of slaughter stock, and so many head were then requested. Unfortunately, the price of cattle fell from £5 a head to £1 a head shortly after this arrangement was made, and the Masai found themelves being asked to pay more and more for what seemed to them to be less and less – for some of the waterworks had already begun to fail. Debt-collection became one of the administration's chief activities, until the balance was taken over by the Native Treasury in 1935, and finally discharged in 1944.

Most of the development schemes undertaken by the British in Masailand – and there were many – met a similar fate. Time and again, efforts to demonstrate a superior way of doing things backfired because some crucial element in the situation had been overlooked. Prestige was repeatedly laid on the line and lost. In 1939 the Tanganyika Forestry Department conducted an 'experiment in controlled burning against the wind' in the presence of the laibon and a large number of Masai, the object being to create a fire-break at the edge of the Roinye forest: disaster was 'only narrowly averted' when the fire got out of control.[43] There were no more experiments. In 1956–7 a mass inoculation campaign in Loliondo division against bovine pleuro-pneumonia went seriously awry and thousands of cattle died.[44] The provision of permanent waters led everywhere to overgrazing and consequent soil erosion, and veterinary quarantine regulations which interfered with the free movement of cattle both within and into and out of the reserves almost certainly contributed to the spread of tsetse fly which occurred during the colonial period.[45]

The biggest fiasco was the most ambitious scheme of all, the Masai Development Plan of the 1950s.[46] This ill-omened project appears to have been undertaken as a sort of consolation to the

Tanganyika Masai after they suffered a series of land losses, to
European settlers and to other tribes, in the late 1940s, when the
Tanganyika government came under pressure to contribute to world
food production. The idea was to clear large areas of tsetse-infested
bush and then set up ranching schemes around permanent waters.
At first, everyone concerned exuded optimism. But two years later
the earth-moving equipment to build the dams had still to arrive,
and the bush-clearing programme, optimistically assigned to the
Masai moran (men of the warrior age-group), had made no progress
at all. A mechanical bush-clearing company was called in, but it
soon became apparent that machines could not accomplish all that
was required, and labourers from other tribes were set to work. They
barely made a dent in the vast area they were supposed to cover.
The rains failed for two years in succession and the fodder crops
planted in the demonstration ranch never materialized. Land was set
aside for another ranch, and this was promptly invaded by vast
herds of plains game when rain finally fell and grass grew. By 1956
the Development Plan funds were almost exhausted – the government had contributed £200,000 – and the District Commissioner
reported that the emphasis had now shifted to attempts 'to achieve
some measure of political, social and economic development among
the Masai themselves'.[47]

Almost equally ambitious development projects were going on in
Kenya at about the same time. All of them failed, from the
disastrous Purko Sheep Ranch, where the sheep died because the
ranch was at too high an altitude[48], to the four big grazing schemes
which went under in the drought of the early 1960s, when people
from outside the schemes, under pressure of need, came in to graze
on the permanent waters and massive erosion occurred.[49]

Was it surprising that the Masai preferred to stick to their own
way of doing things? They generally co-operated with the administration to the extent of providing money for the latest schemes;
participation, of course, was another matter.

A principal object of policy in Kenya Masailand was to break the
military organization of the Masai. Many settlers found the presence
of this armed and organized people on their doorstep unnerving –
Delamere, who treated them with a lordly tolerance, conspicuously
did not – and so, conscious of the injustice which had been done, did
the administration. The Masai moran customarily spent ten to fifteen
years of warriorhood living communally, apart from their families
and under the supervision of specially designated elders, in warrior
villages, or manyattas, at the end of which time they married and
settled down. The obvious course for policy to pursue was to abolish

these manyattas, unleashing in the process the latent energy of the moran for constructive purposes.

Under the energetic Hemsted, orders were issued forbidding the building of manyattas and the carrying of spears, and the graduation ceremonies for the current age-set of warriors were hurried through. The result was a warrior rising in 1922, when the members of the Laitetti manyatta refused to disperse. After killing a number of traders and native policemen, and an elder who had counselled prudence, they took to the hills, where a detachment of the King's African Rifles surprised them and drove them out, with about twenty casualties. 'Enforced labour', wrote Hemsted, commenting upon the episode, 'is the only antidote, and among such a race as the Masai is indispensable to progress.' He did not doubt their 'capacity for culture'; it was their 'environment' which was 'fatal'.[50]

Forced labour was indeed the form taken by the administration's next major effort to deal with what had become known as the moran problem. The warriors of Narok District were put to work in 1935 building a road, the work to count in lieu of payment of taxes. At first all seemed to go well, and photographs were taken for inclusion in the annual report of cheerful and industrious moran wielding their instruments of labour. But they struck just outside Narok township and attacked the District Commissioner, Major Buxton. He ordered his men to fire, and two moran were killed. The officer in charge of the Masai Extra-Territorial District, as the reserve was now called, recommended further efforts to abolish the manyatta system, whose demise had been frequently, but prematurely, announced since 1922.[51]

Moran policy began to change with the arrival of E.H. Windley in Kajiado District in the late 1930s. Fortified with a degree in anthropology from Cambridge, Windley perceived that the significance of the manyattas was not only military but educational. In the manyattas the moran were instructed in the nature of tribal institutions and in appropriate behaviour by their guardian elders, the Ol Piron, and learned the debating skills fundamental to the Masai system of politics; they chose their leaders, or rather, leaders emerged in the democratic fellowship of manyatta life; and they learned personal discipline in observance of the prohibitions traditionally placed on moran.[52] The manyattas, Windley saw, formed 'a useful training ground for the Moran to attain cohesion, corporate spirit and in competition with each other to "Rub corners off" and maintain a degree of their virility'. They served in fact 'certain functions of a public school in this respect'.[53] The correct policy with respect to them was thus not to abolish them but to subject them to constructive supervision.

The same idea occurred to Henry Fosbrooke in Tanganyika at about the same time. He recognized that the manyattas were 'an indigenous school', an integral part of the process whereby a Masai became distinctively a Masai, and recommended that their character-building qualities be respected and adapted.[54] But curiously enough, such articulate recognition of the educational significance of the manyattas was exceptional, though administrators often behaved and wrote in ways which hinted at an implicit acknowledgement of the similarity between what went on in a Masai manyatta and what went on in the English boarding schools they had themselves attended. H.C. Baxter, who was stationed in Tanganyika Masailand in the early 1930s, was fond of using public school metaphors to describe the activities of the moran.[55] References to cattle-raiding as the favourite sport of the moran, in a tone only slightly less indulgent than that which might be used for inter-house cricket matches, were very common. And administrators who remembered the way their own adolescent energies and rivalries had been worked off in school sports tried unsuccessfully, but with remarkable persistence, to introduce football into the manyattas, believing that they were providing the moran with an attractive alternative to stock-raiding. Major Clarence Buxton did not stop at football but – like an enterprising housemaster introducing an Outward Bound programme – organized lion hunts for his moran. The Masai never accepted football as the moral equivalent of war. Their administrators had too readily supposed that the pleasure of kicking a ball across a stretch of grass was an acceptable substitute for the real danger and excitement of a raid. But the fact that they had supposed this at all suggests some appreciation of cattle-raiding's implicit purpose. These men could at least enter imaginatively into the spirit of a male institution such as the manyatta: there was something familiar about it all, even if they were not quite sure what, and this familiarity contributed to the ease they felt in the company of the Masai. Their preoccupation with the military significance of the manyattas kept them, however, from consciously appreciating the extent to which it was there that the Masai received the training responsible for those characteristics which 'we, the British, deeply applaud'.

Having grasped the educational import of the manyattas, Windley cast around for ways in which they might be adapted for administrative purposes. He was of the opinion that the Masai possessed 'a faculty for reasoned intelligence, a pride and a susceptibility to leadership and ideas which made them amenable to sympathetic handling'.[56] But in 1938 he could only suggest that the manyattas be brought as far as possible under administrative control and the moran 'encouraged in any activities to maintain their manliness such as sports, road work, or their lion-hunting with spears'.[57] It was only in 1946 that he came up with a practical scheme for using the manyattas for higher purposes. He proposed a 'Moran training camp' which would 'supplement the indigenous system with more direct educative purpose, introducing some of our ideas on personal training and discipline to ensure bringing the young men of the tribe to hand under our guidance in the early stages of their Moranhood'.[58]

The camp programme was outlined by Windley in some detail. The day would begin with gymnastic exercises before breakfast, the moran being organized in sections, each with a leader chosen by themselves. After breakfast they would

> work for two or three hours on the School of Animal Husbandry bush clearing or fencing. In the afternoon they should have a lecture and alternative football with sports practice. A cinema show or film strip could be shown once a week. Wrestling matches should be held and possibly boxing tried. At the end of each course sports with prizes should be held and a bullock given as a prize to the best drill squad and all round "Sirit" [company] whose instructor might also be rewarded. Two "Il Piron" elders should be chosen as full time retainers to assist in the supervision of the course and the handling of the Moran, giving lectures on Tribal custom. Toxophily might be introduced and possibly elementary reading and writing later on.

Any resemblance to the programme later pursued in the Mau Mau rehabilitation camps was not coincidental. Windley rose to be Chief Native Commissioner of Kenya in the mid-1950s and was one of the moving spirits of re-education.

Windley intended that the first camp should be started just before the next batch of moran formed their manyattas, so that those who passed through it would then be an influence for good on their fellows. A European officer would be in charge, assisted by three African NCOs, one of whom, it was hoped, would be Shartuyan ole Rendeo, the man who had won the Japanese sword. Windley was anxious to avoid any misunderstanding as to the purpose of the camp; the main things, he emphasized, were to be flexible and 'to treat the Moran with the greatest good humour and avoid any suspicion of it being a labour camp. The iron hand in the velvet glove is really the key to handling them.'

The Moran training camp never materialized in quite the form Windley envisaged, the Masai, as usual with administrative projects, declining to extend their co-operation beyond token financial contributions. A number of attempts were made to introduce such courses in the next few years, but as experiments in applied anthropology they were all failures. There were, after all, rather obvious problems of legitimacy involved. If the Masai had an educational system of their own which was functioning well according to their own criteria, there was no reason for them to view with favour the introduction into it, by people whose hegemony they accepted but did not welcome, of alien elements.

In 1948, after a spate of stock-raiding, an officer was appointed with special responsibility for the moran – a Mr Holford-Walker. Policy was now to allow the moran to form manyattas 'and then to exercise control over them, and to use up their surplus energy in making them work'[59], the theory being that if the moran were in manyattas, at least the administration knew where they were. In spite of Holford-Walker's best efforts, the moran evaded his supervision. They built manyattas, but were not to be found in them; they were Potemkin manyattas, the real ones flourishing in inaccessible places.[60] The attempt to bring the moran system under administrative control was deemed a failure, and policy in Kenya shifted once again in the direction of abolition. When independence came in 1963, the moran were there to greet it with their manyattas intact.

Clearly, a sympathetic interest in the Masai was not at all incompatible with the itch to administer, improve, and even, selectively, to destroy. How was it, then, that Masailand acquired its reputation for corrupting those sent to rule over it?

Though the archival evidence shows that if the Masai did not change it was not for want of trying on the part of the administration, it was convenient in some quarters to suppose that it was. There were two groups in East Africa who had a direct interest in discrediting Masai administration and suggesting that officials were 'soft' on the Masai: these were, most importantly, the white settlers who wanted Masai land for farming, and enthusiasts for wildlife conservation who wanted the Masai driven out of areas where their interests were believed to conflict with those of game. District Officers in Masailand regularly defended the Masai against attempts to alienate their land, and in the process acquired a reputation for tender-heartedness. In the eyes of those who believed that the Masai were decorative but unproductive idlers sitting on land that could be put to better use, the unco-operative attitude of district officials was mere romantic obstructionism, proof positive that they had been bewitched by the Masai. But there is evidence to suggest that this was not the case – that it was in fact the district officials who were reasonable men, and not their critics among the settlers and the faunophiles.

In Kenya, though there was relatively little pressure for further alienation of Masai land after the second Masai move, what pressure there was was resisted by the administration, and R.W. Hemsted tried repeatedly to retrieve for the Masai the land alienated to Powys Cobb, which contained streams of crucial importance to Masai stock.[61] In Tanganyika, however, the Masai enjoyed what many Europeans considered to be an absurdly privileged position and envious eyes were cast on Masai District. F.J. Anderson, a settler with a farm at Rasha Rasha, was the spokesman for those who felt that Masai District was wasted on the Masai. In a Legislative Council meeting in 1937 he accused the government of pampering the Masai and condoning such 'vile practices' as 'the repeated rape of immature girls' in manyattas.[62] Nothing was said on this occasion about his interest in Masai land, though he appears to have discussed the subject privately with F.C. Hallier, the Provincial Commissioner of the Northern Province, in October 1937.[63] In 1942, after a long preamble once again accusing the government of 'favouritism' towards the Masai, he asked in the Legislative Council if a thousand square miles of Masailand could be set aside for 'settlement of fighting services personnel, when their job of destroying our foul enemies, who would make slaves of the Masai, is completed'.[64] The request was refused on the grounds that the Masai needed the land – a response which must have confirmed Anderson's dim view of the administration. It seemed to him and other settlers whose views he represented in the Leg. Co. that Masai-loving administrators were allowing these useless people to tie up many thousands of acres of valuable agricultural land.

To the administrators concerned with the welfare of the Masai, however, it seemed that they had a very good case for keeping the enormous area which had been assigned to them. Notwithstanding their impulse to improve, most officials came to recognize, after a year or two in Masailand, that on the whole the Masai made remarkably efficient use of the land. It became apparent to them that the Masai did not wander haphazardly about, ignorantly destroying grazing and oblivious to the control of cattle disease, but had an indigenous system of pasture management and far more understanding of the nature of cattle disease than settlers, and even the Veterinary Department, supposed. The archives contain some extremely impressive examples of recognition by administrators of the fundamental rationality of Masai pastoralism, at a time when pastoralism was generally considered to be merely a primitive prelude to the development of agriculture, and pastoralists obsolete relics of an earlier phase of human history.[65] By the time they left Masailand, most administrators would have agreed with what J.C. Clarke said of the Masai in his annual report for 1950: 'Their advocate', he wrote, 'is Nature.'[66]

Once it was understood that the Masai used a system of rotational grazing, and that the uncertain climate of Masailand demanded flexibility from them in their movements, it was evident that, far from having too much land, they probably had too little. Their administrators then proceeded to act in accordance with what they took to be the finest traditions of their service and stood up for them.

This meant that the District Officers' opposition to the proposals of wildlife conservationists who wanted Masai land was just as uncompromising as their opposition to settlers; and, then as now, the appearance of indifference to the interests of picturesque and harmless animals brought down odium on the heads of those presumed guilty of it. Murrells opposed the creation of a national park in the Ngorongoro crater, and put on record his desire to 'protest most emphatically against the theory that where the interests of game and the Masai clash the Masai must go'.[67] Later administrators simply argued, correctly, that the Masai did no harm to game. Though the exact nature of the symbiosis between pastoralists and plains game has only recently become understood[68], administrators in close contact with the Masai could see that somehow the two did co-exist, and they took exception to the idea that in order for game to thrive the Masai would have to be removed. For their pains, they were written off as sentimental adulators of the noble savage. There could be no better evidence that this was not the case than the careers of Murrells and of S.W. Fraser-Smith, who was District Commissioner of the Tanganyika Masai from 1952 to 1955. Fraser-Smith was a vigorous defender of the tribe's right to live in the Serengeti national park, but deplored the moran system and worked hard in the face of what he repeatedly referred to as their 'stultifying conservatism' to make the Masai appreciate the benefits of modern ranching.[69]

Where administrators might justly be accused of partiality in land questions, however, was in cases involving the relations of the Masai with other tribes. They quite failed to understand, for instance, that the Masai lived, and had always lived, in close interdependence with their agricultural neighbours, who were trading partners and sources of wives and cereals, as need arose. It was common in Kenya for Masai to allow Kikuyu to cultivate a patch of ground within their grazing circuit in return for services rendered; but administrators seeing this practice and not realizing its customary nature tried repeatedly to get rid of the Kikuyu and leave the Masai in undisputed possession of what they supposed to be their sole territory.[70] In doing so they helped to create resentments against the Masai in the minds of those who came to power in the post-colonial state. Administrators also reacted with less than a becoming degree of sympathy to the problems of neighbouring agricultural peoples whose population was outstripping their resources in land. From time to time the Tanganyika government proposed excision of parts of Masailand for the use of other tribes[71], and Masai District Officers could be relied on to oppose these proposals. But it is difficult to know whether their defence of the Masai in such cases should be attributed to the peculiarly seductive qualities of this people, or to the well-documented tendency of District Officers throughout British Africa to become closely identified, in a paternal and proprietary way, with the interests of 'their' tribe.

Whatever might have been the prosaic reason for his initial posting to Masai District, an officer who stayed long enough and had a sufficiently striking personality could expect to become locally famous not only for his love of the Masai but also for the love they bore for him. Men like Murrells and Browne, and Major Clarence Buxton in Kenya, were celebrated as much for the influence they supposedly wielded over the Masai as for their partiality for them – 'Murrells will keep situation under control'. Even so unsentimental a man as Sir Donald Cameron was completely in awe of the Browne legend. He gave it as his opinion in 1926, shortly before Browne's inglorious departure, that the current state of affairs in Masai District represented 'indirect administration in its purest form', and thought this happy circumstance could mostly be credited to Browne, whom the Masai 'greatly respect and honour'.[72] Side by side with the suspicion that Masailand somehow emasculated its administrators, there grew up in East Africa a conviction that the proud Masai could be successfully handled only by the finest type of Englishman, whose qualities of honesty and good judgement they instinctively recognized and respected. The assumption became that the men who were assigned to Masai District were 'picked men', exemplars of the finest ideals of the Colonial Service. 'The Masai, quicker than any race in Africa', wrote an American admirer of the Colonial Service, 'will spot a second-rater. And have no use for him.' After watching a *baraza* conducted by two Masai administrators in Kenya, this observer (Negley Farson) wrote:

> I could not imagine a German, Italian or even a Frenchman being so patient in such a discussion. The British administrators were patient because they knew that the whole of the Masai respect for them lay in

the fact that their judgments – to a fighting race – must come as from honest and intelligent men.[73]

In 1935, after the Murrells *débâcle* and the dawning realization that very little which could be described as administration had gone on in Masai District, the Tanganyika government did in fact begin to give some serious thought to the type of man which should be sent there. The recommendations finally made were of a highly practical nature, but they established a tradition of careful selection which was easily glamorized in both the public and the official mind. The requisites were that

the Masai officers should be of exceptional physique, preferably unmarried (though this has disadvantages) but, if married, then without children; that their wives shd. be happy in solitary surroundings, and that they (the men) should, if possible, be able to pick up Masai and shd. have leanings towards the study of native customs. They must also be willing to go and have their heart in their job.

Frequent leave was recommended 'in order to regain sanity of outlook after long periods of loneliness', and it was later added that: 'Intellectual geniuses are not required, nor anyone with "nerves" or who is likely to become "Masai-astic" . . . i.e. regard themselves as specialists'. A background in anthropology was, however, thought desirable.[74]

Settlers, too, when they got the opportunity, liked to bask in what they supposed to be the approbation of the Masai. It was believed in Kenya that when a Masai came to work for you it was a kind of accolade. 'Members of this tribe were by no means ready to work for any European who asked them to', wrote Elspeth Huxley; 'They were very particular and only entered the service of men whom they liked.'[75] And no one in the administration ever – such is the unfairness of life – quite achieved the renown achieved by Lord Delamere as a great white father to the Masai. Delamere told Margery Perham in 1929 that he 'would take land from the Masai tomorrow for farms. I would take it from any nomads. They don't use it. They can't keep it from those who do.'[76] But he spent his evenings with his Masai shepherds and considered himself, in certain respects, a spokesman for the tribe. He defended the Masai's right not to go to school, and opposed their forcible recruitment into the King's African Rifles during the First World War.[77] When the moran of the Purko section rose in 1918, in protest against recruitment, all operations against them were suspended while

Delamere, at his own request, was allowed to go into the reserve and negotiate with the rebels. He arrived at Narok 'with the intention of using his influence to bring the Moran to reason'[78], and left several weeks later with a promise that the recruits would be forthcoming. 'Government', Denys Finch Hatton wrote to his friend Kermit Roosevelt, '. . . panicked and sent for Delamere who seems to have gone down there with a boy and a cook and settled the whole thing.'[79] But no recruits ever appeared. The Masai promised Delamere everything and delivered nothing.

The foregoing should help to explain why the British so persistently entertained the improbable notion that the Masai were 'loyal': the wish was father to the thought. The Masai, wrote the District Commissioner of Narok in 1955, reciprocate the friendship of 'all races who show themelves to be worthy, in Masai eyes, of this friendship'.[80] The belief that the Masai were loyal followed from the belief that the Masai and the British were capable of appreciating each other's qualities.

It followed, too, from the assumptions that the British made about the Masai's conservatism, it appearing self-evident to them that because the Masai were so conspicuously uninterested in Western civilization they were in all respects content with the *status quo*; so closely were Westernization and agitation linked in the administrative mind. As Westernizing tribes like the Kikuyu became more and more politically active, it was only natural to look to the Masai, who showed no interest in either taxation or representation, as a potential 'counterpoise to the agitator class'.[81] 'The Masai rank as a backward tribe in Kenya', wrote the ever-optimistic Windley,

> but I have been led in my experience to believe that they possess a natural intelligence and character which if properly guided and consistently handled should lead them to play a useful part in the synthesis of tribal life in Kenya . . . as a factor for stability in political development . . .'[82]

H.A. Fosbrooke even believed that it might be possible to educate them without danger to the state. The really bright ones would become genuine leaders, and the drop-outs, who notoriously contributed to agitation in other tribes, would be 'sucked into the vortex of conservatism' and be indistinguishable from their uneducated fellows.[83] Grumble as they might about the Masai's unbudging attachment to their traditional ways, many administrators, particularly in the later years, came to see that it had its advantages. One Kenya Masai official, believing that there was 'a case for the preservation of this people in a fairly pure state as a set off against more politically minded peoples', asked for a doctor to be stationed at Kajiado for this purpose.[84] The fate of this officer is instructive. He was speared to death six years later by a Masai whose favourite bullock he insisted on requisitioning for a government destocking programme.

The administration was always discomposed by evidence of Masai unfaithfulness, reacting to it with pained surprise if not outright disbelief. When the Masai resident in Sanya Chini, stimulated by the activities of the Arusha-Moshi Lands Commission, formed a branch of the Tanganyika African Association in 1946, their DO expressed extreme scepticism about their being really interested: '. . . I cannot believe that the Masai, as I know them, would have applied for membership of an association of which they must be completely ignorant'.[85] A few years later, when Masai rights of occupancy in the Serengeti were at issue, some influential Masai resident in the national park joined the Meru Citizens' Union. The DO at that time assured his superiors that these Masai were highly unrepresentative: the 'Masai tribe as a whole will have nothing to do with political agitators'.[86] When a Masai killed a European farmer in the Sanya corridor – from which the Masai had been evicted – in 1955, it was the shame and distress of all the other Masai which were emphasized by the administration.[87]

But the reddest faces of all blossomed during the Mau Mau Emergency. From the beginning of the Emergency, Nairobi was abuzz with rumours that the government had a secret weapon – the Masai, who, given the chance, would be delighted to take care of the Kikuyu. The only problem was how to set them loose in a manner not too blatantly contravening all the rules of civilized warfare.[88] In the reserve the Masai were 'anxiously watched for signs which would indicate that they had decided to come out actively on our side'.[89] Nothing happened. In January 1953 Holford-Walker, the former Moran Officer, arrived in Kajiado with orders to muster a Masai force for anti-terrorist operations in the Aberdares. In due course, ninety moran marched off to the mountains, embodying, unbeknown to them, the proudest traditions of the British Colonial Service. They were back within a fortnight. What happened is not clear, but it seems the moran displayed a certain lack of enthusiasm: 'in the conditions prevailing one week saw the limit of their usefulness', was the cryptic summary of the Kajiado DO.[90] No more was heard for a while about how the Masai were straining to get at the Kikuyu.

Later on in the Emergency, after insurgents stuck for supplies began stealing Masai cattle, the Masai were persuaded to take a more active role. 'Fighting manyattas' were formed at the request of the administration in 1955, and a 'renaissance of the Masai fighting spirit of old' was detected.[91] Some stolen stock was allowed to be recovered by the traditional method – not, it can be imagined, without amusement on the part of the Masai, who had spent forty years resisting the government's efforts to abolish that fighting spirit which was now deemed so commendable. But by then the military phase of the Emergency was nearly over, and apart from the odd border patrol, the Masai were given no further opportunity to distinguish themselves in battle.

The failure of the Masai to 'come out' on the side of right was embarrassing enough, but that was not the worst of it. Evidence that oathing was going on in the reserve was at first dismissed with the claim that the Masai involved were 'half-and-halfs', that is, the offspring of a Masai father and a Kikuyu mother: the loyalty of the 'pure Masai' was thought to be beyond question.[92] But by 1954 it was confidentially estimated by the Narok administration that at least 85 per cent of the Masai living on the Mau, Melili and the plains had taken the Mau Mau oath.[93] This staggering figure could not easily be explained away. Nevertheless, it was necessary to attempt do so: the alternative was to confess that the administration had failed where it most wanted to succeed.[94]

With the approach to independence, when the game at last was clearly lost, administrators began to permit themselves a certain degree of cynicism about the loyalty of the Masai.[95] They watched with detachment, and even with satisfaction, as the Masai began at the eleventh hour to organize themselves to resist what they feared would be the encroachment of agricultural peoples on their land, not as traditional appendages of the Masai way of life, but as conquerors armed with all the power of the modern state. This was what came, the DOs told the Masai, of ignoring their advice. Failing to be loved, they settled, like disappointed parents, for being right.

In most of Africa and Asia the British could justify their presence in terms of the white man's burden: there was work to do, and justice to be done. In Masailand neither of these considerations very obviously applied. It was never really clear, in any practical sense, just what burden the white man was supposed to take up. The Masai were perfectly adapted to their physical environment. They needed no advice in that quarter. They had also created for themselves a moral environment to which few Englishmen found they could take serious exception. There were no great inequalities of wealth or power, no privileged class whose evil propensities the British felt bound to extinguish. Justice was dispensed mildly, equitably, and democratically: there was no equivalent of the prison-cages of Malaya which fuelled Hugh Clifford's supply of righteous indignation. Paradoxically, it was in this administrative vacuum that many members of the Colonial Service felt they had come into their own.

This surely suggests the extreme importance in the imperial mind of certain forms of display. Though it is mistaken to suppose that the British made no effort to leave the Masai better than they found them, it is clear that their potential emergence from the colonial period much as they had entered it was something their administrators could in the end accept with equanimity. The essential function of the Masai was to provide the perfect opportunity for the British to display what they believed to be their finest characteristics as a ruling race: the ability to understand and to gain the respect of proud traditional peoples, the self-discipline to treat them with courtesy, and the moral authority to guide and control them without resort to brute force. In the Masai the British believed they had found an audience capable of appreciating their own greatness of soul. The almost complete lack of response, one way or the other, from the Masai, only seems to have encouraged these fantasies, because it provided an environment in which fantasy was rarely tested against reality. When reality did begin to break in, as it inevitably did towards the end, the British were unprepared for it. In superfluity, it now became apparent, they had found satisfaction.

6

The Meaning of
Indirect Rule

We can now address ourselves to that much discussed but much misunderstood phenomenon of British imperial thinking in the early decades of the twentieth century, the glorification of 'Indirect Rule' and its elevation into an official doctrine of imperial administration. Indirect Rule was not, as was claimed at the time, just a pragmatic response to circumstances, or a way of breaking the natives in gently to the rigours of civilized living. Still less was it – as it was later perceived to have been – a symptom of a fatal weakening of imperial nerve. It was the culmination of that mystique of rule which had first flowered in the Punjab under John and Henry Lawrence fifty years before, and whose objective basis in reality was now almost universally taken for granted.

Ruling indirectly was of course nothing new for the British. Malaya, the princely states of India, Fiji, Natal, the Gambia, had all experienced some form of indirect administration. In expanding their empire, the British had habitually sought out local agents through whom to impose their authority, and though these arrangements often broke down after the initial period of contact, sometimes they did not. Nor was Britain the only colonial power to incorporate existing native rulers into a system of colonial administration. The Dutch did so in the East Indies, and all the European nations in Africa made use of chiefs to some extent. The British liked to think their system was different from the others, but it is not easy, in examining the literature, to discover exactly where in practice the difference lay. We can only conclude that it was chiefly in the enthusiasm with which the British talked about it all.

It was in the years between the First and Second World Wars that this enthusiasm was at its height. The faithful elucidated the mysteries of Indirect Rule with the theological rapture of early Christians disclosing to themselves the nature of the Trinity. Critics

194

raised their voices with the consciousness of challenging a ruling orthodoxy. All sorts and conditions of native societies were declared to be suitable candidates for it, even when they possessed, to Western eyes, no discernible political organization at all, and so no evident agency through which indirection might be achieved. Such societies were scoured for individuals to whom some shreds of legitimate authority appeared to cling, with sometimes comic, sometimes tragic, results. Like getting wrapped up in the Masai, getting wrapped up in Indirect Rule was not inherently a passive occupation; it seems in retrospect extraordinary that something to which so much energy was in fact devoted should ever have been perceived as a sign of imperial decrepitude.

Indirect Rule with capital letters was born in Northern Nigeria in the first decade of the twentieth century, as a result of Sir Frederick Lugard's compulsion to justify and elaborate in writing his decision to administer the newly conquered Fulani emirates by installing a British Resident at each of the emirate courts. Blessed for a military man with unusual fluency with the pen, Lugard brought to this task a literary energy and a crusading passion which seem to have mesmerized those who heard him into believing that a discovery of the first importance in the field of imperial administration had just been made. Before his appointment to the governorship of Nigeria, Lugard had achieved a modest celebrity as the hero of various military adventures on the imperial frontier, usually of a highly individual and insubordinate kind; by the time he left Nigeria in 1919 his fame as both a practitioner and a theorist of imperialism was assured. His *Political Memoranda*, written for the instruction of his Residents in the period 1902 to 1905 and published in 1906, were revered as the canonical texts of Indirect Rule, and his administrative record, as Hugh Clifford discovered upon succeeding him as governor of Nigeria, was regarded as beyond criticism.

The persuasiveness of Lugard's arguments owed something to his extraordinary personal reputation, which happened to conform to that of the finest imperial type. Uninterested in material things, and conspicuously more at home in jungles than in drawing rooms, he possessed a sweet distinction of bearing which impressed itself on all who met him. One of his Residents reported that in his presence he felt himself become transparent, every aspect of his character laid bare to Lugard's innocent penetration.[1] Like Gordon and Henry Lawrence before him, Lugard was revered as a soldier-saint; like them there was a glory about his head which cast its light on all he did.

Yet nothing could be more surprising than that Sir Frederick Lugard should have been the father of Indirect Rule, a system of administration supposedly distinguished by the judicious delegation of authority. The delegation of authority, as Lugard's admiring but scrupulous biographer, Margery Perham, admits, was quite foreign to his nature. So obsessed was he with the details of administration that he saw nothing inappropriate, while Governor-General of Nigeria, in personally composing a memorandum on the issue of chamber pots to second-class administrative officers: he was, he said, against it.[2] He never developed a proper Secretariat for the Nigerian government and confided in no one but his devoted brother, whom he appointed his Political Secretary. He was a passionate tourer, always in motion, descending on his Residents with floods of instructions which resumed their unceasing flow as soon as he returned to headquarters; and long before Northern Nigeria was brought under effective British occupation, he was composing his *Political Memoranda*, which in addition to his reflections on the subject of Indirect Rule contained instructions to his officers of a comprehensiveness simply beyond satire. At a period when Residents had no clerks and were lucky if they possessed a typewriter, Lugard was listing some thirty different sets of records which either had to be kept or sent in, dealing with every conceivable aspect of a fully developed civil administration from postal matters to canoe registration.[3] This was not a man who was capable of being serious about the devolution of power, and we must seek the reasons for his adoption and promotion of Indirect Rule elsewhere.

Lugard in fact created in Northern Nigeria a type of Residential system which was unprecedentedly (for the British) explicit in its assumption of administrative authority in native affairs. The word Resident normally implied, at least officially, a preponderance of diplomatic over administrative duties, but it was clear from the beginning that a Lugardian Resident was expected to take on a large number of purely administrative tasks. In Nigeria, it was the Resident's task, not the emir's, to assess the people for taxes and to see that the tax was collected. It was the Resident, not the emir, who controlled the police and the army. The emir was not permitted to legislate, to appropriate land for public or commercial purposes, to exercise any control over aliens in his territory, or to appoint or depose his subordinate chiefs. His court of justice, while technically independent and free to operate on traditional lines, was in fact under the close supervision of the Resident, who exercised powers in respect of such courts as to 'enable him', in Lugard's words, 'to entirely control their actions, and, in fact, to use them as auxiliary courts'.[4] It is not obvious, in reviewing this system, exactly where the element of indirection came in, except in so far as the Residents were instructed to maintain at all costs the 'prestige' of the emir.

Lugard also laid down an elaborate protocol for dealing with the emirs and chiefs, who were to be treated by British officers with the precise degree of courtesy – and no more – which their rank deserved.[5] A first-class chief was to be offered a carpet, rather than a rug, to sit on, and the Resident was to rise both to receive him and to dismiss him. He was not to be summoned at short notice or dropped in on, but was to be treated as one would a man whose time was as valuable as one's own. Lugard prided himself on the consideration with which he treated the emirs on his own visits to their courts. 'I am very pleased with my visit to Kano', he wrote to its emir, 'and I am glad to have seen you again, for I regard you as my personal friend, in whom I place entire confidence and trust.' Forwarding a copy of this letter to his wife, he added that 'I quite squirm at the thought lest some successor to me in the near future should treat these chiefs in a different manner from my own'. But, he went on, it was equally if not more dreadful to him to think that this successor might treat the emirs 'as superiors – as Royalties', thereby incurring 'their astonished contempt that the King's representative – the conquering dynasty – should so behave'.[6]

Lugard's sense of the rights of conquest was pronounced, and his belief in Indirect Rule implied no weakening of it. On his entry into Sokoto in 1903 to accept the surrender of the sultan and his chiefs, he addressed them as follows:

> Now these are the words which I, the High Commissioner, have to say for the future. The Fulani in old times under Dan Fodio conquered this country. They took the right to rule over it, to levy taxes, to depose kings and to create kings. They in turn have by defeat lost their rule which has come into the hands of the British. All these things which I have said the Fulani by conquest took the right to do now pass to the British . . .[7]

There was nothing equivocal about that; nor was there about the oath of allegiance the emirs were required to take, which recognized the undisputed sovereignty in all matters, saving that of religion, of the British government. There were a number of episodes of armed resistance to British authority during the early years of occupation, and they were dealt with in a fashion amply sufficient to deter.

Why, then, did Lugard choose to impose his authority in Nigeria through a facade of native institutions, and not in some other fashion? His reasons for adopting Indirect Rule were never, in fact, made very explicit, though it appears that scarcity of administrative manpower, usually considered the determining factor, was not of major importance. In his *The Dual Mandate in British Tropical Africa* (1922) he referred obscurely to considerations of 'policy' as well as of economy which had guided his thinking.[8] He seems to have decided long before assuming responsibility for the government of Northern Nigeria that in general some form of indirect administration was 'in accordance with the spirit of British colonial rule', which was benevolent and not 'arbitrary and despotic'.[9] He went out to Nigeria in 1900 with his mind already made up to employ such a system, once he had conquered the country.[10]

His predisposition was reinforced by further acquaintance with the Fulani, whose 'regeneration' he decided it was worth attempting.[11] He was also aware of the military advantages of creating a nucleus of support for the British among the country's ruling class.[12] But none of these explains the tireless persistence with which he both articulated and sought to reconcile the contradictory aspects of his thinking. The interesting fact was that Lugard united in his person, in an exceptionally dramatic and compulsive fashion, the two opposing but eternally co-existing currents of British imperial thought: the desire to be powerful, and the desire to be good. It is here that we shall find the explanation for the lively inconsistency of his thinking, masked though it was by the illusion of sweet reason he seemed able to create at will.

Both Lugard's parents were missionaries in India, but his father came from a family of soldiers and himself possessed military rank as a chaplain in the Madras establishment of the East India Company. The young Lugard, born in the year after the Mutiny, was brought up, like Henry Lawrence whom he came so much to resemble, in an atmosphere which combined sincere evangelical piety with unquestioning respect for the achievements of the British army and an habitual acceptance of the necessity of command. Though Lugard later lost the simple faith of his childhood, he never lost the evangelical habit of spiritual self-scrutiny which had been so pronounced in him as a boy that his mother at one time feared that 'possibly (though now in perfect health) our Father may be about to remove him to the heavenly garner'. On the morning of his sixth birthday, she wrote,

> he was found to be crying silently in his bed ... Miss Liley [the governess] hearing his quiet sobs went to him. He told her he had been thinking of the text he had just learnt, 'Prepare to meet thy God,' and perhaps he might die tonight, and he did not know if he was ready, if his sins were all forgiven ...
> He told me that ... there were 5 sins he could remember to-day,

besides a great many sins that he knew he had done that he could not remember. The 5 sins were such things as letting his Bible fall by accident, jumping about for a few minutes on the sabbath, forgetting that it was Sunday, and hesitating to lend his sister a book which she asked him for.[13]

Without disparaging the spiritual discipline practised in the Lugard home, it seems fair to say that young Freddy, who even then possessed a lively truculence, studied too assiduously to be good.

As a man, Lugard combined a passionate love of command with an equally passionate desire not to be judged unkindly for it. He was constantly reassuring himself that actions taken in the heat of the moment, and in response to his deepest impulses, possessed a visibly moral quality. 'I love this turgid life of command', he wrote to his wife,

> when I can feel that the sole responsibility rests on me for everything, whether it be a small crisis like this [the Munshi rising], with the necessary action taken to preserve life, and to re-establish prestige or whether it be, as my day's task has been, to confirm the hanging of criminals or the penal servitude, or the petty punishments of others, watching jealously that the executive officer does not inflict punishments which are unfair, or that the legal adviser does not hamper true justice by technical objections.[14]

And he could write after a visit to Kano, with a degree of self-deception which reminds one of Sir Frederick Weld, that, though a mere two years before 'Kano was armed to fight us . . . Today I drank tea alone and unarmed with the Emir as his honoured friend, and I know he is really glad to see me . . .'[15] What had made this miracle possible, in Lugard's view, was Indirect Rule, which, through its generosity of spirit towards the conquered, had transformed militant antagonism into grateful appreciation.

Lugard was later to develop a more elaborate reconciliation of the moral with the amoral aspects of imperialism in *The Dual Mandate in British Tropical Africa*, written after he was removed from the daily turmoil of administration and in retirement in England. With its simple thesis that 'the tropics are the heritage of mankind'[16], to be developed for the benefit of all, including their inhabitants, and its emphasis on the excellence of the British record in these respects and the desirability of prolonging it, the book had an immensely affirmative influence. Reading it, the British discovered that they had been speaking the imperial equivalent of prose all their lives. In *The Dual Mandate* past dominion was justified, present dominion was celebrated, and future dominion looked forward to with serenity. Whatever Indirect Rule meant to Lugard, it never meant the end of the British empire.

Nor did it mean such a thing to any of the other administrators prominently associated with it. Charles Temple, Richmond Palmer, Donald Cameron, Philip Mitchell – none of these were men who showed anything less than enthusiasm for the task of imperial government, and all of them were men of dominant personality and exceptional strength of will. African independence, when they thought of it at all, seemed an eventuality so far into the future as to possess no relevance to their working lives.

The spirit at work in Northern Nigeria was in every respect far closer to that at work in the Punjab in the 1850s than in the United Nations in the 1950s. For what Lugard unintentionally and ironically created through Indirect Rule was an outstanding opportunity for subordinate officials to claim an immense – and to him unwelcome – autonomy within the system. Despite his best efforts to concentrate power effectively within his own hands, the emphasis on local authority implicit in a system purporting to operate through the traditional rulers of a primitive country, which possessed nothing approaching a unitary state co-extensive with its official boundaries, inevitably meant that power would drain away from the centre towards the local administrator, who alone could claim the special knowledge of local conditions, and opportunity for intimate supervision, on which Indirect Rule implicitly depended. The importance attached to maintaining the 'prestige' of the emirs soon translated in practice into the importance of maintaining the autonomy of the Residents, and subsequent governors of Nigeria found almost without exception that Lugard had created an administrative monster which it was beyond their power to control. In the early 1900s the initiative was with those lower down in the governing hierarchy than Lugard, and being the men they were, they took it.

It was during the inter-regnum of 1907 to 1912, when Lugard was occupied as governor of Hong Kong before returning in triumph to be Governor-General of a united Nigeria, that the Northern Residents seized their opportunity to move collectively into a position of virtually unassailable independence from the central government. Two rather weak governors, who regarded Lugard's Residents with some of the reverence they felt for Lugard himself, were ruthlessly overawed and changes introduced – such as the creation of native treasuries – by which the Residents acquired over their little ships of state an ever more complete control.[17]

It did not take long upon his return from Hong Kong for Lugard's sensitive nose to detect an atmosphere of insubordination in Northern Nigeria. A year after his arrival he was complaining to his wife of 'a disloyalty and a swollen-headedness which had spoiled N.N. Every Resident, including the best, writes at large on the policy we must pursue . . . The Governor is left out.'[18] On his tours he felt excluded from direct contact with the emirs and, worse, not particularly welcome in the Residencies. The worst offender in this was Charles Temple, who was senior Northern Resident at the time of Lugard's return. When Lugard arrived in October 1912 on a state visit to Zungeru, Temple not only failed to vacate his headquarters for Lugard's use, as Lugardian protocol apparently demanded, but left the Governor-General to remain on his official train and bake in the African sun. It was an unhappy start to what proved to be a contentious relationship, with Lugard wanting to turn the clock back to the days of his undisputed pre-eminence, and Temple, whose sense of his own consequence was equally developed, treating him as *primus* (barely) *inter pares*.

Temple disagreed with Lugard over almost everything, but above all over the degree of authority to be exercised from the centre. His scheme for the amalgamation of Nigeria, which Lugard had been sent out to accomplish, differed completely from the one proposed by Lugard: Lugard's scheme envisaged a strong governor, Temple's a weak one, with the responsibility for local affairs placed firmly in the hands of the Residents. From this struggle Lugard emerged the official victor. His scheme was the one adopted. But in practice he found himself able to control the Residents only by appointing men he deemed to be sufficiently compliant, an expedient to which he resorted when Temple retired prematurely from the service in 1917.

Less aggravating in manner than Temple, Richmond Palmer, the Resident at Katsina, stood higher in gubernatorial favour. But his career, especially after 1925, when the weak and ailing Sir Graeme Thomson succeeded Hugh Clifford in the governorship, also classically expressed the Residential impulse towards autonomy.[19]

Under Clifford, Palmer bided his time, keeping to himself his misgivings about the governor's achievements in centralization, and exerting himself openly only to oppose Clifford's proposal that lawyers should be allowed to plead in the provincial courts, thereby unacceptably diluting what had been under Lugard the Resident's almost unrestricted jurisdiction over them. No doubt Palmer's restraint was related to the very high and advantageous esteem in which Clifford held him – high enough to appoint him, over the head of a more experienced officer, to the Lieutenant-Governorship of the Northern Provinces. An accomplished traveller, linguist, and student of natives ways, unmasker (in 1924) of a Mahdist plot to eject the British from Northern Nigeria, Palmer was in every way Clifford's idea of what a colonial administrator ought to be.

Once Clifford had departed Palmer set to work to wring from the central government a series of concessions which, had he succeeded in obtaining them all, would have converted Northern Nigeria into a separate state. His persistent returns to the fray helped to drive Thomson to an early grave – though not before he had succeeded in getting Palmer promoted out of Nigeria. Palmer's opening move was to oppose the introduction of a General Tax Ordinance for Nigeria, and, with the support of the Residents, to propose a return to the 1906 Native Revenue Ordinance, which stated that the tax paid in the Northern Provinces was levied by the native authorities with the approval but not at the direction of the governor. He succeeded in wearing down Thomson on this point, but the proposal was eventually rejected by the Colonial Office, with lengthy quotations from Lugard employed to prove its case that the emirs had lost the sovereign right to taxation when defeated on the field of battle. Unrepentant, Palmer shifted his ground to an attack on the format of the Annual Estimates of Nigeria, which he developed into a campaign for the complete decentralization of the Treasury Department. On this he was narrowly over-ruled. One of his more successful campaigns, fought intermittently throughout his Lieutenant-Governorship, was to keep technical officers from the medical, educational, agricultural and public works departments of the central government from enjoying any independent access to the native administrations. In his view, it was the Resident, and the Resident alone, whose task it was to guide the emir along the path of material progress – if such indeed were deemed to be desired.

Palmer's views were shared by the other Northern Residents who, early in his career as Lieutenant-Governor, were organized by him into an effective pressure group known as the Conference of Residents. The Conference's working assumption was that all incursions from Lagos were to be resisted; the reason invariably given was that only the Residents had enough knowledge and experience of the mysteries of Indirect Rule to be entrusted with its execution. It is a tribute to the awe in which Indirect Rule was held in the 1920s that their pretensions were taken seriously: few deliberative bodies in history can have had a higher regard for themselves as repositories of political wisdom than did the Conference of Residents.

So seriously indeed did the Residents take themselves that they were unwilling at first even to allow the stationing of subordinate European officers in the districts. There were District Officers, and there were Assistant District Officers, but they were stationed at regional headquarters where they functioned, not as independent administrators, but as assistants to the Resident: as late as 1921 the Resident at Kano declined to accept the posting of political officers to permanent stations in the districts.[20] When District Officers were eventually allowed into the field they were watched like hawks by their senior officers for signs – an indication, it was said, of inaptitude or inexperience – of running things too directly, and promotions were made or denied on the extent to which they seemed, in the words of the Resident, Adamawa, to be 'imbued with the true spirit of Indirect Rule'.[21] It is significant that one of the first major published attacks on Indirect Rule was written by a Northern Nigeria DO, Walter Crocker, whose animus against the system clearly arose not from disagreement with its basic principles but from the fact that DOs were allowed so little responsibility within it. 'There is a strong case', he boldly suggested,

> for eliminating Residents, and a case for eliminating Lieutenant-Governors. There is an overwhelming case for giving the D.O., the most important unit in the whole machine, more responsibility, and for saving him from dancing attendance on Residents who notoriously dodge responsibility.[22]

It was, and remained, his contention that the pure Lugardian principles of Indirect Rule had been perverted by 'mediocre careerists' in the Northern Residencies after the great man left.[23]

Indirect Rule, then, with its implicit exaltation of the man-on-the-spot over the man in the central office, set the seal of legitimacy on the centrifugal tendencies long at work in the British Colonial Service, and provided them with a rational institutional expression independent of the existence of a frontier. It became, eventually, the cult of the DO writ large, but with delaying actions at each step of the way by men who thought that power should be concentrated at the level in the system they themselves happened to occupy. In Northern Nigeria power did remain in the hands of the Residents, because they possessed' historical claims to legitimacy as the standard-bearers of Indirect Rule – a point always emphasized by Palmer in his dealings with junior officers[24] – and because they were linked with the top men in a *congeries* of feudal autocracies. In other places in which Indirect Rule was attempted, and where no large centralized states existed, such as Tanganyika, the DO enjoyed an undisputed reign.[25]

Both Northern Nigeria and the Punjab were colonies of conquest, untainted by trade or missions, in which the purely administrative outlook could and did bloom unchecked. Both housed defeated, but martial, races who made dominion enjoyable. Both, through a happy combination of theory and circumstances, were places in which enormous responsibilities were entrusted to a handful of inexperienced young men, who proved themselves on the job. And both, as a result of all of the above, provided unparalleled opportunities for the British to convince themselves and show the world – it was remarkable how often Indirect Rulers reported on the esteem in which their system was held by other nations – that they naturally did certain things very, very well.

The distinguished critic of imperialism, E.D. Morel, wrote after a visit to Nigeria in 1910 that the administration of the North was a '*tour de force*' and revealed that, 'with all her faults, Britain does still breed sons worthy of the highest traditions of the race'. 'When one sees', he wrote,

> this man managing, almost single-handed, a country as large as Scotland; when one sees that man, living in a leaky mud hut, holding, by the sway of his personality, the balance even between fiercely antagonistic races, in a land which would cover half a dozen of the large English counties; when one sees the marvels accomplished by tact, passionate interest and self-control, with utterly inadequate means, in continuous personal discomfort, short-handed, on poor pay, out here in Northern Nigeria – then one feels that permanent evil cannot ultimately evolve from so much admirable work accomplished, and that the end must be good.[26]

These are words which could have been written of the Punjab in its heyday. And, as had been so memorably the case with the Punjab, the proof of the pudding was found to be in the eating. The Punjab had stood firm in 1857; the emirs of Northern Nigeria, it was noted with pride, stood firm in 1914, when the British were forced by the outbreak of war with Germany to denude the area of troops.[27]

There were explicit reminiscences of the Punjab, and all it meant in imperial song and story, in the minds of Northern Nigeria's creators as they were creating. Lugard, in his *Political Memoranda*, employed the words of Henry Lawrence to impress upon his officers the importance of constant travel among the people[28], and like him selected his administrators from among the military, believing that their training had taught them, as no other could, the proper exercise of responsibility.[29] Charles Temple almost certainly came to Northern Nigeria with the idea of another Punjab in mind: his father, the distinguished Indian administrator Sir Richard Temple, had been in his youth one of John Lawrence's hard-riding young men, and it was he who wrote in 1901 asking for his son 'to become one of the recruits which Lugard is raising for Nigeria. He might have to sacrifice somewhat of pay for this end but he would not mind that owing to the chance of rising in the Imperial Service.'[30] The old hand could recognize the coming man.

Yet though there were resemblances between Northern Nigeria and the Punjab, there were also differences. Indirect Rule had far more ideological content than the Punjab creed: it was found necessary ceaselessly to draw attention – perhaps because it was a principle coming to be so explicitly disputed by those to whom it was applied – to the long and careful weaning required for the native to shed his primitive mode of thinking and adopt successfully the ways of the modern world. And the men of Northern Nigeria, conscious of themselves as the most refined products of a now self-consciously imperial civilization, were distinctly more inclined than their predecessors in the Punjab to ruminate on what they regarded, rather surprisingly in the circumstances, as the subtleties of their craft. Choosing to overlook the actual blatancy of British power and concentrate instead upon its supposed attenuation, they produced the definitive celebration of the attempt to govern, not through the threat or application of physical force, but through the power of personal influence alone.

The beauty of Indirect Rule was that it created an administrative situation in which personal influence was, in theory at any rate, the administrator's only resource. Because the structure of native authority was supposedly maintained intact, the Resident – supposedly – had to depend for whatever results he achieved on the sway he was able to exercise over his emir. His success could thus be explicitly attributed to that capacity for influence which British administrators had always claimed to possess, but had not normally had the opportunity of conclusively demonstrating. And conversely, in the *exalté* atmosphere of Northern Nigeria, a Resident who admitted defeat at the hands of his emir was deemed to be guilty of two unpardonable sins: he disgraced by his ineptitude the good name of the British Colonial Service; and he brought the whole principle of local administrative autonomy into disrepute. For an officer in Northern Nigeria to complain that his emir refused to take his advice was to put his career at the gravest possible risk; he could expect in due course to be moved to 'easier work' – in other words, to administrative oblivion.[31] It was not unknown in Nigeria for emirs to be removed from office by the British, but only when they committed crimes which brought discredit upon the administration, never for mere recalcitrance. In that case it was the administrator who was removed.

The extreme difficulty of ruling indirectly was pointed out repeatedly by its more successful practitioners, often in terms whose very weightiness implied the triumph of *virtù*. Richmond Palmer was a tireless extemporizer upon this theme. And for a really considered exposition of it we can turn to Charles Temple's *Native Races and their Rulers* (1918), a remarkable work which, though it bears the unmistakable stamp of a mind operating obsessively in isolation, pursuing ideas by their internal logic rather than by the rules of external evidence, can yet be assumed to possess a representative character. A severe critic has acknowledged Temple to be 'both influential and typical among that important body, the Northern Residents'.[32]

The duties of a Resident, Temple asseverated, were such as to give 'opportunities for the exertion of any degree of administrative capacity, tact, and industry', and, amplifying: 'It may readily be supposed that this keeping in touch with the people without impairing the authority of the Emir and consequently of the whole native administration, is no easy task, and one on which any amount of administrative tact and ability can be exerted.' Much more appears in the same vein; but Temple is at his most eloquent in describing the qualifications of the successful Resident. A Resident, he writes, must possess

> an inborn sympathy and liking for the native and his affairs . . . Next after this by far the most important qualification, more important far than special industry or special facility in acquiring native languages for example, is a sense of proportion. To recognise where a reform is urgently required and must be effected at any cost, or where it may be postponed, or where it may be counted on to effect itself without outside influence, and, perhaps most important of all, to be able to recognise the fact that certain reforms would be beneficial could they be effected but that it is not possible to effect them at all; to be able to arrive at a right decision on such points as these is what is chiefly required of a Resident. He must be able to decide rightly whether a native chief's first offence should be punished, or whether patience should be exercised until he has offended ten, nay twenty times – either course may be the right one, it depends entirely on circumstances. He must be able to judge not only when and how, but where his weight should be applied . . .
>
> Such being the principal work which the Resident is called upon to perform under the system of Indirect Rule, it will be seen that he can receive little help from outside sources . . . So subtle are often the

bases on which he arrives at a decision that he may sometimes find considerable difficulty in making a good case on paper for some action he may have taken, even though he feels, and subsequent events may prove, that action to have been perfectly correct. In my humble opinion, he should not be called upon for such justification.[33]

Such was the magnificent ineffability of the Resident, who functioned, if we are to judge by this account, in an atmosphere better described as one of brilliant improvization than of the sober pragmatism for which Indirect Rule was supposedly renowned. If this was pragmatism, it was of a positively mystical kind.

Reading *Native Races and their Rulers*, one becomes aware of the extent to which Indirect Rule, as it came to be practised by Temple and presumably his fellow Residents, implied a special and refined kind of experience of power. Temple was sincere in his desire to preserve native society from too sudden change: he enjoyed its idiosyncrasies, respected its vitality, and greatly loved it as an unkempt garden in which the product of a more ordered civilization might find repose. But the principal argument he produced in favour of ruling indirectly was not that Indirect Rule provided the perfect instrument of intelligent conservation, but that it created the possibility of exercising over the native a far greater degree of control than could be achieved if he were ruled directly. 'The white man', Temple observed, 'can "boss about" the native, there is no doubt about that, but . . . the control thus exerted is very superficial.' If he aspired to something deeper, he must use deeper methods – methods which, alas, could not be applied in bulk. 'A European', Temple wrote, 'cannot exert a personal influence on the characters of more than one hundred to two hundred natives'; but if he concentrated on 'guiding and controlling the native leaders', then his influence would be 'magnified by a natural process a thousand fold' and the result would be that: 'The power thus exerted is infinitely greater in scope than any power or influence which it can be hoped that he will exert under the . . . system of Direct Rule.' In time, Temple believed, the successful Resident would come to take 'the place of public opinion as a controlling force over the Emir's actions'.[34] How far Temple's aspirations coincided with reality may be judged by these observations committed to paper in 1962 by a man who had been his native clerk: 'To speak the gospel truth', this man recalled, 'Mr Temple was very harsh towards the native chiefs . . . really, he did not spare the rod as far as efficient administration was concerned; . . . he was bad-tempered . . . He was strict to the letter, he was very pushful . . .'[35] How unwelcome an epitaph that would have been.

So developed did the cult of personality in Northern Nigeria become that even in dealing with rude and warlike pagans it was bad form to stoop to securing their acquiescence in the will of the government by resort to force. A.C.G. Hastings was reprimanded by High Commissioner Girouard for using military means to effect the subjugation of the cannibal Tula tribe; to redeem himself he volunteered to subdue the equally unruly Awok without firing a shot, and did so – by reminding them of the fate of the Tulas and giving them two hours to surrender their weapons. He spent the interval in full view of the enemy, drinking tea. Looking back on it years later, what struck him most was 'the colossal cheek of it all'.[36]

Hastings' previous dealings with the Tula tribe would seem rather to diminish the role played by force of personality in this affair, but the traveller and eccentric socialist R.B. Cunninghame Graham, who contributed an introduction to Hastings' book, did not for that reason forbear to indicate that force of personality was precisely what it showed. Cunninghame Graham was, however, correct in observing that the expedition against the Awok 'really called for greater nerve than that against the Tulas, which ended in a fight'[37]; and this, as Hastings himself seemed to recognize in recalling first and foremost his 'colossal cheek', was surely the point of it all. Force had been not merely avoided, but transcended.

It will have been noted that, not content with imposing upon themselves the task of ruling through the tendering of advice, which might have been thought difficult enough, the British took upon themselves in Northern Nigeria the even more difficult task of ruling without actually appearing to rule at all – an undertaking whose very absurdity only emphasizes its interest.

The essence of Indirect Rule, wrote a Lieutenant-Governor of Southern Nigeria, was 'authority combined with self-effacement'.[38] 'The Political Officer,' wrote Clifford, 'should be the Whisper behind the Throne, but never for an instant the Throne itself.'[39] The true measure of the Resident's success, wrote Temple, producing as usual the quintessential exposition,

> will be the respect and regard with which the populace hold their own Chiefs and Elders, and not him, combined with general good relations between the private individuals which compose the clan, and the general prosperity of the unit . . . where the policy of the government is to rule indirectly the political officer must be satisfied with the knowledge, locked securely in his breast, that he is very important to the native population although they are not aware of it.[40]

A number of explanations suggest themselves for this strange impulse towards self-effacement in men who loved power, besides the official one that it served to maintain the standing of the native authorities in the eyes of the people. The first is that by positioning himself conspicuously behind a veil, the Resident could leave the population in a state of desirable uncertainty about the degree of influence he actually exercised over their emir: his advice was not seen to be taken, but neither was it seen to be rejected. This was perhaps what was in Temple's mind when he wrote that 'whereas in communities governed by native institutions the white man, *qua* white man, is regarded with great respect, in those districts where the native administrations have been swept away he is regarded as a person of no very great significance'.[41]

Another possible explanation for the embrace of self-effacement is that it created the opportunity for exercising power without accepting responsibility. The less that was known about the political officer's activities, the less was understood about his responsibility for events. Blame was difficult to attach to a person who existed in a state of splendid inscrutability.

But again, too evident delight in surmounting a difficulty which was after all self-imposed suggests that the Resident's obscuration of the nature of his influence was primarily not a form of reticence or uncertainty, but of display. By diminishing the outward evidence of his authority almost to the point of invisibility, he demonstrated to the people and perhaps more importantly to himself that he could perform his duties not only without resort to force but without any discernible support at all: like Hugh Clifford's Sir Philip Hanbury-Erskine choosing to deal with rebellion not as a governor but as 'a man', he was effacing not himself but his institutional context.

The Northern Nigerian Resident's belief in his own self-effacement can usefully be seen in a more general context of fascination with the secret exercise of power. Secrecy sets the imagination free to create unrestrained and guiltless fantasies of consequence in the world, and it was one of the achievements of the men of Northern Nigeria to create a practical milieu in which such fantasies might be enjoyed. But it was not only in Northern Nigeria that the charms of obscurity were known and appreciated; in the late imperial world the passion for secrecy was widespread, and that of the practitioners of Indirect Rule was only one manifestation of it.[42] Cecil Rhodes, whom no one thought of as retiring and who expected to be remembered for a thousand years, chose, it will be remembered, as his instrument to achieve the infinite expansion of the British empire a secret society. In Egypt, Lords Cromer and Milner, enthroned in marble halls and surrounded by British soldiers, thought of themselves as playing, with the utmost discretion, an exceptionally difficult lone hand; they delighted in the formal restrictions placed on British power, though everyone in Egypt knew them to be of no practical consequence.[43] Cromer cherished the thought that he 'remained more or less hidden [and] pulled the strings',[44] and proclaimed his contempt for publicity; yet it was he of whom the fellahin sang as they laboured at their immemorial tasks.

To take an even more famous imperial hero, perhaps the most famous of all, it could be said of T.E. Lawrence that his whole life was a testimony to the fascination of the secret power of the will. In the desert, as his wartime despatches show, he was entranced by the conviction that he was controlling the Arabs without their even realizing it; in his self-imposed obscurity after the war he busied himself secretly, though not too secretly, with pulling strings. His prescription for success in the desert – 'Wave a Sherif in front of you like a banner and hide your own mind and person' – could be taken as a motto for Indirect Rule. 'If you succeed', he went on, 'you will have hundreds of miles of country and thousands of men under your orders, and for this it is worth bartering the outward show.'[45] Nor was he the only imperialist of his day of whom it might have been said, as one of his biographers said of him, that he had 'a genius for backing into the limelight'.[46] It was a curious conceit of imperial memoirists of the time to claim that their labours were unknown to and unappreciated by the British public. Their works were besprinkled with unsolicited testimonials, often from foreigners, and tributes to the splendid work of their brother officers.

Another who was passionately fond of self-effacement was Sir George Goldie, the man who ruled Nigeria in the days of the Niger Company, and whom some credited with being the original progenitor of Indirect Rule. He went to exceedingly great lengths to keep his name out of the public eye, but, as with Lawrence, an extreme desire for secrecy and public contempt for ambition were accompanied by a morbid fascination with the power of the will. He wrote to his biographer that as a young men he

> acquired a settled gloom that nothing could shake . . . I sat down on the sea shore, placing a large black pebble beside me . . . [whilst pretending that] by touching the pebble [I could] wipe out . . . all . . . life on earth . . . so that [it] had never existed. I sat for hours staring at the sea. After a long time . . . I touched the pebble . . . [Then] I started my work in Africa.[47]

This same man wrote that he 'could not remember having ever felt, during my 52 years of life, the slightest symptoms of that curious disease – ambition – which craves for leadership, honour, money, or notoriety'. When he refused a peerage the reason he gave was that he preferred to think his country owed him something.[48]

These ambiguous types found their way into fiction. Kipling (*Kim*, 1901) and John Buchan (*Greenmantle*, 1916) popularized the idea of the imperial hero as secret agent, *Greenmantle* uncannily prefiguring the supposed exploits of T.E. Lawrence in Arabia. Buchan's *A Lodge in the Wilderness* (1906) was a more explicit reflection of the imperial ethos of the day, written after a youthful spell on the periphery of Milner's 'kindergarten' in South Africa. In it a group of senior imperialists, led by a figure modelled on Rhodes, meets in secret conclave in a hunting lodge in Africa to arrange the destiny of the world.

This love of secrecy may have been a reaction to the rapid expansion of Britain's formal power towards the end of the nineteenth century, an attempt to preserve the spirit of the frontier and deny what had become the unexciting obviousness of British dominion. Even more than the exaltation of influence, the love of secrecy was concerned with the exercise of power which had its source not in the collective past but in the force of the individual will. It was Promethean in spirit, and its meaning was the very opposite of restraint.

We must now return to the principal official argument for Indirect Rule and look at it more closely.

The aims of Indirect Rule, Lugard said, were to develop what was best in native institutions and thereby 'to inculcate respect for authority, self-respect, and fair treatment of the lower classes, the weak and the ignorant'.[49] 'If you do not respect your race', said Philip Mitchell in a speech extolling Indirect Rule in Uganda, 'you cannot really respect yourself.'[50] Indirect Rulers ranked self-respect above all the other blessings they could bestow, wealth, health, and the conveniences of modern life paling by comparison, if they were not actually to be regarded as injurious.[51] Probably the main reason why Indirect Rule acquired instant support from the British Government was that this was an assumption deeply rooted in the mental outlook of the English upper classes, who liked their inferiors to be able to think well of themselves. Temple could write with perfect confidence in his audience that though he would not 'strain the reader's capacity by asking him to imagine a native Governor of a Colony or Protectorate' or even a native Colonial Secretary of Nigeria – a proposal which 'does not come within the bounds of practical politics' – he counted it an advantage of Indirect Rule that under it 'the native can and does fill not only positions of great responsibility but the highest positions, positions which place him on the social scale on an equality with the King's representative himself'.[52]

Obviously, self-respect was not the same as disrespect. It went without saying that the truly self-respecting native was the one who understood the indecency of aspiring beyond his station. Thus, though Lugard could not avoid committing himself, in principle, to providing a Western education (that notorious producer of disrespect) to Africans who desired it, he hoped that a system could be devised which would render them 'efficient, loyal, reliable and contented – a race of self-respecting native gentlemen'.[53]

There were peoples in the empire – the Masai, pre-eminently, were one, and the Bedouin Arabs were shortly to be another[54] – who seemed instinctively to possess the right combination of self-respect and pragmatic acceptance of the facts of British power. If the right kind of Masai could be persuaded to act as government headmen, C.E.V. Buxton said, 'the ideal of indirect rule could be achieved'.[55] The inhabitants of Northern Nigeria, however, though coming close to this standard, had with few exceptions to be cured of a certain lack of forthrightness. Thus the element of moral instruction entered Indirect Rule as it was practised in the Nigerian emirates – though in a system so deliberately obfuscatory it was not easy to see how such instruction could be provided. Fortunately, the answer lay close at hand, in that sense of the redeeming power of personal example which had for so long been part of the mental furniture of the British middle classes. 'Our supreme contribution to Africa . . . is not so much what we do as what we are', wrote Walter Crocker.[56] In this spirit, A.C.G. Hastings wrote with pride of the transformation experienced by his cook during ten years of association with him: 'He spoke quite freely at the end. He had his little peccadilloes, the quaint and rather Machiavellian ways to gain his little ends, but he knew me and I knew him, and in essentials he made good.'[57] And when Lugard came to look back on what had been accomplished in the early years of British administration he singled out the improved character of the native rulers, which he attributed to 'the unceasing efforts and devoted ability of the British staff, who have by precept and example made them what they are today'.[58] The inconsistency of demanding frankness and openness from the African while practising a form of government depending largely on influence wielded behind closed doors seems not to have troubled the British; they assumed that it was precisely their own qualities of straightforwardness and transparent honesty which would effect the required transformation in the African character.

As was usual with the rulers of the British empire, moral display served a dual purpose, being intended not only to improve native character but also to stimulate native loyalty. It was always Lugard's assumption that his reception by the emir of Kano as his 'honoured friend' owed as much to the emir's respect for his qualities of character as to gratitude for the restoration of his own eminence. 'The white man's prestige must stand high', wrote Lugard in *The Dual Mandate*,

> when a few score are responsible for the control and guidance of millions. His courage must be undoubted, his word and pledge absolutely inviolate, his sincerity transparent. There is no room for "mean whites" in tropical Africa . . . They lower the prestige by which alone the white races can hope to govern and to guide.[59]

By requiring its practitioners to possess the moral prestige necessary to guide, Indirect Rule seemed to ensure that they also possessed the means whereby, in the absence of any overwhelming display of physical superiority, they could govern. And lest there be any misunderstanding as to the intensity of the attachment Lugard had in mind, it may be noted that his thinking revealed itself quite clearly on the subject of loyalty when he wrote of military matters and the secret of command. Here he abandoned the lofty word 'prestige' and wrote simply of the 'blind devotion' the successful leader might enjoy.[60]

There was something corrupt about the extent to which the British in Northern Nigeria cared about the loyalty of their subjects, and the lengths to which they went to cultivate what could in the end only be an illusion of mutual respect.[61] In Masailand such thoughts could be entertained without abandoning the imperial obligation to attempt improvement; there DO-hood was constantly being born anew, the same irresistible force meeting the same immovable object. But in Northern Nigeria the emotional satisfactions which could be experienced almost incidentally in Masailand could only be experienced at a price, that of being too careful to avoid offence. In spite of all the powers with which he was armed, and routinely used for routine ends, it is clear that the Northern Nigerian Resident too often failed to use them for good: being, rather than doing, good came to define the limits of his aspirations. This is why Hugh Clifford, who was as committed as anyone to indirection, could come to Northern Nigeria in 1921 and be appalled by the state of administrative dereliction which he found there.

Indirect Rule dramatized, sanctified, and institutionalized the belief that backward races should and could be ruled by force of character rather than by force of arms. It was therefore not surprising that at the time Indirect Rule was rising to ideological prominence an emphasis on recruiting the right people should develop in the Colonial Service.

For the Colonial Service, this was something entirely new. The Indian Civil Service and the Sudan Political Service each practised its own system of careful selection, but up to and including the First World War recruitment to the Colonial Service – or rather the assemblage of small local services which made it up – was on a highly casual basis. Candidates either wrote to the Colonial Office or to an influential relative, or, not infrequently, walked in off the street. Callers from the street were dealt with by a doorkeeper who either encouraged or discouraged them, depending on how they looked, and entered his impressions in an official diary: 'not quite a gentleman ... – but would do well for Gold Coast' was a typical entry of 1899.[62] Selection procedures in general were rough and ready, perhaps because selection was scarcely the *mot juste*: over-supply of suitable candidates was not a problem for the Colonial Service until the 1930s, when years of misleading propaganda about difficulty of entry, combined with economic depression, had done their work.[63] Though delighting to read in *Blackwood's* of the exploits of imperial heroes, the educated British public showed little personal inclination for service in the assorted white men's graves which made up the tropical dependencies.

All this was to change with the advent of Sir Ralph Furse, who from 1919 to 1948 was in sole charge of recruitment for the Colonial Service. His achievement was twofold: the unification of the Service in the 1930s, and the eradication from the public mind of any lingering notion of it as a refuge for down-and-outs and ne'er-do-wells. Furse set out to create a Service which would be 'a corps d'elite to which ... the best type of man ... will feel it an honour to belong'[64], and in time and according to his lights, he brought practice into line with theory and made good the boast that those whom England sent out to govern the colonial empire were her finest sons.

Furse had no personal experience of imperial administration, and until he began the series of journeys associated with his work of recruitment, had seen nothing of the empire apart from a brief visit to Ceylon. Drifting into the Colonial Office because deafness prevented him from taking up a career in the regular army, he brought with him a romantic conception of empire stimulated in the first instance by Kitchener's Omdurman campaign and encouraged with appropriate reading matter by his father.[65] This he proceeded to apply directly to the process of recruitment. His achievement was thus in a real sense an imaginative one, and so much was he the right man in the right place at the right time that his procedures and opinions were never seriously gainsaid.

Taking his cue from the Sudan Service and rejecting the written examination, Furse's method of selection was the interview, to which he attached a great mystique. No Northern Nigerian Resident was ever more concerned with the ineffability of the art of judgement than was Furse, who was proud to think of the process by which he reached his decision as one of the *'arcana imperii'*. Asked on one occasion if he would define by what methods he judged a candidate, he replied that it was 'difficult to say. But if I had to choose a hunter for work in a particular type of country I should have a pretty good idea which would be the best animal to pick, though I might not be able to tell you how I went about it.'[66]

Once Furse had perfected his system, no one entered the administrative service – or even the technical services, for he believed the requirements of character to apply just as much to them[67] – without being interviewed by him or one of his small group of assistants. But long before this stage was reached an elaborate, though subterranean, process of screening had gone on. Furse eschewed advertisement – guaranteed, in his opinion, to attract 'a mass of rubbish' – and concentrated on methods which were 'mole-like: quiet, persistent, and indirect'. He and his staff relied on 'personal contacts in the most fruitful quarters' and 'visited, or wrote personally to, a host of individuals who could instruct and influence the young; university tutors, deans of medical schools, school-masters, and so on'.[68] It was all a little like Rhodes' secret society, which was to have 'members placed at our universities and our schools [to] watch the English youth passing through their hands'[69], and may conceivably have been influenced by it. There was a 'secret list' of useful persons who could be relied on to keep an eye open for promising young men. It is said to have included John Buchan.[70]

Furse spread his net wide, but it did not sink deep. His devotion to the ancient universities and the public schools which supplied them – he himself was at Eton and Oxford – was absolute. He wanted the best for his new model Colonial Service, and he was in no doubt as to where he would find it. One of his first undertakings was to transfer the Tropical African Services Course from the Imperial Institute in South Kensington, 'which is not frequented by other students of a kind to make good Administrative officers', to Oxford and Cambridge, where 'it would, I am sure, spread interest in our services among other undergraduates of the type we want'[71]; and the great triumph of his career as a bureaucrat was to persuade the Warren Fisher committee, set up in 1927 to examine methods of recruitment into the Colonial Service, that it was unnecessary to look further afield for men 'who possess the qualities of mind, character and personality which make for success in the leadership of native . . . races'.[72]

What these qualities were Furse was never so vulgar or incautious as to define. But some idea of the general type he was looking for can be gleaned from his memoirs. From these it is clear that he identified completely with the men in the outposts, believing as they did that if all was well in the boma the empire could be left to take care of itself. The vision which entranced him was therefore that of the ideal District Officer, as conceived by the District Officer himself – permanently on tour, manfully resistant to bureaucratic interference from headquarters, and 'winning the trust and loyalty of [his] charges by [his] integrity, fairness, firmness, and likableness'.[73] This was the type of man he was looking for and, by his own account, not infrequently found. If the empire was going to be run on character, Furse was confident he could supply it.

Furse concentrated on the public schools because he believed, like almost everyone else, that they provided an appropriate training in character for future rulers of native races.[74] The time has come to take a closer look at that assumption.

There is now a considerable literature on the public schools[75], none of which unfortunately comes to grips with what seems, with respect to the subject of this book, to be perhaps the central issue: the fact that for a hundred years, from the middle of the nineteenth century to the middle of the twentieth, the British governing classes were educated in an atmosphere which combined the toleration of a merciless brutality with perpetual exhortations to be good. Before Arnold, the public schools were bearpits. After Arnold, they were still bearpits, but with the bears required to put in compulsory attendance at chapel. It is a tribute to the formative power of the experience that by and large the contradiction was internalized. There were very few cynical Englishmen running the empire, or, for that matter, running the country.

Arnold was an evangelical *pur sang*. His concern for the souls of the rich was equalled only by his fear of the impatience of the poor; he lived in daily fear of revolution. When he found himself in charge of a famous school he seized his opportunity and set to work to instil in the offspring of the ruling classes the personally desirable and politically vital sense of sin. This is no exaggeration: though primarily a moralist, Arnold was almost equally a political reformer, and he thought of himself as performing a service to the state. Through him the notion of the responsible use of power by a divinely ordained ruling class was introduced directly into the educational system, and boys were exposed systematically and *en masse* to an idea which only a few of them could have been counted on to pick up informally at home.

The very circumstance, however, which made the public schools a perfect vehicle for propaganda – their isolation, through the boarding system, from the outside world and the idiosyncratic influence of families – ensured that Dr Arnold, in his crusade for the personal salvation of his charges, could enjoy no more than a limited success. There were never enough masters to control the unruly mobs of boys, and the enlistment of prefects to the cause of authority was at best an ambiguous achievement: they were boys, too. As Arnold himself so clearly saw, 'a society formed exclusively of boys, that is of elements each separately weak and imperfect, becomes more than an aggregate of their several defects; the amount of evil in the mass is greater than the sum of evil in the individuals'.[76] Societies of boys were what the public schools essentially remained, with the masters forming no more than a thin crust of adult authority.

The result was apparent in even so cheerful and admiring a representation of public school life as *Tom Brown's School Days*, set in the supposedly reformed Rugby attended by the author. The weak are bullied by the strong, the little by the big, the pious by the irreligious. Strong drink is consumed, fags are roasted, and there is no end of fighting. That reform should extend to the abolition of fighting was not even conceivable to the author. Fighting, he says, is 'the real, highest, honestest business of every son of man' and he advises 'those young persons whose stomachs are not strong, or who think a good set-to with the weapons which God has given to us all, an uncivilized, unchristian, or ungentlemanly affair, just skip this chapter at once, for it won't be to their taste'.[77]

Virtually all the accounts we have suggest that the public schools, in spite of Arnold's efforts, continued to exist in something not far removed from a Hobbesian state of nature – or rather, just far enough removed to allow for the development of tribal ritual. The number of taboos which might unknowingly be broken was terrifying. Some children spent their entire schooldays in unrelieved misery. But matters were so arranged that for most the outlook was not completely bleak; almost everyone could arrive eventually at a state of relative freedom from intimidation and enjoy a measure of authority over others. And when this happy moment arrived, it was crowned with legitimacy, because like many tribal societies the public school was a gerontocracy – an important fact obscured more often than not in the literature by concentration on the oligarchic aspect of the power exercised by favoured groups of senior boys: prefects, athletes, bloods, in slightly differing proportions according to the slightly differing character of the individual schools, but all essentially distinguished by seniority. To think otherwise would be to succumb to the glamour and particularity with which seniority was invested by the boys themselves; the critical fact was that, in the fullness of time, little boys who were beaten by big ones might reasonably expect to do the beating themselves.

The schools were aware of the importance of the gerontocratic process and called it 'learning to command and obey'. But this overlooks what was surely an equally important result of the experience. This was to keep alive, in boys whose privileged background might have encouraged complacent acceptance rather than active pursuit of power, a keen appreciation of what it was like to have it, and what it was like to be without it. The schools claimed to toughen boys, and they did. By making it possible for a vivid and urgent desire for power to exist alongside a consciousness of being the legitimate and predestined possessor of it, they kept the edge on the governing classes.

This was one factor influencing the way in which the teachings of Arnold and his successors were actually apprehended. When boys were given legitimate authority to exercise at last, so eagerly was it anticipated that they were prone to feel it intensely deserved. Thus a consciousness of proved quality rather than a habit of self-questioning, as Arnold had no doubt intended, was often the result of a public school education. 'Confidence', indeed, has been such a marked characteristic of the public school boy that many boys have been sent to public schools mainly to acquire it.

Two other factors seem to have played a part in bringing about a subtle transformation of the Arnoldian message. One was the simple fact that it was directed at and mediated through adolescent boys, whose conception of the significance of their own behaviour is notably dramatic. Thus the evangelical cult of conduct, with its emphasis on the sober virtues, was transformed in the public schools into the much more flamboyant cult of 'manliness' (note the gerontocratic associations of the word), a notion very little different, in its emphasis on courage and strength, from ancient aristocratic ideals of honour, which were thereby incidentally preserved.

The other was the equally simple fact that boys in public schools were chronically deprived of the normal sources of affection. Expelled from the comfort of home usually at the tender age of eight, they were compelled until they left school (or, in some cases, university) to associate almost exclusively with other boys, whose behaviour towards them was unpredictable. Arnold himself deplored the unnatural disruption of the affections in sending a boy away to school. He planned to send his sons to day schools, but weakened at the last.[78] To what extent boys were conscious of the loss of love – in its practical and immediate manifestation – is impossible to say: mechanisms of denial come quickly into operation to deal with such enormities. But what is evident is that they often sought affection from the only source which under the circumstances was available – other boys. Friendships developed of a very intense type, sometimes, inevitably, with an explicitly sexual aspect which seems, in spite of the awful fulminations of headmasters, to have produced remarkably little in the way of enduring guilt or sexual abnormality in adult life: it was the emotional intensity of the experience which was remembered, suggesting how deep a displaced need it in fact fulfilled.

It thus came about that, during the process of a boy's adjustment to public school, two very powerful and not very compatible needs – the need for power and the need for love – were grossly stimulated, in an environment where their satisfaction could not easily be assigned to the usual separate compartments of life. In seeking to satisfy one need, a boy might hopelessly compromise his chances of satisfying the other. If he held his own with other boys in the struggle for power he could hardly help behaving in ways which were unlikely to be lovable – a fact which assumed a definite importance when the only hope of affection came from those same boys. Clearly, not everyone's reaction to the situation was the same. Some boys simply gave up the struggle for power, or scarcely attempted it. Of these a few came to see in friendship the whole meaning of life: Goldsworthy Lowes Dickinson and E.M. Forster were to exemplify this type in English letters. Other boys allowed the need for power to take them over and became bullies; and presumably there were other routes to survival.

But there was one orthodox route, supplied by the school itself. This was to learn to exercise power 'responsibly'. In this way power and love might both be enjoyed, as we see them being enjoyed by the heroes of a thousand school stories. The prefects and captains of the First Eleven, exercising terrific authority for the good of the school, are rewarded, not just with acquiescence but with – blind devotion. By the end of the nineteenth century there was an almost perfect fit between the moral indoctrination pursued by the school and what was perhaps the most obvious way in which an individual boy might try to resolve the conflicting demands which the experience of school made on him. Almost perfect, but not quite: the emotional freighting which it acquired in transmission deprived the Arnoldian message of any remaining austerity. It was good form alone, rooted in ideas of honour, which preserved the appearance of enlightened indifference to the affections of the mob. Public school fiction, avidly written and avidly read, displayed the reality.

The avowed purpose of the public schools was to produce leaders, and if we are to understand by leaders rulers capable of extracting the voluntary compliance of the ruled, we must concede that they produced them. Whether the capacity for leadership extended beyond the special circumstances of school is another question. The fact that it was assumed to do so had its own importance.

The school, indeed, produced an over-supply of leaders. Some of them were absorbed by the empire, where they constructed an administrative system remarkable for the degree of local autonomy exercised within it, and where they pursued, amid uncomprehending but generally unresisting natives, dreams of winning the trust and loyalty of their charges by their integrity, fairness, firmness, and likableness.

In time, and under the influence of Sir Donald Cameron, a man of obscure origin and exceptional ability who had known the delights neither of DO-hood nor of public school, Indirect Rule began to acquire a less exotic coloration and a less inward-looking character than it had had in its glorious beginnings in Northern Nigeria. During his controversial governorships of Tanganyika (1925–31) and Nigeria (1931–5), Cameron developed a system of Indirect Rule – or indirect administration, as he preferred to call it – based wherever possible on local native councils supervised openly but supposedly tactfully by British administrators. In Northern Nigeria, he succeeded in detaching the judicial system and the technical departments from the grip of the administrative service, whose claims to omnipotence and omnicompetence were thereby permanently reduced from the heights to which they had risen a decade before.[79] Professional anthropologists, for whom Lugard and the Northern Residents had had no use, were encouraged to study and to recommend. The whole enterprise of Indirect Rule became more organized, more standardized – the native administrations of Tanganyika, a country of considerable ethnic diversity, were by the end of Cameron's governorship more or less uniform in structure – and more active in intention. Moral authority Cameron did not disregard or despise, but he was more concerned with its educative than with its binding power. The political education of the African, *qua* African, was his first concern, and in his hands Indirect Rule became more genuinely the instrument of regeneration it was supposed to be. But his enthusiasm for system led him too easily to assume that a native administration duly gazetted was a native administration actually functioning as a responsible organ of local government, and this set a limit to his achievements in reform. Though technically shorn of some of his powers, the DO remained substantially in control.

Indirect Rule, then, had several 'meanings', not all of them logically compatible with each other, but there was one thing about it which was entirely clear: the conception of government underlying it was a highly charismatic one. At a time when forces were inexorably at work in Britain itself to produce the bureaucratic form of government we know today, there flourished in the empire a governing ethos which, with its emphasis on character rather than training in its practitioners, its primitive notions of justice, its exaltation of the autonomous agent unhindered by outside control, its demand for loving awe from the governed, was unmistakably the product of an earlier age.[80] The persistence of this primitive conception of the nature of authority, in circumstances which rendered it plausible, was not without its consequences for the future of the empire.

7

The End of Empire

When Charles Temple, impelled by his love of logical discourse, asked himself what might be the ultimate evolution of the system of Indirect Rule, he replied that, by allowing 'natural conditions to exert their influence in a manner modified to meet the requirements of the native group', Indirect rule would 'in due course of time', render that group 'robust enough to stand by itself'.[1]

At first blush this seems, though more cautiously stated, not too different from Macaulay's grand vision of a free and regenerated India, launched into the civilized world by the patient efforts of generations of Englishmen. But there was a fundamental difference between Macaulay's views and those of Temple. Macaulay faced unblinking the prospect that, as a result of his policies, India might be absolutely, if only eventually, free. Temple denied that the policy he advocated posed any significant threat to the integrity of the British empire.

Looking at the long sweep of the historical past, Temple had seen that 'Historical analogies lead us to one conclusion only' – that subject races invariably at some point regain their liberty. But, he asked himself:

> Have we any reason to suppose that yet another solution of the problem is to be found, and that we can introduce a precedent so that the native subject races may remain in existence, unfused with ours, and yet in subjection? If the term subjection be used in its extreme sense I do not for a moment believe that any such solution exists. But if the term be used to designate those relations . . . existing between the masses and the leaders, the relations which exist between a more competent man and a less competent, by virtue of which the more competent can control the actions of the less competent for the

advantage of both, then I think that a solution can be found, and that a return to normality in the case of the conquered sufficient to render existence bearable, honourable, and even enjoyable, can be secured. It depends, however, ... entirely on the attitude which we as conquerors adopt towards the conquered, whether we stop the free circulation in the body politic by our institutions or so organise the dependent races as to leave open opportunities for a proper exercise of the social ambitious instinct [defined previously as the desire to exercise power over others for their own good] on the part of the individual native leaders so endowed.[2]

These cogitations are worth quoting in full, as they so accurately reflect, albeit in a more lucid form than that usually encountered, the thinking of those who in the next few decades were to give away the empire in the belief that they were acting to preserve it.

It will be argued in this chapter that their prideful belief in the capacity to influence, so vividly expressed and so evidently vindicated in Indirect Rule, led the British on to fatal experiment in more and more attenuated forms of imperial control. This is not meant to suggest, of course, that the dismantling of the British empire can be comprehensively explained by the role of 'character' in the formation of imperial policy: a chapter on the end of empire in a book called *Empire and the English Character* must include a disclaimer to that effect. Historians will be occupied for a long time to come in determining the exact balance and interaction of forces – including, to mention only the more obvious, the economic disaster of the Second World War, the rise of America, and the development of nationalism – which contributed to Britain's imperial demise. This chapter confines itself to the intangibles.

Nor is it intended to overlook the existence in the councils of state and elsewhere of men to whom any loosening of the reins was wholly repugnant. Of these Churchill was only the most famous. Such men found themselves, however, fighting what became all too clearly a rearguard action. The emphasis in what follows will be on those who moved the matter forward to its ultimate, if unforeseen, conclusion.

Our story begins in India, where in 1885 what was arguably the only significant nationalist organization with which the British ever had to contend, the Indian National Congress, was founded by – an Englishman.

No doubt if A.O. Hume had never founded the Congress it would have come into existence in some other fashion. But found it he did, and the Congress's early visibility and successes owed something to his organizing talents and access to parliamentary and public opinion at home.

Hume acted in the belief that he was diverting potentially revolutionary energies into channels which would secure the permanence of British rule.[3] A retired administrator who as a young man had single-handedly turned the tide of mutiny in his district in the North-West Provinces, he believed that since those Homeric days British administration had become dangerously out of touch with the people. And indeed, even discounting the role so evidently played by nostalgia in Hume's thinking, it was true that the administration of India, beginning with the viceroyalty of John Lawrence, had become steadily more centralized and more detached. The grain of truth in the myth of the British administrator dispensing justice impervious to the affection of the natives is to be found in this period of the history of British India, of which James Fitzjames Stephen is perhaps the representative figure[4], when a maturing bureaucracy was moving away from a personal to an institutional sense of fairness.

Hume's solution to what he had decided was the problem was the re-introduction, in a form suitable for a more politically evolved society, of the binding power of personal contact. This, rather than a Macaulayish enthusiasm for the export of parliamentary institutions, was the motive for his advocacy, through Congress, of political reform: British authority was to be given a human face by allowing qualified Indians some share in the running of the country. Congress was founded with the blessing of the then viceroy, Lord Dufferin, an unpassionate liberal who saw it as a useful forum for articulate Indian opinion. But Dufferin soon began to feel annoyed with the Congress habit of asking for changes which, however modest, only the government in its wisdom could think of introducing. Pronouncing Congress to be 'a microscopic minority'[5], he began to give thought to ways of preventing this minority from poisoning the minds of the majority, especially those of the vast array of native collaborators – the *patwaris* and the *chowkidars*, the stationmasters and the clerks – on which British rule so visibly depended; and before long attendance by government employees at meetings of Congress or any other political organization was made illegal.[6] Thus began the pattern of alternating concession and repression which marked the Indian path to independence, the British constantly frustrated by their inability to rise permanently above the use of force, the nationalists, with the notable exception of Gandhi, seeing only the adroit employment of the carrot and the stick.

The high-water mark of bureaucratic efficiency in British administration arrived during the viceroyalty of Lord Curzon, from

1899 to 1905. By his very vigour, which left few corners of Indian life uninspected or untouched, Curzon produced disquiet; and by his partition of Bengal, pushed through on its administrative merits with Olympian – the word always comes up with respect to Curzon – disregard for risk, he spectacularly increased the political consciousness of the Bengali middle classes. The result was a passing phase of terrorism and the permanent invigoration of Congress.

The British government's response came in 1909: the Morley-Minto reforms, named after the Secretary of State and the viceroy of the day. These conceded Indian representation on an elective basis in both the central and provincial councils of government, while maintaining intact the principle of the irresponsible executive. Morley denied that they were intended as a prelude to parliamentary government. He appears to have thought of himself, like Hume, as rescuing imperial authority from the life-threatening grip of an insensitive bureaucracy. The Russian revolution of 1905 was much in his mind.[7]

The ensuing *entente* between the government and political India lasted until the First World War. Then, as the war dragged on, and British demands for economic and other kinds of sacrifice – over a million Indians saw military service in Europe and the Middle East – became insupportable, unrest made its appearance again. Positive action was then required. In August 1917 the new Secretary of State for India, Edwin Montagu, announced that the policy of H.M. Government was the 'progressive realisation of responsible government in India as an integral part of the Empire'. This could only mean that, in time, India would attain a status equal to that of the white dominions.

Though the import of the announcement was obvious to Indians, it seems not to have been obvious to the British government, which avoided making any explicit statement on dominion status for India for another twelve years. The 1917 announcement was wrung out of a reluctant and distracted Cabinet by Edwin Montagu, who saw himself at the time as the architect of a new India – an India of 'great self-governing Dominions and Provinces . . . organised and co-ordinated with the great Principalities . . ., federated by one central Government'.[8] Montagu's notion of 'self-government' was not in fact as radical as it might appear. In 1912 he believed that the 'principles of self-government' had already 'been applied in their most extreme form' in Canada and South Africa[9] – a date at which neither of these countries had acquired any formal control over their external relations.

Montagu's stated intention was to 'hold India' not by main force but 'by just institutions, and more and more as time goes on by the consent of the governed'.[10] The 1917 announcement and the reforms of 1919 known as the Montagu-Chelmsford reforms (Chelmsford being the viceroy), which introduced the principle of ministerial responsibility into provincial government, were seen as means to this end. 'Self-government' was thus conceived not as the inevitable prelude to letting India go, as it appeared at the time and has appeared since to eyes less clouded than Montagu's by belief in the possibility of voluntary servitude, but as the natural means of keeping it. Montagu welcomed dissent in India as a sign of blossoming political maturity, and distinguished confidently between legitimate and illegitimate unrest[11] – the latter being that which had for its object 'Home Rule', the former that which aspired to political responsibility to the degree the British saw fit to give it. It was to the former that he believed himself to be responding. When Curzon taxed him with setting in motion 'a revolution . . . which will probably lead by stages of increasing speed to the ultimate disruption of the empire', Montagu replied, aghast: 'Surely you did not mean this!'[12] But he had his moments of self-doubt. A month after the momentous declaration had been made he was asking himself: 'How far can we go in this direction safely? . . . Is there any country in the world that has attempted a half-way house in this, or a quarter-way house? . . . Can you have a form of government administered by an alien agency partly responsible to the people of the country itself?'[13] To these questions he had no answer, and he resolutely put them aside.

In the Montagu declaration we see the first official glimmer of an idea which exercised a vast and perversely inspirational influence on the process of imperial disintegration: the idea of the multiracial Commonwealth.

It is not easy, admittedly, at this point in time, when the Commonwealth seems so obviously a fig-leaf for imperial decline, to credit the extravagant hopes that once were entertained of it as the foundation of everlasting British dominion – influence, as it were, eternally made flesh. Yet the Commonwealth was after all invented at a time when the British were more than ever enamoured of their capacity for effecting the bloodless obedience of subject peoples. The atmosphere reflected in early writings on the subject is unmistakably one of eager, and on the whole, confident experimentation in new forms of political association, in a world in which no absolute diminution of British power appears to be anticipated.

The term Commonwealth referred, of course, originally to a *white* Commonwealth, in which sense we first find it employed by Lord Rosebery in 1884. 'Does this fact of your being a nation', he inquired of an Australian audience, 'imply separation from the Empire? God forbid! There is no need for any nation, however great, leaving the Empire, because the Empire is a commonwealth of nations.'[14] Around the turn of the century, the term began to gain currency among people who wished to acknowledge the increasing political and economic maturity of the colonies of white settlement. One can hardly put it stronger than that, because a certain imprecision appears to have been attached to the word from the beginning. It seems, however, always to have been associated by those who employed it with the idea that Britain's historic policy towards its dependencies had been to lead them along the path towards self-government – a belief which had for its principal inspiration the history of Canada since the Durham report. The most consistent feature of the Commonwealth idea, at all stages of its development, was the principle of consent. In the minds of those who gave positive thought to it, the Commonwealth was to be an organization to which no one who was unwilling need apply, and in which those who had joined were to reach their decisions on the basis of consensus: the goal to be pursued was an uncoerced acknowledgement of Britain as the senior partner in a world-wide enterprise; the position to be sought was the supremely equivocal but potentially supreme satisfying one of *primus inter pares*. When Burma declined to become a member in 1948 – a decision which came as a most unpleasant surprise – comfort was taken in the thought that the voluntary nature of the Commonwealth was thereby confirmed.[15]

There seems to be no sense in which the idea of the Commonwealth can be said to have developed from Indirect Rule, but the similarity of the language employed, and the fact that enthusiasts for one were usually enthusiasts for the other, would appear to suggest that the two ideas sprang from the same rich soil, composted over the years of imperial fact and imperial fancy. When Charles Temple asked himself what form the finally evolved connection between the conquering races and the conquered, now existing in partially evolved form as Indirect Rule, and based on 'the relations which exist between a more competent man and a less competent', might take, he answered that he saw no reason

why in due course, if proper use is made of native institutions, those races which are now subject should not take their places in the ranks of that group of allied nations, as they may I think rightly be called, which forms the [self-governing] British Empire ... I see no reason whatsoever, to take the more organised Filane Emirates and Yoruba chieftainates as examples, why some of the more advanced communities should not enjoy many of the advantages of self-government today, and why powers equal to those wielded in respect to the management of internal and domestic affairs by the Self-Governing Colonies could not, if the policy of Indirect Rule should be consistently and intelligently applied, be granted to such units within one or two generations. In the case of those groups which are less advanced today the process will take longer, but that is all the difference.[16]

To the general public, understandably, it was not always clear whether the creation of a Commonwealth involved a grand gesture of renunciation on Britain's part, or a grand gesture of affirmation on the part of those who took up the option. The inevitable criticism that it was the former was met firmly with the contention that it was the latter, but it had to be admitted that no one could really be sure, and that to embark on such a venture an act of faith was indubitably required. It was thus a boon to the cause that one of its earliest recruits was T.E. Lawrence, who, besides representing to many of his admirers in political circles the very quintessence of those qualities on which the successful transformation of empire into Commonwealth would depend, was an imperial hero to the British public. Had he not, as everyone knew, single-handedly raised and led an Arab army against the Turks? Had he not, through the magnetic influence he was able to exert even over those of his own race, personally seen to it at the Peace Conference that these Arabs were not sent unrewarded away? And had he not, with the utmost delicacy, nurtured in them the impression that they and not he were in control of events?[17] For Lawrence to give his imprimatur to the idea of the Commonwealth seemed sufficient rebuttal to anyone rude enough to associate it with a loss of imperial virility.

In 1919 Lawrence had already written to, of all people, Curzon, confiding that his 'own ambition' was that the Arabs 'should be our first brown dominion and not our last brown colony'. Arabs, he added, 'react against you if you try to drive them . . . but you can lead them without force anywhere, if nominally arm in arm'.[18] In 1920 he was active in writing articles for the press, expounding his version of the 'new Imperialism' and airing his views on the rebellion against the British in Mesopotamia. Of the new imperialism he wrote, in the best Indirect Rule manner, that it involved

an active side of imposing responsibility on the local peoples . . . We can only teach them how by forcing them to try, while we stand by and give advice. This is not for us less honourable than administration: indeed it is more exacting for it is simple to give orders, but

difficult to persuade another to take advice, and it is the more difficult
which is most pleasant doing . . .[19]

Of the rebellion in Mesopotamia he wrote that it could be dealt with
by raising two divisions of volunteer local troops, reducing the
British administrative staff and setting up an Arab government
under the indirect control of a British officer. Such a government,
Lawrence asserted, 'would be child's play for a decent man to run,
so long as he ran it like Cromer's Egypt, not like the Egypt of the
Protectorate. Cromer dominated Egypt, not because England gave
him force, or because Egypt loved us, but because he was so good a
man.'[20] He told Lewis Namier that the rebellion was due to British
administrators becoming accustomed during the war to having
troops to do their will. Only when we learned to rule again without
soldiers, he said, would we be safe.[21] No better summary could have
been provided of what the Comonwealth idea was about.

The Commonwealth became to politicians and men of affairs
what Indirect Rule was to the DO – a chance to display those
qualities which justified them in the possession of an empire, and
thereby ensure its perpetuation. And it is no accident that once the
initiative in this matter had passed, so to speak, to the higher
command, the gradual obscuration of the authority of the District
Officer ensued. As Whitehall began to treat directly with nationalists, doling out to them bits of 'responsibility' as DOs were wont to
do with their native authorities, the mystique of the boma began to
wither away: in the DO's apotheosis lay paradoxically the seeds of his
decline.[22] The story of the last decades of the British empire is thus
the story not only of the attenuation of imperial control, but of the
centralization of imperial authority.

Lawrence's views on brown dominions owed something to his
intimacy with Lionel Curtis, the indefatigable imperial publicist who
was the first person to think seriously about the idea of a multiracial
Commonwealth.[23] Of no mean magnetism himself – Lawrence
thought highly enough of him to make him the recipient of some of
his most excruciating introspections[24] – Curtis was the inspirational
force of that curious organization, the Round Table, in whose
journal of the same name Lawrence published his article on the new
imperialism in the Middle East.

We are still some way from forming a just estimate of the
influence exercised by Curtis and his friends of the Round Table on
the imperial policy of the British government. One obstacle has been
the obsessive discretion of their methods of operation, so appropriately reflecting the imperial mystique which inspired them;

another has been a certain scholarly reluctance to welcome the suggestion that this informal study group composed of intellectuals and men of affairs, who almost never held elective office, and who indeed generally despised it, exercised any significant influence at all. Much remains to be learned of their activities[25], but what is certain is that they had converts in high places – notably Edward Wood (of whom more anon), Leo Amery, and Lord Hailey of *African Survey* fame and immense Colonial Office influence – and that through their publication of a journal widely respected for its seriousness they kept before the eyes of the political establishment the idea of a new kind of empire.

The group had its first incarnation in South Africa as Lord Milner's 'kindergarten', the circle of clever young men, products mainly of New College and All Souls, that Milner gathered around him to assist in the reconstruction and unification of South Africa after the Boer War. They included Curtis, Philip Kerr (later Lord Lothian), Geoffrey Dawson, and R.H. Brand. John Buchan was a peripheral member of the group. Upon their return to England after South African unification in 1910 the kindergarten tackled the next item on what seems to have been an implicit agenda – the unification of the British empire. Under Milner's patronage, they founded for this purpose the Round Table movement, with branches in each of the dominions and a journal published in London.

By imperial unification they meant at this time a federal union of Britain and the white dominions, a scheme differing little in its essentials from other schemes of imperial union which had occupied the minds of the British political classes from time to time during the latter part of the nineteenth century. But the kindergarten's fervour for imperial federation declined during the First World War, when the strength of dominion nationalism became apparent, and they moved towards more informal notions of imperial co-operation. Curtis, meanwhile, as the result of his meditations on how a federated empire might collectively discharge its duty to the backward races under British rule, had begun to reach the conclusion that the answer was to train them for eventual self-government. 'The task of preparing for freedom the races which cannot as yet govern themselves', he wrote, 'is the supreme duty of those who can. It is the spiritual end for which the Commonwealth exists, and material order is nothing except as a means to it.'[26] The practical corollary of this, tirelessly expounded in the *Round Table* in the post-war years, was that the safest place for brown races, for now and the foreseeable future, was within the British empire, where their interests could be looked after and their development, at an appropriately gradual pace, ensured.

Behind all this was discernible the dim outlines of an even grander vision – a vision of an Anglo-Saxon world state, in which Britain, the white dominions and America (realigned with Britain after what Curtis referred to as the 'schism' of 1775[27]) would in concert undertake to ensure the peace and prosperity of the world: Curtis was not called 'The Prophet' for nothing.[28] There was indeed a wild ambition about the Round Tablers' schemes and dreams which belied the unvarying reasonableness of their prose. We get a glimpse of it when Curtis argues, in support of his view that America should have Near Eastern mandates, that this would place her advantageously for the regeneration of post-revolutionary Russia; as 'steward of the Near East', she could 'extend to the blind giant the neighbourly hand of a friendship which is open to no suspicion'.[29] Like their mentor Lord Milner, the Round Tablers were 'British race patriots'[30] dedicated to the maintenance, through the empire, of the world-wide ascendancy of the Anglo-Saxons. History was an inspiration, not a lesson, to them.

The Round Tablers, then, hardly saw themselves as being in the business of imperial decline. On the contrary, they saw the empire as the basis of Britain's claim to world power status, and their commitment to exporting self-government – which they wrote about as if it were merely the current expression of the British administrative genius – was secondary to this. In their South African days the kindergarten showed little interest in the uplift of native races.

India naturally came into focus as a field for Round Table action some time before the other dependencies. By 1915 it had become one of the obsessions by which Curtis was possessed serially in the course of his long and active career[31], and, of all his many projects, the political evolution of India was the one where he could most truly claim to have made a direct contribution to events. He was not, it appears, in any way responsible for the Montagu declaration – though he anticipated its thinking – but came on the scene shortly afterwards as one of the chief architects of the Montagu-Chelmsford reforms. These were of immense consequence in giving elected Indian officials their first real taste of power, and in encouraging them to ask for more – much more, needless to say, than Curtis had either foreseen or intended. Notwithstanding the growing power of the Congress movement, he entertained high expectations of the new policy in fostering the seeds of devotion to the empire in the Indian people, believing in the face of all the evidence that the reforms would create conditions whereby 'one day the greater love of the greater Commonwealth will be found to have come without observation'.[32] Curtis' optimism about this, unlike Montagu's, never wavered. He was by temperament a true believer, who mistook the process of arriving at his own convictions for the unveiling of the eternal verities.

On the eve of his first visit to India Curtis confided to an associate that the great task which lay ahead was 'to renovate the soul of the Indian people'.[33] He spoke with the fervour of discovery, unaware it seems that he was by this date, imperially speaking, reinventing the wheel. He was the kind of man who absorbed ideas unconsciously, made them his own, and pushed them to new limits. In this case he was carrying the task of soul renovation up to an altogether dizzier level of risk and aspiration than had hitherto been attempted. Whole peoples were now to be regenerated, not by the patient labours of obscure administrators toiling at their life's work in obscure places, but by the brilliant schemes of brilliant people flitting about the corridors of power.

Curtis' incipiently multiracial ideas seemed at first rather startling to some other members of the Round Table – his *Project of a Commonwealth* (1915) created dissension in the ranks – but they soon prevailed, and the Round Table brought into currency a new term, the Commonwealth of Nations, which proved popular because it so gracefully combined the idea of imperial unity with that of national autonomy. By the 1920s it was enjoying a wide circulation. Its curiously reassuring suggestiveness helped to prepare British hearts and minds for the possibility of formal, though not final, separation from their subject peoples.

Gandhi has described in *Satyagraha in South Africa* how in the course of the struggle against the Black Act of 1907, which required every Indian over the age of eight in the Transvaal to register and be finger-printed, he developed his doctrine of *satyagraha* or 'truth-force', and its practical application in civil disobedience. The man responsible for introducing the fateful legislation was none other than Lionel Curtis. Curtis was at that time Assistant Colonial Secretary of the Transvaal and he was not motivated in what he did by any particular animus towards Indians. He was as usual training his sights exclusively on the goal currently in view, in this case the unification of South Africa, the kindergarten campaign for which seemed at that moment to require a concession to Afrikaner racial prejudice.[34] In making it Curtis helped to unleash a force which before long would profoundly challenge the British claim to dominion in India.

It is important to try to be clear about what exactly this force was, and the nature of the challenge that it posed to British rule in India – for there was a profound difference between Gandhi's perception of these things and that of the British. To Gandhi, *satyagraha* was a moral force which, by inspiring in the opponent a process of rational empathy with the suffering of the *satyagrahi*, brought him voluntarily to accept the rightness of the *satyagrahi*'s point of view. He thus saw his campaigns of non-violent non-co-operation as a challenge to British confidence in the rightness of their position in India. Indeed, the belief has now passed into the folklore that it was Gandhi's success in appealing to the British conscience, also known as British decency, that led to India's achievement of independence in 1947. This is a belief, however, for which the principal evidence is that this was Gandhi's stated intention.

In acknowledgement of British decency, it must be said that Gandhi possessed the supreme advantage in his campaigns of knowing that, so long as he confined his activities to non-violent protest, he was not risking death at the hands of the authorities. Quite possibly another administration than a British one, less morally aspiring and less legally punctilious, would have arranged for him a quiet accident, or a fatal incarceration. Yet it is remarkable, on the other hand, how morally unmoved the British hierarchy in India seems to have been at the time by civil disobedience: if British officials found it morally painful to see Indians breaking the law and suffering for it, by and large they succeeded in keeping the fact to themselves. Gandhi indeed could count on the British conscience for his personal safety, but he could never count on it for political concessions – and it is clear that at some level he understood this. Otherwise (the point is surely an obvious one) he would have limited himself to verbal argument. The technique of civil disobedience was applied precisely because decency was so evidently not enough, or, looking at it another way, because there was so evidently not enough decency.

The challenge which Gandhi posed to the British, as they perceived it at the time, was not to their consciences but to their authority. The force he unleashed was that of insubordination. Depending, as Dufferin had so clearly perceived, for their ability to govern on the collaboration of a vast class of petty native *fonctionnaires*, and the political apathy of an even vaster class of ignorant peasants, they could in no way afford to see these people aroused to insubordination, even of an ostensibly peaceful kind. And there was in practice a very thin line between peaceful protest and the other variety. The passions aroused in civil disobedience usually expressed themselves before they were spent in acts of more conventional rebellion.

When the situation seemed to warrant it, or the moment seemed opportune, these were dealt with briskly by the forces of law and

order: there was little sign of any paralysis of will in this respect on
the part of the British in India. Though they were as a rule sparing
in the use of force, this was for reasons which seem not to have
included sympathy with civil disobedience.[35] The men who ruled
India were aware that what they referred to as their prestige would
in the end by compromised by too obvious a reliance on resort to
arms. They also knew that the support of Indian 'moderates', that is,
those Indians who were willing to be persuaded of the Raj's essential
righteousness of intent, would be lost if they became too blatantly
repressive. And they had to concern themselves with the possibility
of igniting even greater disturbances which could not be contained
by the forces at hand.

There was, however, a sense in which Gandhi did pose a personal
challenge to the British, as distinct from the institutional challenge of
organized mass disobedience for which he was responsible. In his
manifest ascendancy over millions of Indians, he challenged their
monopoly of the force of personality. It was in meeting him on this
ground that the British came closest to responding to him as a
worthy adversary.

Gandhi, as everyone knows, was a most unusual politician. He
held no office, had no possessions, and came and went from the
political arena at times of his own choosing. Although on occasion he
functioned as leader of the Congress movement, the ascendancy he
achieved over it was purely personal, and he could make it seem as
though he played with it at will. Like the British he preferred to
exercise power without visible institutional support. But he did in
actuality what the British could now do in India only in fantasy. He
truly possessed the charismatic authority to which they, in their too
evidently institutional collectivity, could do little more than aspire.
He thus became, not just an enemy, but that infinitely more
disturbing thing, what they could not but acknowledge to be a rival
for the allegiance of the people of India.

Gandhi's most brilliant demonstrations of this fact were achieved
through his practice of fasting for the attainment of some political
object. As almost everyone except himself perfectly understood, these
fasts were a ruthless exploitation of the power of his own sanctity.
Gandhi only began to undertake serious fasts – that is, fasts where
there was a danger to his life, as opposed to brief fasts for purposes
of spiritual discipline or penance – after he had established a
reputation for sanctity and a large following based to some extent on
that reputation. His first fast unto death occurred in 1918, in support
of the Ahmedabad textile workers' strike, and was employed against
the mill-owning family, who were devoted to him.[36] Gandhi seems
to have felt some flicker of remorse about his treatment of the

Sarabhai family; at any rate, without confessing error, he preoccupied himself with working out rules for what might be termed the
just fast. But such was the genuine power of his personality that his
persistent contention that these fasts were undertaken with the
object of assisting his opponents to accept his point of view on its
merits always received respectful attention, even as it became more
and more evident, with the passage of time, that their success
depended in actuality on the personal capital he had built up: he
was too special, too revered, and eventually too important in the
political consciousness of the Indian masses, to be allowed to die.

It is curious indeed to see in how many ways Gandhi's conception
of power seems a mirror image to that of the British, even if, as in
the case of fasting, he sometimes employed techniques of Hindu
origin to obtain his ends. Like the British he was fascinated by the
thought of obedience willingly given; hence his belief that *satyagraha*
worked because it changed the opponent's mind about the issue at
stake. Like them, too, in their less earthbound moments, he enjoyed
the proud embracing of risk. In South Africa, during the agitation
against finger-printing, he stunned his supporters by declaring that
they must trust Smuts. 'A Satyagrahi', he said, 'bids good-by to
fear.'[37] In this instance, his hopes were first disappointed and then
fulfilled. Smuts was a good choice of opponent. His ultimate
conversion, after long and courteous discussions which added cubits
to Gandhi's stature, provided a timely justification of the latter's
claim to leadership.

These traits in Gandhi were no accident: he was profoundly a
creature of the Anglo-Indian interaction, and a worthy adversary
was indeed just what he aspired to be. His years in England as a
student of law involved him in an earnest effort of adaptation, and it
is clear from his own account that he absorbed through his reading
and his acquaintance a sense of British moral aspiration, for which
he acquired a genuine respect.[38] By what unconscious intelligence
he also acquired an understanding of British moral pride, and how
to set up his own against it, remains a mystery. Though susceptible
to influence, Gandhi was an original.

Like Indian nationalists and reformers of an earlier generation, he
was deeply concerned, in a way which plainly suggests the working
of British influence on his mind, as it had worked on theirs, with the
regeneration of India. He believed as Lionel Curtis did that Indians'
souls had to be renovated before they were fit to govern: he deeply
shocked the American journalist William Shirer by announcing that
'Self-government . . . is inconceivable and unattainable without the
removal of untouchability, as it also is without Hindu-Moslem unity
. . . we shall be unfit to gain independence so long as we keep in

bondage a fifth of the population of Hindustan.'[39] This was a very different type of nationalism from that which had produced the United States of America, and one which it is not easy to explain, as has sometimes been attempted, in terms of Gandhi's attachment to traditional Hindu notions of self-purification. The connection of moral purity with the right to govern was, in the world Gandhi happened to inhabit, a very English one. The long years he spent absorbed in working for the abolition of untouchability and for the reconciliation of Muslim and Hindu, and in innumerable projects of village uplift, testified not only to his genuine goodness but also to the strength of his desire to make India, in the eyes of its alien rulers as well as his own, worthy to be free.

The boldness of Gandhi's political tactics obscured to a large extent the modesty of his political aspirations, which were very much in line with what moderates, taking their cue from the British, had long set their sights upon: self-government within the empire. For one of the unlikeliest converts to the Commonwealth idea was Gandhi himself. He embraced the moral grandeur of it with enthusiasm, and to his dying day aspired to nothing more than Indian membership of the British empire as an equal partner, regarding independence in isolation as a perhaps politically expedient but regrettable alternative. His quarrel with the British was not about whether dominion status was an adequate offer, but over whether they were sincere in making it, and it was only when he concluded, in 1919, that they were not, that he launched mass non-co-operation to get it. This was the man, it should always be remembered, who joined the British army and worked as a stretcher bearer in the Zulu rebellion of 1906, giving as his reason that 'the British empire existed for the welfare of the world'.[40]

It was not until 1915 that Gandhi returned to India from South Africa. By then his triumphs there had given him something of the aura of the awaited one: his following was already in place; he needed only to organize it.

His actions during the war were characteristic. On the one hand, he performed his first Indian act of civil disobedience in support of the oppressed indigo workers of Champaran; on the other hand, he urged Indians to support the British war effort, even engaging in active recruiting in 1918. To the incredulous peasants he explained that 'There can be no partnership between the brave and the effeminate. We are regarded as a cowardly people. If we want to become free from that reproach, we must learn the use of arms.'[41] Presumably he had in mind – nothing else would have been reconcilable with his profession of non-violence – not so much killing as bravely standing up to be killed, but the position was one he felt constrained to apologize for later.[42] It may be that he was influenced in his thinking yet again by the British, whose officer class cultivated the honourable wound, and whose subalterns had lately contributed in altogether disproportionate numbers to the casualties suffered by the British army in France.

Gandhi never fully appreciated how deep, widespread and determined was British resistance to his message of repentance and renunciation, and in what subtle ways this resistance might express itself. He failed always to understand that there was a large area of common ground in British public opinion on India which consisted in the belief that, with a few adjustments, British rule could be made, and remain, acceptable to Indians for ever, and that differences of opinion were to a considerable extent about how this was to be done. We may take, for example, two apparently very different books written by Englishmen serving in India in the 1920s – one by an evident diehard, one by an evident progressive – and see that they meet, in fact, upon this common ground.

The first book, *The Lost Dominion* (1924), by a former ICS officer, Bennet Kennedy, is a powerfully reasoned defence of the *pax Brittanica* and administrative autocracy, and might be described as an unusually uninhibited expression of the ICS point of view. The ICS, as a body, had never been much taken with political reform, sensing correctly that it set in motion a process whereby they could expect only to be replaced, and both reason and sentiment told them that this would never do. As a good ICS man, Kennedy placed the blame for the crisis in India squarely on the service's political masters. He was scathing about the notion that Indians might be pacified by political concession, observing of the Montagu-Chelmsford reforms that: 'If the Indians are capable of providing the directorate, they must surely be capable of providing the agents'. The idea that a free India would remain loyal to the British empire filled him with brilliant scorn. He wrote tolerantly – no doubt to irritate the tender-minded – of 'administrative massacres'.[43]

The other book was *Must England Lose India?* (1930) by Lt. Col. Arthur Osburn, a retired Indian army doctor and member of the Labour party, who hoped one day to see a 'United States of India' dwelling 'contented within the orbit of the British Commonwealth'[44], a hope which Kennedy regarded as absurd. Osburn's points were that his fellow Englishmen in India, whose heartless behaviour towards Indians he described in some detail, failed to 'realize that the British Empire depends for its existence on obtaining the consent and the friendly co-operation of the races governed', and that the demand for independence 'need never have arisen but for the arrogance and want of tact of a large percentage of

Englishmen who, in one capacity or another, are resident in India'.[45] Yet his views and Kennedy's were not so dissimilar as they seemed. Osburn saw hope for the future in Englishmen mending their ways. Kennedy saw it in what he termed a policy of 'constructive repression' – which upon examination turns out to consist mainly in restoring the autonomy of the local official, who will be set free from bureaucratic control to go once again among the people, exercising 'sympathy (in its true and not its debauched sense)', conducting his business in the vernacular, abandoning that 'cold aloofness' which is 'a vice in a ruler', and seeing that the Crown's Indian subjects are well-governed, harmless, and content.[46] Kennedy could have endorsed without difficulty Osburn's remarks that 'We shall not beat the Indian by Indianizing our own sense of decency and justice' and that 'The only real cure for sedition is a just, tolerant and sympathetic rule'.[47]

Shortly after the end of the war an incident occurred which was of critical importance in the development of Gandhi's relations with the British – the massacre at Amritsar. In Amritsar on 13 April 1919 General Dyer broke up a prohibited meeting by firing into the crowd – sustained firing which resulted in 379 people being killed. The iron hand had burst from the velvet glove in unmistakable fashion, and what was more, it was grasped in a congratulatory handshake by large numbers of Englishmen, both in India and in Britain itself. Dyer was eventually censured by a committee of inquiry, but substantial sums were raised for him by public subscription and he was adulated in the press, the House of Commons, and – especially – the House of Lords. The governor of the Punjab praised his initiative. He remained consistently unrepentant, explaining to the investigating committee that his intent had been to produce 'a sufficient moral effect from a military point of view, not only on those who were present, but more specially throughout the Punjab'.[48] He had acted in accordance with the Punjab creed, but with too much enthusiasm and a few decades too late.

These events eventually made plain to Gandhi the existence in both official and unofficial circles of a section of British public opinion which he could not hope to convert, though he came most reluctantly to an acknowledgement of this fact. In spite of Amritsar, he announced himself willing to co-operate with the Montagu-Chelmsford reforms which were unveiled at the end of the year, and only changed his mind as the degree of Dyer's support in British public opinion was borne in upon him, and as he began to find himself isolated by the more radical elements in Congress, who had either already lost their faith in the British, or had never had any. Obliged to seize the initiative, he announced in 1920 his first campaign of mass non-co-operation. British goods were to be boycotted, British courts not resorted to, and British schools not taught in. If non-co-operation remained peaceful, Gandhi promised, self-government would be achieved within a year. Self-government failing to arrive – how extraordinary that he should have thought it would – a campaign for the non-payment of taxes was initiated in Bardoli, near Bombay. This was true civil disobedience rather than mere non-co-operation. A week later a mob set fire to a town hall in Chauri Chaura in the United Provinces, killing 22 policemen. Deeply distressed, Gandhi called off the campaign of civil disobedience. He was then arrested and charged with sedition.

What followed next was an encounter between Gandhi and an Englishman, Judge C.N. Broomfield, which indeed deserves to be remembered in the annals of war for its courtesy, chivalry, and generous sense of occasion. The events in Judge Broomfield's courtroom[49] constitute the element of truth in the myth of Gandhi's successful appeal to the British conscience.

Addressing the court before sentencing, and speaking in that confiding style whose quality of extreme directness made ordinary statements seem extraordinary, Gandhi took upon himself complete responsibility for 'the diabolical crimes of Chauri Chaura' and other disturbances which had broken out in recent weeks. 'I knew that I was playing with fire', he confessed; 'I ran the risk, and if I were set free I would still do the same.' He did not ask for mercy; he did not plead extenuation: he was here, he said, 'to invite and cheerfully submit to the highest penalty that can be inflicted upon me for what in law is a deliberate crime, and what appears to me to be the highest duty of a citizen'. With a high sense not only of justice but of dramatic effect he informed the judge that the only courses open to him were 'either to resign your post, or inflict on me the severest penalty if you believe that the system and law you are assisting to administer are good for the people'. The young judge rose to the occasion. Admitting that it was 'impossible to ignore the fact' that the defendant was 'in a different category from any person I have ever tried or am likely to have to try' and was acknowledged to be 'a man of high ideals and of noble and even saintly life', he took Gandhi gravely to task for his failure to anticipate that violence would be the 'inevitable consequence' of his acts. Asserting, what was palpably untrue, that 'There are probably few people in India who do not sincerely regret that you should have made it impossible for any government to leave you at liberty', he handed down a sentence of six years' simple imprisonment, pointing out – the crowning touch – that the sentence was the same as that given to the nationalist hero Bal Gangadhar Tilak, twelve years before. In a final speech, Gandhi acknowledged the compliment and praised the judge's courtesy. The scene closed with judge and prisoner bowing solemnly to one another, and the latter, after spending half an hour discoursing with his supporters in the courtroom, being led off to prison wreathed in smiles. The British never made the mistake of trying Gandhi again.

Only twenty-two months of the sentence were served, Gandhi being released from prison when his health broke down after an operation for appendicitis. Between 1925 and 1929 he devoted himself to his regenerative projects. In the midst of these, in 1926, there arrived in India the man who was to take up the challenge Gandhi had thrown down to the Englishman's belief in his god-given aptitude for rule – the sixteenth viceroy, Lord Irwin. Confident of his own *mana*, convinced of the legitimacy of his race's presence in India, and equipped with political opinions which met those of Gandhi in a tightly interlocking pattern, in his own way, he, too, was the awaited one. He seems in retrospect the Mahatma's fated antagonist.

The reasons for Irwin's appointment to the viceroyalty are obscure. He was by no means a major figure in British politics at the time, though this had not prevented his being offered in 1920, when he was a mere back-bench MP, the governor-generalship of South Africa – an offer which was withdrawn when the South Africans pressed their desire for someone more important. Aristocratic credentials, the authorship of a biography of John Keble, and a year as Assistant Secretary in the Ministry of National Service did not, in their eyes, seem quite enough. At the time of his appointment to the viceroyalty Irwin was putting in an unremarkable stint as Minister of Agriculture. Yet he had somehow established a reputation in political circles as something out of the ordinary. In 1924 he got a chapter to himself in Harold Begbie's *The Conservative Mind*, a best-selling effort by a popular journalist to identify a Tory tradition representing the best in English life. 'When I say to people that Edward Wood [Irwin's name before his ennoblement on appointment to the viceroyalty] seems to me the highest kind of Englishman now in politics, many of them', Begbie admitted, 'look surprised and perplexed.'

"Edward Wood?" they question; and one can see in their eyes the effort of the memory to attach this name to some sensational event in Parliament or some haunting paragraph in the newspapers . . . "He was Minister for Education in the late Government," I continue. The trouble returns. "Oh, was he!" they say, and dismiss Mr Wood as a nonentity, and me as a pedant or a poseur.

But I have never had this opinion of Edward Wood challenged in the House of Commons. Men of all parties recognise in his personality something which is admirable, something which distinguishes him from other men. Even those who do not share his political opinions readily pay their tribute to the range of his intellect and the graciousness of his character; more remarkable still, even those whose intellectual qualities are the equal of his, but whose moral qualities have degenerated in contact with the sordid atmosphere of politics, never speak of him with an affected amusement as a religious bigot or a narrow-minded moralist; in the remarks of these latter politicians I often detect a tone of rather wistful regret, as if they were conscious in themselves of a loss for which the world they have gained has by no means compensated.[50]

In the absence of any notable achievement, these rather ineffable qualities of character must be counted among the reasons for Irwin's despatch to India.

His political views, however, were presumably not completely irrelevant. He had been sufficiently interested in imperial issues to drift into the Round Table orbit some time after his election to the House of Commons in 1910[51]; and by 1916 his claims to employment were being urged on Milner at the War Office by the Round Table guru F.S. Oliver, who put him unambiguously in a class by himself, above Amery, Brand and Kerr, at the top of his list for preferment.[52] His claims to the viceroyalty were canvassed by another kindergartener, Geoffrey Dawson, who was now in a position of prominence as editor of *The Times*. Dawson was widely credited with influencing Baldwin's decision.[53]

The idea of empire as a voluntary association in which Britain was the respected senior member and acknowledged guiding force appealed strongly to Irwin's self-consciously Disraelian political personality. Blessed with a constituency which returned him unopposed throughout his career in the Commons, and a tenantry which presented him at his wedding with a two-foot high gold cup, it was natural that he should suppose the keystone of the political arch to be a benevolent aristocracy. In Parliament, he was one of the young Conservative MPs who welcomed, from a position of strength as they thought, the accession of Labour into British political life, and set about educating it in the arts of responsible participation in the polity.[54] Like Clifford arguing for natives on the Leg. Co., Edward Wood pointed out that the men on the Labour benches, if a little wild at times, performed an invaluable consultative function in making the views of the masses known to the classes.[55] His pamphlet on modern conservatism (*Conservative Beliefs*, 1924) called

for an end to class warfare and dwelt on the need for reconciliation
in the context of a shared reverence for British political tradition, as
did, in a less philosophical vein, the book he wrote at the end of the
war with his friend George Lloyd (*The Great Opportunity*, 1918). These
attitudes transposed easily to the Commonwealth point of view, class
warfare and nationalist agitation both arousing in him the same
confidently emollient response.[56] When he arrived in India in 1926
he told one of his private secretaries that his aim was to govern in
such a way as 'to keep a contented India in the Commonwealth
twenty-five years hence'.[57]

His conception of the aristocracy was an exalted one; so was his
conception of empire. It is rare to find in his writings any
acknowledgement of the possibility that Britain's dominion overseas
might have had a less than immaculate conception. This would have
compromised the claim to influence. Towards the end of his life,
assessing the course of events in India, Irwin did write that 'Though
they might not have been able to put it into words', the British
people had realized

> that the choice lay between power, which had served us since the days
> of Clive, and influence which, if we could use it aright in the changed
> conditions of the twentieth century, would serve us better. And they
> knew that, of the two, influence was the more securely founded and
> the more enduring.[58]

Perhaps this constitutes such an acknowledgement.

Irwin's policy, then, was amity, meaning the perpetuation of
government by those genetically equipped for it, in what he saw as
the public interest, with public support. In India, where continued
hegemony was now the consideration paramount above all others in
the minds of British politicians, a wholehearted attempt at such a
policy, by one so well qualified to pursue it, must have seemed at
least worth a try.

Before turning to his encounter with Gandhi, certain aspects of
Irwin's character should be particularly noted. These are his charm,
his instrumental attitude towards his own goodness, and his
fundamental opacity of mind – all characteristics which he shared
with Gandhi to some degree.

His charm was universally acknowledged, and was of classically
aristocratic type. Of ascetic countenance (though not particularly
ascetic habits), of grave and rather formal demeanour, he habitually
disarmed people whenever he unbent a little and let them in, as it
were, to his superior private world.[59] He learned to use his charm,
and 'it became', his biographer says, 'so strong a factor in him that it

resembled great beauty in a woman'. Not surprisingly, he possessed
a firm belief in his own judgement, being, in the words of his
biographer again, 'receptive to advice but indifferent to criticism'.
There is one rather startling recorded instance of this charm being
effective at long distance. Years after the event, an Indian revealed
to Irwin's Military Secretary that he was detailed to assassinate the
viceroy on a visit to Lucknow, but, seeing his delightful smile when
he got off the train, changed his mind.[60]

As for his goodness, the attempt to live a Christian life was so
much a part of Irwin's public persona that the legend became
current that, arriving in India on Good Friday, he ignored the
official ceremonies of welcome and went straight to church. He was
brought up in an atmosphere of churchmanship, his revered father
being a prominent layman who devoted his life to the reunification of
the Anglican with the Roman church, and it was perhaps through
him that he acquired what seems to have been an unconscious
appreciation of the utility of goodness in public life; one notes in his
writings a tendency to equate prayer with will.[61]

There is a story told in his otherwise unrevealing autobiography
which nicely illuminates the practical side of this pursuit of
goodness. As a young back-bencher, Irwin dreamed one night of
meeting Lloyd George in a train carrying them both back from
campaigning at a bye-election. 'Your name's Wood, isn't it?' the
great man said.

> I have seen you in the House, and though we haven't met, I have
> taken rather a fancy to you, and would like if I can to help your
> career. Now, I'll tell you what I'll do. There is nothing the House
> loves so much as a personal attack, involving a personal explanation.
> It is the sort of thing that leaves a permanent mark for good or ill on
> the member concerned. So I will make a personal attack on you the
> day after to-morrow, when the House will be full, and I will tell you
> beforehand what I'm going to say and what the right come-back is for
> you to score off me. That won't do me any harm, for my position is
> assured; but you are just beginning your career and it will help you a
> great deal.[62]

For a man without overt ambition, his memorialist in the *Dictionary
of National Biography* was to write, Irwin rose swiftly to high office.
One might question which was the more interesting achievement –
to start with nothing, as Gandhi did, and rise to power on the
strength of personal reputation, or to start with everything, as Irwin
did, and do the same.

Like Gandhi, Irwin possessed a simplicity of demeanour which was deceptive. He seemed open and easy to know, once his aloofness had been put aside, but was not. He gave an impression of penetration, but few people were ever clear about his point of view. His writings and speeches were miracles of ambiguity; he was congenitally even-handed.[63] He never said a foolish thing and usually said a wise one.

All these qualities served him well in the kind of politics he preferred to practise – those of unobtrusive influence and persuasion.

Irwin's first public act upon arriving in India was to appeal, in terms that were for him impassioned, for harmony between Muslims and Hindus. This was a cause dear to Gandhi's heart, and he seems from the beginning to have been sympathetically intrigued by Irwin as a man. There is little contemporary evidence that Irwin ever returned the compliment. His correspondence shows him reacting to Gandhi with the rather detached curiosity he showed for other exotic forms of political life. His recollections are more generous, but notably concerned with the moral impression made on Gandhi, rather than the reverse. It is true that on one occasion, when asked if Gandhi had not been tiresome, he replied that 'Some people found Our Lord very tiresome'[64]; but in the context of general unsympathy it is difficult to know what to make of this very Irwinian rebuke.

Irwin's first big political initiative as viceroy was to extract from the British government permission to make a formal declaration that dominion status was the goal of British policy for India. His reasons for this were simple. In the short run he wished to rally moderate Indian opinion, which had been put out of countenance by its non-inclusion in the Simon Commission, set up to review the Montagu-Chelmsford reforms in 1927; in the long term he wished to save India for the Commonwealth. His underlying thinking, however, was not simple. He assured Lord Salisbury on his visit to England in the summer of 1929 that (according to Salisbury's notes of their conversation[65]), though dominion status might be admitted as the ultimate goal, 'inasmuch as it is impossible to anticipate an India which could defend itself, and as it is unthinkable that a British army could be subject to native control – an essential condition of real Dominion status – the realisation of the aspiration is not within sight'. The difficulty of reconciling this statement with a sincere belief in India's eventual membership of the Commonwealth is apparent. Nevertheless, Irwin appears to have reconciled the two to his own satisfaction, though the arguments to which he resorted owed more to the theological aptitude displayed in his youthful biography of Keble than to ordinary practical intelligence.[66] The political feasibility of dangling before Indians a prize at which they might gaze but which they would never grasp was assured, Irwin told Salisbury, by the fact that Indians in their heart of hearts knew they would always need British administrators to guide them. 'Whenever they are exposed to real difficulty', he pointed out, 'they run for the British umbrella.' It may actually have been Gandhi who was responsible for his optimism about this. In February 1929 Irwin had written to the Secretary of State of a conversation with Gandhi that 'what was interesting' was his statement that, if Indians were at liberty to order their own future, 'we should be astonished by how much they would desire to leave in our hands through lack of self-confidence'. In November 1929 he referred to Gandhi's statement again in a letter to the king explaining his dominion status policy.[67] Salisbury was much struck at this meeting by Irwin's confidence in the future. He himself felt some doubts about the ethics of the proposal, but, 'so great is my regard for Edward', succeeded in suppressing them.

Irwin also canvassed with Salisbury an improved form of dyarchy, the elaborate system set up in 1921 whereby elected Indian ministers in the provincial governments were entrusted with various unexciting portfolios, while British officials remained responsible for the essentials of law, order and taxation. In Irwin's version, all the ministries would nominally be treated alike, with no official restrictions on those which Indians might occupy, 'but the Government [would] be instructed beforehand to take care that certain Departments – e.g., Law and Order – are properly filled'. In the improved atmosphere created by the apparent concession to Indian desires, harmonious relations would transpire. Dyarchy had always depended for its successful working on the exercise of tactful influence by the British governor and his officials, who had their reputations invested in preventing the resignations of their Indian colleagues; but Irwin's formulation took the controlling role allotted to influence much further. Power was to be exercised from behind a veil, as the wilder type of Indirect Ruler aspired to do. One begins to get a clearer idea of what Irwin imagined India's destiny to be.

The dominion status declaration was made in October 1929 and met on the Congress side by what amounted to a demand that it take immediate effect. Irwin, of course, refused, and Gandhi, whose reaction to Irwin's initiative had at first been positive, announced that a campaign of civil disobedience would begin. Gandhi's choice of tactic was a master stroke. In India the production of salt was a government monopoly: he announced that he would walk the 250 miles from Ahmedabad to the sea and break the law by making salt.

Before setting off he wrote to Irwin – 'Dear Friend', the letter began – making a last plea for negotiations. Irwin did not reply.

Nor did he arrest him. The long drama of Gandhi's march to Dandi, accompanied in the end by a crowd several thousand strong, and culminating in the ceremonial collection of a handful of inedible salt, was accomplished without police intervention. Irwin was gambling on Gandhi's inspiration (referred to in a letter to an English friend as 'his silly salt stunt'[68]) falling flat, and was anxious to avoid pushing Indian moderates into the radical camp by dealing with Gandhi more severely than the maintenance of law and order required.[69] His general attitude to civil disobedience was unsympathetic: the General Strike, that affront to Disraelian social harmony, was fresh in his mind.[70] But there is a wisp of evidence that he considered embarking himself on a fast unto death to bring peace to India.[71] This seems very improbable, though it would have been consistent with his character to reject an organized challenge to the social order but to appreciate and even think of emulating and thereby vanquishing a personal one.

On 5 April Gandhi made salt. On 7 April Irwin was writing to the Secretary of State that the Mahatma's health was poor and that his horoscope had predicted he would die that year, which would be, he said, 'a very happy solution'.[72] But still he held off arresting Gandhi, though other leaders were quietly put away, and thousands of Indians were arrested after wading into the sea to collect water for salt. It was not until 30 April, as disturbances mounted throughout India, that Irwin decided that he had no further option but to arrest Gandhi. The arrest was made on 4 May and Gandhi was interned in Yeravda jail. It was then that Irwin showed his steel. The jails were filled and the press muzzled: between April and December 1930 no less than ten ordinances were issued to meet the emergency – the greatest such number that any viceroy had ever promulgated. It was imperative now to show that the British could still govern, and Irwin confounded his critics by showing that he was the man to do it.

Then on 21 May, while Gandhi languished in jail, one of the great set pieces of the civil disobedience movement, more successful perhaps than any other in arousing world-wide sympathy with the Indian cause, took place at the Dharsana salt works. Two thousand five hundred volunteers advanced on the salt depot in successive waves of twenty-five, defying orders to retreat and offering no resistance when the police laid about them with clubs, kicking and beating those who fell. Irwin's response to this spectacular appeal to the viceregal conscience was one of glacial disdain. 'Your Majesty can hardly fail to read with amusement', he wrote to the king, the account of the several battles for the Salt Depot at Dharsana . . . A good many people suffered minor injuries in consequence; but I believe those who suffered injuries were as nothing compared to those who wished to sustain an honourable contusion or bruise, or who, to make the whole setting more dramatic, lay on the ground as if laid out for dead without any injury at all. But of course, as your Majesty will appreciate, the whole business was propaganda and, as such, served its purpose admirably well.[73]

Soon, however, events were to take a different turn. With the Congress leadership in jail, the Round Table conference which met in London in November, at Irwin's initiative, to discuss constitutional advance, came to nothing, and Irwin realized that he must forego the pleasure of seeing the troublemakers in jail for the hope of constitutional development along the lines he had in mind for India. Towards the end of January 1931 he released Gandhi and the other leaders. He did it in style, preparing the ground by a speech to the Legislative Assembly in which he paid tribute to Gandhi's sincerity and asked him to recognize his own.[74] Gandhi wrote to him on 14 February and asked for an interview. 'I would like', he said, 'to meet not so much the Viceroy as the man in you.'[75] This time the request for a meeting was granted.

Gandhi, of course, was wrong in supposing there to be any fundamental conflict in Irwin between the viceroy and the man. Unlike Gandhi's, his was not a divided nature. Temperament and conviction combined to make him see this moment, not as one of intriguing human possibilities, but as one offering an unofficial means to an official end. He understood that Gandhi's challenge was not primarily to his sanctity but to his power, and once he saw on what ground he might meet his antagonist he, like Gandhi, but with more evident calculation, unhesitatingly employed that sanctity in the service of power. He prepared himself to meet the Mahatma on the basis of 'personal appeal and conviction', taking to heart the advice of V.S.S. Sastri, who was acting as intermediary, that Gandhi was '"like a woman; you have got to win him; therefore before you see him, perform all your ablutions, say all your prayers and put on your deepest spiritual robes"'. He intended also to attempt 'some play on what everybody says is characteristic, namely, vanity of power and personality'.[76] Thus equipped, the viceroy met his foe. The result, in terms of the content of the agreement which was reached, was victory: in exchange for a couple of minor concessions, Irwin got everything he wanted. Man to man, the Englishman met the Indian and prevailed.

The terms of the agreement were as follows: that political

prisoners were to be released and the relevant ordinances withdrawn; that civil disobedience was to be stopped; that the boycott of
British goods would cease, though 'peaceful picketing' could
continue; that there would be no change in the salt laws, though
people living by the sea could make some for personal consumption;
and that Congress was to be represented at future sessions of the
Round Table conference, the agreed agenda being federation,
'Indian responsibility', and 'reservations or safeguards in the
interests of India for such matters as, for instance, defence; external
affairs; the position of minorities; the financial credit of India, and
the discharge of obligations'.[77] The last point, far from being the
hardest on which to reach agreement, was the easiest: it was cleared
out of the way at the very beginning[78], Gandhi accepting Irwin's
formulation without demur and apparently feeling no discomfort at
disregarding what he knew to be the views of the Congress Working
Committee. His goal remained, as it had always been, partnership
with Britain within the empire, and he required only to be convinced
of British sincerity in working towards this goal to accept the
principle of reaching it by easy stages.[79] Irwin convinced him.

The point on which Gandhi pressed hardest, and on which the
talks nearly foundered, was that of an inquiry into the conduct of the
police, which he had requested publicly just before the talks began.
Irwin eventually secured his capitulation by confessing to him that,
as head of the government, with no guarantee that civil disobedience
might not start again, he was unable to risk jeopardizing the morale of
the police force. Gandhi was enchanted by the viceroy's frankness, and
recalled to him that Smuts had treated him with similar candour,
recognizing, as he said, the justice of his claim on a certain issue, but
advancing unanswerable reasons from the point of view of government why it was impossible to meet.[80] He could not therefore help
but rise to the occasion, as he had risen to it before. 'I succumbed',
Gandhi said later, 'not to Lord Irwin but to the honesty in him.'[81]

Gandhi was pleased with his agreement, but others on the Indian
side were not so pleased. Nehru wept when he saw the clause
accepting safeguards. Most of the other Congress leaders also had
second thoughts about the wisdom of having allowed Gandhi to
negotiate alone with the viceroy. But they could not at this point
publicly repudiate him. The encounter of 'the two Mahatmas', as
Sarojini Naidu described them[82], had caught the imagination of a
large public, in India as well as England and America. Nehru and
the rest had no choice but to join in the general rejoicing.

Irwin, too, came in for some criticism from his own side, notably
from Churchill, who was famously appalled by the 'spectacle of this
one-time Inner Temple lawyer, now seditious fakir, striding half-

naked up the steps of the Viceroy's palace, there to negotiate and parley on equal terms with the representative of the King-Emperor'[83], but generally he was showered with praise. He congratulated himself on his success in 'carrying Gandhi on the sentimental side' and in persuading him 'to come into line'.[84] Gandhi made no such claims: he had no basis for them.

The importance of Irwin's triumph was that it seemed both classical and prototypical – an exemplification of triumphs past and a portent of triumphs to come. Every Resident, every bush DO, who had ever over-persuaded erring emir or recalcitrant chief, could understand and envy the nature of the viceroy's *coup de théâtre*. Likewise, every enthusiast for Britain's future ascendancy in the world through the Commonwealth could take heart from the fact that a notable nationalist had been charmed into submission by a representative of the Crown. Irwin had triumphed because, as Lawrence had said of Cromer, 'he was so good a man'. To those looking to the future, he had shown what could be done.

He had also, however, as Churchill perceived, conceded to Gandhi and the Congress movement a degree of recognition of their importance which in the long run could do the British no good. Gandhi's great achievement, when all was said and done, was to get the British to pay attention to him, and he did this, first by appealing to their weakness, in threatening the loss of the collaboration on which they depended, and second by appealing to their vanity. He challenged them in a way which in the end they were unable to resist answering on its own terms, countering charisma with charisma. Irwin succeeded in establishing his own, but not in destroying that of Gandhi, which acquired a greater effulgence every time – eight in all – he trudged down Lutyens' great new processional way, opened with brilliant festivity just a week or so ago, carrying only a manila folder and his ever-present staff, to meet the lord of all the world that most of his fellow Indians knew.

In so adroitly 'carrying' Gandhi, Irwin greatly reduced his value as an ally. To ensure his continued ascendancy over Congress, Gandhi had to radicalize himself again. Before long, both sides were accusing each other of breaches of the agreement, and in the autumn of 1931, while Gandhi was in London for the second, inconclusive, Round Table conference, civil disobedience and political violence broke out again. This time the Government of India responded very differently. Lord Willingdon, formerly governor of Bombay and Madras, had replaced Irwin in April, and he was the very embodiment of the ICS point of view. Trouble was something to be nipped in the bud; dangerous agitators people to be kept behind bars. Within a month of his return from London Gandhi found himself in prison, and for several years thereafter his bluffs were resolutely called. If he fasted, he was released from jail; if he attempted civil disobedience, he was back in again. Try as he might to gain entry, the doors of the Viceroy's House remained closed to him. There were to be no negotiations with Willingdon.

Nevertheless, there was constitutional advance, in the form of the Government of India Act of 1935, which provided for responsible government in the provinces. Abandoning its insistence that nothing less than complete independence would do, Congress fought the 1937 elections and took office in seven out of eleven provinces. Gandhi dissociated himself from this development and withdrew from politics until 1939, when the outbreak of the Second World War stirred him to political action again.

In September 1939 the Congress politicians who were enjoying the fruits of office abruptly discovered the limits of their power. Without consulting them, Lord Linlithgow, the viceroy, announced that India was at war with Germany. This he was entitled to do, but the fact that he did it aroused Congress to the realization that Gandhi had been right when he announced upon his retirement that India was still a prison, but now the superintendent was allowing the prisoners to elect the officials who ran the jail. A great surge of confused and ambiguous protest swept India, culminating in the Quit India movement of 1942, when Gandhi, the pacifist, provoked the people to open rebellion. The British showed no sign of indecisiveness in dealing with this outbreak. Fifty-seven and a half battalions of troops restored order in a month with about a thousand Indian casualties, aircraft being used on a number of occasions to machine-gun crowds from the air. After that, India was relatively quiet for the duration of the war.

It is difficult to assess the significance of the various negotiations which went on between the British and the Indians during the early stages of the war. Churchill was prime minister, and though he found it politic in the face of American and Labour pressure to allow negotiations about India's constitutional future to go on, at the same time he ensured that all such negotiations came to nought. When the Cripps offer of 1942, of dominion status – with the all-important right of secession – after the war and representation on the viceroy's Executive Council during the war, looked like being accepted, he joined forces with the viceroy, Linlithgow, behind Cripps' back to persuade the Cabinet that its envoy had exceeded his authority, and the deal was off.[85] Nevertheless, the offer had been made, and at the end of the war, when a Labour government came to power, there was no going back on it.

To the disappointment of some of its supporters, the new Labour government proved to be by no means wedded to the idea that the British empire ought now summarily to come to an end. Indirect Rule and the evolution of the Commonwealth idea had disarmed much left-wing criticism of the empire in the years between the wars and encouraged the development among British radicals of 'responsible' views on imperial subjects, which came naturally to bloom when Labour found itself at last in office.[86] The Cabinet contained no ungovernable enthusiasts for colonial liberation, even Cripps having abandoned his earlier anti-imperialism to become a proponent of using the colonies to close the dollar gap.[87] Bevin had met Lionel Curtis in 1938 and had believed ever since that the Commonwealth was the foundation of a new world order.[88] In combination with his ardent desire to improve the living standard of the British working man, this made for a potent brand of imperialism; few politicians took the Dual Mandate more seriously than Ernest Bevin. Attlee, who had been a member of the Simon Commission and a non-dissenting contributor to its very gradualistic report, had always been extremely cautious in his statements on colonial issues. In 1942 it was he, and not Churchill (who was away), who ordered the wartime internment of Nehru and Gandhi, a move he never regretted.[89]

There was, of course, no question of denying India the freedom which had so often been promised in the irresponsibility of opposition. For one thing, it was now plain that there was little alternative: during the war Indianization of both the ICS and the Indian army had proceeded at such a pace that more than half the ICS and more than half the officers of the Indian army were Indian, and this was not a process to which the brake could suddenly be applied. For another thing, it was evident that, financially speaking, India was a wasting asset. With the development of Indian tariff autonomy starting in the early 1920s – another sop to the moderates – the process had begun whereby Britain was transformed by 1942 from India's creditor into India's debtor. This was not a situation which appealed to the neo-mercantilists in the Cabinet. The issue of Indian freedom thus resolved itself into the problem of how to fulfill the promise of independence in such a way that Britain's position in the rest of Asia and in Africa was not weakened, but strengthened.

The solution was found in making sure that India remained in the Commonwealth. An India in essentially the same relationship to Britain as the great white dominions which had fought by her side in the world war, voluntarily allied rather than involuntarily subjected, could only be, it was reasoned, an asset to British prestige.[90] Extraordinary lengths were therefore gone to to cajole and inspire the rather bewildered Indians, once they had been promised their independence, into requesting Commonwealth membership. The British even, at the eleventh hour, went so far as to change the rules to allow a republic, by definition owing no allegiance to the British Crown, to be a member. But first, someone had to be found to do the cajoling and inspiring, and Attlee's eye alighted upon the martial figure of Lord Louis Mountbatten, then fresh from his victories in Burma.

Mountbatten's career had been a curious one: his reputation as a soldier was founded far less on his record as a commander in the field, which on the whole had been a disastrous one, than on his organizational abilities and his acknowledged brilliance as a leader of men. Sailors who had had the ship shot out from under them because of Mountbatten's recklessness signed up for another tour, such were the inspirational qualities he possessed. It was these qualities which attracted Attlee, who knew that the task he had in mind for his new viceroy would require them all. This was no less than, politically speaking, one of the great strategic withdrawals of history. Mountbatten was to go out to India, announce an early and definite date for British departure, hand over the administrative machine in working order to a unitary government, and secure an alliance with that government in the form of membership of the Commonwealth, preferably with a military treaty.

The daring magnitude of this conception has since been obscured by its almost routine enactment in a series of African countries in the 1960s, but it should never be forgotten that India was the test case, and that at the time success in the execution of such a plan seemed far from assured: only a year before Mountbatten's appointment the then viceroy, Lord Wavell, had been pressing on the Cabinet his 'Breakdown Plan', which consisted simply of the phased evacuation of the British from India without any serious attempt to ensure that a viable, much less friendly, government was installed in their place. 'That would indeed', Attlee told the Cabinet, 'be an inglorious end to our long association with India'[91], and he set his face firmly against such a course. Instead, he gambled on finding someone who could play the last card in the British deck – independence – and then, with nothing further to offer, keep sufficient control of the situation to extricate Britain from India with honour and possibly with glory. The last viceroyalty was thus conceived – by, of all people, a Labour prime minister, but one, it must be remembered, who was at Haileybury – as a supreme test of British adeptness in the gentlemanly art of leadership. When Mountbatten flew off to India, he thought of himself as he had always thought of himself, as a leader of men. 'I want you to regard me not as the last Viceroy winding up the British Raj', he told Nehru, 'but as the first to lead the way to the new India.'[92]

Mountbatten's especial qualification in Attlee's eyes for the job of viceroy was his success in getting the Burmese nationalists to come in on the British side in the closing stages of the war; it was Attlee's firm belief in later life, as indeed it was Mountbatten's, that if Mountbatten had been left in charge in Rangoon, Burma would never have left the Commonwealth.[93] This demonstrated expertise in dealing with nationalists seemed to mark Mountbatten for the job, and when Attlee offered it to him he was sufficiently aware of how much he, and no other, was wanted to attach extraordinary conditions to his acceptance. One of these was that he would go to India only 'at the open invitation of the Indian parties'.[94] Attlee persuaded him that this was impractical. Another was that he be given plenipotentiary powers. These he seems to have been given, or as near as made no difference. Attlee, an astute judge of men, banked on Mountbatten's ambition to provide an adequate counterweight to his proclivity for risk, and in this judgement he was proved to be correct. Though the ascendancy he achieved over Nehru sometimes led Mountbatten to overestimate the extent to which great events lay in the hollow of his hand, he kept himself accountable to the British government throughout.

Within a month of his arrival Mountbatten had decided that the partition of India into separate Hindu and Muslim states was inevitable. This decision may or may not have been correct, but it was understandable. The mounting communal disorder, on a scale unprecedented during British rule, the apparent implacability of the uncharming and uncharmable Jinnah, the tacit acceptance by this stage on the part of most of the Congress leadership of the ultimate partition of the Punjab and Bengal, made the possibility of bringing into being a genuinely united independent India appear slender indeed. But more than that, it was evident that in struggling to attain a communal harmony which was in all likelihood unattainable, Britain ran the risk of throwing away her only chance of retiring from India in good order. It is not quite true to say that the price of Attlee's policy was partition, but it is true to say that its price was the early and firm acceptance of the inevitability of partition. Britain had at all costs to avoid being engulfed in a war of succession between Muslims and Hindus, and the only way to do this was to hand over, while there was still time, not to one but to two successor states. Attlee, therefore, once Mountbatten had concluded that there was no alternative and had produced his Partition Plan, acted with the utmost despatch to get it approved by the Cabinet.[95] It is his haste in this matter which gives colour to the accusation that he was never seriously concerned with the unity of India. This may be; but at the time there was a case to be made for the new policy satisfying the demands both of expediency and humanity. No one, British or Indian, foresaw the scale of the disaster which was to ensue in August 1947.

If Mountbatten failed in one item on his agenda, however, he succeeded triumphantly in the other. Employing with perfect ruthlessness his formidable resources of charm and persuasion, he managed to extract from all parties an affirmation of the desirability of Commonwealth membership. In view of Nehru's repeated rejections of the idea of any further association with Britain, this was a notable achievement, and there is no doubt that Mountbatten felt that it amply compensated for his acquiescence in partition. United or not, he believed, the recruitment of India to the Commonwealth would result in the 'terrific world-wide enhancement of British prestige'.[96] He managed furthermore discreetly to put into circulation the audacious proposal that he should be the first Governor-General of the two independent states. Nehru, having accepted Commonwealth membership, was content to pay Mountbatten the compliment; Jinnah announced that the first Governor-General of Pakistan would be himself. In the event, Mountbatten remained as Governor-General of India, in which capacity, at the invitation of the Congress leaders, he was briefly and secretly to resume executive power in 1947 to deal with the communal violence which threatened to destroy the infant state.

Attlee was ecstatic about the idea of his viceroy staying on, perceiving it as 'a great boost for Britain and for the Commonwealth'[97], a sentiment shared by the now fully evolved Commonwealth statesman – he had been perhaps the first to see the possibilities of the role – General Smuts: 'This does not look like quitting', he cabled to Attlee on hearing the news.[98] No doubt also Attlee correctly judged the effect of this development on the Tory opposition. Churchill indeed was so overcome with the romance of it all that he briefly reconciled himself to the departure of the British from his beloved India.[99]

The actual handing over of power in Delhi was accomplished amid scenes of tremendous enthusiasm, of which the British found themelves, to their delight and astonishment, to some extent the objects.[100] Possessed for once by a spirit of happy hilarity, the Indian crowd unhitched the horses from Mountbatten's carriage and dragged it through the streets; British officers were lifted shoulder high and cheered. For Mountbatten it was unquestionably a great personal triumph. For Attlee it was the vindication of his policy. For many other Englishmen it was a proof that their works in the world had been not evil but good. Attlee was showered with oratorical bouquets in both houses of parliament and from all parties. But it was an Anglophile American who best took the point. This was not, said Walter Lippmann in the *Washington Post*, the work of a decadent people:

> This on the contrary is the work of political genius requiring the ripest wisdom and the freshest vigour, and it is done with an elegance and a style that will compel and will receive an instinctive respect throughout the civilized world. Attlee and Mountbatten have done a service to all mankind by showing what statesmen can do not with force and money but with lucidity, resolution and sincerity.[101]

So the British had come out of India with their egos more or less intact. What next? It was never, as we have seen, the Labour government's intention that the independence of India should be the prelude to a general *nunc dimittis*, and this disposes of the plausible notion that once India was gone the pointlessness of holding on to the rest of the dependent empire, supposedly acquired to protect the sea routes to Bombay, was immediately perceived. So unperceiving, in fact, were the British, that no reappraisal of defence policy consequent upon the departure of India was undertaken.[102] On the contrary, immense efforts were made to secure a military treaty with independent India, the Chiefs of Staff having given it as their opinion that India's manpower resources and location as a staging post made a military understanding with her 'essential from the aspect of imperial strategy'.[103] These were men who had just finished fighting a global war – a war which, it must be remembered, Britain had won – and global habits of mind naturally persisted. Too much is made of the exhaustion of war.

Certain territories, it is true, were disposed of right away, but for reasons which carried no implications for the further demission of power. Ceylon and Burma became independent in 1948, inevitable adjuncts of Indian freedom. In the same year the British abandoned Palestine, never a welcome responsibility and lately become ungovernable, and henceforth took care of their Middle Eastern interests through a group of client states and the fortress colony of Aden. Also in 1948, a State of Emergency was declared in Malaya, but here the British made it clear that they would stand and fight. Malaya had no strategic value but its economic value, as a producer of tin and rubber, was great.[104]

Like the generals, the Colonial Office had had a good war. Civil servants in what was normally one of the sleepier Whitehall departments had enjoyed the intoxicating experience of mobilizing the empire for global conflict. For six glorious years the conscription of labour, the compulsory purchase of agricultural products at below market prices, the unceremonious incarceration of the agitating classes, had all been justified and justifiable. Such habits of interference with colonial lives, once acquired, were not easily given up.[105] Fortunately, they meshed nicely with the neo-mercantilist enthusiasms of the Labour government. If Britain wanted to develop the colonies, the machinery, as never before, was there.

To some extent, the wartime activism of the Colonial Office only reinforced a trend which had begun shortly before the war, when revelations of the poverty-stricken condition of Britain's tropical empire, especially the West Indies, had forced the British government to take a more visible interest in colonial welfare. The result was the Colonial Development and Welfare Act of 1940 and the subsequent erosion of the once sacrosanct idea that the colonies must be, if nothing else, self-supporting. It is hard to exaggerate the importance of this development, which, for reasons purely of financial accountability, involved the Colonial Office intimately in economic planning for the empire and thus helped to bring to an end the old imperial system in which colonies had puttered along as virtually independent satrapies, with the Colonial Office exercising only a watching brief.

The political initiative had also passed to the Colonial Office by the end of the war, though here again the process had begun shortly before the war, with the commissioning by the Royal Institute of International Affairs, or more precisely, its founder and moving spirit, Lionel Curtis, of a comprehensive survey of Africa. This was conceived as potentially the Durham report of Africa, the authoritative statement of the continent's past history, present problems, and possible future lines of political and economic evolution.[106] It was intended, as all Curtis' 'research projects' were, to function ultimately as the basis of policy, and to produce it he selected, not one of the burgeoning African specialists in which Oxford, under his inspiration, was by then abounding, but the sexagenarian Indian civil servant, Lord Hailey. Work on the survey had to await Hailey's retirement, but the choice nevertheless proved to have been an extremely shrewd one, justifying, if nothing else did, Curtis' lifelong faith in himself as a fisher of men. Hailey had exactly the qualities required to make an impact at the Colonial Office, not least among them being, as Curtis astutely realized, the prestige of an immensely distinguished Indian career. Oracular, industrious, and capable of producing as if without effort memoranda of seamless cohesion and judiciousness, Hailey was the Indian civil servant of legendary grasp and authority. When such a man came down from Olympus and applied himself to the problems of Africa, his voice was heard.

The fruit of his labours for the RIIA was a volume of nearly 2,000 pages (*An African Survey*, 1938) which immediately became the basis of intensive discussion at the Colonial Office and which secured for Hailey, until 1943, an unrivalled position of influence in the Office's debate on the future of Africa, which he himself had been instrumental in bringing into being. By the end of the war the Colonial Office was accustomed to thinking synoptically about Africa, to weighing with unaccustomed confidence and delusive clarity the large forces at work there and the ways in which they might be accommodated within a system of administration. One incidental result of this was that Indirect Rule, the proud and mysterious creation of innumerable men-on-the-spot, upon which it was forbidden to the uninitiated to look, was transformed after years of scrutiny by metropolitan experts into a uniform system of local government[107], whereby Britain hoped to bring into the orbit of her unresented influence the non-traditional elements which had made their appearance in African society. At one level – the local level – Indirect Rule was demystified; at another level – the metropolitan level – it was invested with the mystique of *haute politique*.

The frame of reference for all this ferment in the official mind remained the idea of the Commonwealth, which during the war received an impetus from the need to show the Americans, in words if not in deeds, that there would be room for a British empire in the brave new post-war world, and also from the genuine idealism stimulated in some British imperialists – as it had been stimulated in the previous war – by a desire to distinguish themselves from the Germans and their imperial ambitions.[108] To these ends, the most extravagant claims were made. Clement Attlee announced that the British Empire and Commonwealth, being based on Christian principles, was 'the exact contrast to the Nazi conception of a world order', which was the expression of the creed of Antichrist[109], and countless other speeches were made in the same vein. Before the war Lionel Curtis had published an ambitious book entitled *Civitas Dei* (1934–7) in which he sought to prove in three volumes that the British Commonwealth was no less than the ultimate expression in the international social order of the basic principles of Christianity, or, to summarize, 'simply the sermon on the mount translated into political terms'.[110] *Civitas Dei* dismayed many of Curtis' admirers at the time of its publication, but such ideas seemed less ridiculous under the stress of war, when the usual urge was experienced to justify the ways of man to God. It became the common currency of speeches on the empire to advocate the extension of the principle of self-government to all within it, even unto the lowliest. That keeper of the flame, Sir Ralph Furse, to his dying day a believer in the administrative genius of his race, was advocating by 1942 that the territories of the coloured colonial empire be allowed 'to grow up into nations in free association with ourselves'.[111] He seemed unaware that he was thereby announcing the demise of his own service, and indeed for at least some years entertained the illusion that he was not.[112]

The question of the date of everyone's arrival at the gates of the heavenly city was, of course, crucial, and the main contribution of Hailey to the formulation of policy was to keep the question open. Difficult as it is to summarize so majestic a body of work as that produced by Hailey in the days when he reigned supreme as the Colonial Office's oracle on Africa, it seems fair to say that the main impression to be derived from it is of his anxiety to avoid committing the British government to any course of action which might prove to be irreversible. Like a true oracle, Hailey's pronouncements were both authoritative and ambiguous. He firmly allied himself with the forces of change, but was careful to give due weight to the arguments for staying put, the detail in which he did this adding impressively to his reputation for grasp.

In 1939, Hailey was asked by Malcolm MacDonald, the Secretary of State for the Colonies, to write a further comprehensive report on Africa, in which recommendations on the next stage in the political development of the African colonies would be made. This fascinating document, completed in 1941, after its aged author had once again perambulated the African continent, shows the extent to which accommodation to change and the continuation of control were considered to be compatible goals of policy. The question was, as Hailey inimitably put it: 'Can we be sure of the continuance of that degree of acquiescence in our rule which is a necessary condition of administrative progress?'[113], and the answer which he gave was a resoundingly qualified 'Yes'.

Surveying the African scene, Hailey found no sign of the existence of organized mass opposition to British rule, an assessment with which, in fact, most students of the subject would currently agree. But then he was also inclined – on the eve of 'Quit India' – to believe that there was 'perhaps some tendency in England to exaggerate the strength of the forces now opposed to the Government in British India'.[114] This would appear to reflect a chronic tendency to underestimate the enemy: Hailey's record in dealing with political agitation in India suggests, like that of Lord Irwin, with whom he was intimate, a pattern of masterly inactivity arising from over-confidence, followed by repression when the reality of the threat at last became apparent.[115] 'You will have a trying day tomorrow', he once said to his District Magistrate while Chief

Commissioner of Delhi; 'You will be on the alert all day and will probably have a riot. But I have discussed all your arrangements and I approve of them. One embarrassment at least you shall be spared. I am going fishing.'[116]

What Hailey did see in the way of African unrest was a number of scattered local agitations arising from problems connected with land tenure, taxation, conditions of employment, and interference with native custom. All of these problems, falling within the sphere of legitimate unrest, could be dealt with, he believed, by intelligent and sympathetic administrators – were indeed assumed to be, though he did not explicitly say so, their bread and butter: he himself had dealt superlatively with the Punjab rent agitations of 1931.[117] In themselves such problems required no change in the administrative system. However, he did not discount the possibility that larger agitations based on 'racial consciousness' might arise, and these he felt could only be forestalled by making appropriate changes in the structure of administration. The obvious place to begin was by encouraging the evolution of the current native authorities into something which bore a greater resemblance to English local government.

This was not yet, however, the decisive abandonment of Indirect Rule. Nothing drastic or even very specific was proposed. Hailey's reservations about Indirect Rule were based purely upon the practical consideration that in its dogmatic insistence on working only through the authentic traditional leadership it excluded other, possibly more effective, methods of securing the essential 'degree of acquiescence' in British rule. Adherence to tradition, Hailey wrote, in a discreet display of the higher cynicism, 'valuable as it is, is only a means of securing acceptability of the institutions on which we place our reliance, and acceptability is the essential quality which they must possess'.[118] His concern was to ensure that Indirect Rule was sufficiently modernized to function as an instrument of government in an era of rapid social and economic change.

With respect to other aspects of colonial administration, his proposals were a little bolder. Educated Africans, he saw, would only fully accept European rule if they were given some access to the central institutions of government. He therefore proposed that they should be given increased representation in Legislative Councils and that they should be admitted to the administrative services. There was not, however, to be any question of unofficial legislative majorities, and the inevitable requests for development of a parliamentary system must be firmly resisted. Hailey envisaged a system of regional councils, with a nominated membership drawn from native authorities and town councils, functioning initially in a largely consultative capacity but eventually being given legislative powers. Such councils might, conceivably, 'attract the interests of politically minded Africans and thus serve to diminish the demand for representation in a central Legislature by recourse to a system of electorates'.[119] One could only hope that they would; at any rate, they were a relatively safe form of experimentation in power sharing which, unlike a commitment to the development of parliamentary institutions, could if necessary be abandoned. This was all very much in line with the current thinking of the more policy-minded Indirect Rulers: Margery Perham, and even Lugard, supported the formation of regional councils along these lines.[120]

Hailey's chief preoccupations, then, were to find ways of keeping educated Africans (of whose mental capacities he took, incidentally, a dim view[121]) from making a successful bid for power at the centre of the colonial system, and to see that there was no unconsidered rush to reform at the level of the localities. It hardly seems accidental that the extremely imprecise and tentative nature of his proposals allowed the maximum scope for the exercise of political judgement at all levels of the administrative system. Hailey was first and last an administrator, and he intended by his vision of the African future no disrespect to the administrator or diminution of his status. His whole approach to African problems rested indeed on the assumption that there were large reserves of political sagacity within the imperial service, and his aim was to ensure that no situation developed which was beyond the reach of that sagacity.

Unfortunately, Hailey's strategy was to be undone by the very people in whom he reposed his trust.[122] In 1942 Sir Alan Burns, the governor of the Gold Coast, requested the Colonial Office's approval for the appointment of two Africans to his Executive Council. Hailey was, of course, opposed to the idea: in his view the Executive Council was, and should remain, the preserve of officials, who could rise above the narrow sectional interests of other people.[123] But Burns persisted and – his abilities were highly regarded at the Colonial Office – got his way. Bourdillon, the governor of Nigeria, supported the proposal and made a similar request of his own, so by 1943 both the Gold Coast and Nigeria had Africans on their Executive Councils. The force of precedent being what it is, they were joined shortly afterwards by Africans on the Executive Council of Sierra Leone.

The extraordinary thing about these concessions is that they appear to have been made for no particular reason. Certainly they were not made in response to African pressure. Burns believed that the change he proposed would come as a pleasant surprise to the inhabitants of the Gold Coast. Bourdillon thought it would be nice to have Africans on his Council who could advise him of native reactions to government proposals. Neither governor thought of this development as in any way superseding a system of Indirect Rule at the local level. Nor was any very serious thought given to the future constitutional implications of admitting Africans to the holy of holies of colonial government, which they invariably regarded as the precursor of a cabinet. Burns in fact was soon thinking of abolishing the Executive Council altogether, and neither he nor Bourdillon thought that self-government for either of their colonies was visible on the horizon of time. Burns believed, he said, 'in giving people what I think they would like, and should have, before they ask for it'[124]; he seems to have aspired to nothing more than an agreeable atmosphere in which to do business. These important concessions were given with insouciance in a spirit of omnipotence.

This becomes abundantly clear when we consider further developments in the Gold Coast and Nigeria. By the end of 1943 political Africans in the Gold Coast, taking heart from the developments of the previous year, were petitioning for elected majorities in both the Executive and Legislative Councils. Burns compromised by offering them an unofficial majority on the Legislative Council, assuring the Colonial Office as he requested permission to do so that everything remained well in hand.

> I feel confident that the granting of an unofficial majority . . . will be greatly appreciated by the people of the Gold Coast, and, although in some minor matters this may result in some unreasonable and irritating obstruction to Government measures, I do not believe that in the long run the country will be the loser. In major matters the proposed 'reserve powers' of the Governor are adequate, and I should not hesitate to use these powers should circumstances make it necessary.[125]

'Confident' is definitely the right word, and so perhaps would be 'centralizing'. Burns was proposing a political system in which the governor, exercising his reserve powers or not, was the pivotal figure. His patrons and mentors in the Colonial Service had been Lugard, Clifford and Cameron[126]; clearly he had not sat at their feet for nothing.

But the Colonial Office was now beginning to do more than respond to the initiatives of activist governors. When Bourdillon mooted the grand but vague possibility of a scheme of overall constitutional reform for Nigeria, he was rapidly moved by the

Office in the direction of an unofficial majority in the legislature – a development about which he had previously, recalling his experience in Ceylon, expressed the profoundest reservations.[127] He offered little in the way of resistance, however, possibly because of the ill-health which was shortly to drive him into retirement. His successor, Sir Arthur Richards, was also over-ruled on the point, and in Nigeria, too, an unofficial majority on the Legislative Council shortly became an accomplished fact.

The reasons for the decline of Hailey's influence are not entirely clear, but seem to reflect the growing impatience among Colonial Office officials with masterly inactivity in any shape or form. By 1943, when the importance of post-war planning for the colonies was given unambiguous recognition in the form of a massively funded Colonial Development and Welfare Act, they had acquired the taste for action which was to carry matters so swiftly forward after 1945. Hailey's wise evasions were cast aside. Now was the time to be up and doing; and none felt this new ethos more intensely, or evangelized it more successfully, than Andrew Cohen, who by 1945 had replaced Hailey as the dominant force in Colonial Office thinking on Africa.

Cohen brought into the Colonial Office after 1943 a passion for moulding events always latent within him but immensely stimulated by three years spent on wartime secondment as controller of supplies and acting Lieutenant-Governor of Malta.[128] His previous years in the Colonial Office had been disillusioning; nothing ever seemed to get done. But when he returned in 1943 he found the atmosphere more to his liking and was senior enough to make his voice heard. Impervious to the mystique of colonial administration, of which, unlike Hailey, he had no experience at first hand, he plunged right in with radical recommendations for constitutional change in Nigeria, giving as his reasons that:

> Up to now Nigeria has been governed by a benevolent autocracy of officials. At its best this has taken the form almost of a squirearchy. At its worst it has tended to give too much weight to the rigid and rather inhuman outlook of the Secretariat. The day of such autocratic government is passing and more and more educated Africans have got to be brought into the administrative machine.[129]

This was a far cry from anything that Hailey might have said, though the thinking seems recognizably the same as that of A.O. Hume and John Morley, whose hatred of bureaucracy sped India on its constitutional way. In the context of his career and opinions it becomes clear, however, that Cohen's fundamental objection to bureaucracy was not so much that it was inhuman, as that it was inefficient. He was a visionary planner, to whom the judicious calculation of risk was an alien experience; his advent to power in the Colonial Office revealed Hailey to have been, not the herald of a new age, as the simple act of peering into the future had made him appear to be, but the last champion of an old one.

In 1947 Cohen became head of the African division of the Colonial Office, under the Fabian Colonial Secretary Arthur Creech Jones, who had long been the Labour party's parliamentary specialist on Africa. Creech Jones had a strong sense of economic mission to the poor of the world which was basically uncomplicated by political considerations. The important thing, he believed, was not whether Britain ought or ought not to have an empire, but whether, possessing one, she did her best to improve the lives of its inhabitants. He had thus proved amenable during the war to the view of officialdom that self-government was a desirable goal but, in view of the work that remained to be done, the time was not yet. By the end of the war he was advocating political reform as a means of forestalling 'irresponsible nationalism'.[130] But he was captivated by the idea, already developed in Cohen's mind, that if the economic work of the empire were to be done, educated Africans must be actively won to the cause of development. Where Hailey had been mainly concerned to divert the intelligentsia's political impulses into channels which were harmless to the colonial state, Cohen aimed to secure its wholehearted collaboration – a distinction of immense significance, for it seemed to follow that the only chance of doing this was to give Africans, at an early date, a substantial measure of political power. The political and economic lines of thinking in the Colonial Office had converged – with the political one taking a sharp turn to the left.

The first fruit of the new policy was the Local Government Despatch of February 1947, drafted by Cohen and circularized among the African colonies in the name of the Secretary of State. In it Indirect Rule was pronounced dead and its replacement by a democratized system of local government announced. Most African governors responded to it with a marked absence of enthusiasm. They sensed its implicit devaluation of their service's accumulated expertise and authority, and fell back on their commitment to the patiently assisted evolution of the native administration system: many looked forward to the day, not too far distant, when a new generation of chiefs, educated at government schools, would take over their little ships of state and begin to steer them into the modern world, and this seemed enough to be going on with. Philip Mitchell, then governor of Kenya, was particularly scathing about what he regarded as the utopian character of the scheme.[131] Nevertheless, numerous, not very convincing, experiments in forms of partially representative local government were made in the next few years, before the attempt was quietly laid to rest in the early 1950s. The main result was to help prepare the ground for the advocacy of 'multiracialism' by which settler minorities in East and Central Africa fought a rearguard action against independence in the late 1950s and early 1960s; for the argument was inevitably made that the representative principle in local government meant the inclusion of whites.[132]

If the Local Government Despatch made the African governors' flesh creep, the other schemes which were hatching in the Colonial Office would have made their hair stand on end, had they known of them. For an even more radical document was being prepared – the report of the committee set up under Cohen and Sydney Caine, the head of the economic department, to devise a new approach to the economic and political development of Africa. This report, submitted in May 1947, recommended that 'within a generation . . . the principal African territories' should attain 'full responsible government'[133], and outlined four stages through which they were to process. These recommendations were accepted as the basis of policy by the Labour government, but seem never to have been revealed to the Colonial Service, whose opposition was taken for granted. The idea was that power would be gradually conceded to Africans as those who aspired to leadership showed that they had enough popular support to insist on it. This disposed of the usual shibboleth about the unrepresentative nature of African politicians, and was meant to ensure the transfer of power to stable governments. But it also completed the process of placing decisions about the future of Africa in the hands of the Colonial Office. It was the Office which would exercise the necessary judgement about when and how far to proceed, governors being reduced to mere barometers registering the African political weather. To ensure a more reliable reading, five African governors who were coming up for retirement in 1947 were replaced by men in sympathy with the new policy.

This had unlooked-for results of some importance in the Gold Coast, where the new governor, the inexperienced Sir Gerald Creasy, whose professional life had been spent hitherto behind a desk in the Colonial Office, responded to rioting in Accra in 1948 with the conviction that the imperial Armageddon was already at hand. A more old-fashioned governor might have seen the riots for what they were – the expression of economic discontents attendant upon the ending of the war – and, out of professional self-respect if nothing else, kept his response in proportion. But Creasy, abetted by some senior local officials unsettled by the communist takeover in Czechoslovakia a few days before, detected the hand of organized nationalism, and perhaps of international communism, at work, and, forgetting the four stages, panicked and asked for troops. Cohen and Creech Jones had not forgotten, however, and moved swiftly in the face of what they believed to be a revolutionary situation to put their plan into operation. A mere three years later the Gold Coast had direct elections and a proto-ministerial system, which put it at stage three of the master plan. The first elections were held in the belief that victory would go to the moderate United Gold Coast Convention. It went instead to the new Convention People's Party of Kwame Nkrumah, who had to be let out of jail to become leader of government business in the legislature, and a year later, prime minister. It is pertinent to note that Nkrumah might not have fought the election at all had it not been for a consciously Irwinian intervention by Reginald Saloway, the Colonial Secretary of the Gold Coast and formerly of the ICS, who persuaded him in a man-to-man talk to drop his plans for civil disobedience and take the constitutional road instead.[134] Once in office Nkrumah lost no time in organizing his mass base around the demand for independence, and with the assistance of the governor, Sir Charles Arden-Clarke, who, if Saloway saw himself as Irwin, certainly saw himself as Mountbatten, led the Gold Coast to independence in 1957. The occasion was a festive one, and the high life was danced on the Government House lawn.

No one now underestimates the influence of events in the Gold Coast on the rapidity with which other British colonies in Africa achieved their independence: it was critical. Once Nkrumah emerged from jail to become the elected leader of his country the British empire in Africa, notwithstanding a revival of imperialism under the Tory governments of the 1950s, was on its way to being history. The British had put power up for grabs, and political Africans grabbed. In East Africa, the 'second colonial occupation'[135], resulting from the implementation of large-scale develop-ment projects, assisted the process by providing material grievances around which people could be organized. No sooner did the British become serious about the business of government, than it became all too clear that the one white man holding in thrall a million blacks had indeed not been enthralling them at all. In Central Africa, Cohen's well-intentioned plans for federation of the three British territories in the end aroused African opposition which men like Hastings Banda – who had sat at Nkrumah's feet in Accra – and Kenneth Kaunda were able to exploit. By the time Cohen died in 1968 his recommendation that the transfer of power should be completed within a generation had, with the important exception of Southern Rhodesia, where the whites took matters into their own hands, been fulfilled, if not entirely in the graceful fashion he anticipated.

Yet there was a fundamental ambiguity in the Cohen-Creech Jones strategy which remains historically unresolved. Were they trying to give the empire away, or keep it? The answer seems to be that they never really faced up to the question. It was implicit in the strategy that economic collaboration equalled political loyalty, the one being assumed to be impossible without the other; yet the existence of opposition, and the likelihood of its increasing, was also acknowledged. The Plan was justified to Cohen's political masters as strengthening moderate Africans against extremists; and again, the basis for this seems to have been the assumption that those who collaborated in developing the African economies, and who reaped the fruits of development, would be in some sense loyal, though there appears to be no evidence that Cohen had in mind the creation of the comprador class of dependency theory. The ambiguity was resolved in his and Creech Jones' minds by the conviction that their strategy conduced to the creation of the Commonwealth: 'full responsible government' was assumed all along to mean independence within the framework of the Commonwealth.[136] It was thus in the belief that they were building a new form of association hitherto unknown to man, involving a new conception of sovereignty based less on considerations of what could be defended militarily than on a proved capacity for the benevolent use of power, that a Labour government, committed to realizing the full potential of the colonies as the basis for Britain's continued existence as a great power, was able to proceed confidently with a policy of dismantling Britain's imperial authority. If this seems to us now to be so unrealistic as to be unbelievable, we must exercise our historical imagination sufficiently to see that the intellectual weakness of the argument testified to the strength of the political conviction behind it.

The influence of events in India on all of this is extremely hard to assess: it has been often assumed – in one direction or the other – but never fully documented. Hailey's determination not to concede power too early at the centre arose from his concern to avoid the mistakes he believed had been made in India.[137] But Cohen also was anxious to avoid the mistakes of Indian policy – only he believed that the problem in India had been that concessions were made too little and too late[138]; in his own way he was just as keen to secure 'acquiescence' as Hailey was. Opposite lessons were thus drawn from the Indian experience, for no other reason, it seems, than temperamental caution versus temperamental optimism. But Hailey enjoyed his period of ascendancy before Mountbatten had demonstrated the difference that optimism could make. Though the idea of a multiracial Commonwealth was widely accepted in Britain by the end of the war, it was the joyful accession of India which made it a reality, and it is difficult to imagine that this made no difference to the subsequent development of policy. The Cohen-Caine report in fact was completed three months before the independence of India, but at a time when Nehru's acceptance of Commonwealth membership was known to the Cabinet. Its authors presumably at least felt vindicated in their vision of a swift and peaceful collective journey to the City of God.

In only one African colony, Kenya, was this hope substantially disappointed. Here strengthening the moderates against the extremists meant, in the situation the British supposed themselves to be in, arming the former against the latter, and then rewarding the loyalists economically in a fashion which, after independence, made Kenya a prize exhibit in the neo-colonialist case. The resort to force in the end involved the British government in contradictions sufficiently distasteful to precipitate the final decision to retire from Africa. In its lesser way, the judgement of the Devlin Commission that Nyasaland was 'no doubt only temporarily, a police state' also made its contribution. But even then there was no blatant scuttle: constitutions were mongered to the end. Confronted with the probability that formal dominion could be continued only through force, the British gave it up; but they did what they could to create successor regimes over which informal influence could be preserved. This consideration was not neglected even in the economically and strategically insignificant territory of Tanganyika, where Julius Nyerere was hopefully deputed to carry the flag.[139] Britain left Africa in the style in which she had entered it – that of a great power. It was only the substance that was lacking. What helped to disguise the fact, to the world and to the British alike, was their conviction, nurtured over a hundred years and acted upon instinctively to the last, that even without force they possessed the secret of authority.

It was Britain's still unshaken conviction of her great power status, with world-wide interests to defend, that led her into two other messy little wars of the 1950s and '60s, the campaigns for Aden and Cyprus, and also into the *grande débâcle* of Suez. In Cyprus and in Aden the usual attempts at extracting friendly collaboration foundered upon the existence of genuinely determined armed nationalist movements with outside support. Britain's exit in both cases was inglorious, though in Cyprus a military base was secured.

There followed some years of peaceful though increasingly un-dignified resignation to decline, until Margaret Thatcher astonished the world by sending the British navy to recover the Falklands from Argentina. This was magnificent, but it was not imperialism. The point of the exercise was honour, not dominion, and its chief result may have been to show the British that an honourable existence could be led in the world without the great empire on which they had so long relied.

Let us close by returning to a minor but insistent theme emerging at times throughout this book – the sense of nemesis with which British imperialists were periodically afflicted when they thought of their ill works in the world. Plausible as the inference may appear, it would be a mistake to regard this sense of nemesis, though perfectly genuine, as contributing in any intentional fashion to Britain's imperial demise. It rarely resulted in a desire to liberate the subject races, but produced as a rule an urgent desire to be spared retribution – in the form of loss of dominion – by being good. In the words of Kipling's great propitiatory hymn, written at the apogee of empire in 1897,

> Lord God of Hosts, be with us yet,
> Lest we forget – lest we forget!

Nemesis was above all something to be avoided.

There were, of course, few Englishmen who thought that there was anything inherently sinful about empire, and that the mere fact of possession invited retribution. Even that most nemesis-ridden of all Victorian thinkers, that sense of sin incarnate, John Ruskin, regarded the empire not as the problem but as the solution: it was the place where the middle classes could go to redeem themselves, as he tried to show in his study of Herbert Edwardes.[140]

The sense of nemesis can best be seen as the dark side of the British belief in their legitimizing genius for rule. Supposing one were not so to conduct oneself as to inspire the love of subject races? The result, surely, would be the loss of that prestige upon which British rule, unlike that of other races, depended. To emphasize prestige as the British did was to invite, at times, a panic fear of inability to maintain it.

Lugard worried a great deal about the moral putrefaction, national and individual, which ensued from 'the arrogant display of power, or the selfish pursuit of profit'[141], and understood this putrefaction in itself to be the essential nemesis – for no man could hope to rule natives without possessing the qualities required to secure their loyalty and respect. His solution was to choose English gentlemen for the work: 'There is no danger of such men falling a prey to that subtle moral deterioration which the exercise of power over inferior races produces in men of a different type . . . .'[142] Cromer, too, concerned himself with nemesis, as did almost every literate imperialist in a culture so thoroughly conversant with the history of the ancient world. His solution, like Hugh Clifford's, was to make responsible use of imperial power. Thus the British would receive the respect due to their 'superior talents and unselfish conduct' and remain in authority. Otherwise, their empire would fall, and deservedly.[143]

Even if power were inarguably abused, however, all was not irretrievably lost. There was still time for repentance: responsibility, though forsaken, could be resumed. The influential work of J.S. Furnivall on British rule in Burma was founded on, and encouraged, this presumption. To read his chronicle of British offences against Burmese society must have been at first, for a sensitive reader, to despair. But then we find him writing that those who 'destroy a civilization thereby assume responsibilities which they can discharge only by building a new and more highly organized civilization in its place, and, if they fail in this, must pay their reckoning with Nemesis'. If they succeed, however, their reward will be the preservation of 'those established political connections between Europe and the tropics which have come into existence through the temporary incapacity of tropical rulers and peoples to accept the conditions of modern civilization'.[144] The Commonwealth is here implied.

The connection between the extremely personal nature of the British conception of imperial rule and the concern with imperial doom can be seen clearly and appropriately in a curious pamphlet by the rajah of Sarawak, Charles Johnson Brooke, second of his line, in 1907.[147] Brooke looked around him at the state of the British colonies and prophesied that in a matter of decades they would be gone. The 'dark and coloured races', tired of injustice and daily gathering strength, would arise and throw off the imperial yoke, probably under the leadership of China and Japan. Brooke assigned some of the responsibility for this to blunders in high places, but mostly he was inclined to blame the forthcoming cataclysm on the fact that 'the right men to deal with natives are not chosen'. In the days of his youth – he was seventy-eight – such men had been in place, men 'who were accustomed to the civilities and refinements of life more than to the drudgery of office routine', but now, 'though we govern, we only do so by power, and not by friendly intercourse of feeling'. He was inclined furthermore to deplore the excessively

Anglicizing tendencies of British rule, which conveyed to the native loss of respect for his own antique and generally adequate way of doing things. Brooke offered no solution: it was implied in his own state of Sarawak, where English gentlemen ruled ignorant savages benignly and in perpetuity, avoiding by inactivity the otherwise inevitable contradictions of imperial rule.

Epilogue:
Grand Illusions
1900–1940

We might in conclusion ask whether the habits of mind described in this book, having their origin in England but developing exotically outside it, influenced in turn the manner in which English political life not directly connected with imperial matters was conducted. Was there an imperial style in English politics? If by an imperial style we are to understand – what has hitherto been implied – a style the essence of which was the exaltation of the individual agent at work for the good of the state, and operating on its behalf through the power of the unsupported personality, the answer is probably yes – for a brief period and in the work of a minority whose influence may nevertheless have been important.

It was the Round Table group which attempted to import this style of politics into English life. Returning from South Africa after unification in 1910 with their heads seriously turned by the exercise of great, premature and irresponsible authority, and equipped with a world view which saw the empire not as a mere epiphenomenon of British power but as the very foundation of Britain's position in the world, they walked confidently through the doors opened for them by Milner at the top of English political society. Here their extreme concern that the business of the state be in the proper hands, combined with their conviction that those hands were their own and those of their associates, led them to adopt an approach to politics which was profoundly anti-democratic and, ultimately, profoundly anti-realistic. Their methods were those which their campaign for South African unification had taught them were effective in exerting direct and unaccountable influence in a supposedly democratic society[1]: the well-placed newspaper article, the ostensibly detached contribution to the periodical press, in due course the wise and judicious radio broadcast (they were among the first to appreciate the potential of the BBC), and, above all, private

271

displays of sagacity. They were perhaps the closest approximation in reality to Cecil Rhodes' secret society, dedicated, it will be recalled, to 'the furtherance of the British Empire . . . the recovery of the United States . . . the making of the Anglo Saxon race but one Empire'. They wildly over-estimated what politics, thus conceived, could do.

The Round Tablers admired more than anything else political flair – that quality which endowed its possessor with an instinctive sense of what the next move in the political game should be. Like Charles Temple's Resident, they sought to combine guile and utterly disarming pleasantness in a way which made them masters of their fate and that of others. Their approach to politics was elaborated with a high degree of urbanity in the writings of F.S. Oliver, the businessman, man of letters, and highly influential political meddler who was an intimate of Milner. His *The Endless Adventure* (1930–35), a political biography of Robert Walpole, descanted ecstatically on Walpole's sure touch in political warfare and high-minded indifference to democratic political convention. Politics, Oliver declared, was 'the endless adventure of governing men'.[2] In fiction, the adventurous point of view was represented by an old associate of the Round Tablers from South African days – John Buchan. Buchan's heroes all had flair in quantity – sometimes a little too much of it, in the manner of that generation of demi-gods active in Oxford before the First World War and celebrated too extravagantly by their contemporaries, of whom Buchan was one: Sandy Arbuthnot was Aubrey Herbert; Vernon Milburne, Raymond Asquith. Politics, Buchan wrote, was 'the greatest and most honourable adventure'.[3] For all their apparent individualism, what was almost always at stake in his novels was the safety of the state; they were among the earliest prototypes of the spy stories which find such a ready audience in our state-obsessed age.[4]

Though their main concern upon returning to England was imperial federation, the Round Tablers swiftly gravitated towards that traditional concern of political elites – foreign policy. It was here that they contrived to do great damage, for there can be little doubt that in the 1930s they helped to create a climate of worldly, as opposed to pacifistic, support for appeasement.

Under the influence of Milner's view that the imposition of a harsh peace upon Germany in 1919 defeated the object of securing a general settlement in Europe, the Round Tablers decided that the formulation of a statesmanlike policy towards Nazi Germany, leading, it was hoped, to a constructive re-arrangement of Europe as a whole, must proceed from the assumption that the errors of

Versailles had first to be rectified.[5] There was a moral dimension to this decision, but there was an immoral one too: at the heart of the Round Tablers' support for appeasement there was a deep contempt for Europe. As men of empire, architects of the embryonic Anglo-Saxon world state, they found themselves barely able to take seriously the agitations of unpredictable continental politicians, of which they habitually, in their private communications, wrote in terms that might have been employed of uncouth perturbations in some backwater of the empire. Their contempt extended impartially to friends and enemies alike. The French they regarded as utterly irresponsible, and indeed as scarcely white: Lionel Curtis once observed that the skins of Brahmins were 'sometimes no darker than those of Frenchmen'.[6] Czechoslovakia they viewed as a sort of failed South Africa, its unassimilated minorities a standing reproach to the statesmanship of its leaders; they had failed in 'wisdom and prudence'.[7] As for the arch-enemies, Hitler and Mussolini, the Round Tablers were profoundly unimpressed. Personal enthusiasm for the dictators did not feature in their assessments of the situation – and nor, unfortunately, did a realistic appraisal of the threat which they presented.

Accustomed as imperialists to operating in a historical vacuum, where boundary adjustments were made with the flick of a pen, the Round Tablers displayed a marked insouciance about re-drawing the map of Europe. 'I do not myself see what there is to fuss about', wrote John Buchan with authentically proconsular detachment;

> Austria will be much more comfortable economically under Germany's wing. That should have been done long ago in the Versailles Treaty. The chief trouble will be if there is any real threat to Czechoslovakia; but there again, I think the frontier should be rectified. Surely the Versailles arrangement was the most half-witted thing ever perpetrated![8]

'What Europe is witnessing at the moment', Buchan instructed Mackenzie King in 1936, 'is not a conflict of genuine principles so much as the wrangling of ambitious mob-leaders, who have behind them nations who have lost their nerve.' 'This tom-fool Nazi rule' was his description of the government of Germany.[9] In the same spirit, Lothian reported upon his return from a visit to Hitler in 1935 that 'He has a dual personality and creates mass hysteria, but he left me completely cold'.[10] It may well be that one of Britain's misfortunes at this time was that the great disturbers of the peace in Europe bore so striking a resemblance to the colonial agitators whose obsessive sense of grievance her proconsuls were accustomed to manage, and whose ridiculous posturings they were accustomed to ignore.

The steady rise of German military power forced the Round Tablers to acknowledge the need for something substantial to support their efforts at statesmanship, and they therefore became advocates of rearmament. But their conception of rearmament was entirely defensive – the offensives they envisaged remained political. To the end they believed implicitly, in true imperial style, that force was not the extension but the failure of politics. The acknowledgement of German strength stimulated, however, their habitual empiricism and they concluded not too reluctantly that for the safety of the state the game of power politics must now be played. This they proceeded to do, though in general paying but scant attention to the 'power' on which their politics was based. One of the more remarkable fruits of this approach was Lothian's proposal in 1935 for the restoration of Germany's former colonies, in return for an agreement on the limitation of armaments[11]: so much for the glorious responsibilities of the Tanganyika mandate. Another was the inspiration that the way out of the current difficulties was via Anglo-German co-operation in determining the fate of Europe: or, as Geoffrey Dawson put it, 'if the Germans are so powerful as you say, oughtn't we to go in with them?'[12] When Lothian went to visit Hitler in 1935 he recalled to him Cecil Rhodes' great dream that the United States, England and Germany might one day together preserve the peace of the world.[13]

Munich the Round Tablers at first greeted with relief. But when word got out of the fashion in which Hitler had bullied Neville Chamberlain in their second meeting at Godesberg, doubts began to set in.[14] It seemed that Chamberlain had not been treated with the respect he deserved. The dreadful possibility became apparent that Hitler was not as much in awe of British statesmanship as had been supposed. The Round Tablers persevered with appeasement, but the gloss had gone off 'power politics'. Henceforth a more appalling sense of danger began to prevail.

How much influence, if any, did these views, assiduously circulated in the serious press, have upon official policy? To this question there can be no completely satisfactory answer. There was, it is true, a close and well-documented association – at Cliveden[15] and elsewhere – between the Round Tablers and the leading proponents of appeasement in the government. But the evidence tends to suggest that this association was less an influential than an affinitive one. The case which could perhaps be made is not that the Round Table exercised a baleful influence upon official policy, but that official policy reflected to a large extent the same fundamental values and approach to politics.

Recent scholarship has disposed decisively of the notion that Neville Chamberlain was a timid man.[16] His vanity was monstrous, his ambition ruthless, his Cabinet a stranger to collective responsibility. The son of a great imperialist, Joseph Chamberlain, he possessed like his father, and like his acquaintances of the Round Table, a fundamental contempt for Europe: his often-quoted remarks during the Czechoslovakian crisis concerning the 'quarrel in a faraway country between people of whom we know nothing' reveal themselves, in the context of his entire career, to be the product not of ignorance but of an inveterate disdain. Chamberlain was a man who always did his homework, and his policy towards Europe was based, not on irrational anxiety, but on a confident rationality thoroughly, persistently, and ruthlessly employed. Time and again he wore down his opponents in the Cabinet with argument, or outwitted them, in the cause of right, by strategem, and like the Round Tablers, he accorded to politics thus defined an autonomy which he was to learn in the end it could not possess. There is little evidence for the claim, later made so assiduously by his apologists, that Chamberlain's policy was intended to gain time for Britain to re-arm. On the contrary, it is plain that he intended by his own unaided efforts to arrive at no less than that *rapprochement* with Germany which was so dear to the heart of Lord Lothian: his legacy was meant to be a new European order.[17]

Chamberlain's approach to Hitler was anything but abject. Upon his return from Berchtesgaden, he described the *Führer* to the assembled Cabinet at 'the commonest little dog' he ever saw.[18] And when he took to the air on that fateful morning in September 1938 to go and treat with him, he did so in a state of immodest exaltation, conscious to the nth degree of the bold figure he supposed himself to be cutting in the sight of history.[19] After Munich, when he was asked by a fellow guest at a dinner party why Hitler's promise should be trusted, after so many other promises made by him had been broken, he replied that, this time, it was different: 'this time he promised *me*'.[20]

The Round Tablers were firm supporters of Chamberlain. But from the beginning they had their reservations about him. Though he had grasp and he had resolution, he did not have flair. Their real hero in the Cabinet was not Chamberlain but the man who, after the departure of Anthony Eden in February 1938, became his foreign secretary – Lord Halifax.

Halifax was none other than that Lord Irwin who had treated so spectacularly with Gandhi in 1931, further ennobled upon the death of his father in 1934. He owed his appointment to the Foreign Office to the same intangible qualities of address which had secured him the viceroyalty in 1925, now greatly enhanced in the eyes of his associates by the wonders performed in that office. Great expectations appear to have been entertained of him. Might he not, as Samuel Hoare was to write, 'have the same success in Europe that he had won in Asia?'[21]

From the middle of 1936 the idea was being mooted among Halifax's associates that he might go to visit Hitler.[22] Germany had just re-occupied the Rhineland and it seemed there might be something he could do. Halifax himself was more modest, confessing to an acquaintance that: 'I am not sure Hitler is not more difficult than Mr Gandhi.'[23] The idea of sending an imperial statesman to deal with Hitler had at this time fertile ground in which to grow. For some years it had been rumoured that T.E. Lawrence might emerge from his seclusion in the ranks of the armed forces to solve the problems of the world: 'the young men are talking, the young poets writing of him in a Messianic strain – as the man who could, if he would, be a light to lead stumbling humanity out of its troubles', wrote Liddell Hart in 1934.[24] Lawrence's friend Henry Williamson, an enthusiast for Anglo German co-operation, later asserted – with what truth remains unknown – that at the time of his death in 1935 he had been 'considering a scheme for the pacification of Europe', the critical ingredient of which was that he and Hitler should meet.[25]

When the great and famous came to pay their respects to Lawrence at St Paul's on 29 January 1936, it was Halifax who was chosen to give the memorial address. Singling out for approbation Lawrence's 'mastery over life', which gave him a superiority 'unchallenged and unsought',[26] he spoke for the happy few who saw their own qualities brilliantly reflected in him.

The atmosphere of Halifax's eventual visit to Germany in November 1937 was extraordinarily unfraught with seriousness. 'In the minds of his countrymen, peers and colleagues', Arnold Toynbee wrote shortly after the event,

> Lord Halifax was regarded at the time with a certain pride and awe, not unmingled with a spice of sceptical amusement, as a characteristically English exponent of some simple but noble virtues who at the same time had the gift of charming the most outlandishly un-English 'wild men' by the unconscious exercise of an intuitive art which was capable of surpassing the Machiavellian triumphs of cleverer and less scrupulous politicians. To the average Englishman's eye Mr Gandhi and Herr Hitler were two hardly distinguishable specimens of the same species of foreigner in virtue of their being, both of them,

superlatively exotic; and the average member of a British Cabinet may have reasoned in November 1937 that the guileless tamer of Gandhi had at any rate a 'sporting chance' of taming Hitler likewise. Were not both these political 'mad mullahs' non-smokers, non-drinkers of alcohol, non-eaters of meat, and non-practisers of blood sports in their cranky private lives? And did not the German Führer, like the Indian Mahatma, have some bee in his bonnet about the importance of being 'Aryan'?[27]

Halifax's own account opened in the same spirit of fun, with his mistaking the *Führer* upon first sight for a footman.[28] He was not unconscious of the role he was expected to play.

The talks themselves were in the event of a desultory nature, but they seem to have confirmed in Halifax his habitual sense of superiority to the enemy. His descriptions of the Nazi leaders displayed a curious detachment. Of Goering he observed that he was 'immensely entertained at meeting the man. One remembered all the time that he had been concerned with the "clean up" in Berlin on June 30, 1934, and I wondered how many people he had been responsible for getting killed.' The founder of the Gestapo left upon him 'a composite impression of film-star, gangster, great landowner interested in his property, Prime Minister, party manager, head-gamekeeper at Chatsworth'.[29] Goebbels, too, when he came to tea at the embassy, failed to arouse any active sensation of disgust. 'I had expected to dislike him intensely', Halifax recorded, '– but didn't. I suppose it must be some moral defect in me, but the fact remains.'[30] Some remarks of Goebbels' confirmed 'what I had always been inclined to think about part of the Nazi attitude arising from an inferiority complex'.[31] In the context of politics, where the interests of the state enjoyed complete priority, Halifax was as indifferent to Hitler's wickedness as he was to Gandhi's goodness.

To Cabinet discussions of policy towards Germany Halifax contributed in support of appeasement a distinctive and influential note – the sorrowful but infinitely justified worldliness of the decent man.[32] To the public debate, as he thrashed his way through his resolutely thoughtful speeches, he contributed an air of strenuous honesty.[33] He shrank from no unpleasantness that had to be accomplished for the sake of the cause. He it was who explained the facts of life to Haile Selassie when the League of Nations was asked to recognize Italian rule over Abyssinia[34], and he it was who could be relied on to face down the French or put the screws on the Czechs as occasion required.[35] Like Churchill, he was a man who slept well at nights.

Halifax was the foremost exponent in the Cabinet of the usefulness of personal contact with the enemy. Of all the members of the government, he was the only one who from the beginning felt confident about direct dealings with the Nazis. On this matter it was he who led and Chamberlain who followed; the way to Munich was paved with Halifax's good intentions. Notwithstanding his failure to tame Hitler in November 1937 – the *Anschluss* followed punctually in March – we find him in April 1938 once more proposing himself as an emissary to the *Führer*.[36] In May he was suggesting inviting Goering to Sandringham.[37] And in the summer of that year he was responsible for the ill-fated Runciman mission to Czechoslovakia. Like his friends of the Round Table, Halifax believed that in wiser and more experienced hands than those of the Czechs the Sudeten German problem would be capable of solution: before settling on Runciman for his emissary he proposed that the person appointed should be someone who had 'practised experience of administration and of minority problems, such as an ex-governor of an Indian province'.[38] In August Chamberlain allowed him to send a personal appeal to Hitler asking him to cease preparing for war in the interests of peace. This was ignored, leading Chamberlain to conclude, not that such appeals were useless, but that it was time he entered the arena himself.

When Neville Chamberlain took off for Germany on 15 September 1938, accompanied only by his faithful adviser Sir Horace Wilson and an official from the Foreign Office, he acquired by his boldness what in the eyes of the public and the political classes he had never before been acknowledged to possess – the authentic quality of a leader of men. Suddenly, the rolled umbrella, the wing collar, the curate's visage, the shoulderless physique, took on the force of paradox and seemed indicative of the kind of inner strength which required no martial display to make its presence felt. Perhaps it would not be presumptuous to suggest that the long line of imperial heroes who for a hundred years had quelled natives with a word resolved itself that day into a man once described as fit to have been mayor of Birmingham in a bad year.

But fortunately our story does not end here. Even as his master was colloguing with Hitler across the sea, Lord Halifax was experiencing a change of heart. On 23 September he telegraphed to Chamberlain at Godesberg to warn him that the limit of concession had now been reached. On 25 September he argued before the assembled Cabinet that Hitler's demand for the immediate cession of the Sudetenland must not be met. He could not rid his mind, he said, of the fact that Hitler had conceded nothing and was dictating terms as to a vanquished enemy.[39] Lord Halifax was awaking from the long dream of effortless superiority to face the reality of imminent humiliation. During the winter he moved uncertainly and with great agony of mind towards the conviction that the choice which would have to be made was between war with Germany and Britain's abdication as a great power. The occupation of Prague on 15 March 1939 removed all uncertainty. From that point on he moved his country steadily towards war. It was he who was responsible for the unilateral guarantee to Poland which ensured that when Hitler finally moved to satisfy his very evident impulse to add that country to his dominions, Britain would be at war.[40] Believing now that the choice was between doing nothing, which would mean 'a great accession to Germany's strength and a great loss to ourselves of sympathy and support in the United States, in the Balkan countries, and in other parts of the world', and 'entering into a devastating war'[41], Lord Halifax chose the latter course.

Hitler found himself unable to take seriously Britain's intention to go to war over a question – Danzig and the Polish corridor – which only a brief time ago her statesmen had regarded as, of all the contentious questions arising from the settlement of Versailles, the one most amenable to solution in Germany's favour. He had underestimated them as they had underestimated him. He had quite failed to understand that the British will to power had not vanished but only etherealized in the course of Britain's long history of unchallenged consequence in the world. The man who adored *Lives of a Bengal Lancer*, and made it required viewing for his SS because it showed a handful of Englishmen holding a continent in thrall[42], had colossally missed the point. Power had corrupted the British, by making them think it inhered in them personally rather than in the terror of their arms, but in 1939, when everything they admired in themselves seemed suddenly at stake, the qualities they chose to display were those of courage and of reckless pride. Reluctant to fight, they were not afraid to die.

We may ask ourselves in conclusion why it was that in a country where the cult of leadership enjoyed such favour as in England, fascism itself never acquired a hold. The answer surely must be twofold. First, there was the empire to act as an outlet for the very emotions which it inspired: there were always brown races waiting to be led. Second, the mechanisms which developed to ensure that the imperial demand for leadership met with an unfailing supply also operated to rivet upon the British political system a governing class through which the leadership ethos was thoroughly diffused. In a land where the public school system worked to produce *Führers* on the wholesale principle, there was no prospect of any one of them arriving with the consent of his countrymen at supreme power.

Notes

Introduction

1. Stokes, *The English Utilitarians and India* (1959).
2. Temple, *Lord Lawrence*, p. 5.

Chapter 1   Nicholson to Peshawar, Gordon to Khartoum: the Punjab Creed and its Disciples

1. Edwardes and Merivale, *Life of Sir Henry Lawrence*, Vol. I, p. 14. (Vol. I is by Edwardes, who died after completing it; Merivale wrote Vol. II.)
2. Quoted in Kaye, *Lives of Indian Officers*, Vol. II, p. 437.
3. Kaye, *Lives of Indian Officers*, Vol. II, p. 414.
4. Edwardes and Merivale, *Life of Sir Henry Lawrence*, Vol. II, p. 66.
5. Kaye, *Lives of Indian Officers*, Vol. II, pp. 415–19; Khilnani, *The Punjab under the Lawrences*, pp. 31–40. Kaye quotes a letter written to him by Lawrence in which General Littler is named as the officer who took British troops into the field, but this may be a misreading by Kaye as all other authorities give Wheeler. Littler was in command at Lahore and Wheeler in the Jallandhar *doab*.
6. Gibbon, *The Lawrences of the Punjab*, p. 130. See also, e.g., Gough and Innes, *The Sikhs and the Sikh Wars*, p. 148.
7. Kaye, *Lives of Indian Officers*, Vol. I, Preface.
8. Kaye, *A History of the Sepoy War in India*, Vol. I, p. 8.
9. Kaye, *Lives of Indian Officers*, Vol. II, p. 416.
10. Napier, *Defects, Civil and Military, of the Indian Government*, p. 50.
11. Henry Lawrence, *Essays, Military and Political*, p. 310.
12. Kaye, *Lives of Indian Officers*, Vol. II, p. 429.
13. *Westminster Review*, October 1858, quoted in Edwardes and Merivale, *Life of Sir Henry Lawrence*, Vol. II, p. 221.
14. Kaye, *Lives of Indian Officers*, Vol. II, pp. 428–9.
15. Khilnani, *The Punjab under the Lawrences*, p. 112.

16. Napier, *Defects, Civil and Military, of the Indian Government*, pp. 91, 114, 123.

17. Henry Lawrence, 'Sir Charles Napier's Posthumous Work', p. 258.

18. Henry Lawrence, *Essays, Military and Political*, p. 5.

19. Garrett and Grey, *European Adventurers in the Punjab*, pp. 131–2.

20. Edwardes and Merivale, *Life of Sir Henry Lawrence*, Vol. I, p. 296.

21. Henry Lawrence, *Adventures of an Officer in the Service of Runjeet Singh*, Vol. I, p. 45. *Adventurers of an Officer* was first published in serial form in the *Delhi Gazette* in 1840 and was later published as a book. Quotations are from the Oxford reprint of the 1845 edition.

22. Ibid., Vol. II, p. 158.

23. Henry Lawrence, *Essays, Military and Political*, p. 245.

24. Edwardes and Merivale, *Life of Sir Henry Lawrence*, Vol. II, pp. 172–3.

25. Balcarres Ramsey, quoted in Bosworth Smith, *Life of Lord Lawrence*, Vol. I, p. 171.

26. Bosworth Smith, *Life of Lord Lawrence*, Vol. I, p. 181.

27. Herbert Edwardes, *A Year on the Punjab Frontier*, Vol. I, p. 352.

28. Emma Edwardes, *Memorials of the Life and Letters of Major-General Sir Herbert B. Edwardes*, Vol. I, p. 65.

29. Ibid., p. 83.

30. Herbert Edwardes, *A Year on the Punjab Frontier*, Vol. I, pp. 118, 236–8.

31. Ibid., pp. 135–6.

32. Ibid., p. 226.

33. Ibid., pp. 242–5.

34. Ibid., p. viii.

34. Edwardes and Merivale, *Life of Sir Henry Lawrence*, Vol. II, pp. 172–3.

36. Ibid., Vol. I, p. 55.

37. Ibid., p. 255. Pp. 251–6 contain extracts from 'Anticipatory Chapters of Indian History'.

38. *Westminster Review*, October 1858, quoted in ibid., p. 221.

39. Emma Edwardes, *Memorials of the Life and Letters of Major-General Sir Herbert B. Edwardes*, Vol. I, pp. 57, 58.

40. Gibbon, *The Lawrences of the Punjab*, p. 119.

41. Kaye, *Lives of Indian Officers*, Vol. II, p. 627.

42. Ibid., p. 588.

43. Ibid., p. 687–8.

44. Trotter, *The Life of John Nicholson*, pp. 161–2.

45. Ibid., p. 180.

46. Ibid., p. 181.

47. Ibid., p. 43.

48. Ibid., p. 127.

49. Ibid., pp. 314–5.

50. Henry Lawrence, *Adventures of an Officer in the Service of Runjeet Singh*, Vol. I, pp. 122–5.

51. William Napier, *The Life and Opinions of General Sir Charles James Napier*, Vol. IV, p. 228.

52. Henry Lawrence, 'Sir Charles Napier's Posthumous Work', p. 287.

53. Carrington, *The Life of Rudyard Kipling*, p. 106; Lumsden and Elsmie, *Lumsden of the Guides*, pp. 67–8.

54. Herbert Edwardes, *A Year on the Punjab Frontier*, Vol. II, pp. 721–2.
55. Ruskin, 'A Knight's Faith', pp. 386, 478.
56. Herbert Edwardes, *A Year on the Punjab Frontier* Vol. II, p. 722.
57. Ibid., Vol. I, p. 569.
58. Ibid., Vol. II, p. 727.
59. See Low, *Lion Rampant*, p. 19; Robinson, 'Non-European Foundations of European Imperialism'; and Touval, 'Treaties, Borders, and the Partition of Africa', pp. 286–7.
60. Kaye, *Lives of Indian Officers*, Vol. II, p. 423.
61. See his appreciation of Henry Lawrence in Edwardes and Merivale, *Life of Sir Henry Lawrence*, Vol. II, pp. 146–54.
62. Khilnani, *The Punjab under the Lawrences*, pp. 93–5. For evidence that Abbott's hold over the Pathans was less than complete, see Nicholson to Resident at Lahore, 13 September 1848, in Singh, *Private Correspondence relating to the Anglo-Sikh Wars*, pp. 425–7.
63. Edwardes and Merivale, *Life of Sir Henry Lawrence*, Vol. II, pp. 191–2.
64. Kaye, *Lives of Indian Officers*, Vol. II, p. 439.
65. Ibid., p. 488.
66. Bosworth Smith, *Life of Lord Lawrence*, Vol. II, p. 272.
67. This appears to be the import of Kaye, *Lives of Indian Officers*, Vol. II, p. 641.
68. *Third Punjab Administration Report (1854–1856)*, p. 117, cited in Khilnani, *The Punjab under the Lawrences*, p. 128.
69. Beames, *Memoirs of a Bengal Civilian*, p. 103.
70. Cust, *Life Memoir*, p. 30.
71. Sen, *Eighteen Fifty-Seven*, p. 327.
72. Hibbert, *The Great Mutiny*, p. 293.
73. Bosworth Smith, *Life of Lord Lawrence*, Vol. II, p. 63.
74. Ibid., p. 156.
75. Cooper, *The Crisis in the Punjab*, pp. 167–8.
76. Ibid., p. 167.
77. John Lawrence to Lord Canning, 4 December 1857, in Edwardes, *The Necessary Hell*, p. 174.
78. Bosworth Smith, *Life of Lord Lawrence*, Vol. II, p. 227.
79. Ibid., p. 312.
80. *Mutiny Reports from Punjab and N.W.F.P.*, passim. See also Chaudhuri, *Civil Rebellion in the Indian Mutinies*, pp. 235–40. I am not concerned here with the controversy over whether or not the Mutiny was a national revolt. What is clear is that there was disaffection in the Punjab to a degree which belied the government's claims about the loyalty of the population.
81. Edwardes, *The Necessary Hell*, p. 164.
82. *Mutiny Reports from Punjab and N.W.F.P.*, Vol. II, pp. 340–41.
83. Bosworth Smith, *Life of Lord Lawrence*, Vol. II, p. 304.
84. Ibid., p. 308.
85. Memorandum of Governor-General, 20 January 1868, in Stokes, *The English Utilitarians and India*, p. 271.
86. My source for the debate on reorganization is Mason, *A Matter of Honour*, pp. 317–28.
87. Ibid., p. 321.

88. Ibid., p. 324.
89. Cooper, *The Crisis in the Punjab*, p. 7.
90. *Mutiny Reports from Punjab and N.W.F.P.*, p. 343.
91. Mason, *The Men Who Ruled India*, Vol. I, pp. 324–5.
92. See Farewell, *Queen Victoria's Little Wars*, pp. 364–71; Kiernan, *From Conquest to Collapse*, passim; Low, *Lion Rampant*, pp. 21–2.
93. For an estimate of relative numbers, see Kirk-Greene, 'The Thin White Line'.
94. Mundy, *Narrative of Events in Borneo and Celebes*, Vol. II, p. 5. Mundy's book consists mostly of extracts from Brooke's journals; references to it are to the journals.
95. Mannoni's *Prospero and Caliban: The Psychology of Colonisation* is the *locus classicus* of the view that colonialism springs from a 'Prospero complex'; parts of Mannoni's argument have been effectively criticized, but the book remains immensely suggestive.
96. Mundy, *Narrative of Events in Borneo and Celebes*, Vol. I, p. 196.
97. Crisswell, *Rajah Charles Brooke*, pp. 62–3.
98. Poem written by Brooke 'about 1830', in Tarling, *The Burthen, the Risk, and the Glory*, p. 13.
99. Mundy, *Narrative of Events in Borneo and Celebes*, Vol. II, pp. 27–8.
100. Letters to Henry Wise and James Gardner, in James Brooke, *A Vindication of His Character*, pp. 12–15.
101. Mundy, *Narrative of Events in Borneo and Celebes*, Vol. I, pp. 272–3.
102. *Dictionary of National Biography*.
103. Pringle, *Rajahs and Rebels*, pp. 66–7.
104. Tarling, *The Burthen, the Risk, and the Glory*, p. 57.
105. Mundy, *Narrative of Events in Borneo and Celebes*, Vol. II, p. 84.
106. Hahn, *James Brooke of Sarawak*, p. 146.
107. Runciman, *The White Rajahs*, p. 116.
108. Helms, *Pioneering in the Far East*, p. 190.
109. Allen, 'Malayan Civil Service', p. 157. For Colonial Office interest in Sarawak, see Reece, *The Name of Brooke*.
110. Chevenix Trench, *The Road to Khartoum*, p. 53.
111. Gordon, *Khartoum Journals*, pp. 144–5 (5 October 1884).
112. Gordon, *Letters to his Sister*, p. 116 (3 January 1876).
113. Gordon, *Khartoum Journals*, p. 189 (12 October 1884). His views may have owed something to Sir John Seeley's *The Expansion of England*, published in 1883.
114. Wilson, *The 'Ever-Victorious Army'*, pp. 184–5.
115. Spence, *To Change China*, pp. 67, 83.
116. Nutting, *Gordon of Khartoum*, p. 50.
117. Charles, *Three Martyrs of the Nineteenth Century*, pp. 188–9. The other martyrs are Livingstone and Patteson.
118. Chevenix Trench, *The Road to Khartoum*, p. 53.
119. Keegan, *The Face of Battle*, p. 186–92.
120. *Pall Mall Gazette*, 9 January 1884, in Marlowe, *Mission to Khartoum*, pp. 121–2.
121. Ibid., p. 125.
122. Chevenix Trench, *The Road to Khartoum*, p. 195.
123. Ibid., p. 218.
124. Holt, *The Mahdist State in the Sudan*, pp. 111–2.

125. See, e.g., Emerson, *General Gordon*, p. 161; Hake, *Gordon in China and the Soudan*, p. 326.
126. I first became aware of this process of distortion from Douglas H. Johnson's article, 'The Death of Gordon: A Victorian Myth'.
127. Haines, 'Gordon's Death', p. 133.
128. Johnson, 'The Death of Gordon', p. 307.
129. Hake, *The Story of Chinese Gordon, with Additions*, p. 357; and see also Haines, 'Gordon's Death', pp. 136–7.
130. Johnson, 'The Death of Gordon', pp. 286–9.
131. Ibid., pp. 289–92.
132. Hake, *Events in the Taiping Rebellion*, p. 5.
133. Collins, 'The Sudan Political Service', p. 294.
134. Gordon, *Letters to his Sister*, p. 384. (14 December 1884).

Chapter 2 Frederick Courtenay Selous, Adventurer

1. The episode is described in Chevenix Trench, *The Road to Khartoum*, pp. 174–9, and Flint, *Cecil Rhodes*, pp. 56–7.
2. It can be found in Flint, *Cecil Rhodes*, pp. 248–52.
3. Ibid., pp. 216–8.
4. Rhodes to W.T. Stead, 19 August 1891, Rhodes House Micr. Afr. 413.
5. Brett to Rhodes, 15 November 1892, Rhodes House Mss. Afr. s. 229/V.
6. Flint, *Cecil Rhodes*, p. 57.
7. Ibid., p. 218.
8. See Anthony Storr's convincing essay on Churchill in Taylor et al., *Churchill: Four Faces and the Man*, pp. 204–46.
9. E.A. Maund, quoted in Keppel-Jones, *Rhodes and Rhodesia*, p. 104.
10. Williams, *Cecil Rhodes*, p. 146; also, notes by Williams on interview with Selous, 15 June 1914, Rhodes House Mss. Afr. s. 134.
11. Millais, *Life of Frederick Courtenay Selous*, pp. 96, 353–7. Apart from Selous' own writings, Millais is the main biographical source for this chapter. For a Boer estimate of Selous' prowess as a hunter, see Le Roux, *Pioneers and Sportsmen of South Africa*, pp. 180–81.
12. Millais, *Life of Frederick Courtenay Selous*, p. 153.
13. Quoted in ibid., p. 361.
14. Selous, *A Hunter's Wanderings*, p. 400.
15. Ibid., pp. 15–23.
16. Millais, *Life of Frederick Courtenay Selous*, p. 132.
17. Selous, *A Hunter's Wanderings*, pp. 17, 287, 141, 68, 340, viii, 232, 142.
18. Ibid., pp. vii, viii, ix.
19. Millais, *Life of Frederick Courtenay Selous*, pp. 13–55.
20. Haggard, *The Private Diaries of Sir H. Rider Haggard*, pp. 74, 93–4.
21. Haggard, *King Solomon's Mines*, p. x.
22. See Bryden, 'Captain Frederick Courtenay Selous, D.S.O.,' p. 478; and E. Heawood's obituary of Selous in the *Geographical Journal*, p. 222.
23. Haggard, *Allan Quatermain*, pp. 272–3.

24. Millais, *Life of Frederick Courtenay Selous*, pp. 14, 17, 31, 40.
25. Ibid., pp. 2, 13–50.
26. *The Times*, 8 January 1917, p. 9.
27. A.R. Morkel, quoted in Millais, *Life of Frederick Courtenay Selous*, p. 196.
28. Sclater, 'Captain Selous', p. 198.
29. R.M. Haines, quoted in Millais, *Life of Frederick Courtenay Selous*, pp. 348–9.
30. Loveday, *Three Stages of History in Rhodesia*, p. 107.
31. Vambe, *An Ill-Fated People*, pp. 88–90; personal information from David Hatendi. In a speech to the Royal Colonial Institute in 1894, Selous publicly deprecated the idea that white men lost caste with Africans by liaisons with native women (Selous, 'The History of the Matabele, and the Cause and Effect of the Matabele War', p. 259).
32. Selous, *A Hunter's Wanderings*, p. 245.
33. Ibid., pp. 246–7.
34. Selous, *Travel and Adventure in South-East Africa*, p. 322. The letter is reproduced in full on pp. 313–25.
35. Ibid., p. 204.
36. Ibid., pp. 205–6.
37. Selous, 'The History of the Matabele, and the Cause and Effect of the Matabele War', p. 288.
38. His ensuing adventures are described in *Travel and Adventure in South-East Africa*, Chapters XI, XII and XIII, and also in articles in *The Field* in 1888 and 1889 and in the *Proceedings of the Royal Geographical Society*, Vol. XI, 1889.
39. Letter dated 13 November 1888, reproduced in the *Proceedings of the Royal Geographical Society*, Vol. XI, 1889.
40. Cary, *Charter Royal*, p. 46. In the space available in this chapter I can only touch briefly on the complicated manoeuvrings which took place among the various parties competing for what then appeared to be the glittering prize of south central Africa. Of the many books on the subject, the three which I found most useful were Robert Cary's *Charter Royal*, J.S. Galbraith's *Crown and Charter*, and Arthur Keppel-Jones' *Rhodes and Rhodesia*. None of these books can be considered a definitive account; much went on which was not recorded or was deliberately mis-recorded, and the historian must often rely on intelligent surmise.
41. Johnson, *Great Days*, p. 69.
42. Selous, 'Mr Selous' Further Explorations in Matabele-land', p. 296.
43. Michell, *The Life and Times of the Right Honourable Cecil John Rhodes*, Vol. I, pp. 280, 306; Williams interview with Selous, 15 June 1914, Rhodes House Mss. Afr. s. 134. Michell, an early biographer of Rhodes, had access to his papers.
44. Cary, *Charter Royal*, p. 64.
45. Selous, 'Mashunaland and the Mashunas', pp. 662, 675, 664, 675, 676.
46. Keppel-Jones, *Rhodes and Rhodesia*, p. 44.
47. Verschoyle to Cawston, undated, Rhodes House Mss. Afr. s. 73.
48. Selous, 'Mashunaland and the Mashunas', p. 675.
49. See works by D.N. Beach, Terence Ranger and Father Christopher Devlin listed in the bibliography.
50. Selous, 'Further Explorations in the Mashuna Country', pp. 269–70.

51. Selous, 'Mr F.C. Selous' Explorations in Central South Africa', p. 285.
52. Selous, 'Mashunaland and the Mashunas', pp. 665, 676.
53. Selous, 'Twenty Years in Zambesia', pp. 308–10, and *Travel and Adventure in South-East Africa*, pp. 331–5. And see also Blennerhassett and Sleeman, *Adventures in Mashonaland*, p. 196.
54. Millais, *Life of Frederick Courtenay Selous*, p. 330.
55. Selous, *Travel and Adventure in South-East Africa*, p. 286.
56. See his *Sunshine and Storm in Rhodesia*, p. 67.
57. Selous, *Travel and Adventure in South-East Africa*, p. 383.
58. Ranger, 'The Rewriting of African History During the Scramble', p. 273.
59. Selous to Selous Exploration Syndicate, 2 October 1889, in ibid., pp. 273–4.
60. Selous to Selous Exploration Syndicate, 28 October 1889, in Selous, *Travel and Adventure in South-East Africa*, p. 311.
61. Williams interview with Selous, 15 June 1914, Rhodes House Mss. Afr. s. 134.
62. Rhodes to Abercorn, 31 March 1890, Colonial Office Confidential Print, C.O. 879/32, No. 392.
63. Lippert to Colonial Office, 14 March 1890, Colonial Office Confidential Print, C.O. 879/32, No. 392.
64. 'Memorandum on the Origin and Operations of the British South Africa Chartered Company' by Sidney Olivier, Colonial Office Confidential Print, C.O. 879/37, No. 439, p. 15.
65. Johnson to Rhodes, 7 January 1892, Rhodes House Mss. Afr. s. 228, C3B.
66. Selous to his mother, 22 December 1889, quoted in Ranger, 'The Rewriting of African History During the Scramble', p. 275.
67. Selous to Thomas Leask, 6 July 1890, in Wallis (ed.), *The Southern African Diaries of Thomas Leask*, p. 242. See also a list of persons to whom shares of the BSAC were allotted between 21 April and 8 December 1890, catalogued as Item 90 in Rhodes House Mss. Afr. s. 228, C3A.
68. Sir Frederick Young, introducing a talk given by Selous at the Royal Colonial Institute on 13 June 1893. See Selous, 'Incidents of a Hunter's Life in South Africa', p. 347.
69. Blake, *A History of Rhodesia*, p. 71.
70. Leyds, *The Transvaal Surrounded*, p. 444; Axelson, *Portugal and the Scramble for Africa*, p. 218.
71. Article by Selous in the *Manchester Guardian*, 20 January 1891, reproduced in *Travel and Adventure in South-East Africa*, pp. 387–94.
72. Beach, 'The Adendorff Trek in Shona History', pp. 42–3; Selous, *Travel and Adventure in South-East Africa*, pp. 374–7.
73. Jameson to Rutherfoord Harris, 3 August 1890, in Beach, 'The Adendorff Trek in Shona History', p. 43.
74. Selous, *Travel and Adventure in South-East Africa*, p. 426.
75. Tanser, *A Scantling of Time*, p. 253.
76. By early 1891, 'Rhodesia' was the name used in the press, though the chartered company did not adopt the name till 1895. See Blake, *A History of Rhodesia*, p. 114.
77. Selous to Selous Exploration Syndicate, 28 October 1889, in *Travel and Adventure in South-East Africa*, p. 311.
78. Fripp and Hiller (eds.), *Gold and the Gospel in Mashonaland*, p. 22.

79. Selous to his mother, 11 November 1893, in Millais, *Life of Frederick Courtenay Selous*, p. 204.
80. See his letter to *The Times*, 19 February 1894.
81. Selous, 'The History of the Matabele, and the Cause and Effect of the Matabele War', p. 273.
82. Ibid., pp. 273–4; and see also *Travel and Adventure in South-East Africa*, p. 384.
83. Selous, 'Introductory Review of the War', pp. 2–3.
84. Marquis of Lorne, concluding remarks to talk given by Selous to the Royal Colonial Institute on 13 March 1894, in Selous, 'The History of the Matabele, and the Cause and Effect of the Matabele War', p. 288.
85. Ibid., p. 259.
86. Great Britain, *Southern Rhodesian Commission* [Cave Commission], Cmd 1129, 1921, p. 302.
87. Cust, *The Matabéle-Scandal*, pp. 13, 22, 25, 41.
88. Ibid., p. 46.
89. Fripp and Hiller (eds.), *Gold and the Gospel in Mashonaland*, p. 111.
90. Selous, 'Introductory Review of the War', p. 6; Glass, *The Matabele War*, p. 76; Harris, *The Chartered Millions*, p. 101.
91. Selous, 'Introductory Review of the War', p. 2.
92. *Truth*, 8 February 1894, p. 309.
93. Selous, 'The History of the Matabele, and the Cause and Effect of the Matabele War', p. 279.
94. Selous, letter to *The Times*, 19 February 1894.
95. Ibid.
96. Labouchere, letter to *The Times*, 21 February 1894.
97. Great Britain, *Correspondence Respecting Death at Tati of Two Indunas in October 1893*, C. 7284, 1894, pp. 5, 12–13.
98. Glass, *The Matabele War*, pp. 202–3, 204.
99. Great Britain, *Correspondence Respecting Death at Tati of Two Indunas in October 1893*, C. 7284, 1894, pp. 12–13.
100. Labouchere, letter to *The Times*, 22 March 1894.
101. Ibid.; *Truth*, 22 February 1894, p. 420.
102. Williams interview with Selous, 15 June 1914, Rhodes House Mss. Afr. s. 134.
103. Rhodes to Stead, 19 August 1891, Rhodes House Micr. Afr. 413.
104. British South Africa Company, *Report of the Directors*, 1894, p. 20; Phimister, 'Rhodes, Rhodesia and the Rand', p. 82; Stigger, 'Volunteers and the Profit Motive in the Anglo-Ndebele War, 1893', p. 21.
105. *Truth*, 11 October 1894, pp. 836–7.
106. Selous, *Sunshine and Storm in Rhodesia*, pp. 10–12.
107. The basic source for the 1896 rising remains Terence Ranger's *Revolt in Southern Rhodesia 1896–7*, though Julian Cobbing has challenged Ranger's view that the revolt was organized by priests of the Mwari cult. See Cobbing, 'The Absent Priesthood'.
108. Stent, *A Personal Record of Some Incidents in the Life of Cecil Rhodes*, p. 18.
109. Ibid., p. 37.
110. Ranger, *Revolt in Southern Rhodesia*, p. 245.
111. Ibid., p. 246.
112. Selous, *Sunshine and Storm in Rhodesia*, pp. 137, 30, 64, 193, 66–7.

113. Ibid., p. 88.
114. Ibid., p. 245.
115. Reuter's interview, *The Times*, 23 November 1896; Selous, letter to *Daily Graphic*, 17 December 1896.
116. Selous, letter to *Daily Chronicle*, 4 August 1897.
117. Selous, speech given at the British Association meeting in Toronto, 24 August 1897, reported in the *Toronto Globe*, 25 August 1897.
118. Selous, letter to *Daily Graphic*, 17 December 1897.
119. Blake, 'Second Thoughts on Rhodesia', p. 121.
120. Selous, speech given at the British Association meeting in Toronto, 24 August 1897, reported in the *Toronto Globe*, 25 August 1897.
121. Selous, *The War in South Africa*; Koss, *The Pro-Boers*, pp. 81–3.
122. Swinburne, 'The Transvaal', *The Times*, 11 October 1899.
123. Lewsen (ed.), *Selections from the Correspondence of John X. Merriman*, p. 156.
124. Quoted in Keppel-Jones, *Rhodes and Rhodesia*, p. 430.
125. Selous, letter to J.G. Millais, 1 January 1900, in Millais, *Life of Frederick Courtenay Selous*, p. 235.
126. Selous, *Travel and Adventure in South-East Africa*, pp. 9–10.
127. Koss, *The Pro-Boers*, pp. 85–9.
128. Selous, *Recent Hunting Trips in British North America*, pp. 349–50.
129. Millais, *Life of Frederick Courtenay Selous*, p. 376; Haggard, *King Solomon's Mines*, p. 3.

Chapter 3   Hugh Clifford, Administrator

1. Barr, *Taming the Jungle*, pp. 85–6. Syphilitic dementia has a very varied symptomatology and may include both mania and depression; and it can have an incubation period of up to forty years. See Bruetsch, 'Neurosyphilitic Conditions: General Paralysis, General Paresis, Dementia Paralytica', p. 136.
2. Vincent Thompson ('Sir Hugh Clifford and the National Congress of British West Africa: A Reconsideration') and J.A. Ballard ('Administrative Origins of Nigerian Federalism', p. 338) succumb rather too easily to the temptation to attribute Clifford's unconventional opinions to insanity.
3. Gailey, *Clifford: Imperial Proconsul*, p. 9. Gailey's book is the only full-length biography of Clifford and is a useful source of information, but is very much the authorized version. A valuable short study of Clifford can be found in J. de V. Allen's 'Two Imperialists: A Study of Sir Frank Swettenham and Sir Hugh Clifford'; and further biographical information may be found in two articles by A.J. Stockwell – 'Sir Hugh Clifford's Early Career (1866–1903) as Told from his Private Papers' and 'Hugh Clifford in Trinidad 1903–1907'.
4. Clifford to Eve Hall, 12 May 1925, pp. 5–6, Rhodes House Mss. Brit. Emp. s. 440.
5. Ibid., p. 2.
6. Detailed descriptions of this process can be found in Sadka, *The Protected Malay States, 1874–1895*, and Thio, *British Policy in the Malay Peninsula, 1880–1910*.
7. Sinclair, *A History of New Zealand*, p. 143.

8. Lovat, *The Life of Sir Frederick Weld*, p. 61.
9. Ibid., p. 380.
10. Ibid., p. 318.
11. Ibid., pp. 315–6.
12. Weld, 'The Straits Settlements and British Malaya', p. 311.
13. Bird, *The Golden Chersonese*, p. 323. And see also *Verandah*, by Low's descendant, James Pope-Hennessy.
14. St Pol Lias, *Pérak et les Orang-Sakèys*, p. 176; quoted in translation in Sadka, *The Protected Malay States*, p. 189.
15. Clifford, 'Autobiographical Preface' to second edition of *In Court and Kampong*, pp. 12–13.
16. Quoted in Sheppard, 'Clifford of Pahang', p. 54.
17. Clifford, preface to *The Further Side of Silence*, p. viii.
18. Clifford, 'Autobiographical Preface' to second edition of *In Court and Kampong*, p. 23.
19. Ibid., p. 24
20. Ibid., p. 46.
21. Clifford, 'Up country', *East Coast Etchings*, pp. 225–6, 229, 230, 228, 231, 232–3.
22. Clifford, '*Since the Beginning*', p. 283.
23. Clifford, 'The East Coast', *East Coast Etchings*, pp. 1–2.
24. Stockwell, 'Sir Hugh Clifford's Early Career', p. 93; Thio, *British Policy in the Malay Peninsula, 1880–1910*, p. 89.
25. Linehan, 'History of Pahang', pp. 124–5; Gailey, *Clifford*, p. 19.
26. Clifford, 'At the Court of Pĕlĕsu', *In a Corner of Asia*, p. 13. In his 'Autobiographical Preface' to the second edition of *In Court and Kampong*, Clifford refers (p. 35) to this story as a factual account.
27. Clifford to Clementi Smith, 7 June 1888, reproduced in Stockwell, 'Sir Hugh Clifford's Early Career', p. 108.
28. Clifford, 'At the Court of Pĕlĕsu', *In a Corner of Asia*, p. 9.
29. Clifford, 'Autobiographical Preface' to second edition *In Court and Kampong*, p. 37.
30. Clifford, *Annual Report for the State of Pahang (1890)*, quoted in de Silva, 'British Relations with Pahang, 1884–1895', p. 23.
31. Clifford, 'Bush-whacking', *Bush-whacking*, pp. 48–50.
32. Clifford, preface to *The Further Side of Silence*, p. ix; 'Autobiographical Preface' to second edition of *In Court and Kampong*, pp. 31–2.
33. Quoted in Linehan, 'History of Pahang', p. 150; Clifford, 'Expedition to Trengganu and Kelantan', passim.
34. Clifford, 'One Who had Eaten my Rice', *The Further Side of Silence*, p. 287. The story also appears under the title 'Ûmat' in *Studies in Brown Humanity*, pp. 36–53.
35. Reproduced in Stockwell, 'Sir Hugh Clifford's Early Career', pp. 109–12. For Clifford in Borneo, see also Tregonning, *A History of Modern Sabah*, p. 58, and 'The Mat Salleh Revolt', p. 97.
36. Gailey, *Clifford*, p. 29; Stockwell, 'Sir Hugh Clifford's Early Career', p. 97.
37. Clifford, 'Bush-whacking', *Bush-whacking*, pp. 86–7.
38. Clifford, 'British and Siamese Malaya', p. 53.

39. Clifford, 'Life in the Malay Peninsula; As it was and is', pp. 373–85.
40. Ibid., pp. 395–6.
41. Ibid., p. 399. See also Allen, 'The Ancien Regime in Trengganu' for how Clifford exaggerated the horrors of pre-colonial rule in that state.
42. Clifford, 'The Flight of Chêp the Bird', *In Court and Kampong*, p. 107.
43. Clifford, 'His Little Bill', *Studies in Brown Humanity*, pp. 64–5.
44. Clifford, 'The Vigil of Pa'Tûa, the Thief', *In a Corner of Asia*, pp. 253–79.
45. Clifford, preface to *Studies in Brown Humanity*, p. vii.
46. Swettenham, *Malay Sketches* (1895) and *The Real Malay* (1900).
47. Clifford, 'In the Heart of Kalamantan', p. 27. Quotations from 'In the Heart of Kalamantan' are from the version found in *In Days that are Dead*, pp. 24–74. The original version, published in *Blackwood's* in October 1900, has minor differences in wording.
48. Clifford, 'In the Heart of Kalamantan', *In Days that are Dead*, p. 26.
49. Clifford to directors of British North Borneo Company, 12 February 1900, in Tregonning, 'The Mat Salleh Revolt', p. 32.
50. Clifford, 'In the Heart of Kalamantan', *In Days that are Dead*, pp. 39, 60, 72–4.
51. Clifford, 'The Quest of the Golden Fleece', *Malayan Monochromes*, pp. 187–225; first published in *Blackwood's*, January 1903. O'Hara's consciousness of what he was doing is implied rather more strongly at the end of the earlier version, which otherwise is substantially the same.
52. Clifford, 'A Dying Kingdom', pp. 107, 113.
53. Clifford, *A Free Lance of To-day*, pp. 8, 14, 18, 103, 121, 194, 199.
54. Clifford, 'The Familiar of Megat Pendîa', pp. 274–5.
55. Ludowyk, *The Modern History of Ceylon*, p. 104. And see also, e.g., Clifford, speech to the Nigerian Council, 29 December 1920, in Coleman, *Nigeria*, p. 193.
56. Quoted in Gailey, *Clifford*, p. 37.
57. Clifford, *A Free Lance of To-day*, pp. 89–90. The interested reader is referred to similar insights in the works of black writers such as Frantz Fanon and W.E.B. DuBois.
58. Tregonning, 'The Mat Salleh Revolt', p. 32; Clifford, 'Bush-whacking', *Bush-whacking*, pp. 48–50.
59. Gailey, *Clifford*, p. 41.
60. Clifford, 'British and Siamese Malaya', p. 67.
61. See, e.g., Clifford, 'Since the Beginning', pp. 28–31.
62. Sadka, *The Protected Malay States*, p. 208.
63. See, e.g., Clifford, 'Dutch Colonial Administration in Theory and Practice'; 'Chinese Immigration'; and 'British and Siamese Malaya', p. 52.
64. Clifford, 'Rival Systems and the Malayan Peoples', pp. 403–4.
65. Allen, 'Johore 1901–1914'; Thio, *British Policy in the Malay Peninsula*, p. 187.
66. Clifford, 'Chinese Immigration'.
67. Clifford, *Further India*, p. 346.
68. Clifford, 'The Destiny of the Philippines', pp. 155–6.
69. Clifford, 'Life in the Malay Peninsula; As it was and is', p. 395.
70. Smith, *Arthur Lionel Smith*, pp. 145–6, 164.
71. Clifford, 'The Destiny of the Philippines', p. 156.
72. Clifford, 'Sally: A Study', *Sally, A Study, and Other Tales of the Outskirts*, p. 89.

73. Clifford, *Saleh: A Sequel*, pp. 284, 288, 298–9.
74. Clifford to Sir Arthur Steel-Maitland, 12 June 1917, quoted in Gailey, *Clifford*, pp. 105–6.
75. Clifford, 'The Breath upon the Spark', *Bush-whacking*, p. 338.
76. Clifford, 'Saigon', p. 601. See also Clifford, 'The Problem of the West Indies', p. 143.
77. Clifford, *Further India*, p. 68.
78. Clifford, 'Lesson from the Malay States', p. 598.
79. Stockwell, 'Hugh Clifford in Trinidad', p. 8.
80. Clifford to Secretary of State for the Colonies, 25 August 1904, in ibid., p. 14.
81. Memorandum by Clifford to Sir Alfred Moloney, 24 January 1904, in ibid., p. 15.
82. Ibid., pp. 27–8.
83. Secretary of State to acting Governor (Clifford), 21 June 1906, in ibid., p. 28.
84. Clifford, 'Memorandum on the Existing Condition of Race-Feeling in the Island of Trinidad', 20 May 1905, CO 295/435.
85. Stockwell, 'Hugh Clifford in Trinidad', p. 29.
86. Clifford, 'America's Problem in the Philippines', pp. 519–20.
87. Clifford, 'The Problem of the West Indies'.
88. Gailey, *Clifford*, pp. 62–4, 76, 169; Ludowyk, *The Modern History of Ceylon*, p. 138.
89. Ibid., p. 131.
90. Clifford, 'In Kambodia', p. 789.
91. Clifford, 'The Tragedy of Angkor', p. 506.
92. Ibid., p. 509.
93. Gailey, *Clifford*, p. 71.
94. Extract from despatch from Clifford to Secretary of State for the Colonies, read in Legislative Council debate in 1917, in Kay, *The Political Economy of Colonialism in Ghana*, p. 248.
95. Extract from despatch from Clifford to Secretary of State, read in Legislative Council debate in 1917, in ibid., pp. 247–8.
96. Wraith, *Guggisberg*, pp. 79, 94; Kimble, *The Political History of Ghana*, p. 49.
97. Clifford, speech in Legislative Council, 28 October 1918, in Metcalfe, *Great Britain and Ghana*, pp. 569–70; Gailey, *Clifford*, pp. 88–9.
98. Clifford, 'Recent Developments in the Gold Coast', p. 245.
99. Clifford, speech in Legislative Council, 25 September 1916, in Metcalfe, *Great Britain and Ghana*, pp. 558–9; Wraith, *Guggisberg*, p. 92.
100. Clifford, speech in Legislative Council, 25 September 1916, in Metcalfe, *Great Britain and Ghana*, p. 559.
101. Gailey, *Clifford*, pp. 92–3, 110–11.
102. Clifford, speech in Legislative Council, 2 November 1918, in Metcalfe, *Great Britain and Ghana*, p. 571.
103. Clifford, 'Recent Developments in the Gold Coast', p. 252.
104. Clifford, speech in Legislative Council, 28 October 1918, in Wraith, *Guggisberg*, p. 83.
105. Clifford, *The Gold Coast Regiment in the East African Campaign*.
106. Clifford, *German Colonies*, p. 113.
107. An account of the Armitage affair can be found in Gailey, *Clifford*, pp. 98–105.

108. Clifford to Sir George Fiddes, 15 September 1916, CO 96/570, p. 3.
109. Clifford, 'At the Heels of the White Man', *Studies in Brown Humanity*, p. 136.
110. Clifford, '"Our Trusty and Well-Beloved"', *Malayan Monochromes*, pp. 17–18, 27–8, 31–2.
111. Burns, *Colonial Civil Servant*, p. 55; Gailey, *Clifford*, p. 154.
112. Clifford, '"Cast"', pp. 622–3.
113. The best coverage of Clifford's policy in the south is found in Gailey, *Clifford*, Chapters VIII and IX. Clifford's response to the Abeokuta affair is also discussed in detail in the last chapter of Gailey's *Lugard and the Abeokuta Uprising*.
114. Clifford to Sir Williams Gowers, 30 November 1924, Rhodes House Mss. Afr. s. 1149; Allen, 'Sir Hugh Clifford in Malaya and Nigeria', p. 313.
115. Clifford, 'United Nigeria', p. 10; Clifford to Sir William Gowers, 30 December 1923, Rhodes House Mss. Afr. s. 1149; Cookey, 'Sir Hugh Clifford as Governor of Nigeria', pp. 534–6. Clifford's criticisms of northern administration are discussed in detail in Okonjo, *British Administration in Nigeria*, Chapter IV.
116. Clifford, minute addressed to the Lt. Governor of the Northern Provinces, 18 March 1922, reprinted in Kirk-Greene (ed.), *The Principles of Native Administration in Nigeria*, pp. 174–86.
117. Heussler, 'British Rule in Africa', p. 583; Okonjo, *British Administration in Nigeria*, pp. 257–60.
118. Clifford's account of this episode can be found in his letter to the Secretary of State for the Colonies of 16 March 1923 (CO 583/118).
119. Clifford, speech to the Nigerian Council, 29 December 1920, in Coleman, *Nigeria*, p. 193.
120. Cookey, 'Sir Hugh Clifford as Governor of Nigeria', p. 543.
121. Cook, *British Enterprise in Nigeria*, pp. 263–4.
122. The memorandum is extracted in Buell, *The Native Problem in Africa*, Vol. I, pp. 771–4.
123. Hancock, *Survey of British Commonwealth Affairs*, Vol. II, Part II, pp. 194–7; information from Gene Tidrick.
124. Quoted in Apter, *The Gold Coast in Transition*, p. 51.
125. Quoted in Cookey, 'Sir Hugh Clifford as Governor of Nigeria', p. 546.
126. Clifford to Eve Hall, 12 May 1925, pp. 1–2, 8, Rhodes House Mss. Brit. Emp. s. 440.
127. Diary of Lady Moore, 7 May 1925, and note attached to letter from Clifford to Moore, 5 May 1925, Rhodes House Mss. Brit. Emp. s. 466.
128. Note appended by Lady Moore to diary entry of 7 May 1925, Rhodes House Mss. Brit. Emp. s. 466 (but see also postscript by Sir Henry Monck-Mason Moore to Hulugalle, *British Governors of Ceylon*, p. 219); Prince of Wales to Leo Amery, 27 April 1925, in Gailey, *Clifford*, p. 166.
129. Ibid., pp. 171–4.
130. Hulugalle, *Don Stephen Senanayake*, p. 67.
131. Clifford to Eve Hall, 12 October 1927 and 12 January 1928, Rhodes House Mss. Brit. Emp. s. 440; Walker, 'Sir Hugh Clifford', p. 705.
132. Some contemporary evidence of this process can be found in the issues of *British Malaya* for 1927 to 1929; and see also Victor Purcell's recollections in *The Memoirs of a Malayan Official*, p. 275.

133. Clifford, speech to the Federal Council, 16 November 1927, in Emerson, *Malaysia*, pp. 174–5.
134. Heussler, *British Rule in Malaya*, p. 272.
135. Allen, 'Sir Hugh Clifford in Malaya and Nigeria', p. 320.
136. Stockwell, *British Policy and Malay Politics during the Malayan Union Experiment, 1942–1948*, p. 3.

Chapter 4   Kenya: White Man's Country

1. Reproduced in Leakey, *Defeating Mau Mau*, p. 63.
2. See Robinson and Gallagher, *Africa and the Victorians*, Chapter XI.
3. For the conquest of Kenya, see Maxon, *John Ainsworth and the Making of Kenya*, Chapters II and III; Sorrenson, *Land Reform in the Kikuyu Country*, pp. 16–17; Rosberg and Nottingham, *The Myth of 'Mau Mau'*, pp. 13–16; John Lonsdale, 'The Politics of Conquest: The British in Western Kenya'; and Ochieng, 'Colonial African Chiefs', p. 63.
4. Huxley and Perham, *Race and Politics in Kenya*, p. 129.
5. Ibid., p. 136.
6. Cranworth, *Profits and Sport in British East Africa*, p. 25.
7. Huxley, *White Man's Country*, Vol. I, pp. 147–8, 299.
8. Ross, *Kenya from Within*, pp. 162–3; Trzebinski, *The Kenya Pioneers*, pp. 96–7.
9. Farrant, *The Legendary Grogan*, pp. 112–3; Trzebinski, *The Kenya Pioneers*, pp. 156–7.
10. Van Zwanenberg, *Colonial Capitalism and Labour in Kenya*, pp. 2–3.
11. Cranworth, *Profit and Sport in British East Africa*, p. 299 and passim.
12. Spencer, 'Settler Dominance, Agricultural Production and the Second World War in Kenya'.
13. Norden, *White and Black in East Africa*, p. 104.
14. Trzebinski, *Silence Will Speak*, pp. 69, 75, 187.
15. *Comment*, 18 January 1951, p. 15.
16. Cranworth, *Profit and Sport in British East Africa*, p. 254.
17. Ibid., p. 248.
18. Sorrenson, *Origins of European Settlement in Kenya*, p. 103.
19. Van Zwanenberg, 'The Economic Response of Kenya Africans to European Settlement', p. 206.
20. Approximate size of African population of Kenya between the early 1900s and the Second World War.
21. Sorrenson, *Origins of European Settlement in Kenya*, pp. 246–7.
22. Bennett, *Kenya*, p. 48.
23. Dealt with comprehensively in Sorrenson, 'Land Policy in Kenya'; *Origins of European Settlement in Kenya*; and *Land Reform in the Kikuyu Country*. And see also Tignor, *The Colonial Transformation of Kenya*.
24. Both 'pledges' are quoted in Sorrenson, 'Land Policy in Kenya', p. 681.
25. Evans, *Law and Disorder*, p. 15.
26. Frost, *Race Against Time*, p. 116.
27. Sorrenson, *Origins of European Settlement in Kenya*, p. 105.

28. Redley, 'The Politics of a Predicament', p. 56.
29. Brett, *Colonialism and Underdevelopment in East Africa*, pp. 192–3. See also Van Zwanenberg, *Colonial Capitalism and Labour in Kenya*, p. 78–80, and Spencer, 'The First World War and the Origins of the Dual Policy of Development in Kenya'.
30. See especially Lonsdale and Berman, 'Coping with the Contradictions', pp. 497, 501–2.
31. Bennett, *Kenya*, p. 44.
32. Berman and Lonsdale, 'The Development of the Labour Control System in Kenya', p. 76.
33. Sorrenson, *Origins of European Settlement in Kenya*, pp. 243–5.
34. Ross, *Kenya from Within*, pp. 113–4.
35. Annual Report of Nyanza Province, 1913, K.N.A. [Kenya National Archives], PC/NZA 1/3; Ainsworth to Chief Secretary, 9 October 1912, K.N.A., PC/NZA 2/3; Ainsworth, 'Memo re: Native Labour', 13 September 1911, quoted in Maxon, *John Ainsworth and the Making of Kenya*, pp. 225–6. And see also Ainsworth, memorandum entitled 'East African Protectorate Native Policy', 4 June 1913, K.N.A., PC/NZA 2/3.
36. Maxon, *John Ainsworth and the Making of Kenya*, Chapter V.
37. Ibid., pp. 372–5.
38. Ibid., pp. 307–28; Sorrenson, *Origins of European Settlement in Kenya*, p. 254.
39. Grogan, *From the Cape to Cairo*, pp. 359, 369–71.
40. Farrant, *The Legendary Grogan*, pp. 116–26; Trzebinski, *The Kenya Pioneers*, p. 129.
41. Cranworth, *Kenya Chronicles*, pp. 64–5.
42. Ross, *Kenya from Within*, pp. 114–5.
43. Trzebinski, *The Kenya Pioneers*, p. 125.
44. Courtney, *Africa Calling*, pp. 44, 61.
45. Trzebinski, *The Kenya Pioneers*, pp. 54–5, 84.
46. Redley, 'The Politics of a Predicament', is a comprehensive source on these events.
47. Robinson, 'The Moral Disarmament of the African Empire', pp. 94–5.
48. Masai Annual Report, 1937, K.N.A., PC/SP 1/2/1.
49. Ross, *Kenya from Within*, p. 346.
50. Bennett, *Kenya*, p. 51.
51. Redley, 'The Politics of a Predicament', p. 138. For a settler denunciation of the 'sheer hypocrisy' of trusteeship, see Davis and Robertson, *Chronicles of Kenya*, p. 243.
52. Huxley, *White Man's Country*, Vol. II, pp. 192, 194.
53. Coryndon to Sir Sidney Henn, 5 May 1924, quoted in Brett, *Colonialism and Underdevelopment in East Africa*, p. 183.
54. Huxley, *White Man's Country*, Vol. I, pp. 216–23, 72, Chapter IX, 64, 24.
55. Huxley and Perham, *Race and Politics in Kenya*, pp. 114, 122.
56. Ibid., pp. 71, 54–5, 120, 124, 105.
57. For an example which sounds extreme but may not have been, see Brodhurst-Hill, *So This is Kenya*, p. 212.
58. Cranworth, *Kenya Chronicles*, p. 272.
59. Dinesen [Blixen], *Out of Africa*, pp. 36, 212, 223, 157.

60. Ibid., p. 352; and see also p. 215.
61. See Judith Thurman, *Isak Dinesen: The Life of a Storyteller*.
62. Dinesen, *Letters from Africa*.
63. Cranworth, *Kenya Chronicles*, p. 187.
64. See, e.g., Portsmouth, *A Knot of Roots*, p. 271.
65. Trzebinski, *Silence Will Speak*, pp. 44, 55. The reasons for Cyril Connolly's fascination with Kenya settlerdom will be readily apparent.
66. Fox, *White Mischief*, pp. 32, 46–7; Grant, *Nellie's Story*, p. 105.
67. Simpson, *The Land that Never Was*, p. 158.
68. Powys, *Black Laughter*, p. 133.
69. Van Zwanenberg, *Colonial Capitalism and Labour in Kenya*, Chapter VIII; Tignor, *The Colonial Transformation of Kenya*, pp. 191–4.
70. Lipscomb, *White Africans*, p. 118.
71. Koinange, *The People of Kenya Speak for Themselves*, pp. 25–6.
72. Brett, *Colonialism and Underdevelopment in East Africa*, pp. 208–11.
73. The Electors' Union, *Kenya Plan*, p. 14.
74. Clayton, *Counter-Insurgency in Kenya*, pp. 31–2; Mitchell, *African Afterthoughts*, pp. 264–5.
75. For a useful summary of the evidence, see Buijtenhuijs, *Essays on Mau Mau*, pp. 35–9, and also Chapter I of Barnett and Njama, *Mau Mau from Within*. I find by far the most astute contemporary account of the Emergency to be Evans, *Law and Disorder*; and in spite of its inevitable shortcomings in the realm of historical analysis, the Corfield report (*Historical Survey of the Origins and Growth of Mau Mau*, 1960, Cmnd. 1030) remains an indispensable source for anyone interested in the Emergency.
76. The most notable of these is Karari Njama's memoir, published in Barnett and Njama, *Mau Mau from Within*. For the war in the forest see also Itote ('General China'), *'Mau Mau' General*; Wamweya, *Freedom Fighter*; Mathu, *The Urban Guerrilla*. Other 'Mau Mau' memoirs by people not personally involved in forest fighting are Kaggia, *Roots of Freedom*; Kariuki, *'Mau Mau' Detainee*; Kabiro, *Man in the Middle*; Muchai, *The Hardcore*.
77. For a portrait of Kimathi in action, or rather inaction, see Barnett and Njama, *Mau Mau from Within*.
78. Kitson, *Gangs and Counter-Gangs*, p. 63.
79. Itote, *'Mau Mau' General*, pp. 148–9.
80. For a discussion of who the Kikuyu loyalists were, see Ogot, 'Revolt of the Elders: An Anatomy of the Loyalist Crowd in the Mau Mau Uprising 1952–1956'.
81. Sorrenson, *Land Reform in the Kikuyu Country*, pp. 80, 100–101. Sorrenson argues (p. 100) that Mau Mau became 'a Kikuyu civil war'.
82. Kenya Colony and Protectorate, *Prisons Department Annual Reports*, 1956–1959. In 1959, 3,690 persons were committed to prison under the Emergency regulations.
83. Clayton, *Counter-Insurgency in Kenya*, p. 31.
84. Buijtenhuijs, *Essays on Mau Mau*, pp. 35–6.
85. See particularly Berman, 'Bureaucracy and Incumbent Violence: Colonial Administration and the Origins of the "Mau Mau" Emergency in Kenya'.
86. The question of KAU involvement in Mau Mau remains unresolved, but it is

noteworthy that the only KAU leader who later claimed to have been a member of the 'Mau Mau Central Committee' was Bildad Kaggia, who says explicitly that the only KAU officials on the committee were himself and Fred Kubai, and that Kenyatta, while aware of the existence of the committee, was unaware of its composition (Kaggia, *Roots of Freedom*, pp. 113–4).

87. For Mitchell's policies see Fay Carter's chapter on him in King and Salim (eds.), *Kenya Historical Biographies*, and Mitchell's own *African Afterthoughts*.

88. Berman, 'Bureaucracy and Incumbent Violence', p. 169.

89. On Baring, see Douglas-Home, *Evelyn Baring: The Last Proconsul*, and Blundell, *So Rough a Wind*, pp. 98–103.

90. Ibid., p. 101.

91. Clayton, *Counter-Insurgency in Kenya*, p. 5; Douglas-Home, *Evelyn Baring*, p. 231.

92. Baring to Secretary of State, 9 October 1952, reproduced in Douglas-Home, *Evelyn Baring*, pp. 227–31.

93. Ibid., p. 78.

94. *Hansard*, 5th series, House of Commons, *507*, c. 1865, 19 November 1952; *508*, c. 1544, 3 December 1952.

95. Rawcliffe, *The Struggle for Kenya*, p. 58.

96. Ibid., p. 57.

97. Clayton, *Counter-Insurgency in Kenya*, p. 15.

98. Sorrenson, *Land Reform in the Kikuyu Country*, p. 102.

99. My figures on executions are derived from the following sources: Kenya Colony and Protectorate, *Prisons Department Annual Reports*, 1952–1959; and *Hansard*, 5th series, House of Commons, *530*, c. 35, 14 July 1954; *530*, c. 119, 21 July 1954; *533*, c. 1244, 24 November 1954; *551*, cc. 154-6, 25 April 1956. Figures for executions under Emergency Regulations are not given separately in the 1959 report; there were 22 executions overall in the colony in that year.

100. *Hansard*, 5th series, House of Commons, *531*, c. 47, 28 July 1954.

101. Clayton, *Counter-Insurgency in Kenya*, p. 38.

102. *Hansard*, 5th series, House of Commons, *514*, c. 2121, 29 April 1953.

103. Descriptions of the better-known cases can be found in Clayton, *Counter-Insurgency in Kenya*, pp. 44–5; and Evans, *Law and Disorder*, pp. 260–77.

104. Clayton, *Counter-Insurgency in Kenya*, pp. 57–9; Majdalany, *State of Emergency*, pp. 225–6.

105. Clayton, *Counter-Insurgency in Kenya*, pp. 6, 51; Rawcliffe, *The Struggle for Kenya*, p. 66.

106. Farrant, *The Legendary Grogan*, pp. 221–2.

107. Ibid., p. 224.

108. *East African Standard*, 23 April 1953, quoted in Evans, *Law and Disorder*, p. 179.

109. This view was first put forward explicitly by Donald L. Barnett in his introduction to Barnett and Njama, *Mau Mau from Within*, but it is implicit in much of Peter Evans' *Law and Disorder*.

110. Murray-Brown, *Kenyatta*, p. 256.

111. For an explicit statement, see the Fairn Committee report (Kenya Colony and Protectorate, *Report of the Committee on Emergency Detention Camps*), p. 2

112. Carothers, *The Psychology of Mau Mau*; Leakey, *Mau Mau and the Kikuyu*, and *Defeating Mau Mau*.

113. See his *Kenya: Contrasts and Problems* (1937).

114. The comparison would be an enlightening one to pursue; for a start, see Berman, 'Bureaucracy and Incumbent Violence', pp. 172–3.

115. Carothers, *The Psychology of Mau Mau*, p. 15.

116. Huxley, 'The Cause and Cure of Mau Mau', p. 812.

117. The Corfield report, pp. 134–5.

118. Kenya Colony and Protectorate, *Annual Report of the Department of Community Development and Rehabilitation*, 1954, p. 23.

119. Kenya Colony and Protectorate, *Community Development Organization Annual Report*, 1953,p. 3. See also Jesse Kariuki's description of a camp programme in *'Mau Mau' Detainees*, p. 131.

120. Kenya Colony and Protectorate, *Annual Report of the Department of Community Development and Rehabilitation*, 1955, p. 21.

121. As the Church of England, among others, pointed out; see Driberg, *The Mystery of Moral Re-Armament*, p. 213.

122. Ibid., p. 300; and see also *MRA Pictorial*, no. 21, New Year 1960, pp. 12–13.

123. Clayton, *Counter-Insurgency in Kenya*, p. 17.

124. Mathu, *The Urban Guerrilla*, pp. 65–71; Muchai, *The Hardcore*, pp. 42, 47; Kariuki, *'Mau Mau' Detainee*, p. 127.

125. Rosberg and Nottingham, *The Myth of 'Mau Mau'*, pp. 341–2.

126. Great Britain, *Documents Relating to the Deaths of Eleven Mau Mau Detainees at Hola Camp in Kenya*, Cmnd. 778, 1959,pp. 27–8; Rosberg and Nottingham, *The Myth of 'Mau Mau'*, p. 344.

127. Great Britain, *Further Documents Relating to the Deaths of Eleven Mau Mau Detainees at Hola Camp in Kenya*, Cmnd. 816, 1959, p. 22

128. Douglas-Home, *Evelyn Baring*, pp. 295–6.

129. Great Britain, *Record of Proceedings and Evidence in the Inquiry into the Deaths of Eleven Mau Mau Detainees at Hola Camp in Kenya*, Cmnd. 795, 1959, pp. 63–4.

130. Great Britain, *Documents Relating to the Deaths of Eleven Mau Mau Detainees at Hola Camp in Kenya*, Cmnd. 778, 1959, p. 28.

131. Kitson, *Gangs and Counter-Gangs*, pp. 126–7, and passim; Henderson, *Man Hunt in Kenya*, pp. 149–50.

132. Itote, *'Mau Mau' General*, pp. 187–8.

133. Carothers, *The Psychology of Mau Mau*, p. 28.

134. Chandos [Oliver Lyttelton], *The Memoirs of Lord Chandos*, p. 397.

135. Ibid., p. 398.

136. See Richard Frost's *Race Against Time*, especially Chapter IX. Frost was the British Council representative in Nairobi from 1947 to 1955 and during 1963, and was involved in many efforts at bridge-building between the races. He may have exaggerated the prevalence of such efforts, but his description of them suggests a valuable corrective to the view that the people involved in them or supporting them were never more than a tiny minority in Kenya.

137. Hill, *The Dual Policy in Kenya*, pp. 53–4.

138. Blundell, *So Rough a Wind*, pp. 178, 285.

139. Clayton, *Counter-Insurgency in Kenya*, p. 45; Wasserman, *Politics of Decolonization*, pp. 29, 41.

140. See Portsmouth, *A Knot of Roots*; and Griffiths, *Fellow Travellers of the Right*.

141. Farrant, *The Legendary Grogan*, pp. 222, 225; Frost, *Race Against Time*, p. 222;

and see also Grogan's 1958 estimate of Kenyatta on p. 58 of his memoir, 'Sixty Years in East and Central Africa'.

142. See 'An Appreciation' by Colonel the Honourable Ewart Grogan, printed as Appendix I in Williams, *Paradise Precarious*; and Farrant, *The Legendary Grogan*, p. 227.
143. Huxley and Perham, *Race and Politics in Kenya*, pp. 247, 266.
144. Capricorn Africa Society, *The Capricorn Declarations*, pp. 9–11.
145. Wood, *Kenya*, pp. 12–13.
146. Ibid., p. 125.
147. Rosberg and Nottingham, *The Myth of 'Mau Mau'*, p. 338; and see also Kenya Colony and Protectorate, *Annual Report of the Department of Community Development and Rehabilitation*, 1957, p. 24.
148. Commissioner for Community Development and Rehabilitation, 'Rehabilitation' (unpublished report of 6 January 1954), quoted in Rosberg and Nottingham, *The Myth of 'Mau Mau'*, p. 338.
149. Throup, 'The Origins of Mau Mau', pp. 432–3.
150. Wasserman, *Politics of Decolonization*, pp. 168–9.

Chapter 5   The Masai and their Masters

1. Farson, *Last Chance in Africa*, p. 29.
2. See, e.g., Merrill, 'Resistance to Economic Change: The Masai'; Gulliver, 'The Conservative Commitment in Northern Tanzania: The Arusha and Masai'; Tignor, 'The Maasai Warriors: Pattern Maintenance and Violence in Colonial Kenya'.
3. Annual Report of Narok District, 1955, K.N.A. [Kenya National Archives], DC/NRK 1/1/3.
4. Annual Report of Narok District, 1929, K.N.A., DC/NRK 1/1/2.
5. Annual Report of Masai Extra-Territorial District, 1937, K.N.A., PC/SP 1/2/1. G.H. Mungeam ('Masai and Kikuyu Responses to the Establishment of British Administration in the East Africa Protectorate', pp. 129–30) suggests that the British overestimated Masai military power on the basis of stories from Arabs interested in maintaining a trade monopoly in the interior. Alan Jacobs ('The Traditional Political Organization of the Pastoral Maasai', pp. 37–48) suggests that the British failed to distinguish between the peaceful pastoral Masai and their warlike semi-pastoral cousins, the Kwavi.
6. Hanley, *Warriors and Strangers*, p. 220.
7. Assistant District Officer Loliondo to District Officer Monduli, 6 February 1934, T.N.A. [Tanzania National Archives], Acc. 17:287.
8. Interview with E.G. Rowe, 18 August 1977.
9. Farson, *Last Chance in Africa*, p. 29.
10. Thomson, *Through Masailand*, pp. 90, 93.
11. H.C. Baxter, 'The Three-Pronged Drive', p. 56, Rhodes House Mss. Afr. s. 609.
12. For some sociological observations on the Englishman's desire to maintain the integrity of his personal space, see Hall, *The Hidden Dimension*, pp. 129–34.
13. West, *The White Tribes of Africa*, p. 33.

14. Annual Report of Kajiado District, 1961, K.N.A., DC/KAJ 2/1/12.
15. Annual Report of Narok District, 1939, K.N.A., DC/NRK 1/1/3.
16. Fosbrooke, 'An Administrative Survey of the Masai Social System', p. 50.
17. Annual Report of Masai District, 1955, T.N.A., 471/R.3/5/1.
18. Annual Report of Masai Province, 1927, K.N.A., PC/SP 1/2/1.
19. Provincial Commissioner of the Northern Province to Member for Agriculture and Natural Resources, no date but apparently 1950, T.N.A., SMP 37560/1.
20. Fosbrooke, untitled report on the Masai social system, 1938, pp. 98, 120, 130, T.N.A., Acc. 468:4/1.
21. Annual Report of Masai Extra-Territorial District, 1937, K.N.A., PC/SP 1/2/1.
22. Browne to Chief Secretary, 30 March 1926, T.N.A., Acc. 17:43.
23. DO Moshi to Provincial Commissioner of the Northern Province, 16 May 1928, T.N.A., Acc. 17:37.
24. Browne to Chief Secretary, 1 March 1926, T.N.A., Acc. 17:43.
25. See, for example, Annual Report of Arusha District, 1920, T.N.A., 1733/1.
26. Browne to Chief Secretary, 15 March 1926, T.N.A., SMP 7794/7/A.
27. Note from Murrells to Philip Mitchell, Provincial Commissioner of the Northern Province, quoted in Mitchell to Chief Secretary, 16 March 1927, T.N.A., SMP 7077/4.
28. Browne to Chief Secretary, 15 March 1926, and 'Memorandum on the Formation of the Masai Reserve and the Administration of the Masai, 1916–1925', by E.D. Browne, T.N.A., SMP 7794/7/A.
29. Baxter (Acting DO, Monduli) to Provicial Commissioner of the Northern Province, 5 August 1933, T.N.A., SMP 11528.
30. Murrells to Provincial Commissioner of the Northern Province, 28 February 1927, T.N.A., Acc. 17:43.
31. Mitchell to Murrells, 16 March 1927, T.N.A., Acc. 17:43.
32. Mitchell to Chief Secretary, 16 March 1927, T.N.A., SMP 7077/4.
33. Minute by Cameron, 29 March 1927, T.N.A., SMP 7077/4.
34. Minute by Mitchell, 29 September 1933, T.N.A., SMP 11528.
35. Murrells to Provincial Commissioner of the Northern Province, 16 September 1930, T.N.A., Acc. 69:47/MS.
36. Perham, *East African Journey*, pp. 127–8.
37. Memorandum by Murrells, 20 July 1930, T.N.A., SMP 13477.
38. Provincial Commissioner of the Northern Province to 'Secretary, Dar es Salaam', 16 January 1928, T.N.A., Acc. 62:47/MS/1.
39. Perham, *East African Journey*, p. 126.
40. Mitchell diaries, 29 January 1930, and passim 1927–33, Rhodes House Mss. Afr. r. 101.
41. Hallier (Provincial Commissioner of the Northern Province) to Chief Secretary, 3 February 1936, T.N.A., SMP 23075.
42. Murrells to Provincial Commissioner of the Northern Province, 7 August 1931, T.N.A., Acc. 69:47/MS; Page-Jones, 'Water in Masailand', p. 55.
43. 'Forestry' section, Masai District Book, T.N.A., MF.13.
44. Annual Report of Masai District, 1956, T.N.A., 471/R.3/5/1; Jacobs, *The Pastoral Masai of Kenya*, p. 47. According to Jacobs, estimates of the number of stock deaths ranged from 4,000 (official) to 24,000 (unofficial).
45. A deduction based on the pioneering works of John Ford (*The Role of*

Trypanosomiases in African Ecology, 1971) and Helge Kjekshus (*Ecology Control and Economic Development in East African History*, 1977).

46. Information on the Masai Development Plan can be found in the Annual Reports of Masai District for 1950 to 1957 (T.N.A., 69/63/20, 69/63/21 and 471/R.3/5/1) and in the following files: Acc. 17:289, Vol. III; 37560/1; Acc. 471:D.3/2, Vols. I and II.
47. Annual Report of Masai District, 1956, T.N.A., 471/R.3/5/1.
48. Annual Reports of Narok District, 1956–60, K.N.A., DC/NRK 1/1/3 and 1/1/5, PC/SP 1/6/1 and AA/13/1/8/6, Vol. II.
49. Annual Report of Kajiado District, 1961, K.N.A., DC/KAJ 2/1/12; Kajiado District Handing Over Report, June 1962, K.N.A., DC/KAJ 3/2.
50. Annual Report of the Masai Reserve, 1922–3, K.N.A., PC/SP 1/2/2/; Tignor, *The Colonial Transformation of Kenya*, p. 81.
51. Annual Report of the Masai Extra-Territorial District, 1935–6, K.N.A., PC/SP 1/2/1; Tignor, *The Colonial Transformation of Kenya*, pp. 84–5.
52. For further information on the manyattas, see Jacobs, 'The Traditional Political Organization of the Pastoral Masai', and Saitoti, *Maasai*.
53. Kajiado District Handing Over Report, December 1938, K.N.A., DC/KAJ 3/1.
54. Fosbrooke to Provincial Commissioner of the Northern Province, 2 March 1953, T.N.A., Acc. 471:960; and see also his unpublished (1939) survey of the social organization of the Masai in T.N.A., Acc. 468:4/1. Fosbrooke's training in anthropology was the reason for his posting to Masai District in 1936.
55. Baxter, 'The Three-Pronged Drive', p. 53; 'The Pack-Saddle', pp. 141, 143; 'Masai Warfare (19th Century)', p. 152, Rhodes House Mss. Afr. s. 609.
56. Kajiado District Handing Over Report, December 1938, K.N.A., DC/KAJ 3/1.
57. Annual Report of Kajiado District, 1938, K.N.A., ARC (MAA) 2/3/5.
58. Narok District Handing Over Report, March 1946, K.N.A., DC/NRK 2/1/1.
59. Narok District Handing Over Report, February 1951, K.N.A., DC/NRK 2/1/1; Kajiado District, Handing Over Report of the Moran Officer [June 1952?], K.N.A., DC/KAJ 3/2.
60. Annual Reports of Narok District, 1950 and 1951, K.N.A., DC/NRK 1/1/3; Moran Officer to O/in/C Masai District, 23 May 1952, K.N.A., PC/SP 6/2/1B.
61. Hemsted to unnamed official, 3 February 1914, in Ngong Political Record Book, Part A, K.N.A., DC/KAJ 1/2/1.
62. Copies of questions asked by F.J. Anderson in the Legislative Council, and circular letter from Chief Secretary to all Provincial Commissioners, 21 December 1937, T.N.A., SMP 23075.
63. Hallier diaries, 14 October 1937 and 20 February 1939, Rhodes House Mss. Afr. s. 1072.
64. 'Extract from Questions and Answers in the Legislative Council, DSM, 9.12.42', T.N.A., SMP 23075.
65. Outstanding among these is H. St. J. Grant, 'Masai History and Mode of Life – A Summary Prepared for the Committee of Enquiry into the Serengeti National Park, 1957', Rhodes House Mss. Afr. s. 1237.
66. Annual Report of Masai District, 1950, T.N.A., 69/63/20.
67. Murrells to Acting Provincial Commissioner of the Northern Province, 15 December 1930, T.N.A., SMP 13477.

68. See, for example, Jacobs, 'Maasai Pastoralism in Historical Perspective'.

69. Annual Reports of Masai District, 1952, 1953, 1955, T.N.A., 69/63/21 and 471/R.3/5/1; file entitled 'Board of Trustees of the National Park and Board of Management, 1952–3', T.N.A., Acc. 17:150/A/II; file entitled 'Development – Masai Plan, 1953–55', T.N.A., Acc. 471:D.3/2.

70. See, for example, Annual Report of Narok District, 1959, K.N.A., DC/NRK 1/1/5. On Masai-Kikuyu relations, see, for example, Berntsen, 'The Maasai and their Neighbours: Variables of Interaction'.

71. The more important of these proposals were those contained in the following documents: *Land Development Survey, Fourth Report, 1930, Mbulu District* (Dar es Salaam: Government Printer, 1931) and *Report of the Arusha-Moshi Lands Commission* (Dar es Salaam: Government Printer, 1947).

72. Copy of memorandum on 'Masai Question' by Cameron, 11 June 1926, T.N.A., Acc. 17:43.

73. Farson,*Last Chance in Africa*, pp. 170–71.

74. Minute by 'G.F.S.', 13 December 1935; Hallier (Provincial Commissioner of the Northern Province) to Chief Secretary, 3 February 1936, T.N.A., SMP 23075.

75. Huxley, *White Man's Country*, Vol. I, p. 151.

76. Perham, *East African Journey*, p. 138.

77. Tignor, *The Colonial Transformation of Kenya*, p. 82, and 'The Maasai Warriors', p. 281; Huxley,*White Man's Country*, Vol. II, p. 39.

78. Annual Report of the Masai Reserve, 1918–19, K.N.A., PC/SP 1/2/2.

79. Trzebinski, *Silence Will Speak*, p. 137.

80. Annual Report of Narok District, 1955, K.N.A., DC/NRK 1/1/3.

81. Kajiado District Handing Over Report, March 1939, K.N.A., DC/KAJ 3/1.

82. Annual Report of Kajiado District, 1944, K.N.A., PC/SP 1/5/3.

83. Fosbrooke, memorandum on 'Sociological Implications of Masai Development', 19 June 1953, T.N.A., Acc. 471:960.

84. Kajiado District Handing Over Report, 10 May 1940, K.N.A., DC/KAJ 3/1.

85. DC Masai to DC Moshi, 26 November 1946, T.N.A., Acc. 17:21.

86. Annual Report of Masai District, 1952, T.N.A., 69/63/21.

87. Annual Report of Masai District, 1955, T.N.A., 471/R.3/5/1.

88. Evans, *Law and Disorder*, p. 163.

89. Annual Report of Narok District, 1953, K.N.A., DC/NRK 1/1/3.

90. Annual Report of Kajiado District, 1953, K.N.A., PC/SP /1/5/3; Moran Officer's Monthly Report, January-February 1953, K.N.A., PC/SP 6/2/1B. For a fantasy version of what was expected to occur but did not, see Ruark, *Something of Value*, pp. 442, 452–63.

91. Annual Report of Narok District, 1955, K.N.A., DC/NRK 1/1/3.

92. Annual Report of the Southern Province, 1953, K.N.A., PS/SP 1/1/1; Annual Report of Kajiado District, 1953, K.N.A., PC/SP 1/5/3; Annual Report of Narok District, 1953, K.N.A., DC/NRK 1/1/3.

93. Annual Report of Narok District, 1954, cited in King, 'Molonket ole Sempele', p. 25. The 1954 report is missing from the series microfilmed by Syracuse University in 1966, which forms the basis of the Kenya part of this study (see Gregory et al., *A Guide to the Kenya National Archives*, pp. 72–3). See also King, 'The Kenya Maasai and the Protest Phenomenon, 1900–1960'.

94. Narok District Handing Over Report, June 1954, K.N.A., DC/NRK 2/1/1.

95. Annual Report of Narok District, 1960, K.N.A., DC/NRK, 1/1/5.

Chapter 6 The Meaning of Indirect Rule

 1. Sir Charles Orr, quoted in Perham, *Lugard: The Years of Authority*, p. 180.
    Margery Perham's massive work remains the indispensable source on Lugard.
    More critical studies are to be found in Nicolson, *The Administration of Nigeria,
    1900–1960* and Muffett, *Concerning Brave Captains*. A notably fair-minded
    treatment of Lugard by a Nigerian is to be found in Okonjo, *British
    Administration in Nigeria, 1900–1950*.
 2. Perham, *Lugard: The Years of Authority*, p. 609.
 3. Ibid., p.157.
 4. Lugard, *Political Memoranda* (1906), pp. 10–11, quoted in Nicolson, *The
    Administration of Nigeria*, p. 138. The *Political Memoranda* were first published in a
    very limited edition in 1906. In 1919 a revised and expanded edition was
    published, and it is this edition which I have consulted directly.
 5. Lugard, *Political Memoranda* (1919), pp. 308–10.
 6. Lugard to his wife, 6 January 1905, in Perham, *Lugard: The Years of Authority*,
    pp. 201–2.
 7. Quoted in ibid., p. 128.
 8. Lugard, *The Dual Mandate in British Tropical Africa*, p. 95.
 9. Lugard, *The Rise of our East African Empire*, Vol. II, p. 651.
10. Undated note by Lugard, in Perham, *Lugard: The Years of Authority*, p. 140.
11. Annual Report of Northern Nigeria, 1902, quoted in ibid., pp. 148–9.
12. Okonjo, *British Administration in Nigeria*, pp. 29-36.
13. Quoted in Perham, *Lugard: The Years of Authority*, pp. 17–18.
14. Lugard to his wife, 2 January 1906, in ibid., p. 248.
15. Lugard to his wife, 4 January 1905, in ibid., p. 201.
16. Lugard, *The Dual Mandate in British Tropical Africa*, p. 61.
17. Bull, 'Indirect Rule in Northern Nigeria', pp. 68–9.
18. Lugard to his wife, 28 December 1913, in Perham, *Lugard: The Years of Authority*,
    p. 479.
19. A detailed review of Palmer's career in the North can be found in Okonjo,
    British Administration in Nigeria, pp. 128–67.
20. Hill, *Population, Prosperity and Poverty*, p. 26.
21. Circular issued by G.S. Browne, Resident Adamawa, November 1928, quoted
    in Okonjo, *British Administration in Nigeria*, p. 140.
22. Crocker, *Nigeria*, p. 256.
23. Crocker, *On Governing Colonies*, pp. 68–81.
24. Okonjo, *British Administration in Nigeria*, p. 137.
25. Robert Heussler, in *British Tanganyika*, characterizes Indirect Rule in Tan-
    ganyika as 'D.O. rule'. Notwithstanding Heussler's proneness to accept the DO
    version of events in all matters, the characterization is apt.
26. Morel, *Nigeria, its Peoples and its Problems*, pp. 6–7, 41.
27. Okonjo, *British Administration in Nigeria*, p. 139; and see also Hastings, *Nigerian
    Days*, p. 117.
28. Lugard, *Political Memoranda* (1919),p. 14.

29. Nicolson, *The Administration of Nigeria*, p. 132.
30. Sir Richard Temple to Sir George Goldie, 1 October 1901, Rhodes House Mss. Afr. s. 141.
31. Crocker, *Nigeria*, p. 122.
32. Perham, foreword to Kirk-Greene (ed.), *The Principles of Native Administration in Nigeria*, p. x.
33. Temple, *Native Races and their Rulers*, pp. 63, 68–70.
34. Ibid., pp. 58–9, 69, 71–3.
35. Letter to D.N. Muffett, 1962, quoted in Muffett, *Concerning Brave Captains*, pp. 157–8.
36. Hastings, *Nigerian Days*, pp. 78–83.
37. Ibid., introduction by R.B. Cunninghame Graham, p. xv.
38. Ruxton, 'An Anthropological No-Man's Land', p. 8.
39. Clifford, minute addressed to the Lt. Governor of the northern provinces, 18 March 1922, reprinted in Kirk-Greene (ed.), *The Principles of Native Administration in Nigeria*, p. 184.
40. Temple, *Native Races and their Rulers*, p. 70.
41. Ibid., p. 73.
42. Hannah Arendt (*Imperialism*, pp. 87–101) noted and discussed this phenomenon, arriving at conclusions somewhat different from mine.
43. See Cromer's *Modern Egypt* and Milner's *England in Egypt*.
44. Cromer to Rosebery, 22 February 1893, in Zetland, *Lord Cromer*, p. 192.
45. Lawrence, *Secret Despatches from Arabia*, p. 128.
46. Lowell Thomas, in A.W. Lawrence (ed.), *T.E. Lawrence by his Friends*, p. 215.
47. Quoted, with excisions as given, in Muffett, *Empire Builder Extraordinary*, p. 22.
48. Ibid., pp. 20, 21.
49. Lugard, *Political Memoranda* (1919), p. 318.
50. Mitchell, 'Indirect Rule', p. 105.
51. See Temple, *Native Races and their Rulers*, p. 71, for a typically explicit statement of this view.
52. Ibid., p. 58.
53. Lugard, *Political Memoranda* (1919), p. 131.
54. See my *Heart-Beguiling Araby*, pp. 212–3.
55. Annual Report of Masai District, 1937, K.N.A., PC/SP 1/2/1.
56. Crocker, *Nigeria*, p. 249.
57. Hastings, *Nigerian Days*, pp. 177–8.
58. Lugard, *Political Memoranda* (1919), p. 315.
59. Lugard, *The Dual Mandate*, p. 59.
60. Ibid., p. 577; and see also p. 585.
61. An important book which shows the extent to which an administrator could allow his concern for correctness of feeling between the natives and the British to influence his work is *The Making of Northern Nigeria* (1911) by Lugard's favourite Resident, Charles Orr.
62. Desk diary of Colonial Office patronage secretary, 10 March 1899, Rhodes House Mss. Brit. Emp. r. 21.
63. See Kuklick, *The Imperial Bureaucrat*, for information regarding the Gold Coast.
64. Furse, untitled memorandum, 1 April 1920, Rhodes House Mss. Brit. Emp. s. 415.

65. Furse, *Aucuparius*, Chapter I.

66. Colonial Office, *Appointments Handbook*, p. 15; and also Furse, *Aucuparius*, p. 233.

67. Furse, 'Recruitment and Training of Colonial Civil Servants' (1927), p. 4, Rhodes House Mss. Brit. Emp. s. 415.

68. Furse, *Aucuparius*, pp. 233–4.

69. Rhodes, 'Confession of Faith' (1877), in Flint, *Cecil Rhodes*, p. 250.

70. Kirk-Greene, 'John Buchan and Empire'.

71. Furse, untitled memorandum, 1 April 1920, Rhodes House Mss. Brit. Emp. s. 415.

72. Furse, 'First Memorandum Prepared for the Warren Fisher Committee', 27 April 1929, Rhodes House Mss. Brit. Emp. s. 415.

73. Furse, *Aucuparius*, p. 263.

74. Though he was outraged when the American scholar Robert Heussler, in an extremely sympathetic study of the Colonial Service (*Yesterday's Rulers*, 1963), exposed the extent of his preference to the light of day (Furse, notes on draft of Heussler's *Yesterday's Rulers*, Rhodes House Mss. Brit. Emp. s. 415).

75. The most interesting examples known to me are Jonathan Gathorne-Hardy's *The Old School Tie*, J.R. de S. Honey's *Tom Brown's Universe*, J.A. Mangan's *Athleticism in the Victorian and Edwardian Public School*, and Rupert Wilkinson's *Gentlemanly Power*. Of these the best, because most comprehensive and most alive to the variety of possible outcomes to a public school education, is *The Old School Tie*.

76. Quoted in Honey, *Tom Brown's Universe*, pp. 6–7.

77. Hughes, *Tom Brown's School Days*, pp. 265–6.

78. Honey, *Tom Brown's Universe*, p. 22.

79. For Cameron's achievements, see Gailey, *Sir Donald Cameron: Colonial Governor*; Okonjo, *British Administration in Nigeria*, Chapter VII; Austen, 'The Official Mind of Indirect Rule: British Policy in Tanganyika, 1916–1939'; and Cameron's oddly titled memoir, *My Tanganyika Service and Some Nigeria*. Cameron was ably supported in print at the time by Margery Perham (see her 'A Restatement of Indirect Rule' and *Native Administration in Nigeria*). Perham saw Cameron as a worthy successor to Lugard; he saw himself as correcting Lugard's mistakes.

80. The reader is referred to Max Weber's extensive writings on charismatic versus bureaucratic authority, and, at this point, also to Joseph Schumpeter's immensely intriguing but frustrating *Imperialism and Social Classes*.

Chapter 7   The End of Empire

1. Temple, *Native Races and their Rulers*, p. 78.

2. Ibid., p. 23.

3. On Hume's career and opinions, see Wedderburn, *Allan Octavian Hume*.

4. See especially his *Liberty, Equality, Fraternity* (1872).

5. Quoted in Spear, *India*, p. 315.

6. Spangenberg, 'Altruism Versus Careerism', p. 21. On the importance of collaborators to the British, see, for example, Gallagher, Johnson and Seal,

Locality, Province and Nation; Brown, 'Imperial Facade: Some Constraints upon and Contradictions in the British Position in India, 1919–1935'; Dewey, '*Patwari* and *Chaukidar*: Subordinate Officials and the Reliability of India's Agricultural Statistics'.

7. Hyam, *Britain's Imperial Century*, p. 241; Minto, *India, Minto and Morley*, pp. 30, 239–40.

8. Montagu, *Speeches on Indian Questions*, p. 305.

9. Ibid., p. 250.

10. Ibid., p. 252.

11. Ibid., pp. 26–9, 50–1.

12. Correspondence between Curzon and Montagu, July 1918, in Waley, *Edwin Montagu*, pp. 172–4.

13. Montagu to Chelmsford, 21 September 1917, in ibid., pp. 137–8.

14. Quoted in Mansergh, *The Commonwealth Experience*, p. 19.

15. For some indication of the mixed feelings arising from the defection of Burma, see Carrington, *The Liquidation of the British Empire*, p. 69, and Mansergh, *The Commonwealth and the Nations*, p. 20. These two books belong to the Whiggish tradition of imperial historiography inspired by the Commonwealth idea and finding its most impressive expression in Keith Hancock's *Survey of British Commonealth Affairs* (1937–42).

16. Temple, *Native Races and their Rulers*, pp. 78–9.

17. For the Lawrence legend, see Lowell Thomas' *With Lawrence in Arabia* (1924) and Robert Graves' *Lawrence and the Arabs* (1927). And for the debunking, see Richard Aldington's *Lawrence of Arabia* (1955), which has survived the sound and fury which greeted its publication to become a classic of the *genre*.

18. Lawrence to Curzon, 27 September 1919, in Lawrence, *The Letters of T.E. Lawrence*, pp. 291–2.

19. Lawrence, 'The Changing East', pp. 771–2.

20. Lawrence, letter to *The Times*, 22 July 1920, and article in *The Observer* entitled 'France, Britain and the Arabs', 8 August 1920, reprinted in Lawrence, *The Letters of T.E. Lawrence*, pp. 308, 311–15.

21. A.W. Lawrence (ed.), *T.E. Lawrence by his Friends*, p. 232.

22. For a DO's lament over the decline of the putative alliance between chiefs and boma, see Robin Short's *African Sunset* (1973).

23. Lavin, 'Lionel Curtis and the Idea of Commonwealth'; Knightley and Simpson, *The Secret Lives of Lawrence of Arabia*, pp. 37–9, 182–3. Lawrence claimed to have had a brown dominion in mind throughout the war; perhaps he did.

24. Lawrence, *The Letters of T.E. Lawrence*, pp. 410–21.

25. Useful sources are Kendle, *The Round Table Movement and Imperial Union*; Nimocks, *Milner's Young Men: The 'Kindergarten' in Edwardian Imperial Affairs*; and Allison, 'Imperialism and Appeasement: A Study of the Ideas of the Round Table Group'.

26. Curtis, *The Problem of the Commonwealth*, p. 206.

27. Curtis, 'Windows of Freedom', p. 29.

28. The idea of bringing in America may actually have originated with Kerr. See his letter to Curtis, 15 October 1918, reproduced in Butler, *Lord Lothian*, pp. 68–70.

29. Curtis, 'Windows of Freedom', p. 34.
30. Milner, 'Credo', *The Times*, 27 July 1925.
31. Lavin, 'Lionel Curtis and the Idea of Commonwealth', pp. 108–9.
32. Curtis, *Letters to the People of India*, p. 54.
33. Curtis to Henri Bourassa, 2 September 1916, in Kendle, *The Round Table Movement and Imperial Union*, p. 205.
34. Toynbee, *Acquaintances*, p. 138.
35. For strategic restraint in the use of force, see Low, 'The Government of India and the First Non-Cooperation Movement, 1920-1922'; and see also Brown, 'Imperial Facade: Some Constraints upon and Contradictions in the British Position in India, 1919-1935'.
36. In his otherwise disappointing *Gandhi's Truth*, Erik Erikson rightly treats the Ahmedabad fast as a critical event in Gandhi's life.
37. Quoted in Fischer, *Gandhi*, p. 36.
38. See Gandhi's *Autobiography*, and other writings.
39. Quoted in Shirer, *Gandhi*, p. 116, also p. 132; and for an extreme example of this ambivalent type of nationalism see Chaudhuri, *Autobiography of an Unknown Indian*.
40. Gandhi, *Satyagraha in South Africa*, p. 383.
41. Quoted in Fischer, *Gandhi*, p. 56.
42. Ibid., p. 57.
43. Kennedy ['A. Carthill'], *The Lost Dominion*, pp. 93, 316, 327–30.
44. Osburn, *Must England Lose India?*, pp. 21, 221.
45. Ibid., p. 6.
46. Kennedy, *The Lost Dominion*, pp. 237–8, 241.
47. Osburn, *Must England Lose India?*, pp. 254, 256.
48. Quoted in Spear, *India*, p. 348.
49. Described in detail in Watson, *The Trial of Mr Gandhi*.
50. Begbie, *The Conservative Mind*, pp. 47–8. And cf. Furse, *Aucuparius*, p. 86.
51. Allison, 'Imperialism and Appeasement', p. 138.
52. Gollin, *Proconsul in Politics*, pp. 331, 376.
53. Campbell-Johnson, *Viscount Halifax*, p. 133. Irwin's name was also put forward by the king (Nicolson, *King George the Fifth*, p. 504), and by Lord Winterton (*Orders of the Day*, pp. 133–4).
54. See Cowling, *The Impact of Labour*, passim.
55. Begbie, *The Conservative Mind*, p. 50.
56. For an early example, see Irwin's maiden speech in the House of Commons, in Birkenhead, *Halifax*, pp. 96–7.
57. Quoted in *Dictionary of National Biography*; see also Zinkin and Zinkin, *Britain and India*, p. 93.
58. Halifax, *Fullness of Days*, p. 150.
59. For an example, see the interviews excerpted in Watson, *The Trial of Mr Gandhi*.
60. Birkenhead, *Halifax*, pp. 71, 190, 277.
61. See, e.g., Halifax, *Speeches on Foreign Policy*, p. 104.
62. Halifax, *Fullness of Days*, p. 62.
63. For an early example, written before he went into politics, see his *John Keble* (1909).

64. Quoted in *Dictionary of National Biography*.

65. The source for Salisbury's notes is Peele, 'A Note on the Irwin Declaration', from which the following account is taken.

66. For a glimpse of these, see Halifax, *Fullness of Days*, pp. 118–19, and Campbell-Johnson, *Viscount Halifax*, pp. 230–34.

67. Brown, *Gandhi and Civil Disobedience*, p. 42; Campbell-Johnson, *Viscount Halifax*, p. 233.

68. Irwin to G.R. Lane-Fox, 31 March 1930, in Bakshi, *Gandhi and Salt Satyagraha*, p. 61.

69. Birkenhead, *Halifax*, p. 281.

70. Halifax, *Indian Problems*, p. 92.

71. Halifax, *Fullness of Days*, p. 161; Morris, *Farewell the Trumpets*, p. 291.

72. Quoted in Birkenhead, *Halifax*, p. 282.

73. Ibid., p. 284.

74. Halifax, *Indian Problems*, pp. 110–11; and see also Gopal, *The Viceroyalty of Lord Irwin*, p. 98.

75. Quoted in Birkenhead, *Halifax*, p. 296.

76. Irwin to Secretary of State, 16 February 1931, in ibid., p. 296.

77. Clause 2 of the Gandhi-Irwin agreement, in Campbell-Johnson, *Viscount Halifax*, p. 305.

78. Bernays, *Naked Fakir*, p. 141.

79. Brown, *Gandhi and Civil Disobedience*, pp. 186–7; Gopal, *The Viceroyalty of Lord Irwin*, p. 110.

80. Halifax, *Fullness of Days*, p. 148; Bernays, *Naked Fakir*, p. 168.

81. Quoted in Gopal, *The Viceroyalty of Lord Irwin*, p. 106.

82. Watson, *The Trial of Mr Gandhi*, p. 198.

83. Quoted in Fischer, *Gandhi*, p. 103.

84. Irwin to Secretary of State, 9 March 1931, in Birkenhead, *Halifax*, p. 303.

85. Moore, *Churchill, Cripps and India*.

86. See, e.g. Hinden (ed.), *Fabian Colonial Essays*.

87. Pearce, *The Turning Point in Africa*, p. 96.

88. Bullock, *The Life and Times of Ernest Bevin*, Vol. I, pp. 627–34.

89. Williams, *A Prime Minister Remembers*, p. 204.

90. For a full treatment of Cabinet thinking on India at this time, see Moore, *Escape from Empire: The Attlee Government and the Indian Problem*.

91. Quoted in Harris, *Attlee*, p. 372.

92. Quoted in Cambell-Johnson, *Mission with Mountbatten*, p. 45.

93. Williams, *A Prime Minister Remembers*, pp. 212–5; Harris, *Attlee*, p. 373; Ziegler, *Mountbatten*, p. 323.

94. Mountbatten to Attlee, 20 December 1946, in Ziegler, *Mountbatten*, p. 354.

95. Harris, *Attlee*, pp. 382–3.

96. Mountbatten to Ismay, 11 May 1947, in Ziegler, *Mountbatten*, p. 383.

97. Quoted in Harris, *Attlee*, p. 384.

98. Quoted in Moore, *Escape from Empire*, p. 355.

99. Ziegler, *Mountbatten*, pp. 384–5.

100. For a vivid description of these, see Lapping, *End of Empire*, pp. 90–91.

101. Quoted in Ziegler, *Mountbatten*, p. 428.

102. Kennedy, *The Rise and Fall of British Naval Mastery*, p. 326.

103. Quoted in Moore, *Escape from Empire*, p. 226.
104. For Britain's misconceived constitutional experiment in Malaya after the war, the Malayan Union, see Allen, *The Malayan Union*, and Stockwell, *British Policy and Malay Politics during the Malayan Union Experiment, 1942–1948*.
105. The major source for wartime and immediate post-war developments in the Colonial Office is, at the time of writing, R.D. Pearce, *The Turning Point in Africa: British Colonial Policy, 1938–48*; but see also Pearce's controversies with John Cell and John Flint (Cell, 'On the Eve of Decolonization: the Colonial Office's Plans for the Transfer of Power in Africa, 1947'; Pearce, 'The Colonial Office in 1947 and the Transfer of Power in Africa: An Addendum to John Cell'; Flint, 'Planned Decolonization and its Failure in British Africa'; Pearce, 'The Colonial Office and Planned Decolonization in Africa').
106. Lavin, 'Lionel Curtis and the Idea of Commonwealth', pp. 114–15.
107. Anticipated to some extent by Sir Donald Cameron in Tanganyika; see Chapter VI, [pp. 220–21], and Gailey, *Sir Donald Cameron*, p. 84.
108. See Louis and Robinson, 'The United States and the Liquidation of the British Empire in Tropical Africa, 1941–1951', in Gifford and Louis (eds.), *The Transfer of Power in Africa*; and Robinson, 'Conclusion', in Kirk-Greene (ed.), *Africa in the Colonial Period, III – The Transfer of Power*.
109. Quoted in Pearce, *The Turning Point in Africa*, p. 84.
110. Curtis, *Civitas Dei*, Vol. I, p. 164.
111. Furse, 'The Fifth British "Empire" – Is it the Last?', speech to the Eton Political Society, 25 February 1942, Rhodes House Mss. Brit. Emp. s. 415.
112. Furse, 'Review of the Position in Regard to Recruitment and Training at the End of the First Two Years of Post-War Recruitment', 9 November 1947, Rhodes House Mss. Brit. Emp. s. 415.
113. Hailey, *Native Administration and Political Development in British Tropical Africa*, p. 5. This version of the report is that printed confidentially by the Colonial Office in 1944; it contains, apparently, some changes from an earlier version, which I have not read.
114. Ibid., p. 8.
115. Low, '"Civil Martial Law": The Government of India and the Civil Disobedience Movements, 1930–34'; Halifax, *Fullness of Days*, pp. 116–7.
116. Mason, *The Men who Ruled India*, Vol. II, p. 290.
117. Low, '*The Contraction of England*', p. 6.
118. Hailey, *Native Administration and Political Development in British Tropical Africa*, p. 14. These comments throw some light on Hailey's often-quoted characterization of Indirect Rule as 'first, . . . a useful administrative device; then . . . a political doctrine; and finally . . . a religious dogma' (Pearce, *The Turning Point in Africa*, p. 45).
119. Hailey, *Native Administration and Political Development in British Tropical Africa*, p. 55.
120. Flint, 'Planned Decolonization and its Failure in British Africa', p. 402; and see also Perham's *Native Administration in Nigeria* (1937).
121. See the entries for 19 February 1940, 25 February 1940 and 28 February 1940 in Hailey's unpublished diary of his African tour (Rhodes House Mss. Brit. Emp. s. 342).
122. This account of events in the Gold Coast and Nigeria is based on Pearce, *The*

Turning Point in Africa, pp. 76–81; and Hargreaves, 'Toward the Transfer of Power in British West Africa', in Gifford and Louis (eds.), *The Transfer of Power in Africa*.

123. Hailey, *Native Administration and Political Development in British Tropical Africa*, pp. 60–61.

124. Minute by Burns, 13 January 1945, in Pearce, *The Turning Point in Africa*, p. 78.

125. Burns to Secretary of State, 21 August 1944, in ibid., p. 80.

126. See his autobiography, *Colonial Civil Servant*.

127. Okonjo, *British Administration in Nigeria*, p. 303.

128. On Cohen, see articles by Ronald Robinson, including 'Sir Andrew Cohen: Proconsul of African Nationalism (1909–1968)', and 'Andrew Cohen and the Transfer of Power in Tropical Africa, 1940–1951'. A biography is awaited.

129. Minute by Cohen, 14 October 1943, in Pearce, *The Turning Point in Africa*, p. 155.

130. Quoted in ibid., p. 104.

131. Pratt, *The Critical Phase in Tanzania*, pp. 15–17.

132. See especially, ibid., Chapter II.

133. Report of the Cohen-Caine Commitee, 22 May 1947, summarized in Robinson, 'Andrew Cohen and the Transfer of Power in Tropical Africa, 1940–1951', pp. 62–3.

134. Saloway, 'The New Gold Coast', pp. 470–71.

135. Low and Lonsdale, 'Introduction: Towards the New Order 1945–1963'.

136. Robinson, 'Sir Andrew Cohen: Proconsul of African Nationalism (1909–1968)', p. 359; and 'Andrew Cohen and the Transfer of Power in Tropical Africa, 1940–1951', p. 62.

137. Pearce, *The Turning Point in Africa*, p. 77.

138. Pearce, 'The Colonial Office and Planned Decolonization in Africa', p. 92.

139. Pratt, *The Critical Phase in Tanzania*, Chapter III.

140. Ruskin, 'A Knight's Faith'.

141. Lugard, *The Dual Mandate in British Tropical Africa*, p. 59.

142. Ibid., p. 132.

143. Cromer, 'The Government of Subject Races'.

144. Furnivall, *Colonial Policy and Practice*, pp. 538, 550.

145. Charles Brooke [The Rajah of Sarawak], *Queries: Past, Present, and Future*.

Epilogue   Grand Illusions 1900–1940

1. The fullest account of the kindergarten's campaign is to be found in Nimocks, *Milner's Young Men*.

2. Oliver, *The Endless Adventure*, p. 3.

3. Buchan, *Pilgrim's Way*, p. 232.

4. On the spy story, see Colin Watson's *Snobbery with Violence: English Crime Stories and their Audience*, especially his remarks (pp. 250–51) on the 'spy' as secret policeman.

5. Gollin, *Proconsul in Politics*, Chapter XX; Allison, 'Imperialism and Appeasement', pp. 310–13.

6. Curtis, *Civitas Dei*, Vol. I, p. 13.
7. Anon, 'The Crisis and the Future', pp. 2–4. This article constituted the entire December 1938 issue of the *Round Table* and can be taken as the considered view of the movement's inner circle.
8. Quoted in Smith, *John Buchan*, p. 443.
9. Quotes from ibid., p. 452.
10. Quoted in Butler, *Lord Lothian*, p. 203.
11. Allison, 'Imperialism and Appeasement', pp. 357–9.
12. Quoted in Rowse, *Appeasement*, p. 28.
13. Butler, *Lord Lothian*, p. 337.
14. Ibid., p. 226; Allison, 'Imperialism and Appeasement', pp. 391–401.
15. The idea of a 'Cliveden set' is now regarded with such contempt by historians – succumbing perhaps to the same judiciousness which afflicted its supposed members – that I hesitate to mention the place at all. Lady Astor's ambitions as a political hostess went high and wide (see Tom Jones, *A Diary with Letters, 1931–1950*, pp. xxiv–xl, for a famous description) but Lothian and his friends were among her most welcome and frequent guests, and the house was a favoured venue for Round Table 'moots'. Waldorf Astor, because of his proprietorship of *The Observer*, was drafted into Milner's circle in the days of the 'Monday night cabal' (Gollin, *Proconsul in Politics*, p. 325).
16. Larry Fuchser's study, *Neville Chamberlain and Appeasement: A Study in the Politics of History* (1982), expounds fully the view of Chamberlain as a man who felt himself to be in control of events.
17. This part of Martin Gilbert's and Richard Gott's *oeuvre* on appeasement (*The Appeasers*, 1963; *The Roots of Appeasement*, 1966; 'Horace Wilson: Man of Munich?', 1982), appears so far to have withstood criticism. Revisionist scholarship on Chamberlain and appeasement may be said to have been officially inaugurated with D.C. Watt's 'Appeasement, the Rise of a Revisionist School?' in 1965.
18. Quoted in Cooper, *Old Men Forget*, p. 229.
19. See Douglas, *In the Year of Munich*, p. 49; Fuchser, *Neville Chamberlain and Appeasement*, p. 138; and Scott, 'Neville Chamberlain and Munich', p. 354.
20. Quoted in 'Cato', *Guilty Men*, pp. 59–60.
21. Templewood [Hoare], *Nine Troubled Years*, p. 280.
22. Gannon, *The British Press and Germany*, p. 101.
23. Halifax to Agatha Harrison, 13 March 1936, in Tinker, *The Ordeal of Love*, p. 282.
24. Liddell Hart, *'T.E. Lawrence' in Arabia and After*, p. 448.
25. Williamson, 'Lawrence of Arabia and Germany'. See also Knightley and Simpson, *The Secret Lives of Lawrence of Arabia*, pp. 307–8; Mack, *A Prince of our Disorder*, pp. 408–9; Griffiths, *Fellow Travellers of the Right*, pp. 134–7.
26. Halifax, *T.E. Lawrence*, pp. 7–8.
27. Toynbee, *Survey of International Affairs, 1937*, Vol. I, pp. 338–9. For some relevant material on the development of British public opinion on Hitler, see Brigitte Granzow's interesting study, *A Mirror of Nazism: British Opinion and the Emergence of Hitler 1929–1933*.
28. Birkenhead, *Halifax*, pp. 368–74, gives an account based on Halifax's private papers. Halifax, *Fullness of Days*, pp. 186–93, reproduces his diary entries for 19

and 20 November 1937, which cover his talks with Hitler at Berchtesgaden and subsequent visit to Goering. Ivone Kirkpatrick, an official at the Berlin embassy at the time, who was present at the meeting with Hitler, describes it in his *The Inner Circle*, pp. 94–8.

29. Halifax, diary entry for 20 November 1937, in *Fullness of Days*, pp. 192–3.
30. Quoted in Birkenhead, *Halifax*, p. 373.
31. Halifax, *Fullness of Days*, p. 193.
32. Cowling, *The Impact of Hitler*, p. 278.
33. See Halifax, *Speeches on Foreign Policy*.
34. Cowling, *The Impact of Hitler*, p. 274.
35. This comes out very clearly in Birkenhead's account of Halifax's foreign secretaryship.
36. Middlemas, *The Strategy of Appeasement*, p. 227.
37. Cowling, *The Impact of Hitler*, p. 276.
38. Halifax to British Minister in Prague, 18 June 1938, in Gilbert and Gott, *The Appeasers*, p. 124.
39. Middlemas, *The Strategy of Appeasement*, p. 378.
40. My source for the Polish guarantee, and Halifax's influence, is Newman, *March 1939: The British Guarantee to Poland*. Though at times excessively deferential in its attitude towards official documentation – on this general point with respect to studies of the period, see Skidelsky, 'Going to War with Germany', p. 58 – Newman's book makes sense of the otherwise completely quixotic-seeming course taken by British policy in the last two weeks of March 1939. See also Mearsheimer, *Conventional Deterrence*, pp. 82–7.
41. Quoted in Newman, *March 1939*, p. 153.
42. Kirkpatrick, *The Inner Circle*, p. 97.

Bibliography

The following is a list of works cited in the text. With a few exceptions, documents are not listed; full references for these are given in the Notes.

Aldington, Richard. *Lawrence of Arabia*. London, 1955.

Allen, J. de Vere. 'Two Imperialists: A Study of Sir Frank Swettenham and Sir Hugh Clifford'. *Journal of the Malaysian Branch of the Royal Asiatic Society*, 1964, *37*, pp. 41–73.

——. *The Malayan Union*. New Haven, 1967.

——. 'The Ancien Regime in Trengganu, 1909–1919'. *Journal of the Malaysian Branch of the Royal Asiatic Society*, 1968, *41*, pp. 23–53.

——. 'Malayan Civil Service, 1874–1941: Colonial Bureaucracy/Malayan Elite'. *Comparative Studies in Society and History*, 1970, *12*, pp. 149–78.

——. 'Johore 1901–1914'. *Journal of the Malaysian Branch of the Royal Asiatic Society*, 1972, *44*, pp. 1–28.

——. 'Sir Hugh Clifford in Malaya and Nigeria'. *Kenya Historical Review*, 1976, *4*, pp. 312–22.

Allison, George Richard, 'Imperialism and Appeasement: A Study of the Ideas of the Round Table Group'. Unpublished Ph.D. thesis, Harvard University, 1965.

Anon. 'The Crisis and the Future'. *Round Table*, 1938, *29*.

Apter, David E. *The Gold Coast in Transition*. Princeton, 1955.

Arendt, Hannah. *Imperialism*. New York, 1968. First published 1951.

Askwith, T.G. *The Story of Kenya's Progress*. Nairobi, 1953.

Austen, R.A. 'The Official Mind of Indirect Rule: British Policy in Tanganyika, 1916–1939'. In Prosser Gifford and Wm. Roger Louis (eds.), *Britain and Germany in Africa*, New Haven, 1967, pp. 577–606.

Axelson, Eric. *Portugal and the Scramble for Africa*. Johannesburg, 1967.

Bakshi, S.R. *Gandhi and Salt Satyagraha*. Kerala, 1981.

Ballard, J.A. 'Administrative Origins of Nigerian Federalism'. *African Affairs*, 1971, *70*, pp. 333–48.

Barnett, Donald L. and Njama, Karari. *Mau Mau from Within: Autobiography and Analysis of Kenya's Peasant Revolt*. Modern Reader edition, New York, 1970.

Barr, Pat. *Taming the Jungle: The Men who Made British Malaya*. London, 1977.

313

Beach, D.N. 'The Adendorff Trek in Shona History'. *South African Historical Journal*, 1971, *3*, pp. 30–48.

——. 'Ndebele Raiders and Shona Power'. *Journal of African History*, 1974, *15*, pp. 633–51.

Beames, John. *Memoirs of a Bengal Civilian*. London, 1961.

Begbie, Harold. *The Conservative Mind*. London, 1924.

Bennett, George. *Kenya: A Political History: The Colonial Period*. Nairobi, 1978.

Berman, B.J. 'Bureaucracy and Incumbent Violence: Colonial Administration and the Origins of the "Mau Mau" Emergency in Kenya'. *British Journal of Political Science*, 1976, *6*, pp. 143–75.

Berman, B.J. and Lonsdale, J.M. 'Crises of Accumulation, Coercion and the Colonial State: The Development of the Labour Control System in Kenya, 1919–1929'. *Canadian Journal of African Studies*, 1980, *14*, pp. 55–81.

Bernays, Robert. *Naked Fakir*. London, 1931.

Berntsen, John. 'The Maasai and their Neighbours: Variables of Inter-action'. *African Economic History*, 1976, *2*, pp. 1–11.

Bird, Isabella. *The Golden Chersonese, and the Way Thither*. Kuala Lumpur, 1967. First published 1883.

Birkenhead, Lord. *Halifax: The Life of Lord Halifax*. Boston, 1966.

Blake, J.Y.F. 'Second Thoughts on Rhodesia'. *National Review*, 1898. *31*, pp. 118–29.

Blake, Robert. *A History of Rhodesia*. New York, 1978.

Blennerhassett, Rose and Sleeman, Lucy. *Adventures in Mashonaland, by Two Hospital Nurses*. London, 1893.

Blundell, Michael. *So Rough a Wind*. London, 1964.

Bosworth Smith, R. *Life of Lord Lawrence*. New York, 1883.

Brett, E.A. *Colonialism and Underdevelopment in East Africa: The Politics of Economic Change 1919–1939*. London, 1973.

British Malaya, 1927–9, *2–4*.

British South Africa Company. *Report of the Directors*, 1894. London, 1895.

Brodhurst-Hill, A.M.E. *So This is Kenya*. London, 1936.

Brooke, Charles [The Rajah of Sarawak]. *Queries: Past, Present, and Future*. London, 1907.

Brooke, James. *A Vindication of his Character and Proceedings in Reply to Statements Privately Printed and Circulated by Joseph Hume, Esq. M.P.* London, 1853.

Brown, Judith. 'Imperial Facade: Some Constraints upon and Contradictions in the British Position in India, 1919–1935'. *Transactions of the Royal Historical Society*, 1976, *26*, pp. 35–52.

——. *Gandhi and Civil Disobedience: The Mahatma in Indian Politics, 1928–34*. Cambridge, 1977.

Bruetsch, Walter L. 'Neurosyphilitic Conditions: General Paralysis, General Paresis, Dementia Paralytica'. In *American Handbook of Psychiatry*, New York, 1975, vol. IV, pp. 134–51.

Bryden, H.A. 'Captain Frederick Courtenay Selous, D.S.O.' *Cornhill Magazine*, 1917, *43*, pp. 470–83.

Buchan, John. *Greenmantle*. London, 1916.

——. *Pilgrim's Way: An Essay in Recollection*. Boston, 1940.

Buell, Raymond, L. *The Native Problem in Africa*. New York, 1928.

Buijtenhuijs, Robert. *Essays on Mau Mau*. Leiden, 1982.

Bull, Mary. 'Indirect Rule in Northern Nigeria 1906–1911'. In Kenneth Robinson and Frederick Madden (eds.), *Essays in Imperial Government*, Oxford, 1963, pp. 47–87.

Bullock, Alan. *The Life and Times of Ernest Bevin. Volume One, Trade Union Leader 1881–1940.* London, 1960.

Burns, Alan C. *Colonial Civil Servant.* London, 1949.

Butler, J.R.M. *Lord Lothian, 1882–1940.* London, 1960.

Cameron, Donald. *My Tanganyika Service and Some Nigeria.* London, 1939.

Campbell-Johnson, Alan. *Viscount Halifax.* New York, 1941.

——. *Mission with Mountbatten.* London, 1951.

Capricorn Africa Society. *The Capricorn Declarations: A Statement of Principles and Aims for East and Central Africa.* Salisbury, 1952.

Carothers, J.C. *The Psychology of Mau Mau.* Nairobi, 1954.

Carrington, C.E. *The Life of Rudyard Kipling.* New York, 1955.

——. *The Liquidation of the British Empire.* London, 1961.

Carter, Fay. 'Sir Philip Mitchell'. In Kenneth King and Ahmed Salim (eds.), *Kenya Historical Biographies*, Nairobi, 1971, pp. 29–44.

Cary, Robert. *Charter Royal.* Cape Town, 1970.

'Cato'. *Guilty Men.* New York, 1940.

Cell, John. 'On the Eve of Decolonization: The Colonial Office's Plans for the Transfer of Power in Africa, 1947'. *Journal of Imperial and Commonwealth History*, 1980, *8*, pp. 234–57.

Chandos, Lord [Oliver Lyttelton]. *The Memoirs of Lord Chandos.* London, 1962.

Charles, Elizabeth R. *Three Martyrs of the Nineteenth Century: Studies from the Lives of Livingstone, Gordon, and Patteson.* London, 1886.

Chaudhuri, Nirad C. *Autobiography of an Unknown Indian.* London, 1951.

Chaudhuri, S.B. *Civil Rebellion in the Indian Mutinies (1857–1859).* Calcutta, 1957.

Chevenix Trench, Charles. *The Road to Khartoum: A Life of General Gordon.* New York, 1978.

Clayton, Anthony. *Counter-Insurgency in Kenya 1952–60.* Nairobi, 1976.

Clifford, Hugh Charles. 'Expedition to Trengganu and Kelantan'. *Journal of the Malayan Branch of the Royal Asiatic Society*, 1961, *34*, pp. xi–162. Reprint of Cifford's report of 7 August 1895.

——. *East Coast Etchings.* Singapore, 1896.

——. *In Court and Kampong: Being Tales and Sketches of Native Life in the Malay Peninsula.* London, 1897.

——. *'Since the Beginning': A Tale of an Eastern Land.* London, 1898.

——. *Studies in Brown Humanity: Being Scrawls and Smudges in Sepia, White, and Yellow.* London, 1898.

——. 'The Familiar of Megat Pendîa'. *Living Age*, 1898, *217*, pp. 273–9.

——. 'Life in the Malay Peninsula; As it was and is'. *Proceedings of the Royal Colonial Institute*, 1898–9, *30*, pp. 369–401.

——. *In a Corner of Asia: Being Tales and Impressions of Men and Things in the Malay Peninsula.* London, 1899.

——. 'Lessons from the Malay States'. *Atlantic Monthly*, 1899, *84*, pp. 587–99.

——. 'A Dying Kingdom'. *Macmillan's Magazine*, 1902, *86*, pp. 106–14.

——. '"Cast"'. *Cornhill Magazine*, 1902, *86*, pp. 613–34.

——. 'Chinese Immigration'. *The Times*, 23 and 30 August 1902.

——. 'Dutch Colonial Administration in Theory and Practice'. *The Times*, 1 January 1902.

——. 'The Destiny of the Philippines'. *Macmillan's Magazine*, 1902, *87*, pp. 153–60.

——. 'British and Siamese Malaya'. *Proceedings of the Royal Colonial Institute*, 1902–3, *34*, pp. 45–75.

——. 'Rival Systems and the Malayan Peoples'. *North American Review*, 1903, *177*, pp. 399–409.

——. *Further India*. New York, 1904.

——. *Sally: A Study, and Other Tales of the Outskirts*. London, 1904.

——. 'America's Problem in the Philippines'. *Living Age*, 1906, *251*, pp. 515–25.

——. 'The Problem of the West Indies'. *Fortnightly Review*, 1907, *82*, pp. 135–47.

——. *Saleh: A Sequel*. Edinburgh, 1908.

——. 'Saigon'. *Blackwood's Magazine*, 1909, *186*, pp. 593–605.

——. 'In Kambodia'. *Blackwood's Magazine*, 1910, *187*, pp. 777–89.

——. 'The Tragedy of Angkor: A Fragment of Obscure History'. *Cornhill Magazine*, 1910, *102*, pp. 498–509.

——. *The Downfall of the Gods*. New York, 1911.

——. 'Sir William Butler'. *Cornhill Magazine*, 1912, *106*, pp. 827–39; and 1913, *107*, p. 144a.

——. *Malayan Monochromes*. New York, 1913.

——. *The Further Side of Silence*. New York, 1916.

——. *German Colonies: A Plea for the Native Races*. London, 1918.

——. 'Recent Developments in the Gold Coast'. *Journal of the African Society*, 1919, *18*, pp. 241–53.

——. *The Gold Coast Regiment in the East African Campaign*. London, 1920.

——. 'United Nigeria'. *Journal of the African Society*, 1921, *21*, pp. 1–14.

——. *In Days that are Dead*. New York, 1926.

——. 'An Autobiographical Preface to the 1927 Edition'. In *In Court and Kampong*, second edition, London, 1927, pp. 9–49.

——. *A Free Lance of To-Day*. Second edition, London, 1928. First published 1903.

——. *Bush-whacking and Other Asiatic Tales and Memories*. London, 1929.

Cobbing, Julian. 'The Absent Priesthood: Another Look at the Rhodesian Risings of 1896–1897'. *Journal of African History*, 1977, *18*, pp. 61–84.

Coetzee, J.M. *Waiting for the Barbarians*. London, 1980.

Coleman, James S. *Nigeria: Background to Nationalism*. Berkeley, 1958.

Collins, Robert. 'The Sudan Political Service'. *African Affairs*, 1972, *71*, pp. 293–303.

Cook, A.N. *British Enterprise in Nigeria*. Philadelphia, 1943.

Cook, E.T. and Wedderburn, Alexander (eds.). *The Works of John Ruskin*. London, 1907.

Cookey, S.J.S. 'Sir Hugh Clifford as Governor of Nigeria: An Evaluation'. *African Affairs*, 1980, *79*, pp. 531–47.

Cooper, Duff. *Old Men Forget*. New York, 1954.

Cooper, Frederic H. *The Crisis in the Punjab*. London, 1858.

Courtney, Roger. *Africa Calling*. London, 1935.

Cowling, Maurice. *The Impact of Labour 1920–1924: The Beginning of Modern British Politics*. Cambridge, 1971.

——. *The Impact of Hitler: British Politics and British Policy, 1933–1940*. Cambridge, 1975.

Crane, Robert I. and Barrier, N. Gerald (eds.). *British Imperial Policy in India and Sri Lanka 1858–1912*. New Delhi, 1981.

Cranworth, Lord. *Profit and Sport in British East Africa*. London, 1919. Revised and expanded version of *A Colony in the Making*, London, 1912.

——. *Kenya Chronicles*. London, 1939.

Crisswell, Colin N. *Rajah Charles Brooke: Monarch of All He Surveyed*. Kuala Lumpur, 1978.

Crocker, Walter R. *Nigeria: A Critique of British Colonial Administration*. New York, 1971. First published 1936.

——. *On Governing Colonies: Being an Outline of the Real Issues and a Comparison of the British, French and Belgian Approach to them*. London, 1947.

Cromer, Lord. *Modern Egypt*. London, 1908.

——. 'The Government of Subject Races'. *Edinburgh Review*, 1908, *207*, pp. 1–27.

Curtis, Lionel. *The Project of a Commonwealth*. London, 1915.

——. *The Problem of the Commonwealth*. Toronto, 1916.

——. *Letters to the People of India on Responsible Government*. Calcutta, 1917.

——. 'Windows of Freedom'. *Round Table*, 1918, *9*, pp. 1–47.

——. *Civitas Dei*. London, 1934–7.

Cust, Robert Needham. *The Matabéle-Scandal and its Consequences: By one who (1) Remembers the Punishment which Fell upon Cain for Killing his Brother, and (2) is Jealous of the Honour of Great Britain*. Cambridge, 1894.

——. *Life Memoir*, Hertford, 1899.

Davis, A. and Robertson, H.G. *Chronicles of Kenya*. London, 1928.

De Silva, J. 'British Relations with Pahang, 1884–1895'. *Journal of the Malayan Branch of the Royal Asiatic Society*, 1962, *35*, pp. 1–50.

Devlin, Christopher, 'The Mashona and the Portuguese'. *The Shield*, May 1961, pp. 7–12.

——. 'The Mashona and the British'. *The Shield*, June 1961, pp. 5–11, 24.

Dewey, Clive and Hopkins, A.G. (eds.). *The Imperial Impact: Studies in the Economic History of Africa and India*. London, 1978.

Dewey, Clive. *Patwari* and *Chaukidar*: Subordinate Officials and the Reliability of India's Agricultural Statistics'. In Clive Dewey and A.G. Hopkins (eds.), *The Imperial Impact: Studies in the Economic History of Africa and India*, London, 1978, pp. 280–314.

Dinesen, Isak [Karen Blixen]. *Out of Africa*. Vintage edition, New York, 1972. First published 1937.

——. *Letters from Africa, 1914–1931*. Chicago, 1981.

Douglas, Roy. *In the Year of Munich*. New York, 1977.

Douglas-Home, Charles. *Evelyn Baring: The Last Proconsul*. London, 1978.

Driberg, Tom. *The Mystery of Moral Re-Armament*. New York, 1965.

Edwardes, Emma. *Memorials of the Life and Letters of Major-General Sir Herbert B. Edwardes, K.C.B., K.C.S.I.* London, 1886.

Edwardes, Herbert B. *A Year on the Punjab Frontier, in 1848–49*. London, 1851.

Edwardes, Herbert B. and Merivale, Herman. *Life of Sir Henry Lawrence*. London, 1872.

Edwardes, Michael. *The Necessary Hell: John and Henry Lawrence and the Indian Empire*. London, 1958.

Electors' Union. *Kenya Plan*. Nairobi, 1949.

Emerson, George R. *General Gordon: Soldier, Administrator, and Christian Hero*. London, 1885.

Emerson, Rupert. *Malaysia: A Study in Direct and Indirect Rule*. New York, 1937.

Erikson, Erik. *Gandhi's Truth: On the Origins of Militant Nonviolence*. New York, 1969.

Evans, Peter. *Law and Disorder, or, Scenes of Life in Kenya*. London, 1956.

Farrant, Leda. *The Legendary Grogan*. London, 1981.

Farson, Negley. *Last Chance in Africa*. New York, 1950.

Farwell, Byron. *Queen Victoria's Little Wars*. New York, 1972.

Fischer, Louis. *Gandhi: His Life and Message for the World*. Mentor edition, New York, 1954.

Flint, John. *Cecil Rhodes*. Boston, 1974.

——. 'Planned Decolonization and its Failure in British Africa'. *African Affairs*, 1983, *82*, pp. 389–411.

Ford, John. *The Role of Trypanosomiases in African Ecology*. Oxford, 1971.

Fox, James. *White Mischief*. Vintage edition, New York, 1984.

Fripp, Constance E. and Hiller, V.W. (eds.). *Gold and the Gospel in Mashonaland, 1888. Being the Journals of (1) The Mashonaland Mission of Bishop Knight-Bruce, (2) The Concession Journey of Charles Dunell Rudd*. London, 1949.

Frost, Richard. *Race Against Time: Human Relations and Politics in Kenya before Independence*. London, 1978.

Fuchser, Larry Williams. *Neville Chamberlain and Appeasement: A Study in the Politics of History*. New York, 1982.

Furnivall, J.S. *Colonial Policy and Practice: A Comparative Study of Burma and Netherlands India*. Cambridge, 1948.

Furse, Ralph. *Aucuparius*. London, 1962.

Gailey, Harry A. *Sir Donald Cameron: Colonial Governor*. Stanford, 1974.

——. *Clifford: Imperial Proconsul*. London, 1982.

——. *Lugard and the Abeokuta Uprising: The Demise of Egba Independence*. London, 1982.

Galbraith, J.S. *Crown and Charter: The Early Years of the British South Africa Company*. Berkeley, 1974.

Gallagher, John, Johnson, Gordon and Seal, Anil (eds.). *Locality, Province and Nation: Essays on Indian Politics*. Cambridge, 1973.

Gandhi, M.K. *Autobiography: The Story of my Experiments with Truth*. Washington, D.C., 1954. First published 1927–9.

——. *Satyagraha in South Africa*. Madras, 1928.

Gann, Lewis and Duignan, Peter (eds.). *African Proconsuls*. New York, 1978.

Gannon, Franklin Reid. *The British Press and Germany, 1936–1939*. Oxford, 1971.

Garrett, H.L.O. and Grey, C. *European Adventurers in the Punjab, 1785 to 1849*. Lahore, 1929.

Gathorne-Hardy, Jonathan. *The Old School Tie: The Phenomenon of the English Public School*. New York, 1978.

Gibbon, Frederick P. *The Lawrences of the Punjab*. London, 1908.

Gifford, Prosser and Louis, Wm. Roger (eds.). *Britain and Germany in Africa*. New Haven, 1967.

—— *France and Britain in Africa*. New Haven, 1971.

———. *The Transfer of Power in Africa: Decolonization 1940–1960*. New Haven, 1982.

Gilbert, Martin. 'Horace Wilson: Man of Munich?' *History Today*, 1982, *32*, pp. 3–9.

Gilbert, Martin and Gott, Richard. *The Appeasers*. Boston, 1963.

———. *The Roots of Appeasement*. New York, 1966.

Glass, Stafford. *The Matabele War*. London, 1968.

Gollin, A.M. *Proconsul in Politics: A Study of Lord Milner in Opposition and in Power*. New York, 1964.

Gopal, Sarvepalli. *The Viceroyalty of Lord Irwin*. Oxford, 1957.

Gordon, Charles G. *The Journals of Major-Gen. C.G. Gordon, C.B., at Khartoum*. A.E. Hake, ed., London, 1885.

———. *Letters of General C.G. Gordon to his Sister, M.A. Gordon*. London, 1888.

Gough, Charles and Innes, Arthur D. *The Sikhs and the Sikh Wars: The Rise, Conquest, and Annexation of the Punjab State*. Patiala, 1970. First published 1897.

Granzow, Brigitte. *A Mirror of Nazism: British Opinion and the Emergence of Hitler 1929–1933*. London, 1964.

Graves, Robert. *Lawrence and the Arabs*. London, 1927.

Gregory, Robert G., Maxon, Robert M. and Spencer, Leon P. *A Guide to the Kenya National Archives*. Syracuse, 1968.

Griffiths, Richard. *Fellow Travellers of the Right: British Enthusiasts for Nazi Germany, 1933–9*. London, 1980.

Grogan, Ewart S. *From the Cape to Cairo*. London, 1909. First published 1900.

———. 'Sixty Years in East and Central Africa'. In F.S. Joelson (ed.), *Rhodesia and East Africa*, London, 1958, pp. 53–9.

Gulliver, P.H. (ed.). *Tradition and Transition in East Africa: Studies of the Tribal Element in the Modern Era*. London, 1972.

———. 'The Conservative Commitment in Northern Tanzania: The Arusha and Masai'. In P.H. Gulliver (ed.), *Tradition and Transition in East Africa: Studies of the Tribal Element in the Modern Era*, London, 1972, pp. 223–42.

Haggard, Henry Rider. *King Solomon's Mines*. London, 1956. First published 1885.

———. *Allan Quatermain*. London, 1956. First published 1887.

———. *The Private Diaries of Sir H. Rider Haggard, 1914–25*. New York, 1980.

Hahn, Emily. *James Brooke of Sarawak*. London, 1953.

Hailey, Lord. *An African Survey: A Study of Problems Arising in Africa South of the Sahara*. London, 1938.

———. *Native Administration and Political Development in British Tropical Africa*. Nendeln, Liechtenstein, 1979. Reprint of 1944 edition with introduction by A.H.M. Kirk-Greene.

Haines, C.R. 'Gordon's Death. What is the Truth?' *United Services Magazine*, 1890, *2*, pp. 130–37.

Hake, A.E. *The Story of Chinese Gordon, with Additions, bringing the Narrative down to the Present Time*. New York, 1884.

———. *Events in the Taiping Rebellion*. London, 1891.

———. *Gordon in China and the Soudan*. London, 1896.

Halifax, Lord [as Edward Wood]. *John Keble*. London, 1932. First published 1909.

———. *Conservative Beliefs*. London, 1924. Reprinted from *The Times*, 14 March 1924.

Halifax, Lord [as Lord Irwin]. *Indian Problems*. London, 1932.

Halifax, Lord. *T.E. Lawrence*. New York, 1936.

———. *Speeches on Foreign Policy*. London, 1940.

——. *Fullness of Days*. New York, 1957.

Hall, E.T. *The Hidden Dimension*. New York, 1966.

Hancock, W.K. *Survey of British Commonwealth Affairs*. London, 1937–42.

Hanley, Gerald. *Warriors and Strangers*. New York, 1971.

Hargreaves, John D. 'Toward the Transfer of Power in British West Africa'. In Prosser Gifford and Wm. Roger Louis (eds.), *The Transfer of Power in Africa: Decolonization 1940–1960*, New Haven, 1982, pp. 117–140.

Harlow, Vincent and Chilver, E.M. (eds.). *History of East Africa*, Vol. II. Oxford, 1965.

Harris, John H. *The Chartered Millions: Rhodesia and the Challenge to the British Commonwealth*. London, 1920.

Harris, Kenneth. *Attlee*. London, 1982.

Hastings, A.C.G. *Nigerian Days*. London, 1925.

Heawood, E. Obituary of Selous. *Geographical Journal*, 1917, *49*, pp. 221–3.

Helms, L.V. *Pioneering in the Far East*. London, 1969. First published 1882.

Henderson, Ian [with Philip Goodhart]. *Man Hunt in Kenya*. New York, 1958.

Heussler, Robert. *Yesterday's Rulers: The Making of the British Colonial Service*. Syracuse, 1963.

——. 'British Rule in Africa'. In Prosser Gifford and Wm. Roger Louis (eds.), *France and Britain in Africa*, New Haven, 1971, pp. 571–92.

——. *British Tanganyika: An Essay and Documents on District Administration*. Durham, 1971.

——. *British Rule in Malaya*. Westport, 1981.

Hibbert, Christopher. *The Great Mutiny: India 1857*. Penguin edition, London, 1982.

Hill, Mervyn F. *The Dual Policy in Kenya*. Nakuru, 1944.

Hill, Polly. *Population, Prosperity and Poverty: Rural Kano 1900 and 1970*. Cambridge, 1977.

Hillmer, Norman and Wigley, Philip (eds.). *The First British Commonwealth: Essays in Honour of Nicholas Mansergh*. London, 1980.

Hinden, Rita (ed.). *Fabian Colonial Essays*. London, 1945.

Holt, P.M. *The Mahdist State in the Sudan, 1881–1898*. Oxford, 1970.

Honey, J.R. de S. *Tom Brown's Universe: The Development of the English Public School in the Nineteenth Century*. New York, 1977.

Hughes, Thomas. *Tom Brown's School Days*. London, 1857.

Hulugalle, H.A.J. *British Governors in Ceylon*. Colombo, 1963.

——. *Don Stephen Senanayake*. Colombo, 1975.

Huxley, Elspeth. *White Man's Country: Lord Delamere and the Making of Kenya*. New York, 1967. First published 1935.

——. 'The Cause and Cure of Mau Mau'. *New Commonwealth*, 1954, *27*, pp. 62–4.

——. *The Flame Trees of Thika*. London, 1959.

——. *The Mottled Lizard*. London, 1962.

——. *Nellie: Letters from Africa*. London, 1984.

Huxley, Elspeth and Perham, Margery. *Race and Politics in Kenya*. Second edition, London, 1956. First published 1944.

Hyam, Ronald. *Britain's Imperial Century, 1815–1914: A Study of Empire and Expansion*. London, 1976.

Innes, Emily. *The Chersonese with the Gilding Off*. Kuala Lumpur, 1974. First published 1885.

Itote, Waruhiu ['General China']. *'Mau Mau' General*. Nairobi, 1974. First published 1967.

Jacobs, A.H. *The Pastoral Masai of Kenya: A Report of Anthropological Field Research*. London, 1963.

——. 'The Traditional Political Organization of the Pastoral Masai'. Unpublished Ph.D. thesis, Oxford University, 1965.

——. 'Maasai Pastoralism in Historical Perspective'. In Théodore Monod (ed.), *Pastoralism in Tropical Africa*, London, 1975, pp. 406–25.

Joelson, F.S. (ed.). *Rhodesia and East Africa*. London, 1958.

Johnson, Douglas H. 'The Death of Gordon: A Victorian Myth'. *Journal of Imperial and Commonwealth History*, 1982, *10*, pp. 285–310.

Johnson, Frank. *Great Days: The Autobiography of an Empire Pioneer*. London, 1940.

Jones, Tom. *A Diary with Letters, 1931–50*. London, 1954.

Kabiro, Ngugi. *Man in the Middle*. Richmond, 1973.

Kaggia, Bildad. *Roots of Freedom 1921–1963*. Nairobi, 1975.

Kariuki, J.M. *'Mau Mau' Detainee*. Nairobi, 1975. First published 1963.

Kay, G.B. *The Political Economy of Colonialism in Ghana*. Cambridge, 1972.

Kaye, J.W. *Lives of Indian Officers*. London, 1904. First published 1867.

——. *A History of the Sepoy War in India 1857–1858*. New York, 1896. First published 1880.

Keegan, John. *The Face of Battle*. New York, 1977.

Kendle. *The Round Table Movement and Imperial Union*. Toronto, 1975.

Kennedy, Bennet ['A. Carthill']. *The Lost Dominion*. Edinburgh, 1924.

Kennedy, Dane. 'Climatic Theories and Culture in Colonial Kenya and Rhodesia'. *Journal of Imperial and Commonwealth History*, 1981, *10*, pp. 50–66.

Kennedy, Paul M. *The Rise and Fall of British Naval Mastery*. London, 1976.

Keppel-Jones, Arthur. *Rhodes and Rhodesia: The White Conquest of Zimbabwe 1884–1902*. Kingston, 1983.

Khilnani, N.M. *The Punjab under the Lawrences*. Simla, 1951.

Kiernan, V.G. *From Conquest to Collapse: European Empires from 1815 to 1960*. Leicester, 1982.

Kimble, David. *The Political History of Ghana: The Rise of Gold Coast Nationalism, 1850–1928*. Oxford, 1963.

King, Kenneth and Salim, Ahmed (eds.). *Kenya Historical Biographies*. Nairobi, 1971.

King, Kenneth, 'Molonket ole Sempele'. In Kenneth King and Ahmed Salim (eds.), *Kenya Historical Biographies*, Nairobi, 1971, pp. 3–28.

——. 'The Kenya Maasai and the Protest Phenomenon, 1900–1960'. *Journal of African History*, 1971, *12*, pp. 117–38.

Kipling, Rudyard. *Kim*. London, 1901.

Kirk-Greene, A.H.M. (ed.). *The Principles of Native Administration in Nigeria – Selected Documents, 1900–1947*. London, 1965.

——. *Africa in the Colonial Period, III – The Transfer of Power: The Colonial Administrator in the Age of Decolonisation*. Oxford, 1979.

——. 'John Buchan and Empire'. *The John Buchan Journal*, 1980, *1*, pp. 9–10.

——. 'The Thin White Line: The Size of the British Colonial Service in Africa'. *African Affairs*, 1980, *79*, pp. 25–44.

Kirkpatrick, Ivone. *The Inner Circle.* London, 1959.

Kitson, Frank. *Gangs and Counter-Gangs.* London, 1960.

Kjekshus, Helge. *Ecology Control and Economic Development in East African History: The Case of Tanganyika 1850–1950.* London, 1977.

Knightly, Philip and Simpson, Colin. *The Secret Lives of Lawrence of Arabia.* Panther edition, London, 1971.

Koinange, Mbiyu. *The People of Kenya Speak for Themselves.* Detroit, 1955.

Koss, Stephen. *The Pro-Boers: The Anatomy of an Antiwar Movement.* Chicago, 1973.

Krieger, Leonard and Stern, Fritz (eds.). *The Responsibility of Power.* London, 1968.

Kuklick, Henrika. *The Imperial Bureaucrat: The Colonial Administrative Service in the Gold Coast, 1920–1939.* Stanford, 1979.

Lapping, Brian. *End of Empire.* New York, 1985.

Lavin, Deborah. 'Lionel Curtis and the Idea of Commonwealth'. In Frederick Madden and D.K. Fieldhouse (eds.), *Oxford and the Idea of Commonwealth*, London, 1982, pp. 97–121.

Lawrence, A.W.(ed.). *T.E. Lawrence by his Friends.* New York, 1937.

Lawrence, Henry. *Adventures of an Officer in the Service of Runjeet Singh.* Karachi, 1975. Reprint of 1845 edition.

——. 'Sir Charles Napier's Posthumous Work'. *Calcutta Review*, 1854, 22, pp. 208–90.

——. *Essays, Military and Political, Written in India.* London, 1859.

Lawrence, T.E. 'The Changing East'. *Round Table*, 1919–20, 10, pp. 756–72.

——. *Secret Despatches from Arabia.* London, 1939.

——. *The Letters of T.E. Lawrence.* David Garnett, ed., New York, 1939.

Leakey, L.S.B. *Kenya: Contrasts and Problems.* London, 1936.

——. *Mau Mau and the Kikuyu.* London, 1952.

——. *Defeating Mau Mau.* London, 1954.

Le Roux, Servaas D. *Pioneers and Sportsmen of South Africa, 1760–1890.* Salisbury, 1939.

Lewsen, Phyllis (ed.). *Selections from the Correspondence of John X. Merriman, 1899–1905.* Cape Town, 1966.

Leyds, W.J. *The Transvaal Surrounded.* London, 1919.

Liddell Hart, B.H. *'T.E. Lawrence' in Arabia and After.* London, 1934.

Linehan, W. 'History of Pahang'. *Journal of the Malayan Branch of the Royal Asiatic Society*, 1936, 14.

Lipscomb, J.F. *White Africans.* London, 1955.

Lloyd, George and Wood, Edward [Lord Halifax]. *The Great Opportunity.* London, 1918.

Lonsdale, J.M. 'The Politics of Conquest: The British in Western Kenya, 1894–1908'. *Historical Journal*, 1977, 20, pp. 841–70.

Lonsdale, J.M. and Berman, B.J. 'Coping with the Contradictions: The Development of the Colonial State in Kenya, 1895–1914'. *Journal of African History*, 1979, 20, pp. 487–505.

Louis, Wm. Roger and Robinson, Ronald. 'The United States and the Liquidation of the British Empire in Tropical Africa, 1941–1951'. In Prosser Gifford and Wm. Roger Louis (eds.), *The Transfer of Power in Africa: Decolonization 1940–1960*, New Haven, 1982, pp. 31–55.

Lovat, Alice. *The Life of Sir Frederick Weld, G.C.M.G., a Pioneer of Empire.* London, 1914.

Loveday, A.F. *Three Stages of History in Rhodesia.* Cape Town, 1960.

Low, D.A. 'The Government of India and the First Non-Cooperation Movement, 1920–1922'. *Journal of Asian Studies*, 1965–6, *25*, pp. 241–59.

——. *Lion Rampant: Essays in the Study of British Imperialism*. London, 1973.

——. (ed.). *Congress and the Raj*. London, 1977.

——. '"Civil Martial Law": The Government of India and the Civil Disobedience Movements, 1930–34'. In D.A. Low (ed.), *Congress and the Raj*, London, 1977, pp. 165–98.

——. *'The Contraction of England'*. Cambridge, 1985.

Low, D.A. and Smith, Alison (eds.). *History of East Africa*, Vol. III. Oxford, 1976.

Low, D.A. and Lonsdale, J.M. 'Introduction: Towards the New Order 1945–1963'. In D.A. Low and Alison Smith (eds.), *History of East Africa*, Vol. III, Oxford, 1976, pp. 1–63.

Ludowyk, E.F.C. *The Modern History of Ceylon*. London, 1966.

Lugard, F.D. *The Rise of our East African Empire*. London, 1968. First published 1893.

——. *Political Memoranda: Revision of Instructions to Political Officers on Subjects Chiefly Political and Administrative, 1913–1918*. London, 1970. Reprint of 1919 edition with introduction by A.H.M. Kirk-Greene.

——. *The Dual Mandate in British Tropical Africa*. Edinburgh, 1923. First published 1922.

Lumsden, Peter S. and Elsmie, George R. *Lumsden of the Guides: A Sketch of the Life of Sir Harry Burnett Lumsden, K.C.S.I., C.B.* London, 1900.

Mack, John E. *A Prince of our Disorder*. Boston, 1976.

Madden, Frederick and Fieldhouse, D.K. (eds.). *Oxford and the Idea of Commonwealth*. London, 1982.

Majdalany, F. *State of Emergency*. Boston, 1963.

Mandelstam, Nadhezda. *Hope Abandoned*. London, 1974.

Mangan, J.A. *Athleticism in the Victorian and Edwardian Public School: The Emergence and Consolidation of an Educational Ideology*. Cambridge, 1981.

Mannoni, O. *Prospero and Caliban: The Psychology of Colonization*. London, 1956.

Mansergh, Nicholas. *The Commonwealth and the Nations*. London, 1968. First published 1948.

——. *The Commonwealth Experience*. London, 1969.

Marlowe, John. *Mission to Khartoum: The Apotheosis of General Gordon*. London, 1969.

Mason, Philip. *The Men who Ruled India*. London, 1953–4.

——. *A Matter of Honour: An Account of the Indian Army, its Officers and Men*. Penguin edition, London, 1976.

Mathu, Mohamed. *The Urban Guerrilla*. Richmond, 1974.

Maxon, R.M. *John Ainsworth and the Making of Kenya*. Washington, D.C., 1980.

Mearsheimer, John J. *Conventional Deterrence*. Ithaca, 1983.

Merrill, Robert S. 'Resistance to Economic Change: The Masai'. *Proceedings of the Minnesota Academy of Science*, 1960, *28*, pp. 120–31.

Metcalfe, G.E. *Great Britain and Ghana: Documents of Ghana History, 1807–1957*. London, 1964.

Michell, Lewis. *The Life and Times of the Right Honourable Cecil John Rhodes, 1853–1902*. New York, 1977. First published 1910.

Middlemas, Keith. *The Strategy of Appeasement*. Chicago, 1972. Published in England as *Diplomacy of Illusion*.

Millais, J.G. *Life of Frederick Courtenay Selous, D.S.O.* London, 1919.

Milner, Lord. 'Credo'. *The Times*, 27 July 1925.

Minto, Lady. *India, Minto and Morley, 1905–1910*. London, 1935.

Mitchell, Philip. 'Indirect Rule'. *The Uganda Journal*, 1936, *4*, pp. 101–7.

——. *African Afterthoughts*. London, 1954.

Monod, Théodore (ed.). *Pastoralism in Tropical Africa*. London, 1975.

Montagu, Edwin S. *Speeches on Indian Questions*. Madras, no date.

Moore, R.J. *Churchill, Cripps and India, 1939–1945*. Oxford, 1979.

——. *Escape from Empire: The Attlee Government and the Indian Problem*. Oxford, 1983.

Morel, E.D. *Nigeria, its People and its Problems*. London, 1968. First published 1911.

Morris, Jan. *Farewell the Trumpets: An Imperial Retreat*. Harvest edition, New York, 1978.

Morris-Jones, W.H. and Fischer, G. (eds.). *Decolonization and After: The British and French Experience*. London, 1980.

MRA Pictorial, 1960.

Muchai, Karigo. *The Hardcore*. Richmond. 1973.

Muffett, D.J.M. *Concerning Brave Captains*. London, 1964.

——. *Empire Builder Extraordinary: Sir George Goldie, his Philosophy of Government and Empire*. Douglas, 1978.

Mundy, Rodney. *Narrative of Events in Borneo, down to the Occupation of Labuan*. London, 1848.

Mungeam, G.H. 'Masai and Kikuyu Responses to the Establishment of British Administration in the East Africa Protectorate'. *Journal of African History*, 1970, *11*, pp. 127–43.

Murray-Brown, Jeremy. *Kenyatta*. Fontana edition, London, 1974.

Mutiny Reports from Punjab & N.W.F.P.. Lahore, 1976. Reprint of 1911 edition.

Napier, Charles. *Defects, Civil and Military, of the Indian Government*. New Delhi, 1977. First published 1853.

Napier, William. *The Life and Opinions of General Sir Charles James Napier, G.C.B.* London, 1857.

Newman, Simon. *March 1939: The British Guarantee to Poland*. Oxford, 1976.

Nicolson, Harold. *King George the Fifth: His Life and Reign*. London, 1952.

Nicolson, I.F. *The Administration of Nigeria, 1900–1960: Men, Methods and Myths*. Oxford, 1969.

Nimocks, Walter. *Milner's Young Men: The 'Kindergarten' in Edwardian Imperial Affairs*. London, 1970.

Norden, Hermann. *White and Black in East Africa*. London, 1924.

Nutting, Anthony. *Gordon of Khartoum: Martyr and Misfit*. New York, 1966.

Ochieng', William R. 'Colonial African Chiefs – Were They Primarily Self-Seeking Scoundrels?' In Bethwell A. Ogot (ed.), *Politics and Nationalism in Colonial Kenya*, Nairobi, 1972, pp. 46–70.

Ogot, Bethwell A. (ed.). *Politics and Nationalism in Colonial Kenya*. Nairobi, 1972.

——. 'Revolt of the Elders: An Anatomy of the Loyalist Crowd in the Mau Mau Uprising 1952–1956'. In Bethwell A. Ogot (ed.), *Politics and Nationalism in Colonial Kenya*, Nairobi, 1972, pp. 134–48.

Okonjo, I.M. *British Administration in Nigeria 1900–1950: A Nigerian View*. New York, 1974.

Oliver, F.S. *Ordeal by Battle*. New York, 1916.

———. *The Endless Adventure: Personalities and Practical Politics in Eighteenth-Century England*. Boston, 1931.

Orr, Charles. *The Making of Northern Nigeria*. New York, 1966. First published 1911.

Osburn, Arthur. *Must England Lose India? (The Nemesis of Empire)*. London, 1930.

Owen, Roger and Sutcliffe, Bob (eds.). *Studies in the Theory of Imperialism*. London, 1972.

Page-Jones, F.H. 'Water in Masailand'. *Tanganyika Notes and Records*, 1948, *26*, pp. 51–9.

Pearce, R.D. 'The Colonial Office in 1947 and the Transfer of Power in Africa: An Addendum to John Cell'. *Journal of Imperial and Commonwealth History*, 1982, *10*, pp. 211–5.

———. *The Turning Point in Africa: British Colonial Policy, 1938–48*. London, 1982.

———. 'The Colonial Office and Planned Decolonization in Africa'. *African Affairs*, 1984, *83*, pp. 77–93.

Peele, Gillian. 'A Note on the Irwin Declaration'. *Journal of Imperial and Commonwealth History*, 1972–3, *1*, pp. 331–7.

Perham, Margery, 'A Re-Statement of Indirect Rule'. *Africa*, 1934, *7*, pp. 321–34.

———. *Native Administration in Nigeria*. London, 1937.

———. *Lugard: The Years of Adventure, 1858–1898*. London, 1956.

———. *Lugard: The Years of Authority, 1898–1945*. London, 1960.

———. *East African Journey*. London, 1976.

Phimister, I.R. 'Rhodes, Rhodesia and the Rand'. *Journal of Southern African Studies*, 1974, *1*, pp. 74–90.

Pope-Hennessy, James. *Verandah: Some Episodes in the Crown Colonies, 1867–1889*. New York, 1964.

Portsmouth, Lord. *A Knot of Roots*. London, 1965.

Powys, Llewellyn. *Black Laughter*. London, 1953. First published 1925.

Pratt, Cranford. *The Critical Phase in Tanzania 1945–1968: Nyerere and the Emergence of a Socialist Strategy*. Cambridge, 1976.

Pringle, R. *Rajahs and Rebels: The Ibans of Sarawak under Brooke Rule, 1814–1914*. Ithaca, 1970.

Purcell, Victor. *The Memoirs of a Malayan Official*. London, 1965.

Ranger, Terence O. *Revolt in Southern Rhodesia 1896–97: A Study in African Resistance*. Evanston, 1967.

———. 'The Rewriting of African History During the Scramble: The Matabele Dominance in Mashonaland'. *African Social Research*, 1967, *4*, pp. 271–82.

Rawcliffe, D.H. *The Struggle for Kenya*. London, 1954.

Redley, M.G. 'The Politics of a Predicament: The White Community in Kenya, 1918–32'. Unpublished Ph.D. thesis, Cambridge University, 1976.

Reece, R.H.W. *The Name of Brooke: The End of White Rajah Rule in Sarawak*. Kuala Lumpur, 1982.

Robinson, Kenneth and Madden, Frederick (eds.). *Essays in Imperial Government*. Oxford, 1963.

Robinson, Ronald. 'Non-European Foundations of European Imperialism: Sketch for a Theory of Collaboration'. In Roger Owen and Bob Sutcliffe (eds.), *Studies in the Theory of Imperialism*, London, 1972, pp. 117–40.

——. 'Sir Andrew Cohen: Proconsul of African Nationalism (1909–1968)'. In Lewis Gann and Peter Duignan (eds.), *African Proconsuls*. New York, 1978, pp. 353–64.

——. 'Conclusion'. In A.H.M. Kirk-Greene (ed.), *Africa in the Colonial Period, III – The Transfer of Power: The Colonial Administrator in the Age of Decolonisation*, Oxford, 1979, pp. 178–81.

——. 'Andrew Cohen and the Transfer of Power in Tropical Africa, 1940–1951'. In W.H. Morris-Jones and G. Fischer (eds.), *Decolonization and After: The British and French Experience*, London, 1980, pp. 50–72.

——. 'The Moral Disarmament of African Empire 1919–1947'. In Norman Hillmer and Philip Wigley (eds.), *The First British Commonwealth: Essays in Honour of Nicholas Mansergh*, London, 1980, pp. 86–104.

Robinson, Ronald and Gallagher, John, with Alice Denny. *Africa and the Victorians: The Official Mind of Imperialism*. London, 1961.

Rosberg, Carl G. and Nottingham, John. *The Myth of 'Mau Mau': Nationalism in Kenya*. Meridian edition, New York, 1970.

Ross, W. McGregor. *Kenya from Within: A Short Political History*. London, 1968. First published 1927.

Rowse, A.L. *Appeasement: A Study in Political Decline*. New York, 1961. Published in England as *All Souls and Appeasement*.

Ruark, Robert. *Something of Value*. New York, 1955.

Runciman, Steven. *The White Rajahs: A History of Sarawak from 1841 to 1946*. Cambridge, 1960.

Ruskin, John. 'A Knight's Faith: Passages in the Life of Sir Herbert Edwardes'. In E.T. Cook and Alexander Wedderburn (eds.), *The Works of John Ruskin*, Vol. XXXI, London, 1907. First published 1885.

Ruxton, F.H. 'An Anthropological No-Man's Land', *Africa, 3*, pp. 1–12.

Sadka, Emily. *The Protected Malay States, 1874–1895*. Singapore, 1968.

Saitoti, Tepilit Ole. *Maasai*. New York, 1980.

Saloway, Reginald. 'The New Gold Coast'. *International Affairs*, 1955, *31*, pp. 469–76.

Schumpeter, Joseph. *Imperialism and Social Classes*. London, 1951. First published in German in 1919.

Sclater, W.L. 'Captain Selous: A Memoir'. *Journal of the African Society*, 1919, *18*, pp. 198–201.

Scott, William E. 'Neville Chamberlain and Munich: Two Aspects of Power'. In Leonard Krieger and Fritz Stern (eds.), *The Responsibility of Power*, London, 1968, pp. 353–69.

Seeley, John. *The Expansion of England*. Chicago, 1971. First published 1883.

Selous, Frederick Courtenay. *A Hunter's Wanderings in Africa*. London, 1881.

——. 'Further Explorations in the Mashuna Country'. *Proceedings of the Royal Geographical Society*, 1883, *5*, pp. 268–71.

——. 'Mr F.C. Selous' Explorations in Central South Africa'. *Proceedings of the Royal Geographical Society*, 1884, *6*, pp. 284–5.

——. 'A Journey with Donkeys across the Zambesi'. *The Field*, 1888, *72*, pp. 610, 653–5.

——. 'Mr Selous' Further Explorations in Matabele-land'. *Proceedings of the Royal Geographical Society*, 1888, *10*, pp. 293–6.

——. 'Letters from Mr F.C. Selous on his Journeys to the Kafukwe River, and on the Upper Zambesi'. *Proceedings of the Royal Geographical Society*, 1889, *11*, pp. 216–23.

——. 'Mashunaland and the Mashunas'. *Fortnightly Review*, 1889, *51*, pp. 661–76.

——. 'Notes of a Journey to the Barotse Valley'. *The Field*, 1889, *73*, pp. 227, 278–9.

——. 'Incidents of a Hunter's Life in South Africa'. *Proceedings of the Royal Colonial Institute*, 1892–3, *24*, pp. 347–63.

——. *Travel and Adventure in South-East Africa*. London, 1893.

——. 'Twenty Years in Zambesia'. *Geographical Journal*, 1893, *1*, pp. 289–324.

——. 'The History of the Matabele, and the Cause and Effect of the Matabele War'. *Proceedings of the Royal Colonial Institute*, 1893–4, *25*, pp. 251–90.

——. 'Introductory Review of the War'. In W.A. Wills and L.T. Collingridge, *The Downfall of Lobengula*, London, 1894, pp. 1–13.

——. *Sunshine and Storm in Rhodesia*. New York, 1969. First published 1896.

——. *The War in South Africa*. London, 1899.

——. *Recent Hunting Trips in British North America*. London, 1907.

——. *African Nature Notes and Reminiscences*. London, 1908.

Sen, Surendra Nath. *Eighteen Fifty-Seven*. Delhi, 1958.

Sheppard, M.C. ff. 'Clifford of Pahang'. *Straits Times Annual*, 1956, pp. 54–9.

Shirer, William. *Gandhi: A Memoir*. Pocket Book edition, New York, 1979.

Short, Robin. *African Sunset*. London, 1973.

Simpson, Alyse. *The Land that Never Was*. London, 1937.

Sinclair, Keith. *A History of New Zealand*. London, 1980.

Singh, Gandâ. *Private Correspondence relating to the Anglo-Sikh Wars*. Amritsar, 1955.

Skidelsky, Robert. 'Going to War with Germany'. *Encounter*, 1972, *39*, pp. 56–65.

Smith, Alison. 'The Immigrant Communities (1): The Europeans'. In D.A. Low and Alison Smith (eds.), *History of East Africa*, Vol. III, Oxford, 1976, pp. 423–66.

Smith, Janet Adam. *John Buchan*. Boston, 1965.

Smith, Mary Florence. *Arthur Lionel Smith*. London, 1928.

Smith, Vincent A. *The Oxford History of India*. Third edition, edited by Percival Spear. Oxford, 1958.

Sorrenson, M.P.K. 'Land Policy in Kenya, 1895–1945'. In Vincent Harlow and E.M. Chilver (eds.), *History of East Africa*, Vol. II, Oxford, 1965, pp. 672–89.

——. *Land Reform in the Kikuyu Country*. Nairobi, 1967.

——. *Origins of European Settlement in Kenya*. Nairobi, 1968.

Spangenberg, Bradford. 'Altruism versus Careerism: Motivations of British Bureaucrats in Late Nineteenth Century India'. In Robert I. Crane and N. Gerald Barrier (eds.), *British Imperial Policy in India and Sri Lanka 1858–1912*, New Delhi, 1981, pp. 12–26.

Spear, Percival. *India: A Modern History*. Ann Arbor, 1961.

Spence, Jonathan. *To Change China: Western Advisers in China 1620–1960*. Boston, 1969.

Spencer, I.R.G. 'Settler Dominance, Agricultural Production and the Second World War in Kenya'. *Journal of African History*, 1980, *21*, pp. 497–514.

——. 'The First World War and the Origins of the Dual Policy of Development in Kenya 1914–1922'. *World Development*, 1981, *9*, pp. 735–48.

Stent, Vere. *A Personal Record of Some Incidents in the Life of Cecil Rhodes*. Cape Town, 1924.

Stephen, James Fitzjames. *Liberty, Equality, Fraternity*. London, 1872.

Stigger, P. 'Volunteers and the Profit Motive in the Anglo-Ndebele War, 1893'. *Rhodesian History*, 1971, *2*, pp. 11–23.

Stockwell, A.J. 'Sir Hugh Clifford's Early Career (1866–1903) as Told from his Private Papers'. *Journal of the Malaysian Branch of the Royal Asiatic Society*, 1976, *49*, pp. 89–112.

——. 'Hugh Clifford in Trinidad 1903–1907'. *Caribbean Quarterly*, 1978, *24*, pp. 8–33.

——. *British Policy and Malay Politics during the Malayan Union Experiment, 1942–1948*. Kuala Lumpur, 1979.

Stokes, Eric. *The English Utilitarians and India*. Oxford, 1959.

Storr, Anthony. 'The Man'. In A.J.P. Taylor et al. *Churchill: Four Faces and the Man*, London, 1973.

Swettenham, Frank. *Malay Sketches*. London, 1895.

——. *The Real Malay: Pen Pictures*. London, 1900.

Swinburne, Algernon Charles. 'The Transvaal'. *The Times*, 11 October 1899.

Tanser, G.H. *A Scantling of Time: The Story of Salisbury, Rhodesia, 1890–1900*. Salisbury, 1965.

Tarling, Nicholas. *The Burthen, the Risk, and the Glory: A Biography of Sir James Brooke*. Kuala Lumpur, 1982.

Taylor, A.J.P. et al. *Churchill: Four Faces and the Man*. Penguin edition, London, 1973.

Temple, C.L. *Native Races and their Rulers: Sketches and Studies of Official Life and Administrative Problems in Nigeria*. Cape Town, 1918.

Temple, Richard. *Lord Lawrence*. London, 1889.

Templewood, Lord [Samuel Hoare]. *Nine Troubled Years*. London, 1954.

Thio, Eunice. *British Policy in the Malay Peninsula, 1880–1910*. Singapore, 1969.

Thomas, Lowell. *With Lawrence in Arabia*. New York, 1924.

Thompson, Vincent B. 'Sir Hugh Clifford and the National Congress of British West Africa: A Reconsideration'. *Kenya Historical Review*, 1975, *3*, pp. 109–25.

Thomson, Joseph. *Through Masailand*. London, 1887.

Throup, David. 'The Origins of Mau Mau'. *African Affairs*, 1985, *84*, pp. 399–433.

Thurman, Judith. *Isak Dinesen: The Life of a Storyteller*. New York, 1982.

Tidrick, Kathryn. *Heart-Beguiling Araby*. Cambridge, 1981.

Tignor, Robert L. 'The Maasai Warriors: Pattern Maintenance and Violence in Colonial Kenya'. *Journal of African History*, 1972, *13*, pp. 271–90.

——. *The Colonial Transformation of Kenya: The Kamba, Kikuyu, and Maasai from 1900 to 1939*. Princeton, 1976.

Tinker, Hugh. *The Ordeal of Love*. Delhi, 1979.

Touval, Saadia. 'Treaties, Borders, and the Partition of Africa'. *Journal of African History*, 1966, *7*, pp. 279–92.

Toynbee, Arnold J. *Survey of International Affairs, 1937*. London, 1938.

——. *Acquaintances*. London, 1967.

Tregonning, K.G. 'The Mat Salleh Revolt (1894–1905)'. *Journal of the Malayan Branch of the Royal Asiatic Society*, 1956, *29*, pp. 20–36.

——. *A History of Modern Sabah 1881–1963*. Singapore, 1965.

Trotter, L.J. *The Life of John Nicholson, Soldier and Administrator*. London, 1897.

Trzebinski, Errol. *Silence Will Speak: A Study of the Life of Denys Finch Hatton and his Relationship with Karen Blixen*. London, 1977.

——. *The Kenya Pioneers*. London, 1985.

Vambe, Lawrence. *An Ill-Fated People: Zimbabwe before and after Rhodes.* London, 1972.

Van Zwanenberg, R.M.A. 'The Economic Response of Kenya Africans to European Settlement: 1903–1939'. In Bethwell A. Ogot (ed.), *Politics and Nationalism in Colonial Kenya*, Nairobi, 1972, pp. 206–32.

——. *Colonial Capitalism and Labour in Kenya 1919–1939.* Nairobi, 1975.

Waley, S.D. *Edwin Montagu: A Memoir and an Account of his Visits to India.* New York, 1964.

Walker, R.P.S. 'Sir Hugh Clifford'. *Malaya*, 1953, *2*, pp. 704–5.

Wallis, J.P.R. (ed.). *The Southern African Diaries of Thomas Leask, 1865–1870.* London, 1954.

Wamweya, J. *Freedom Fighter.* Nairobi, 1971.

Wasserman, Gary. *Politics of Decolonization: Kenya Europeans and the Land Issue 1960–1965.* Cambridge, 1976.

Watson, Colin. *Snobbery with Violence: English Crime Stories and their Audience.* London, 1979. First published 1971.

Watson, Francis. *The Trial of Mr Gandhi.* London, 1969.

Watt, D.C. 'Appeasement, the Rise of a Revisionist School?' *Political Quarterly*, 1965, *36*, pp. 191–213.

Wedderburn, William. *Allan Octavian Hume.* New Delhi, 1974. First published 1913.

Weld, Frederick A. 'The Straits Settlements and British Malaya'. *Proceedings of the Royal Colonial Institute*, 1883–4, *15*, pp. 266–311.

West, Richard. *The White Tribes of Africa.* London, 1965.

Wheeler-Bennett, John W. *Munich: Prologue to Tragedy.* New York, 1964. First published 1948.

Wilkinson, Rupert. *Gentlemanly Power: British Leadership and the Public School Tradition.* New York, 1964.

Williams, Basil. *Cecil Rhodes.* New York, 1968. First published 1921.

Williams, Francis. *A Prime Minister Remembers.* London, 1961.

Williams, Howard. *Paradise Precarious.* Nairobi, 1956.

Williamson, Henry. 'Lawrence of Arabia and Germany'. *Anglo-German Review*, 1937, *1*, pp. 107, 144.

Willis, W.A. and Collingridge, L.T. *The Downfall of Lobengula.* London, 1894.

Wilson, Andrew. *The 'Ever-Victorious Army': A History of the Chinese Campaign under Lt.-Col. C.G. Gordon, C.B., R.E., and of the Suppression of the Tai-ping Rebellion.* San Francisco, 1977. First published 1868.

Winterton, Lord. *Orders of the Day.* London, 1953.

Wood, Susan. *Kenya: The Tensions of Progress.* Second edition, London, 1962. First published 1960.

Wraith, R.E. *Guggisberg.* London, 1967.

Zetland, Lord. *Lord Cromer.* London, 1932.

Ziegler, Philip. *Mountbatten.* Perennial Library edition, New York, 1986.

Zinkin, Maurice and Taya. *Britain and India: Requiem for Empire.* Baltimore, 1964.

Index